THE ACLU
ON TRIAL

THE ACLU
ON TRIAL

William H. McIlhany II

ARLINGTON HOUSE·PUBLISHERS
NEW ROCHELLE, NEW YORK

ISBN 0–87000–337–2

Manufactured in the United States of America

Library of Congress Cataloging in Publication Data

McIlhany, William H
    The ACLU on trial.

    Includes bibliographical references and index.
    1. American Civil Liberties Union.   I.   Title.
JC599.U5M23   323.4'06'273   76–10995
ISBN 0–87000–337–2

Contents

Part II

History of the ACLU: Inconsistency or Conspiracy?

Preface

In approaching a discussion or evaluation of any major nationwide organization that has been active throughout most of this century, one becomes aware of an overwhelming need to limit the range and concerns of one's investigation. Such an organization is the American Civil Liberties Union. Examining its detailed and complex public record requires on the part of anyone—including myself—the formulation of well-defined purposes in advance of study to serve as guidelines for limiting the relevant material to a manageable quantity. And the reader should certainly know an author's goals for his inquiry, as well as his qualifications and sources of evidence, so as to judge with accuracy the success of the intended demonstration.

Just what is meant by such terms as rights, civil liberties, crime, and justice is a matter unfortunately absent from many contemporary discussions of legal controversies and the organizations crucially involved in them. Much has been written by admirers and detractors of the American Civil Liberties Union that exhibits this omission. If for no other reason, I intend to avoid repeating that practice.

In the literature prepared during the half century of the Union's existence, two general trends of commentary have emerged. The ACLU and its supporters have prepared records of its legislative lobbying and courtroom actions and their corresponding results appraised on the assumption that all such efforts were in support of the constitutionally guaranteed liberties of American citizens. Just as this literature has varied between professionally prepared legal writing on an academic level and admittedly polemical essays for public consumption, so also has accumulated a mountain of work correspondingly prepared for diverse audiences that seeks to condemn the Union's leaders and the overall effect they have had on the nation as being consistently un-American because of documented left-wing affiliations, if not asserting that the organization has always been a Communist front.[1]

Although this last body of criticism has usually distinguished between the laudatory, if misguided, ideals motivating the ACLU's membership and the supposed malevolent purposes of its top directors, one is unable to find a critical analysis of the group's record derived from any systematic explanation of the meaning of its professed values and the consistency, or lack of same, between the two. Such an examination is the fundamental concern of this study, although the Union's leadership is examined in an effort to understand the relationship between its words and deeds. This requires an initial delving into political theory, most especially the philosophy of law, in order to obtain some objective criteria for the judgments that must be made on the ACLU's contributions.

After the theoretical framework is briefly presented and defended, its standards are applied to test the results of the Union's work against the meaning of its asserted ideals. In many ways, the analysis views the ACLU and its inconsistences as a particularly influential consequence of the state of philosophy of law today as it is communicated through the teaching and practice of law.

The approach here is from philosophical and historical perspectives, rather than that of a law school study of particular cases, statutes, precedents, and their uses in court. There are two reasons for this. I am qualified to discuss the subject of law, if at all, only from the two stated viewpoints; I am not a law graduate. And most of the Union's work has been exclusively in the field of American constitutional law, the subject matter and controversies of which are substantially the basic questions of the major branches of philosophy reappearing in the context of the relationships between individuals living in some reasonably close proximity to each other.

In addition to the authors of the published sources I have cited, I am especially indebted to Dr. Delos Hughes of the Politics Department of Washington and Lee University's undergraduate School of Commerce, Economics and Politics, who allowed me to develop some of these ideas in two courses under his supervision. Of course, Dr. Hughes should not be associated necessarily with the conclusions of my work.

I am also thankful to my editors at Arlington House, David Franke and Karl T. Pflock, and its president, Neil McCaffrey, for giving me this opportunity to pursue a favorite subject. Mr. McCaffrey was most helpful in introducing me to Clifford Forster and C. Dickerman Williams, to both of whom I owe many thanks for assistance with first-hand observations.

I want to thank the following persons for helping me while I was obtaining factual documentation on the Union and its positions: Sidney Cardwell and archivist Richard Gibboney, New York ACLU headquarters, and Ron Ridenour, former Public Relations Director of the ACLU of Southern California, Los Angeles office. My friend and legendary rare bookfinder, H. E. Burroughs, was most helpful, as usual, in locating a number of scarce volumes used in this study.

My thanks go especially to Myril Creer who is in charge of the John Birch Society's Research Department at San Marino, California, where there is located much of the primary source material collected by the late George W. Robnett of the Church League of America, a specialist on the ACLU and similar organizations. My good and very knowledgeable friend, Mrs. J. Walter Larkin, of Phoenix, Arizona, was kind enough to acquaint me with the ACLU research done by Charles C. Polenick. I was once again greatly assisted by a fine typist, Rosemary Carroll, of Newport Beach, California.

This theoretical journey is solely under the author's guidance, although many of the ideas were derived from the work of others. Where these sources are indicated, the reader should assume that the application of others' ideas to current issues is my own work, and I alone should be judged for any inaccurate association.

September 1975
  Newport Beach, California   WILLIAM H. MCILHANY

11

Part I

The Work of the ACLU As a Reflection of Contemporary Legal Philosophy

1

The Philosophical Foundations
of the Natural Law Tradition

Evaluation of an organization, regardless of size or scope, is a project that can only be so successful as its method is properly conceived in advance. In the case of a nationwide organization with over fifty years of accumulated operations, the importance of one's approach is amplified. It would be possible, at least, to record all the significant details concerning the informal sports club formed by five youths two weeks ago. But the American Civil Liberties Union is a subject so vast that it must be approached in a more limited or partial context for purely practical considerations.

Approaching an Organization

One's discerning judgment enters the picture when the particular context is selected for study. The problem is to approach clearly what constitute the essential characteristics of the organization, those that can fairly be weighed against certain principles one has accepted as valid in the area relevant to the organization under study. Of course, those principles must be defined before they can serve as clear standards against which the group's record is compared. In the case of the ACLU, the relevant area is political and legal philosophy, that being ultimately derived from alternatives in the more fundamental branches of philosophy: metaphysics, epistemology, logic, and ethics.

Further caution is needed at the outset in determining how to select the data on an organization that will allow an examination of the group's essential quality in terms of the principles that are accepted and defended. It is much easier to recognize that the appropriate contextual arena of the ACLU is the corpus of American constitutional law and its understanding than it is to say which facts about the Union provide valid premises for a generalized judgment of its value or success in promoting its expressed ideals.

Most everyone wishes to avoid hasty generalizations. Any organization could have as members a few individuals who commit murders during or after their association with the group. Such alone would be recognized easily as unsatisfactory grounds for referring to that group as being composed of killers. However, that same perceptiveness seems harder for some critics of the ACLU to observe when they package a description of it based on an observation of some of its members adorned with long hair and beards, untidy appearances, and smoking marijuana.[1]

To focus clearly on the essential qualities of an organization requires several advance assumptions on the part of the observer. He must first realize that the organization is no more than the sum of its parts; its advocacies and actions are the ideas and work of its members, usually the more energetic and influential ones. Only those most influential in it, its leadership at various times and on various levels, can be held responsible for initiating its positions and accomplishments. Individual members do not necessarily support all the programs of a national or local body of leadership. Nor does the past record of actions and accomplishments of the group's leaders indicate the limit of their or the organization's potential for the future. Practically speaking, in studying the record of a group's accomplishments, one can only measure the statements and work of its moving or influential personalities against an understanding of their professed goals.[2]

Such qualifications as these are not reviewed to insult the intelligence of the reader, but to declare that I was trying to pay attention to them as my analysis commenced, because there will be times in this study when one could employ these distinctions as possible questions or objections against what will be presented. Therefore, I acknowledge their importance in advance. They constitute fundamentals for an epistemology (or theory of knowledge) for the study of groups, abstractions denoting a plurality of individual persons.

The goal here is to avoid confusions that result from talking about such abstract concepts as "group," "organization," or "society" as if one were referring to individually existing things, such as chairs and tables. I use the term "concrete-concept fallacy" to refer to such confusions, which I have found to cloud discussions on a multitude of topics. A group exists only as a mental concept isolating and integrating one's knowledge of a number of living and nonliving things, as well as their actions, ideas, and physical characteristics. Consequently, it is necessary to talk about groups in terms of their constituent parts, those individual things whose sum total is known of as the group. Perhaps this makes clear why I prefer to discuss such "social phenomena" from the perspective of the history of ideas and individuals, rather than using the impersonal language and mathematics of empirical sociology, which speaks of such abstractions as groups and societies as if they were primary entities, avoiding any focus on influential individuals as if, metaphorically speaking, one cannot see the trees for the forest.[3]

Another vital consideration at the outset, one which more than justifies the discussion that follows, is the fact that groups exist both in time and in particular cultures, two more abstractions not to be confused with concretes and in need of definition. An organization such as the American Civil Liberties Union is not limited in its potential accomplishments only by the "laws" of physical science. It is also limited by the amount of antecedent facts and the developed level of expertise in its field, in this case, American constitutional law. This reservoir of experience and knowledge is accumulated over time; the concepts employed in a field of study are just so advanced and integrated with other concepts at any point in time.

This certainly allows for new integration of knowledge and discoveries at any point in the future, but it demands that we not forget that whatever limitations and failures can be charged to a group are to some extent a reflection of the previous level of input available to those acting, influential members of the group from their accumulated study and experience. These persons cannot be blamed realistically for lacking knowledge or methodology that was not actually or potentially available to them at the time being evaluated. Just as one cannot reasonably criticize the Wright brothers for failing to achieve supersonic flight, we must try to understand how many grounds for criticizing the ACLU are equally applicable to the philosophy and practice of law before and during its lifetime. On this basis we should now begin to review the legacy that the Union inherited in its field of crucial concerns. Then we will be in a better position to judge the merits of what it has done with it.

Certainly there are very basic questions that arise during contemporary discussions of particular laws, their justifications, and the record of their enforcement. Many arguments over the desirability of particular laws often dissolve into seemingly fruitless debates over such problems as "But what makes this particular law, or any other, truly *legal* or just?" "What is *law* itself apart from any particular statute or piece of legislation?" "Is constitutional government anything other than a political state, the legislative and judicial action therein, and a fully or partly written description of how it operates?" "If so, what is it?" "If not, what is your basis for saying that certain laws are unconstitutional even though they are upheld by the courts and sanctioned by the legislature as specified in the document outlining "the Supreme Law of the Land?" "Don't those nations that you call 'totalitarian' function as loosely under written constitutions as we do under our own?'' ''Just what are you referring to as legal or constitutional apart from either the written documents themselves or the past history of their application as enforced rules?''[4]

At this point, in order to resolve such problems (which will seem hopeless to many entangled in them), it is necessary to discuss the basic controversies underlying the subjects of natural law and constitutionalism.

Metaphysics, Epistemology, and Ethics

In the study of philosophy we find a hierarchy of branches, each discipline building on whatever assumptions or conclusions have been reached on the more fundamental levels. The first branch, metaphysics, concerns itself with basic and all-inclusive questions in reference to the entire Universe: What is the nature of man? What is the nature of reality? What is the relationship between the two? How are all events caused to happen? One basic question in metaphysics with crucial relevance to the philosophy of law is: Do individual men possess minds with the capacity of free will or volitional control over their thoughts and actions?[5]

Next follows the theory of knowledge, or epistemology, which concerns itself with the criteria of knowledge, truth, and facts, such questions as ''How do you know that which you claim about man and his world is true?'' Establishing that nature and requirements for knowledge of reality, epistemology leads directly into the closely related science of validity and proof: logic. One of the most important philosophical issues in history, and a dispute that has significantly influenced popular notions of law as well as practically every other subject, is the epistemological problem of universals.[6]

Before entering that dispute at some length, it should be mentioned that from an accepted defense of his metaphysical conclusions in the arena of epistemology and logic, the philosopher quite naturally enters other realms. With his (hopefully) well-reasoned conclusions he realizes that he is doing little more than mental exercise and usually notices that he must answer the question ''What should one do about that which one knows?'' Here his focus is shifted from the *is* (what exists) to the *ought* (what I should do), and if he chooses to wrestle with the matter, he has embarked on the subject of ethics, or morality. The fact that he must *choose* to concern himself with such issues underlies the importance of resolving clearly at the very outset such problems of metaphysics as free will. In addition, all discussions in the field of ethics naturally presuppose that human beings possess the faculty of volition, from which arises the fact that alternative courses of behavior are possible to them. This is why we do not talk about the morality of rocks, automobiles, and forms of life below man exhibiting none of the consequences of free will.[7]

18

Applications to Political Economy

After arriving at general principles for the efficacious guidance of his own conduct—those principles being rightly derived from his basic nature and resulting needs and desires—the philosopher can advance to the application of such norms to the condition of two or more individuals living in association with one another: the abstraction *society*. Here again, moral philosophy for multitudes of men must be as well rooted in individual nature as moral philosophy for one man. This is because such characteristics as personalities, needs, and desires are only possessed by individual things. There is no "tall" apart from things that are tall in relation to others.

As a consequence of the faculty of free will, all human beings learn to value, as well as seek to gain or keep, many tangible and intangible objects. Examples range from a person's sports car to his reputation to his knowledge of how to fly a plane. When any such values are attained, they become his personal property, in addition to what was already his: his life, mind, and body, with all their potentially useful capacities. A great deal of one's property can be freely exchanged between consenting individuals on the basis of a mutual interest in the transaction. However, it is also possible for transactions of property to occur that either do not involve any genuine consent on the part of an involved party or that are examples of the use of force to deprive a person of his property or to injure it.

It is precisely because some men throughout history have always chosen to use fraud and physical force or the threat of it to take or harm another's property, that a specialized field of ethics has developed to deal with this problem. Generally at issue is "How do individual men in a society go about protecting the property of each person without creating a situation in which some or all persons' property needs to be protected from the protectors?" The study is today called political economy by many of its practitioners.

The field of politics concerns itself with the means by which an individual's rights (or inalienable property, as will be discussed later) can be protected from fraud or force on the part of other individuals. The abstract institutions that constitute the major part of this study are government and law. This has been properly done with the preliminary understanding that governments are composed of individual men and such men draft, pass upon, and enforce laws. Not only does this fact ensure imperfection, but it implies that private property must be protected from both those in and out of government. There is no separate groundwork for a morality unique to government, another one of those illusive concepts so often equated with the existing status of individual things making it up. In applying morality to government in a study of politics, we are only realistic if we hold fast to our earlier findings on human nature. In this connection, it is parenthetically interesting that those ideologists who insisted that individual morality has no application in politics, for whatever "reasons," have usually been some of the most accomplished violators of private property.

The other subcategory of political economy focuses on the exchange of property between individuals: economics. Due to the manner in which economics is so widely taught today (politics also for that matter), it is quite understandable that students in the field have no idea that their subject is a branch of philosophy.

Premises Will Out: Universals

Perhaps the reader is wondering if this discussion of abstract philosophy is really necessary to a critical analysis of an organization concerned with issues of political and legal controversy. Assuming that this approach may not have been sufficiently justified thus far, it might be well to discuss two crucially important political alternatives that shall concern us throughout this examination. In doing so, we can demonstrate the importance of a philosophical approach by showing that two famous advocates of these alternatives were logically led to them by their most fundamental differences in metaphysics and epistemology.

As has been already stated, the issue as to whether or not individual men have volitional control over their thoughts and actions is of fundamental importance in ethics, since that subject would have little meaning outside a context involving living beings with the potential of following ethical alternatives. The view of man as a being possessing a mind over which he has the power of free will has been countered classically by variants of determinism. From ancient astrologers to modern behavioral psychologists, this view has presented (with varying degrees of consistency) a portrait of men as robots, passively reacting to a host of determinating forces, either within each man or in the surrounding environment. Certainly the position which one takes in the volition-determinism debate will have profound consequences for one's views in political theory and issues of law. The notion of a person being truly guilty of a criminal action logically presupposes that he was the controlling initiator of that action; it is possible that he could have acted otherwise.[8]

Two very influential British political philosophers of the past well represented the opposing sides of this argument. The thinker who left such a mark on the framers of the U.S. Constitution, John Locke, acknowledged human free will, each person's capacity to control his conceptual faculty:

1. *Made by the mind out of simple ones.*—We have hitherto considered those ideas, in the reception whereof the mind is only passive, which are those simple ones received from sensation and reflection before mentioned, whereof the mind cannot make one to itself, not have any idea which does not wholly consist of them. [But as the mind is wholly passive in the reception of all its simple ideas, so it exerts several acts of its own, whereby out of its simple ideas, as the materials and foundations of the rest, the other are

20

framed. The acts of the mind wherein it exerts its power over its simple ideas are chiefly these three: (1) Combining several simple ideas into one compound one; and thus all *complex ideas* are made. (2) The second is bringing two ideas, whether sinple or complex, together, and setting them by one another, so as to take a view of them at once, without uniting them into one; by which way it gets all its *ideas of relations*. (3) The third is separating them from all other ideas that accompany them in their real existence; this is called abstraction: and thus all its *general ideas* are made. This shows man's power and its way of operation to be much the same in the material and intellectual world. For, the materials in both being such as he has no power over, either to make or destroy, all that man can do is either unite them together, or to set them by one another, or wholly separate them. . . .]

2. *Made voluntarily.*—In this faculty of repeating and joining together its ideas, the mind has greater power in varying and multiplying the objects of its thoughts infinitely beyond that sensation or reflection furnished it with; but all this still confined to those simple ideas which it received from those two sources, and which are the ultimate materials of all its compositions. For, simple ideas are all from things themselves; and of these the mind can have no more nor other than what are suggested to it. It can have no other ideas of sensible qualities than what come from without by the senses, nor any ideas of other kind of operations of a thinking substance that what it finds in itself. But when it has once got these simple ideas, it is not confined barely to observation, and what offers itself from without; it can, by its own power, put together those ideas it has, and make new complex ones which it never received so united.[9]

Locke's earlier contemporary, Thomas Hobbes, had advanced the view of man as a relatively passive automaton:

Every *deliberation* is then said to *end* when that whereof they deliberate is either done or thought impossible, because till then we retain the liberty of doing or omitting according to our appetite or aversion.

In *deliberation,* the last appetite or aversion immediately adhering to the action or to the admission thereof is that we call the WILL—the act, not the faculty, of *willing*. And beasts that have *deliberation* must necessarily also have *will*. The definition of the *will* given commonly by the Schools, that it is a *rational appetite,* is not good. For if it were, then could there be no voluntary act against reason. For a *voluntary act* is that which proceeds from the *will,* and no other.[10]

Here it is important to mention that Hobbes defined *voluntary acts* as those which are determined by the *will* and *vital acts* as those which need no assistance from mental functioning, including all automatic physiological body processes. With that clear, we can return to his statement.

But if instead of a rational appetite we shall say an appetite resulting from a precedent deliberation, then the definition is the same that I have given here. *Will,* therefore, *is the last appetite in deliberating.* And though we say in common discourse a man had a will once to do a thing that nevertheless he forbode to do, yet that is properly but an inclination which makes no action voluntary, because the action depends not of it but of

21

the last inclination or appetite. For if the intervenient appetites make any action voluntary, then by the same reason all intervenient aversions should make the same action involuntary; and so one and the same action should be both voluntary and involuntary.[11]

Without taking time to explicate fully the entanglements in which Hobbes found himself, we can fairly observe that he denied the reality of any truly volitional capacity in man, however circuitous an argumentative route he chose for his defense.

By what persuasions were Locke and Hobbes led to such divergent metaphysical conclusions concerning man's autonomy? We should hardly expect such positions to be assumed as initial postulates by competent philosophers. They were not. The dispute between Locke and Hobbes over the existence or nonexistence of free will in man arose from a consistent application of their respective conclusions concerning the nature of man's knowledge. It was precisely Locke's conviction that man's knowledge is of a conceptual nature that allowed his acknowledgement of the concepts *mind* and *volition*. For Hobbes such concepts were inadmissible, since he denied the existence of the process of concept-formation.

Realism and Its Problems

The first major contributions to this issue, the problem of universals, came from the outstanding Greek "realists," Plato and Aristotle.[12] In answer to the question "What is the manness essential to all men?" Plato held that all individual men were illusory projections of the universal manness, existing as an ideal form in another dimension. Most people only see the illusory projections and conclude that they constitute reality. But the mind of the philosopher has access to the world of ideal forms, the true reality. Aristotle differed by claiming that the manness common to all men was a tangible element within each man. Although John Locke knew that his ancient colleagues were mistaken in their assumption that there is anything strictly identical between the physical structures of two men, he held that the concept of manness is known to human minds by the same process advanced by the Greek sages. He agreed with them that a concept is a mental representation or reflection of a particular thing with its nonuniversal characteristics somehow omitted. They primarily differed on the issues of the location and existential status of the universal, the "stuff" of which concepts are made. Plato and Aristotle thought universals possessed the existential status of tangible concrete objects, differing only as to their spatiotemporal location in reference to the existing particulars named by them. By giving concepts the metaphysical quality of individual concretes, rather than distinguishing their existential status as epistemological or ideational, the explanations of realism advanced by both Plato and Aristotle exhibited what we have already dubbed "the concrete-concept fallacy."

Locke was too wise to avoid noticing this problem, and his realist explanation of concepts was formulated with the intention of correcting the error, as Brand Blanshard has written:

Locke held roundly that both Platonic and Aristotelian universals were fictions. 'All things that exist are only particulars'; 'general and universal belong not to the real existence of things; but are the inventions and creatures of the understanding made by it for its own use, and concern only signs, whether words or ideas.' How, then, does the illusion that there are universals arise? It arises out of the projection into things of our own abstract ideas. And why do we 'invent' such ideas? Because they are extremely convenient tools. It is in theory possible that everything we experience should have its own name, but that would call for a supply of proper names running into the millions. What happens is that when a new object is very like something we know already, we call it by the same name, 'man' for example, and this name comes to be associated with the thought of the qualities common to these objects. With its help, we can think, if we wish, of a set of qualities in which all men are alike. We can then, by dropping out some, go on to think of the qualities in which all animals are alike, attaching the name 'animal' to this thinner group. But the unity or identity of such classes lies in the idea itself, not in the nature of men or of animals. Each man, as we experience him, is a bundle of particular qualities; there is nothing in him over and above these qualities, in the way of manness or humanity, in which he is identical with other men. Thus the only 'universal' involved is the idea, which we devise for our own convenience and whose locus is our own mind.[13]

In this characteristically well-stated passage, Blanshard is making basically the same point for Locke that is contained in what I have called the concrete-concept fallacy. Namely, that universals, or concepts, exist only in an epistemological status as objects of thought or organized knowledge. The group of characteristics or qualities common to all men are not located in another dimension, as Plato claimed. Nor are they material things which could be extracted from an individual man with the result of leaving behind an example of the wider class, animal. Perhaps the best contemporary definition of concept formation as an epistemological activity was posited by Ayn Rand: the mental integration of two or more concretes on the basis of their common essential characteristics with their particular measurements omitted.[14] Such a formulation as that of Locke or Rand provides, at least, a starting point that is not vulnerable to the same objections which rose against the realism of Plato and Aristotle.

The "nominalists," of which Thomas Hobbes is a leading example, challenged the validity of realist universals on several grounds, which probably encouraged Locke to modify his presentation. Their criticisms included the fact that any such explanation as Aristotle's apparently claimed that what is essential to a thing exists separately from that thing, opening the way for the illogical step of removing or isolating a chair's chairness and still expecting it to remain what it is. And Aristotle's position that we recognize all trees to be such by a special faculty that strips away from our perception all that is not "treeness" in each one we encounter brought both questions about the nature and function of that capacity as well as the protest that this meant man's knowledge was composed only of universal, not particular, characteristics. Thus, on this road, one had no ability to make physical descriptions or measurements. What would one do with those concepts that are obvious matters of degree? How would one's special faculty recognize that number of years at which a person first becomes "old" or that temperature immediately below which it becomes "cold"? Obviously, Locke and others sought to avoid such quagmires.[15]

However, Locke's formulation is subject to much criticism for its flaws, as Professor Blanshard writes:

> Now this theory, as it is stated, is inconsistent with itself. It says first that things possess nothing in common and then that we form abstract ideas by fixing our attention on what they have in common. But if they really have nothing in common, how could we fix attention on it? Presumably what Locke means is that they are similar, and that we fix attention on the points in which they resemble each other. Will the theory serve as thus amended?
>
> Not quite. (1) It was offered as a theory of universals generally; but we have seen reason to believe that specific universals are genuine identities, not merely sets of similar characters. Locke seems, indeed, to admit this when he talks of 'the same colour being observed today in chalk or snow, which the mind yesterday received from milk.' But this 'same' is inconsistent with his general theory that there are no universals among things. If he is to carry that theory through consistently he must hold that not even such a specific universal as this shade of whiteness is ever the same in two cases. And we have found this an unplausible view.
>
> (2) Even with regard to qualitative, and generic universals, the theory is imperfectly worked out. Locke assumes that, though there are no Aristotelian universals, thought acts as if there were. We have found his saying that we abstract 'common' properties. Is this surrender to the universal to be averted by substituting 'similar' for 'the same?' The case certainly calls for argument. In saying that Socrates and Plato are alike, we ordinarily assume that they are alike in some respect, namely in being men. This *respect* in which they are alike seems to be common property. In the very attempt to make clear what we mean by calling them alike, we seem to be carried back to the universal we sought to avoid. It is obvious that some account must be given of the relation between being similar and being the same. Locke never gave it. He was content to say that from merely similar particulars the mind could glean the concept of an identity which was not there. And of course if it was not among the events of nature, it was also not among the events of one's own mind. No two thoughts of 'the same thing,' held by different persons or successively by the same person, ever had anything in common. Nor did we ever use the same word. 'Man', as used a second time, was just another particular, which had nothing whatever in common with the first.[16]

The fact that Locke never satisfactorily answered these objections in defending his positions led to the collapse of conceptualism in philosophy and the rise of nominalist views, particularly from the early nineteenth century onward, the consequences of which have had the most profound, though little known, effects on all fields of study, including law.

Nominalism As Destroyer

By abandoning any interest in universals, the nominalists found themselves inheriting problems far more complex than those they attacked. Perhaps the most unpleasant implications contained in nominalist epistemology concerned the validity of deductive and inductive reasoning. The student of logic is familiar with the classic "barbara" form of the syllogism: "All men are mortals. Socrates is a man. Therefore, Socrates is mortal." This translates algebraically into: "All As are Bs. C is an A. Therefore, C is B." Therein is contained the method of human reasoning that has been found to be quite in concord with reality. However, this process presupposes that identities or universals can be identified in more than one particular thing, as it says, "All As are Bs," rather than, "All As are similar to Bs." Thus, a consistent nominalist would have to admit that deductive and inductive reasoning must be scrapped for something else. But there are, and probably never have been, any fully consistent nominalists among philosophers, as such would be a terrible task. Certainly Thomas Hobbes was not fully committed to the application of his assumptions. And logicians of nominalist persuasion, when confronted with the above dilemma, have generally replied that logical expressions, such as a classical syllogism, do not refer to anything in the material world anyway, but merely illustrate a habit philosophers have adopted for dealing with the relationship between certain markings on paper.[17]

So the nominalists, in claiming that there is no basis in reality for our grouping of disparate concretes in the category labeled by a word, were left with the weak and compromising stance that such gatherings are collected on the basis of rough similarities or "family resemblances" somehow "common" to all the members. And it has been such weak nominalism that has so profoundly influenced the majority of philosophers since the time of Immanuel Kant and has lent much to the approaches taken by adherents of empiricism, logical positivism, and linguistic analysis.

Consequences of Conceptualism Abandoned

It has been the reader's patient attention to a rather technical issue of academic philosophy that now allows me to discuss more meaningfully the consequences of this trend as it has been applied in the philosophy of law. Although we shall return shortly to the problem of universals in an effort to formulate a defensible conceptualism where Locke failed, in passing by the subject momentarily, the reader might keep in mind the alternatives thus far presented, if for no other reason than for noticing how often the ancient dispute arises in the day-to-day clothes of myriad discussions.[18]

The reason I have belabored this philosophical discussion so far should be now easily understood. In fact, it should finally come home dearly to the reader. Thomas Hobbes and John Locke both thought that human government should conform to man's nature, although the former would have been unlikely to have expressed it that way. The fact that Locke affirmed man's conceptual faculty and the potentially efficacious functioning of his mind led him to realize that man was in control of himself in a very fundamental way. Therefore, he held, to reflect this, government must be limited sufficiently to allow for self-government by individuals. Because Hobbes rejected all abstract universals, including mind and free will, he was left with a view of man as a helpless robot, pushed and pulled by external sensory pressures over which he had no effective control. Man was in a state of involuntary, uncontrollable chaos, the slave of forces beyond himself. This condition, Hobbes believed, would place him eternally in physical conflict with his fellows. The only remedy for the tranquility of society could be an absolute dictatorship over all human machines, for ordering them in the proper directions.

In today's world the followers of Thomas Hobbes are winning. For our purposes, the degree to which the advocates of human liberty were successful is the degree to which they are consistent in and improve upon the Lockean tradition. We must examine the American Civil Liberties Union by that standard. There is no other more crucial issue, as the history of constitutionalism reveals. And there is precious little time.

26

2

Constitutionalism and the Rise of Nominalist-Positivist "Law"

When we turn to the field of politics and law, particularly constitutional law, we enter the subject matter of concern to such organizatons as the American Civil Liberties Union. As comparatively recent phenomena in the history of constitutionalism, the ACLU and its approach to issues of constitutional law have been greatly influenced by the prevailing legal treatment of the subject they inherited. It is therefore necessary to discuss briefly the evolution of constitutionalism to uncover what persuasions we might expect to find operative in the Union's orientation and policies. As justification for having just led the reader through rather viscous, but hopefully comprehensible, waters, my comments on constitutionalism will be in the context of the ascendancy of nominalism over conceptualism in philosophy by the end of the nineteenth century.

The central issue in American constitutionalism is one of universals, the subject of natural law. To appreciate the philosophy of natural law that inspired those who wrote the U.S. Constitution, we must trace its Greek, Roman, and British roots.

Natural Law

Fundamental to constitutionalism is the effort to make the actions of those administering a political state conform to a set of standards beyond their control. Since this implies an origin for such standards beyond the transitory whims of individual rulers, constitutionalism has always started with a quest for a higher law than that passed by legislatures or handed down by kings, a set of principles of law against which all such legislation or edicts would be judged. Here we have the concept of two different kinds of law. One variety, statute, or *positive,* law is the product of legislative bodies, or "the law the King makes." The other, constitutional law, is "the law that *makes* the King." Clearly, the latter serves as a standard against which each of the former is judged.

Limited Government in Athens and Rome

Although modern constitutionalism is usually associated with the purpose of limiting the power of a government by proscribing numerous actions of its leaders on the basis of a higher principle, to the Greeks a constitution was merely a description of the characteristics and mechanics of a political state, no matter how powerful it was. In spite of this, the Greeks saw truth in law as a reflection of that which was right in ethics. Such truth was to be discovered by the same method used in all other investigations.[1]

Because Aristotle believed "there really is, as everyone to some extent divines, a natural justice . . . that is binding on all men," he advised lawyers "to appeal to the law of nature" if they found that they did not have a secure case in statutory law, arguing with Sophocles that "an unjust law is not a law."[2]

The attorney preeminent of the ancient world followed this advice. Cicero wrote, "*True Law* is right reason in agreement with nature; it is of universal application, unchanging and ever lasting. . . ."[3] By this he meant higher, *natural,* law was not subject to amendment by legislatures. Indeed, natural law was as immutable as the law of gravitation. He continued:

> . . . We cannot be freed from its obligations by Senate or people . . . and there will not be different laws at Rome and at Athens, or different laws now and in the future, but one eternal and unchangeable law will be valid for all nations and all times, and there will be one master and ruler, that is God, over us all, for He is the author of this law, its promulgator, and its enforcing judge. . . . It is a *sacred obligation* not to attempt to legislate *in contradiction* to this law."[4]

Fully consistent in practice with his convictions, Cicero often pleaded in the courts of Rome that a statute of the Roman Senate was invalid because it violated natural law. At this point, any reader who has had American courtroom experience knows that we are talking about a method of practicing law quite removed from present-day norms.

28

Reaffirmation of Medieval Church Fathers

The tradition that the ultimate source of natural law was divine relevation lasted from the pagan Roman Republic into the Christian Middle Ages, being defended by neo-Platonists like Saint Augustine and other early Church fathers. The Aristotelian approach was brightly renewed by the ablest philosophical mind of this remote period, Saint Thomas Aquinas. Echoing Cicero, Saint Thomas professed with regard to a statute that "if on any point [it] is in conflict with the law of nature, it at once ceases to be a law; it is a mere perversion of law."[5]

The recognition by most great thinkers from the Roman Republic through the Renaissance that there was a *natural law* to which man-made law must conform, did not prevent a number of persisting controversies surrounding its nature and use. If, indeed, the natural law came from God, was it all contained in the existing Holy Scriptures, or was it continually revealing itself to men through an earthly spokesman for God? Obviously, there would be conflict as to the sources of natural law between Catholics and Protestants. The natural law for Moslems would come from a different deity and scriptures than those of Christians and Jews. And yet, the concept of natural law presupposes that such law is valid for all men everywhere.

A further problem arose from fraudulent misuses of natural law to justify tyrannical actions of government, the sort of thing natural law was thought to prohibit. Monarchs could pose as equal interpretors of the law with jurists, claiming their actions to be of the order divinely ordained in man and his world. Medieval constitutionalism did not produce any systematic means for obligating rulers to place themselves under the constraint of true natural law. This problem was a source of the criticism so well made by Enlightenment thinkers: "natural law" could easily be used to justify any edict, however despotic, and it provided a specious support for the "divine right of kings" doctrine.

Thus, the great unsolved dilemma of medieval constitutionalism remained as follows: The actions of rulers must be restricted by obedience to a higher, or divine, natural law because men are sinful and prone to abuse power. However, just who is now present on earth to proclaim, reveal, or rule in accord with the natural law other than individual men? Obviously, one man cannot claim special status to know true law better than his fellows by virtue of a position he holds which is not equally esteemed by all. If such a condition prevailed, all that remained of "natural law" would soon become a license for whatever *he* wanted to do. If he is the verbal source of law, he alone must know the extent to which he is subject to it. We can recognize the tendency of this problem to arise as we examine the English contribution to constitutionalism.[6]

29

The English Tradition Through Coke

Cicero's concept of law was brilliantly reflected in the writings of John of Salisbury, a twelfth century political thinker. He wrote that "there are certain precepts of the law which have perpetual necessity, having the force of the law among all nations and which absolutely cannot be broken. . . ."[7] Not only must the judges observe the natural law, but the monarch "may not lawfully have any will of his own apart from that which the law or equity enjoins, or the calculation of the common interest requires."[8]

About 1256, Henry of Bratton reaffirmed the king's obligation to observe the limits on his power imposed by the law of nature, concluding that all authority was derived from, and limited by, a law higher than the king's will. Almost two centuries later a leading jurist, Sir John Fortescue, stated that statutes or positive laws were like "a sanction added by the state to a precept of natural law." Such precepts were not subject to the king's tampering; he could not take from the people what was theirs without their consent. Sir John further isolated the monarch from manipulation of the law by urging that only jurists with much study and experience were qualified to interpret the law.[9]

The development of the view that the king was as much subject to the law as were his people led to the famous English constitutional crisis of 1608, which grew out of the confrontation between the towering legal scholar Sir Edward Coke and King James I. The dispute resulted from Coke's defense of judicial review for deciding all conflicts in law. It seems that King James, a scholar in his own right, thought "the law was founded on reason and that he and others had reason as well as the judges."[10] James was offended bitterly by the notion that "he should be under the law, which was treason to affirm."[11] Whereas Coke contended (at the time quite futilely)

> that the King hath no prerogative, but that which the law of the land allows. . . . And it appears in our books, that in many cases, the common law will control acts of Parliament, and sometimes adjudge them to be utterly void; for when an act of Parliament is against *common right and reason,* or repugnant, or impossible to be performed, the common law will control it and adjudge such an act to be void.[12]

The influence of Coke's emphasis on natural law in early American jurisprudence may be understood when one realizes that his *Institutes* was the principal text studied by the new nation's first legal graduates. It remained for them to secure and strengthen his goal of judicial review.

In sixteenth century England, Richard Hooker advanced the Thomist natural law position decades before Coke's *Institutes* appeared. According to Hooker, "In laws, that which is *natural* bindeth universally, that which is *positive* not so."[13] Another contemporary of Coke, Algernon Sydney, lost his head in 1683 for

30

voicing his position during the Stuart Restoration and adding this imperative: "that which is not just is not law and that which is not law ought not to be obeyed." [14]

The Contributions of John Locke

But the English thinker who was most influential on later American institutions was John Locke, the subject of our earlier comments. Locke not only was oriented toward the Newtonian perspective on a universe governed by knowable principles or laws. He also was in harmony with Alexander Pope's unity of metaphysics and ethics, as expressed, "whatever is, is right." [15] Locke even thought he knew how such truths might be derived! His premises led him directly to a formulation on law closely resembling that of Cicero: "The law of nature stands as an eternal rule to all men, legislators as well as others." [16] This conviction motivated him to suggest institutional principles that might be employed to prevent political rulers from abridging natural law.

To quote some from Locke on these prescriptions for limiting government will serve to show his influence on American constitutionalism. Here Locke explains that government must be limited because those in government have no just powers to do anything for their subjects that those subjects were not justly able to do for themselves prior to the establishment of the state.

> For nobody can transfer to another more power than he has in himself, and nobody has an absolute arbitrary power over himself, or over any other, to destroy his own life or take away the life or property of another. A man, as has been proved, cannot subject himself to the arbitrary power over the life, liberty, or possessions of another, but only so much as the law of nature gave him for the preservation of himself and the rest of mankind, this is all he doth, or can give up to the commonwealth, and by it to the legislative power, so that the legislative can have no more power than this. [17]

Acknowledging rights to be inalienable characteristics of all living persons, Locke further proposed a number of principles of procedural natural law. The law of the realm must rightly be applied to all and grant equal protections to all, regardless of personal status or condition. Laws must be understandable, possible to obey, and known by those subject to them prior to their enforcement. They must not be passed and then enforced retroactively. Laws must be enforced in the courts and a prohibition placed on the legislature exercising any judicial function. Legislatures cannot transfer the powers that have been delegated only to them by their constituents. Because Locke recognized the right to one's property as absolute, he held that it could not be taken by anyone in or out of government without direct or indirect consent. Should those in government act contrary to these principles of natural law, Locke claimed that by doing so they have subverted the purpose of government and those who have delegated their powers, the citizens, are free to remove the misrulers by whatever means necessary. [18]

31

Manifestation in the New World

The English tradition of constitutionalism from the Magna Carta, which came to be regarded as a fundamental statement of natural law,[19] to Coke and Locke was heavily borrowed by the numerous legal minds among the Founders of the United States to accomplish the limited government goal that Britain never achieved. Thomas Jefferson, Alexander Hamilton, James Madison, John Adams, Sam Adams, James Otis, Patrick Henry, George Wythe, and William Patterson were most prominent among these attorneys of the Coke tradition.[20] They were joined by other staunch advocates of natural law, including Benjamin Franklin and George Mason. Hamilton put it beautifully:

> The sacred rights of mankind are not to be rummaged for among old records or musty parchments. They are written, *as with a sunbeam, in its whole volume of human nature, by the hand of Divinity itself, and can never be erased or obscured by mortal power.*
> . . .When the first principles of civil society are violated, and the right of a whole people are invaded, the common forms of municiple law are not to be regarded. *Men may then betake themselves to the law of nature; and, if they but conform their actions to that standard,* all cavils against them betray either ignorance or dishonesty. There are some events in society, to which human laws cannot extend, but when applied to them, *lose all their force and efficacy.* In short, when *human laws contradict or discountenance the means which are necessary to preserve the essential rights of any society, they defeat the proper end of all laws, and so become null and void.*[21]

Well reflecting the same sentiments was Hamilton's frequent opponent Thomas Jefferson, who wrote:

> Every man, and every leader of men on earth, possess the right of self government. *They receive it with their being from the hand of nature.* Individuals exercise it by their single will; collections of men by that of the majority; for the law of the majority is the natural law of society. . . . It is to secure our rights that we resort to government at all. . . . The idea is quite unfounded that on entering society we give up any natural rights. . . . All natural rights may be abridged in their exercise by Law. . . . Laws abridging the natural right of the citizen should be restrained by *rigorous constructions within their narrowest limits.* . . . The mass of the citizens is the safest depository of their own rights.[22]

The leading Pennsylvania lawyer of the Revolutionary War and one of the first American professors of law, James Wilson, defined natural law as having *"its foundations in the constitution and state of man."*[23] This statement reveals the degree to which this eloquent Founding Father was in accord with the philosophical approach outlined earlier, in which one's rational conclusions concerning ethics and politics are derived logically from one's findings concerning the nature of man. Wilson continues:

This law, or right reason as Cicero calls it, is thus beautifully described by that eloquent philosopher. It is, indeed, a true law, conformable to nature, diffused among men, unchangeable, eternal. By its commands, it calls men to duty; by its prohibitions it deters them from vice. *To diminish, to alter, much more to abolish this law, is a vain attempt.* Neither by the Senate, nor by the people, can its powerful obligations be dissolved. It requires no interpreter or commentators. It is not one law at Rome, another at Athens; one law now, another hereafter; it is the same eternal and immutable law; given at all times and to all nations: for God, who is its author and promulgator, is always the sole master and sovereign of mankind.[24]

Indications of this focus on natural law as the essence of American constitutionalism can be easily found in James Otis' arguments in the 1761 *Writs of Assistance case;* his pamphlet, *The Rights of the British Colonists Asserted and Proved* (1764); the Massachusetts Circular Letter of 1768; the documents of the First Continental Congress; the documents of the 1776 Town Meeting of Concord, Massachusetts; the debates before the constitutional conventions established in 1784; the preambles to both the Declaration of Independence and the Constitution; and *The Federalist Papers.*[25]

The Return to Legislative Supremacy

Unfortunately, at the same time that a conceptualist view of natural law was forming the philosophical base for the first successful experiment in *limited* constitutional government, a different and antithetical outlook was gaining acceptance among jurists and philosophers in general.

The legal deviation arose from the works of a towering writer on the law, Sir William Blackstone (1723–1780). His *Commentaries on the Laws of England,* published between 1765 and 1769, became the standard work on the history of the common, or unwritten, law. While acknowledging the supremacy of a higher, fundamental law, Blackstone's factual errors of research led him to advocate the legislative supremacy of Parliament:

It hath sovereign and uncontrollable authority in the making, conforming, enlarging, restraining, abrogating, repealing, revising, and expounding of laws . . . this being the place where that absolute, despotic power which must in all governments reside somewhere, is entrusted by the constitution of these kingdoms. All mischiefs and grievances, operations and remedies that transcend the ordinary course of the laws, are within the reach of this extraordinary tribunal. . . . It can, in short, do everything that is *not naturally impossible,* and therefore some have not scrupled to call its power by a figure rather too bold, the omnipotence of Parliament. True it is, that what the Parliament doth no authority on earth can undo.[26]

33

Much to the distress of American natural law advocates, such as Jefferson, the fact that all attorneys and "educated gentlemen" were likely to be students of Blackstone's work meant that his confusions and ill-conceived thesis would become tremendously influential in Britain and America. His influence remains with us today. Blackstone, by quite wrongly advocating the doctrine of legislative supremacy, reduced the concept of a philosophically knowable natural law to an equation with whatever positive laws or statutes are approved by the lawmakers. The tyranny that Lockean natural law advocates had strived to prevent by limiting the king or executive with a set of moral prohibitions was replaced in Blackstone's system with an all-powerful legislature restricted only by the laws of the physical and biological sciences.

One obviously influential factor in the growth of collectivism in modern-day Britain is the heritage it received from Blackstone. His rule of the majority through their unlimited representatives effectively overturned the constraints of the Magna Carta and the common law tradition, bringing to that nation precisely the dangers inherent in unbridled democracy that our Founding Fathers had so feared and obstructed with a system of checks and balances.

But since the publication of his *Commentaries,* Blackstone has been winning the battle against natural law among philosophers and jurists. British and American legal theorists after 1789 transferred their interest from the conceptualist approach to law taken by those followers of Coke who founded the United States to a purely factual and superficially historical study of past statutes, precedents, and judicial decisions. The analysis, quite the same as the "case method" used today in most law schools, approached positive or written laws and court decisions as *the given,* to be noted and learned for future employment in courtroom argumentation. No longer was there anything further to consider, such as philosophical conclusions regarding the nature of man and his rights. Those rights were whatever the legislature and courts had held them to be. Soon it was popular to think of old-fashioned natural law theories as pleasant pastimes for those who might be interested. Increasingly, natural law ideas have become less persuasive, if not inadmissible, in formal arguments before judges and juries in both civil and criminal disputes. The esteemed career of Cicero would come to failure in the legal profession today. Legal education and practice have moved far from the natural law orientation of those who designed American constitutionalism. Commenting on the light dismissal of the former natural law emphasis, Lon L. Fuller writes:

> The view, common among modern scholars, that in the quoted passage Coke betrays a näive faith in natural law, tells us little that will help us understand the intellectual climate of the seventeenth century. It tells us a great deal about our own age, an age that in some moods at least thinks itself capable of believing that no appeal to man's nature, or to the nature of things, can ever be more than a cover for subjective preference, and that under the rubric "subjective preference" must be listed indifferently propositions as far apart as that laws ought to be clearly expressed and that the only just tax is one that makes the citizen pay the exact equivalent of what he himself receives from government.

34

Those who actually created our Republic and its Constitution were much closer in their thinking to the age of Coke than they are to ours. They, too, were concerned to avoid repugnancies in their institutions and to see to it that those institutions should suit the nature of man. Hamilton rejected the "political heresy" of the poet who wrote:

> For forms of government let fools contest—
> That which is best administered is best.[27]

While most influential personally in propagating the doctrine that the true law was whatever the legislature issued, Blackstone was only a catalyst for this change. He well foreshadowed what was coming anyway to legal theory as a result of the philosophical revolution that was earlier introduced to the reader.

The Legacy of Legal Positivism

Blackstone's departure from the natural law tradition occurred about the same time that many philosophers—Immanuel Kant being the most important by far—were discarding Locke's defense of universals, or conceptualism, in favor of nominalism.[28] The resulting popularity of a strict empiricism in philosophy led to the rise of legal positivism.[29] The positivist jurists henceforth regarded legality as illustrated by the actions of any political authority, regardless of the quality of those actions. From the natural law position of "that which is true of man is law," the positivists switched to the rule "that which is done by those in authority in any area is law."

With the method of concept-formation ignored in an effort to escape "superstitions," philosophers forsook the challenge to defend the validity of all universals, including those that had so long been respected as abstract principles of natural law. For their discussions of law they were left with no subject matter other than the directly perceivable products of human government. The law became one and the same with the tangible written statute. There were no more fine theoretical distinctions or debates over the degree of legality inherent in a particular law. All statutes everywhere were equally *legal* to positivists and their later philosophical kinsman, the legal realists[30] and the new analytical jurists,[31] as long as they were authored by an existing political state and being enforced. Professor Fuller comments on this contemporary trend:

> It is truly astounding to what an extent there runs through modern thinking in legal philosophy the assumption that law is like a piece of inert matter—it is there or not there. It is only such an assumption that could lead legal scholars to assume, for example, that the "laws" enacted by the Nazis in their closing years, considered as laws and in abstraction from their evil aims, were just as much laws as those of England and Switzerland. An even more grotesque outcropping of this assumption is the notion that the moral obligation of the decent German citizen to obey these laws was in no way

affected by the fact that they were in part kept from his knowledge, that some of them retroactively "cured" wholesale murder, that they contained wide delegations of administrative discretion to redefine the crimes they proscribed, and that, in any event, their actual terms were largely disregarded when it suited the convenience of the military courts appointed to apply them.[32]

I think it is rather easy to see that legal positivism leads to a sanction of brutal totalitarianism and a position diametrically opposed to the views of those who formulated American constitutionalism. The problem is that legal positivism also rules the teaching and practice of modern American law. After the first-year law student completes his "history" course in constitutional law, with the exception of only a few law schools, he may never again hear or have occasion to participate in a discussion of natural law. He certainly will be unlikely to make use of what he has *not* learned after passing the bar exam. If this is the case with the overwhelming majority of those who make and practice the law in America today, is it any wonder that we find at every turn the problem of human rights being violated by unlimited government action?

Knowing that our institutions of legal instruction, lawmaking, and jurisprudence have lost all consistency with the foundation of American constitutionalism should make it easier to understand why individual liberties remain so greatly imperiled. It should also make it easier for us to understand some of the reasons for the inconsistency we shall discover between what is necessary to ensure the goals of one organization in this modern tradition and what that organization has actually accomplished. It should help us understand why the opposite of human liberty has been so generally promoted by the work of the American Civil Liberties Union.

3

Alternatives in the Philosophy of Law in Today's Legal Education and Practice

To better clarify the alternatives that exist in the philosophy of law today, it is necessary to illustrate them by means of a model applying their approaches to legality as solutions to a problem. The model presented here is an adaptation of another, from which I gained understanding of this subject.[1]

Crime Out of Time

The year is A.D. 2000. The people of the United States have managed in two decades to restore, strengthen, and expand their constitutional-republican system of government, with far greater built-in limitations and institutionalized mechanical restraints on governmental power at all levels than existed a century earlier. The disastrous drift toward statism, national bankruptcy, and crushing bureaucracy that advanced after 1930 has been overwhelmingly reversed. A popular interest in the American constitutional heritage has taken hold of influential citizens in all fields as a result of the grass-roots educational movement that was established in the 1950s by a retired business executive, then widely scorned but now venerated after his death.

The issue of individual rights is paramount in all newspaper editorials, judicial decisions, and political campaign speeches. There are no higher "priorities." Government has been reduced to a system of national defense and local police and courts for punishing those who violate the rights of others—but only *after* such violations have happened.

This radical transformation of the United States has produced incredible prosperity, now that the long depression of the late 1970s is behind the nation. Government has been separated completely from the economic sphere of people's lives, except for actions against those initiating force and fraud. The changes in the United States have encouraged a number of formerly statist nations to emulate the new American example. Many have little choice now that U.S. foreign aid has been abolished.

The freeing of technology from dictatorial restraints did far more than just solve the pollution and energy problems. Private corporate firms are preparing to send astronauts to nearby solar systems where advanced life is thought to exist. An inventor has announced that he has finally perfected the world's first machine capable of time travel. He stated that the design was completed in early 1980, but it could not be tested due to the lack of significant venture capital and because of the bureaucratic ban that existed until recently on certain nutritional supplements that are necessary for the physiological well-being of persons experiencing time-frame transfer.

Recently, a corporation was formed to finance the world's first expedition through time. Five accomplished scientific and professional persons were chosen for the voyage. The time-travel device, in outward appearance little more than a room with a floor area of four hundred square feet and no windows was quickly readied for the initial test.

The members of the expedition reviewed extensively their project routine, for they were not to be in communication with the corporate directors or the inventor until their "return" from a past age. Naturally, the corporation and the inventor did not make known the workings of the wondrous contraption. For in the United States of A.D. 2000, all private property, tangible and intellectual, is protected. It was assumed that everything had been checked and was in working order, and that all contingencies were understood.

The time voyagers remained in the device for what seemed to observers in the year 2000 but a few hours. They emerged appearing quite healthy, and two of the men actually seemed to have lost several facial characteristics of aging. They were greeted by the President, and the ceremony was broadcast throughout the world. Of course, it was necessary to have them undergo thorough medical checks to guarantee they were none the worse for the extraordinary wear.

The chronicle of the mission was recorded in personal log books and diaries, which were processed and studied during the following weeks. It was announced that in a month or two information on the trip would be available for sale to the various private communications media.

Two days later, newspapers across the country featured the resignation of the

Time Travel Corporation's board of directors and the inventor, and reported the company's formal dissolution.

A stunned public waited eagerly to know the reason. Within a few days, it was revealed that the tumult has resulted from a reading of the log diaries kept by the time travelers and voluntary truth-machine tests to which they had submitted to confirm the factual nature of their writings.

These writings revealed that the expedition members, upon arriving at a distant point in the earth's past, had encountered an ancient tribal culture of very peaceable tendencies, primitives who neither posed nor offered any threat to the travelers. However, possessed and overcome by long-accumulated feelings of insecurity, three of the time explorers had initiated an unprovoked, all-out campaign of murder, rape, and plunder on these helpless ancients, committing every bestial brutality and violation of rights conceivable in the context of that primitive culture. Two expedition members had voiced objection to the violations at the outset, but they were outnumbered. The three plunderers had threatened to kill them and leave them in the past to die eons before they were born. This was enough to make the two outraged voyagers offer no resistance for the remainder of the trip. They had been able to record the events in their diaries while the other three were ravaging the countryside. No attempt was made to breach the language barrier with the ancient victims, or to learn anything of their culture, traditions, and laws. The mission had turned into an orgy of destruction and violence.

The shocked American people demanded swift justice for the brigands-in-time. The President appointed an investigating commission to study the records and recommend a constitutional course for securing a solution, its findings to be merely recommendations for lower-court action. The deliberations of the commission soon were bogged down in what seemed to be an insurmountable quandary: Could the persons on the time-travel voyage be punished for actions that are clearly criminal under our present system but may not have been proscribed by whatever unknown laws were observed by the people of earth at that distant past time when they were perpetrated?

The presidential commission heard several different arguments on this problem and then broke down in hopeless controversy. Let us listen to the advocates:

FIRST ADVOCATE: Distinguished Commissioners, I am here to appeal to what is purely common sense. There is no way we can do anything legal against the members of the time-travel expedition. All of the available factual evidence shows that they committed actions which we would appraise in our time as horribly criminal. But only when such actions are committed in our time, or another in which laws similar to ours obtain. The primitive culture encountered by the crew, our primordial ancestors perhaps, showed no signs of possessing any systematic body of law—certainly none explicitly prohibiting the actions of those on the mission. In the absence of such evidence to the contrary, we must assume that such acts were not illegal in that time. We certainly cannot call the voyagers actions unlawful. How silly that would be in the absence of any laws at all!

Now, of course, the crude accusation will be made against me that I am totally insensitive to the miseries inflicted by the crew members on the defenseless natives. Such is rubbish, as no one in our time has a record as a more staunch defender of the downtrodden and oppressed in the courts than I.

Attacks of personal invective against me for making this case thusly accomplish precious little. We should all face the future, not the past, rejoicing that our culture is more humane than that of our ancestors and has molded that which is law to endanger all who would bring violence without reason to their fellow men. The course I am advising you to take, that of freeing the crew members from any punishment, will provoke discontent from the vulgar, who fancy the law as something inherently *theirs*. But taking this advice will protect the law from the peculiar nature of men who would destroy our institutions before ever understanding them.

SECOND ADVOCATE: It may surprise you gentlemen to learn that I concur fully with the conclusion of my noted colleague, who has just spoken—but for entirely different reasons.

I, too, should stress at the outset that I abhor the acts with which the three time travelers have been charged, as well as the cowardly submission of their companions. But one's moral sentiments have nothing to do with the law.

In recent centuries those of our profession have come to realize that that which constitutes a state's legality is the position of authority or power it holds over its citizens. With few exceptions, this authority has been maintained by brute force. Our nation's renewed tradition of limited government implies that our government's authority is voluntarily granted by the vast majority of our citizens. But we are a rare social experiement in the history of our race. Most governments have derived their authority from superior power over their subjects. And there has probably never been any political state in which the wishes of some individual were not subordinated to those of the majority, as expressed by the rulers in power. Those who would suggest that the actions of those in power must conform to some vague list of "principles" to qualify for the category of legality are like nervous children hunting ghosts in an old house. They can never agree on just what those "principles" are, and the attempts which have been made to codify them are miserably unsatisfactory. The "principles" are either too inflexible to apply to specific cases with much success or are written so generally that they are susceptible to a dozen different interpretations. No such "principles" of legality amount to anything tangible or scientifically verifiable. Fortunately, preoccupation with the subject of legality as something other than the actions of those in positions of power and authority has been left to those still interested in vague philosophizing, while we of the legal profession concern ourselves with the serious business of the law.

All of this discussion has been necessary to remind you of our outlook as practitioners of law, as opposed to whatever contrasting moral or emotional sentiments we feel. When we apply this background to the case of the time travelers and their morally objectionable actions, we find that they themselves constituted a temporary government in the ancient time they visited during their presence among the people of that era. This they did simply by virtue of the fact that they were in a position, owing to their advanced weapons and knowledge, of superior power and authority. The primitive tribe on which they inflicted the violence over which we are now deliberating may have had leadership before the crew arrived. But that tribal government was, temporarily, replaced by a more powerful group, which alone could command the submission of the natives. That new government legally was the time-travel crew. As morally objectionable as its actions were, they were, temporarily the law. On this basis, there is nothing we can do in the law against the moral offenders. We can voluntarily express our disapproval of their actions by no longer associating with them. But we cannot prosecute them for legal violations when, under their unique circumstances, whatever they chose to do was the law. Certainly might never makes right, but it does make law. We are fortunate today to be governed by benevolent, reasonable and moral men.

THIRD ADVOCATE: Thus far, Distinguished Commissioners, you have had the same recommendations argued from two opposite poles of thought. My position would not be that there was no law in existence during the maiden voyage of the Time Travel Corporation. Neither would I hold that the crew members became the lawful authority in that ancient time they visited. To avoid a hasty or extreme conclusion, we must consider a number of issues more carefully. In the first place, we do not know that all of the crew's violent actions would be at odds with our present standards. Indeed, after the commencement of hostilities the voyagers may have committed many acts of violence in self-defense. The ancient natives, armed with their spears and clubs, did eventually resist the onslaught against them. This was recorded in the mission's diaries and later admitted by the offenders. Therefore, we cannot say that everything of a violent nature done by the crew was worthy of punishment by our standards. Indeed, if we knew more about the ancient tribe itself, we would very likely discover that many of its members who were victimized by the crew had records of activities which we would consider equally criminal. Beyond that, even the expedition members who took these actions also provided some worthy contributions by their other actions. They took a great risk by agreeing to participate in the mission. Their danger was increased by their arrival in a primitive and forbidding environment. In spite of all this, they managed to prove that time travel is possible, and their work at the outset, before the violence began, consisted of collecting invaluable medical and historical data. Any blanket prosecution of them merely for their outrages against the ancients would blind itself to these facts. Not everything they did was immoral. And some of the violence may have been quite reasonably justified, as it is difficult to believe that they would have continued it so long otherwise.

Because of these factors, I would propose that we study carefully the record of the crew's actions, perhaps by detailed hypnotic interviews, to discover which ones really were criminal according to our contemporary consensus. This is the only means for certain protection of the innocent and punishment of the guilty.

Approaching a Verdict

As anyone familiar with these issues would know, there are numerous other controversies that would arise in the discussion of this fanciful illustration, many issues not mentioned in the three illustrative recommendations that have been heard. One could propose the solution offered by the third speaker and meet the objection that such selective prosecution would be unavoidably unjust since it would depend on ultimately untrustworthy evidence and since the selection of which actions to punish could easily be made on the basis of emotional whim. To solve this problem, someone else could propose that a comprehensive law be written concerning the actions of the expedition members, one that would apply in this case and all others in the future. Then all the time travelers would be prosecuted on the basis of this new all-encompassing statute. Immediately, objections would arise that such would be an ex post facto law, a tool of tyranny specifically prohibited by the U.S. Constitution. Perhaps government could stay out of the matter entirely, another might suggest, and allow civic-minded fellows to dispatch the explorers late one night. It would not matter who carried out this act of retribution, it might be claimed, since we would be hard-pressed to determine who living today is a direct descendant of the survivors in the ancient tribe. But let us avoid all this and get back on the track.

This whole illustration was to serve the purpose of clarifying alternatives in the philosophy of law, including those influential in contemporary American legal education and practice, the context in which the American Civil Liberties Union exists. Understanding those alternatives will definitely help us understand an organization which tends to follow one of them.

The first speaker was an advocate of what might be called the subjectivist theory of law. In holding that what constitutes legality is the product of a particular culture or society at a particular point in time, this advocate is really arguing that there is no natural law objectively rooted in the unchanging characteristics of all human beings regardless of time or place. With such an implied denial of natural law, this viewpoint would favor the position that there is no basis for evaluating one society's statutes by themselves or against any others in the past, present, or future. All such systems result from their appropriateness to their particular time and place and have their origins in the ideas of their people. In other words, there are no objective principles of truth or legality that can be applied favorably or unfavorably to such systems.

Oddly enough, the advocates of this position would be likely to argue it with a conviction that would impress the observer as an attempt to prove its absolute truth! Such a position is closely related to currently fashionable notions in the social sciences that insist that it is wrong or worse to compare critically the life style of African headhunters with American entrepreneurs.

The subjectivist theory also tends to avoid a focus on the individual person as the

42

exclusive source and identification of human rights. After one denies that there are objectively knowable principles of human nature from which we may derive principles of natural law, as does any consistent subjectivist, the only remaining source for the identification of "human rights" is the collective expression of various groups. The rights of these group members, not being identified on the basis of individual characteristics common to all, must then be selected on the basis of behavior that is observable as being undertaken by most or all persons in each group. The result is discussion of the rights peculiar to: men, women, children, workers, unemployed persons, prisoners, doctors, lawyers, accountants, teachers, students, magicians, et cetera. We shall return to this perspective and its influence in the ACLU shortly. But it was necessary to apply it in a fictitious illustration with bizarre particulars to convey in a rather exaggerated manner the way in which this theory inevitably results in the sanction of injustice.

The second advocate represented an explicit version of positivist legal theory. He is a spokesman for the philosophy of law that has been most influential in the United States during this century, a development of the ideas first associated with Blackstone, as has been already mentioned. The ramifications of this approach are dramatically obvious. Starting with an outright denial of the validity of any principles of natural law, the positivist is left with only one alternative standard of legality. That is whatever those in command of superior power choose to do. The positivist may prefer personally, but not for scientific or legal reasons, the record of one set of rulers over another. But all are equally *legal* by virtue of the fact that they are in authority and obeyed. With this single stipulation as the only relevant factor for the positivist, it really does not matter whether such a government is given the consent of its citizens by virtue of affection or at the point of a sword. And it is because of this peculiar qualification for legality that the consistent positivist will regard brutal totalitarian dictatorships as legally equal with any benevolent monarchy or limited constitutional republic.

We should not be surprised that the rise of positivism in law and other fields has accompanied the growth of government power and the loss of individual freedom. The influence of posivitism has been a powerful tool in the hands of those seeking police-state power for themselves because it legally sanctions whatever they may wish to do. Like the subjectivist, the positivist does not focus on the individual as the source of such concepts as rights or legality. He looks rather to the actions of those who compose the state and views issues on the basis of whether there is a "state's interest" in the matter. The state is the perceivable entity that the positivist has substituted for the abstract characteristics of the individual. What the positivist would call "rights," if anything at all, would be the privileges granted by those in power, and just as easily taken away.[2]

Another logical consequence of positivist legal philosophy is the reinterpretation of what the concept of human rights includes, the reference points in reality that are appropriate for the familiar expression "one's right to . . ." Because the positivist is inclined toward the recognition of only those things that are tangible, that can be experienced by more than one person, his interest in rights is not with the characteristic attributes, such as the actions, of a human being. This would be on far too abstract a conceptual level, or "too ghostly," to suit him. Therefore, if the positivist is disposed to use the term "rights" in any meaningful way at all, it must for him refer to tangible or material things, such as physical products or services.

This is, perhaps, more important than it may seem at first. It will tend to make the positivist who discusses man's right to life, for instance, think of things quite different from, say, an advocate of a conceptualist natural law, which we shall soon define. The positivist would find no meaningful content in the right to life other than the necessary physical requirements for remaining alive. These would be appropriate food, clothing, shelter, and any*thing* else beyond subsistence to luxury. The positivist's version of the right to life could only mean the "right" to the *things* necessary to remain alive, regardless of how or from whom they were obtained. This does not mean that the positivist would volunteer his support for robbery. But he would say that the source of one's means of survival was irrelevant to, or a separate question entirely from, one's "right" to those *things*.

From a positivist viewpoint "rights" or any other term can only refer to measurable quantities, such as goods and services. From this premise and the previous one concerning collective or group status of "rights," it is but a short step for one to speak about the economic rights of minority groups to the property of others. And the American Civil Liberties Union, as we shall see, quite in the present tradition of positivist legal theory in America, has conducted a crusade in the name of human rights that has resulted quite predictably in the overwhelming advocacy of the violation of the rights of others. Such is almost inevitable when one's conception of legality is whatever those in power do, when the tradition of philosophical understanding of natural law is forgotten or shunned, and the positivist alternative partly accepted or substituted. What is most tragic for those sincere persons in such organizations as the ACLU and other movements is that, as long as the positivist approach remains dominant in American legal education and practice, there is precious little hope for an idealistic attorney to win justice in a civil or criminal court action, particularly on the lower levels of the judicial system, when he must argue philosophical concepts of natural law necessary for the logical demonstration that some existing statute or precedent is implicitly unconstitutional. Until that is changed, our legal system will remain in many ways immune to justice.

A close philosophical relative of positivism was somewhat represented in the remarks of the third and final spokesman before our make-believe commission. He was advocating an examination of the facts, to the fullest extent that they could be obtained, so that the sum total of criminality of each of the time travelers could be weighed against their other actions and the extenuating circumstances during the voyage. We might call this the "case method," or empiricism. A legal application of it is taught in most law schools as how lawyers are supposed to think. Like

44

positivist legal theory, with which it has developed, it pays no attention to any philosophical arguments over the nature of man. Rather, those who follow this approach seek to examine each new crisis or legal dispute purely on the basis of the historical facts, without "coloring" their perception by applying to it any general principles about anything which may have been abstracted in the past. They expect to conclude their examination with a judgment. If they are legislators, it becomes a statute. If they are judges, it becomes a ruling or precedent.

As these statutes, rulings, and precedents accumulate over time, they are surveyed by lawyers of this particular persuasion, who select from the multitude what seems helpful to form an argument. Thus legal argumentation becomes a mechanical assembly of previous decisions that were based on previous decisions, most of which were made without any reference or pleading on the basis of natural law. As this process continues, there is accumulated a huge quantity of statutes and precedents with a positivist origin, namely, based simply on prior statutes and precedents. What original influence natural law argumentation had in a body of law such as that in the United States, is eroded and watered down to a virtually untraceable strength amid the flood of legal rulings formulated from other juggled legal rulings.

Certainly, a process of considering the facts of each case on its own merits avoids the gross injustice of an arbitrary system in which the same punishments are meted out to everyone on whom the regime frowns regardless of their deeds. A process such as this is often effective in maintaining fairly well, or giving more prominent lip service to, what Professor Fuller has called the "internal morality of law" or, in American constitutional terms, due process and equal protection under the laws. No discussion of abstract natural law is necessary to perpetuate the traditions of trial by jury, habeas corpus, the issuance of warrants for search and seizure, the avoidance of ex post facto statutes and bills of attainder, the securing of a court order prior to seizure of property, and all the other mechanical functions that constitute what is known as equitable procedural enforcement of the laws. Most of these protections are rooted in the U.S. Constitution and are upheld as standards for the *enforcement* of laws.

The Contradiction of Empiricism

Although equally derived from natural-law principles, these constitutional safeguards, which remain popular in the positivist-empiricist legal world of today, have precious little to say concerning the *content* or *subject matter* of various laws. It is as if all of American constitutionalism in our courts has become a concern over the means of statutory law, but not the ends. This is because the empiricist-oriented attorney or judge does not have to follow an abstract philosophical argument to discover that a man has been deprived of his right to trial, or to know the charges on which he is being held, or to establish his freedom from self-incrimination. Such things are perceivable within the positivist-empiricist framework. However, should an idealistic attorney make a plea against the content of a statute on the books on the basis of several principles abstracted and explicated from several different portions of the Constitution, even if he does so with obviously careful logic, his appeal is likely, by past experience, to go unattended by the Supreme Court, or to be declared inadmissible for jury consideration by a judge in a lower state or federal court. Indeed, it is quite frustrating to observe sincerely committed individuals and a few attorneys of the same persuasion attempting to attack what is, by natural-law standards, clearly unconstitutional in the content of many state and federal laws and administrative regulations, only to find the courts immune to their kind of argumentation.

Americans are going to prison today for attempting this futile utilization of a judicial system that has had removed from it the philosophical base required for justice. Americans are going to jail today from lost arguments before unlistening judges whose careers have been molded in the positivist-empiricist legal climate. Those same Americans would have won their cases less than two centuries ago. Perhaps this background will make it not too difficult to understand why those steeped in contemporary legal thinking find issues of due process and equal protection far easier to recognize and understand than they do the substantive-content issues of laws judged against the prohibitions on government activities contained in the Bill of Rights.[3]

Of course, the positivist and empiricist approaches in legal theory suffer from the same inherent, but generally unnoticed, logical contradictions found in their basic philosophical counterparts. Both schools of thought deny the existence of abstract or universal principles derivable objectively from reality by man's reason. They insist that the only realistic and scientific approach to all subjects, including law, is a process of factual verification that consists of searching for an observable correspondence between one's claims and the facts "out in the open." The problem here is that this process of verification is claimed to be the only valid approach for all occasions. It is thus a universal, or abstract, principle which subsumes all concrete instances in its category. But for the positivist or the empiricist, there can be no universal principles!

The Consequent Loss of Justice

While we can now leave the positivists and empiricists trying in vain to untangle this, their own untyable knot of illogic, we should note a particular legal consequence of this as a judicial method. When the ultimate success of a legal argument must depend on an attorney's ability to convince a judge or jury of a purely factual matter, when that jury is instructed officially not to consider any issues concerning the validity of the statute over which the case is brought, and when the unquestioned statute that imposes the penalty on the offender is, by natural law standards *illegal,* then such a system as ours is currently will, in every equal application of the enforcement of this law, make escape from injustice judicially impossible.

What then would be a proper approach to a legal controversy such as the one posed in our science fiction story? What principles might be applied in a conceptualist natural law framework to seek substantive, as well as procedural, justice? Most thinkers on this subject today cannot imagine that an objective and clear alternative in this direction would be possible, or at least widely accepted. But these two requirements are quite different. Ideas have rarely been both true and popular. And after criticizing the assumptions and results of what is taught and practiced as law so widely today, we must at least briefly outline the rational alternative. Such is worthwhile because it embodies the approach to law that was in the minds of the framers of the U.S. Constitution, the protection of whose labors is ostensibly the outstanding work of the American Civil Liberties Union. We need to discuss it not just for the solution to our hypothetical problem. Indeed, in a society of renewed individual freedom, it would by necessity be the accepted norm once again, while today's popular legal theories would be rapidly on the decline. We need to discuss it because it is a vital key to the reestablishment of justice in America and because it is conspicuously absent from the statements and publications of the ACLU.

4

Basic Foundations for a Libertarian-Conceptualist Theory of Law

For us to be able to arbitrate a legal problem such as that posed in the last chapter, that is, in a manner essentially different from the suggested solutions that were examined, we must build a new framework of legal concepts that will lead us in a different direction. This can be done by answering a hierarchy of questions that arise when a new recommendation is made.[1]

We would suggest that a natural law, constitutionalist approach to the case of the time travelers would focus primarily on their actions, to determine what actions are appropriate for us to take in applying the principle of justice. Immediately there is the question: "What in the world is justice?"

Method of Definition

To begin with, we must remember what is necessary for the formulation of a correct definition of justice, or any other concept. We have already noted the definition of a concept as the mental integration of two or more concretes in reality on the basis of their common characteristics and with their particular measurements omitted. By this process, we recognize individual chairs to be chairs, although we may have never seen these particular chairs before. In a verbal definition it is impossible to list all the common characteristics of the subject being defined. We therefore must try to select the essential characteristics of the subject, those that differentiate the subject from all other definable subjects in the next larger conceptual category. Aristotle called that larger category, the *genus*, and the distinguishing essential characteristics, the *differentia*. For man, the *genus* is animal, the *differentia*, rational. That application of rational means the possession normally of the faculty of reason, not necessarily its consistent utilization!

All such definitions are valid or invalid on the basis of a correct *genus* and *differentia*. An example of too broad a definition of man would be a "form of life that transports and reproduces itself." This is true of man, but also includes one-celled microorganisms. We would also err by defining man as the only animal capable of destroying its entire species. This may also be true, but the ability to produce devastating weapons is not an essential characteristic, rather, it is a consequence of the ability to think abstractly, or reason. It is necessary to remind ourselves of this method of proper definition and the pitfalls that result from not using it. If kept in mind, it holds the key to understanding much of the confusion that we hear all around us. And certainly we would not be reminded of it otherwise, particularly when we open all dictionaries to find a definition, only to receive a list of undefined synonyms.

Justice As a Characteristic Human Action

There are other good rules for accurate definition, but one principle makes itself obvious when we consider justice. Unlike the positivist, we note immediately that the subject of our definition of justice belongs in a *genus* not of physical objects. Justice is not a kind of physical thing. It is not the buildings and people who compose a system of courts. If all those people were asleep (as some judges occasionally are) in those buildings, we would agree that the people and the buildings were present, but not justice. Because we know the buildings and the people were there in Nazi Germany, without justice, we realize that we are not referring to material things when we speak of justice, as we would be with a definition of rocks.

This leaves us with the remaining category of possibilities for the *genus*, namely, characteristics, or attributes. This would include physical characteristics of objects, such as the color or shape of rocks. For things which move, either in response to other things acting on them or on their own initiation, such as men, the category of characteristics includes actions. And justice obviously must refer to the action characteristics of acting beings. But such justice can be recognized in different senses.

49

Social Justice As the Marketplace

A man who ventures into the desert with limited supplies and little knowledge is acting at the peril of his nature, that is, his inherent requirements for food, water, and protection from a dangerous environment. These requirements are necessary for his healthy survival because he is a human being. And, if he runs out of supplies and does not use his remaining strength to seek a return to those requirements, he will perish.

In a sense this is justice. "Justice" here denotes the principles of human action necessary for man's preservation of himself according to his nature. Notice that the context of this definition, the particular arrangement in reality that is being defined, involves one man and the physical environment. The context obviously changes when more than one man is involved, and so does the *differentia* of the definition. Thus we recognize that the *differentia* of all definitions are contextual; a change of circumstances changes the selection of common characteristics of a concept that are appropriate, or essential.

In the context of many men living together within the political boundaries of a nation, the concept of justice can be applied in both a moral and legal sense. In the same manner that natural justice for the loner in the desert consisted in choosing to act or not to act in accord with the reality of his nature and the nature of his surroundings, so justice in a moral and legal context among pluralities of men denotes the principles of their actions that are appropriate and consistent for their natural requirements in their relationships with each other.

What is entailed in this is discovered by attending to the essentials of those relationships. Human beings, by virtue of their reasoning capacity and faculty of free will, seek to obtain, preserve, avoid, or dispose of, various tangible and intangible things. All of those things, virtually everything that exists, are known as "values." Of course, if they are objects that men seek to avoid or rid themselves of, we would refer to them as negative values, or disvalues. But all are still the object or target of our actions as men. And things that are valued obtain their value not just because of any intrinsic attribute or utility, but by virtue of the fact that they are desired by men because of something about them. Thus the concept of value denotes a characteristic relationship between that which is valued and that which does the valuing, or acts toward the valued object, all of which is abstracted into the concept of value in a particular context. Indeed, that which is valued in a value relationship may not be a physical concrete at all, but rather a characteristic, such as one's beauty or reputation.

In the lives of most all men, the predominant activity is the pursuit of positive values and the avoidance of negative ones. The vast majority of the values one seeks are not available by the actions of oneself alone. They must be obtained from other men who are also seeking values for themselves. For all men to live in accord

50

with their value-seeking nature, they must agree to exchange their values on mutually acceptable terms. There is justice built into this principle of the exchange of values. Namely, the terms or price one sets for the exchange of his values for those of others must be at least reasonable enough that some others will participate in the exchange. If not, the unreasonable person will "price himself out of the market," not obtain the values he needs for his physical or financial survival, and perish.

We should immediately notice that, if what a person values or seeks is not in accord with his nature as a healthy and happy individual, then the achievement of that value will be mistaken and result in something which would, by itself, be a negative value. A great deal of alcohol may be mistakenly valued by a person for some reason, but the hangover is not.

Definition of Crime

There are two basic ways by which a person's values may be taken by another without his honest consent. In both cases we say his rights have been violated. The two means are (1) the use or threat of physical force and (2) misrepresentation of the transaction, fraud. Both actions amount to the unjust appropriation of someone's values. And such is the definition of crime.

Notice that this definition of crime says nothing about any requirement to the effect that the particular action must be contrary to the wording of a statute issued by an existing political authority. In other words, it is not a positivist definition of crime. Neither does it imply that it would be valid everywhere except on some distant and uncharted desert isle populated by two people, the criminal and his victim. This is because the same metaphysical source of the concepts employed would still be present: human beings and their nature. The same observation would apply to the distant past. We are likewise not concerned with any abridgement of our recognition of the criminality of certain actions because other actions committed by the same person may have been praiseworthy. Justice implies that we would recognize that, unless a man is shown to have been psychotic during the commission of an act, the actions he takes, the alternatives he selects, are to some degree his personal choice. And thus he is to be evaluated, positively or negatively, from a moral perspective for each action and commensurate with each action to the degree of its good or evil. Once again, the standard for that good or evil that all men, including the most confused atheist, can easily reason, is temporal: the requirements for a person's healthy and happy life.

In a legal context, we appraise each action only on the basis of its relevance to our definition of criminality. Actions that do not result in the deprivation of another's values or violation of another's rights may receive our attention from a moral perspective, but not from a legal one. Unless they qualify for it by virtue of our definition, they fall "outside the purview of the law." If the actions are essentially criminal, just as morally we would wish to reward someone to the extent of his virtues, we are obliged to punish the criminal to the extent of his wrongs.

Retribution and Punishment

An understanding of how this is justly done can be arrived at if we remember that crimes are essentially involuntary transactions of values by force or fraud. Were such a transaction voluntary, but one party to the transaction failed to meet his part of the bargain, he would clearly establish himself as that much in debt to the other party. Because crimes are transactions in which one party has, so to speak, deliberately defaulted, he has also created a debt that he owes to his victim. The only person to whom he could owe the debt is the victim, because the victim was the other party to the transaction.

Thus is exploded the legal fiction of a criminal satisfying his "debt to society" by doing his time. Since justice consists in the restoration of the criminally appropriated values to the victim and the penalizing of the criminal by making him pay for those values with his own of equal or commensurate measure, it is the responsibility of those who would institute a just society to see that such is done whenever there has been a criminal deprivation. To do this, those who compose the government of a political entity might forcefully deprive a person proven guilty of robbery or fraud of an amount from his property equal to that which he stole from his victim. This would be an act of deprivation, but not unjust deprivation, because the criminal had actually established a debt to his victim for that stolen amount. By not repaying that debt, or forcing the legal authorities to apprehend him, he had effectively refused to satisfy the transaction that he initiated.

The victim is entitled to forgive the criminal his debt, since it is his debt to forgive. But if the debt is not forgiven and the criminal, as just explained, refuses to pay, he automatically forfeits his right to that part of his property equal in value to that taken from the victim. It is of this forfeited property that the victim, or the government on behalf of the victim, justly deprives the criminal.

The Death Penalty As Justice

Immediately there are problems. This view seems to hold well in all cases of stolen physical property. Indeed, the criminal's debt to the victim might be increased due to the loss of the property's commercial utility during the time in which the victim was separated from it. But what if the property is something that cannot be returned to the victim as easily, or at all? What if the victim has been murdered, raped, or his reputation ruined by libel or slander? Obviously, we cannot return the right to life unviolated to a victim of homicide. But justice can be reflected, not in the impossible recompensation of the irreplaceable value, but by the fulfillment of the other half of the transaction. That is, by making the criminal pay the penalty equal in damage to his own values as that which he brought upon his victim. It is at this point that we can see the logic and justice of capital punishment in all cases of total and irreparable damage done by criminal actions. One cannot regain one's life or one's virginity, as one can slowly but surely act to restore one's reputation.

It is quite important to note that this is the *only* reason why capital punishment in such cases is just. It may be true that capital punishment or life sentences protect society from future murders by homicidal criminals. It may also be true, as common sense would dictate, that the institution of capital punishment is the most powerful psychological deterrent to criminals considering the commission of capital crimes, particularly if such sentences are made mandatory in every case. But all such considerations are peripheral considerations, quite ancillary, if not totally irrelevant, to the reason why capital punishment is just for crimes that inflict commensurate damage to human values.

The Concept of Rights

The essential legal and moral concept just employed, and which needs still further elaboration, is that of rights. In spite of the fact that the essentials of a conceptualist natural law and justice—beyond their conceptualist roots in metaphysics and epistemology, to which we have already made reference for the reader's pursuit—are contained in the understanding of the nature of crime, which is the sole focus of natural legal reasoning as outlined above, there still remains room for doubt over just what is referred to by the concept of rights.

Because we referred to a particular criminal action, murder, as the deprivation of an irreparable value as well as a violation of one's right to life, we see that the two concepts, rights and values, are closely related. To begin once again by avoiding the concrete-concept fallacy, we note that the *genus* of both values and rights are abstract characteristics of particular human actions. The concept of value, we have seen, denotes an abstracted combination of several aspects of reality: the valuer, that which is valued, and the relationship of potential or initiated action between them. A person who values a good job will act to seek one for himself, or keep and improve the one he has. But an individual might be said to have a right to life, or a good standard of living (the consequence of a good job, at least in part), entirely apart from any action he takes or does not take to bring it about. His right to such amounts to his capacity or ability to value that object and act toward it. From this we derive that human rights are moral *characteristics of human action* consequent to the potential opportunities for the expression of natural human capacities.

You have a right to life because you are alive. Your right to freedom of thought and action is a direct consequence of your possession of free will. Contradicting

Kant's disastrous contribution to the subject of ethics, we might say of rights that, following your nature, what you can do, you *rightly* do.

Please note several things. First, the possession of characteristic rights during a person's life is defined, or limited, by what some would call equal responsibilities. Because your rights are derived directly from your nature, and because the essentials of that nature are common to all, you have no consequent right to take any action against others which, if exercised against you, would violate your rights or deprive you of your values. Next, the only entities that possess rights as characteristics are those that possess capacities that may be exercised rightfully, namely individual persons. Thus, it would be nonsense to speak of "group rights," the "rights" of majorities or minorities (except the smallest minority, the individual), or "states' rights" if something was meant other than the simple arithmetical sum of the rights possessed by the individuals who compose those pluralities. If one ever speaks of the "right" of a group that is at odds with an individual's right, we know that, whatever his purpose, he is *not* talking about *rights*.

Similarly, we should note that the aspect of human life to which the term rights exclusively refers, by the definition already defended, is human action. We have the right to live, think, speak, and act, so long as we do so in such a manner that we do not forfeit the right to those free actions by any act that puts us in debt to someone by our violation of his same rights. Our right to think and act, to mental and physical activity, allows us to pursue our values by performing the actions, usually called work, that are necessary to obtain what we value from others. What we obtain by such work, mental or physical, is the accomplishment of our values, our private property. That includes the car we save for and purchase, the idea we originate that commercially remunerates us when merchandised as a new invention, and the life we possess and are able to maintain after we have worked to earn from others the values that are its basic requirements.

The delicate distinction being made here is that rights pertain only to the free opportunity to express those capacities for thought and action that we naturally possess, to choose to pursue our values or decline to do so. Our rights do not refer to the valued things themselves, which we may accomplish or obtain if we exercise our capacities, but only to the free opportunity to act in pursuit of them, as long as we do nothing forceful or fraudulent along the way to impede another's opportunity.

What this means is illustrated in two very different senses of "the right to work." By our approach, we would say that, because every normal person has the capacities for certain types of work, everyone has the right to seek employment and, in the exchange of values inherent in any work relationship between employer and employee, to try to perform satisfactorily to keep that employment, to improve his ability or performance to seek better compensation, or to end the exchange by looking for a better job elsewhere. On the other hand, a positivist approach to "the right to work" would likely be that one has a right to be able to find a job and keep it, regardless of the wishes of whoever else is involved in the activity, including whoever furnishes his own property for the creation of the job. Rejecting an abstract approach to rights as being immediately consequential to human characteristics, the positivist can only look to the ends of the work as that to which the person has a right. This leads to talk of one's "right" to a certain standard of living, a guaranteed annual income, a home, a car, et cetera. Such are the premises underlying all talk of one's "economic rights," usually by persons who do not understand the implications of what they are saying. However, since such a view amounts to one person's claim to the products of another's labor, with or without his consent, there are undoubtedly some who do intend the consequences of the self-contradictory doctrine so precisely characterized by Ayn Rand as the "right to enslave."[2] And it will become increasingly obvious, as we examine the positions taken by spokesmen for the ACLU, that such mistaken positivist notions of "rights" allow for the promotion of what must be injustice, though wittingly or unwittingly called the reverse.

The true relationship between natural law and human rights was lucidly expressed several decades ago by Jacques Maritain:

> We must now consider the fact that natural law and the light of moral conscience within us do not prescribe merely things to be done and not to be done; they also recognize rights, in particular, rights linked to the very nature of man. The human person possesses rights because of the very fact it is a person, a whole, master of itself and of its acts, and which consequently is not merely a means to an end, but an end, an end which must be treated as such. The dignity of the human person? The expression means nothing if it does not signify that by virtue of natural law, the human person has the right to be respected, is the subject of rights, possesses rights. These are things which are owed to man because of the very fact that he is man. . . . The true philosophy of the rights of the human person is therefore based upon the idea of natural law. . . .
>
> Another altogether opposite philosophy has sought to base the rights of the human person on the claim that man is subject to no law other than that of his will and his freedom, and that he must "obey only himself," as Jean-Jacques Rousseau put it, because every measure or regulation springing from the world of nature (and finally from creative wisdom) would destroy at one and the same time his autonomy and his dignity. This philosophy built no solid foundation for the rights of the human person, because nothing can be founded on illusion; it compromised and squandered these rights, because it led men to conceive them as rights in themselves divine, hence infinite, escaping every objective measure, denying every limitation imposed upon the claims of the ego, and ultimately expressing the absolute independence of the human subject and a so-called absolute right—which supposedly pertains to everything in the human subject by the mere fact that it is in him—to unfold one's cherished possibilities at the expense of all other beings. When men thus instructed clashed on all sides with the impossible, they came to believe in the bankruptcy of the rights of the human person. Some have turned against these rights with an enslaver's fury; some have continued to invoke them, while in their inmost conscience they are weighed down by a temptation to skepticism which is one of the most alarming symptoms of the present crisis. A kind of intellectual and moral

revolution is required of us, in order to re-establish on the basis of a true philosophy our faith in the dignity of man and in his rights, and in order to rediscover the authentic sources of this faith.[3]

Accepting the above ideas, we would conclude that any legal application of a positivist or other false definition of crime or rights, because it must be essentially at odds with human nature, will result in injustice. This injustice will convince many of the "bankruptcy of the rights of the human person" and other examples of philosophical skepticism, which disillusionment will grow, and has since the French Revolution's Age of Unreason, into "an enslaver's fury."

The Jury Returns

To bring justice to the case of the Time Travel Corporation explorers we would be required to determine their factual guilt and punish them to the commensurate extent of the wrongs they inflicted, not being swayed by any consideration unique to the fact of their actions taking place in the distant past. Because the victims of the travelers, particularly those who were not killed or raped and able theoretically to have their values restored, are no longer alive, justice can only be illustrated, and must be, by the just deprivation of commensurate values from the expedition members, both replaceable and irreplaceable. Were the victims still alive, they or an independent arbitrator could decide on an arbitrary property value to be repaid as the debt for an assault or physical injury. However, since they are no longer alive, the violators must suffer the same deprivation for justice to be done, even though the possibility no longer remains that the victim's debt can be satisfied. Such forceful deprivation is a just function of government.[4] The difference between this approach and the positivist approach to law in fashion today pertains primarily to a different manner of determining in arguments in court what is the law based on human rights and their violation by criminal actions, as opposed to the prevailing standard of a person's actions being "criminal" because of factual disobedience to the wording of a positive law or judicial precedent issued by a government.

What Justice Would Bring

Other aspects of legal education and practive would be modified with the rise of a libertarian-conceptualist natural law. The influence of methodological empiricism in legal "rules of evidence" would be less constricting on factual determinations in a case. This would result from the increased admissibility and recognized validity of factual conclusions, as well as legal conclusions, based on deductive and inductive reasoning. In many ways, the theories of factual detection that thrilled millions in the stories of Sherlock Holmes would return to the courtroom, and objective reasoning would replace the utility of thought-paralyzing objections over "hearsay" and "circumstantial" evidence. But these matters are at least somewhat less essential to the substantive redefinition of the nature of law, rights, and crime, which is absolutely necessary for a return of the viability of justice to the American judicial system, and to accomplish the "intellectual and moral revolution" of which Maritain wrote.

Such a return to justice would bring the full admissibility in court of philosophical arguments on natural law in both criminal and civil cases. Persons who argued cases of law would no longer be limited to a closed and privileged fraternity of state-sanctioned attorneys. This would be because cases would no longer be won or lost due to an attorney's ability to compose an argument based on the assembly of prior statutes and precedents, or to judges' rulings in the lower courts based on the same grounds. Judicial review of statutory law would be once again distributed to every local court and jury of citizens throughout the land. And laymen who have studied the conceptual issues here discussed are just as capable of arguing them before other laymen as are professional manipulators of statutes and precedents. All local juries would effectively determine principles of natural law and their application in the context of each case, the facts of which, as today, they would also decide. This would amount to a return to the system of judicial and executive review that has existed with erratic success in English legal history since the Magna Carta as the common-law courts.[5] The challenge would be for such an experiment fully to succeed.

Other considerations are possible and noteworthy. Such a system would open the field of law to full free enterprise competition. Local courts could hire classical logicians for independent advice to deliberating juries on the conceptual consistency of the arguments they had heard. It might even be suggested that such competition in the practice of law would be an impetus to improved performance and moral conscience on the part of many attorneys, who now feel protected by monopolistic professional institutions such as the bar.

To those who might object that such a drastic change would destroy the legal profession and allow for inept charlatans to practice as amateur lawyers and ignorant or ill-conducted courts to legalize such things as murder, I would suggest the following: In a totally free society, the market of exchanges between individuals will always provide what people want. Very few people want murder and other crimes to be decriminalized because they do not want to be victims of those crimes. To say that such a system would enourage injustice is to say that people, when presented with logical arguments, will opt for injustice. If this is true, what remains is only in the hands of God. I am sure that it is not. What mounting injustice has developed in the United States, including the legal decriminalization of infanticide as abortion on demand, has all taken place in the context of the positivist legal institutions that my recommendations would replace. The only heritages of natural-law constitutionalism, those of the short-lived Roman Republic and England before Parliament became supreme legislatively, which our

Founding Fathers drew upon in shaping our system, were grounded in the principles we are recommending. Who can say that a return to those principles would not constitute a return to justice to a far greater extent than is possible under our present practice?

Certainly, one form of widespread contemporary legal injustice would likely go out the window with a popular return to common law traditions, namely, the practice of what might be called "anticipatory punishment." This consists of such cases as a man being declared legally insane and involuntarily confined in an institution because he says he is Napoleon. The thinking here is that this person has shown that he is likely in the future to harm someone, or himself (whom he does have a right to harm). Similarly, a man gets an injunction from a court that temporarily forces his neighbor to refrain from cutting down a tree on his own property because the person with the injunction believes that further cutting will result in the tree falling on his house. Applying our natural-law understanding of crime to such situations, we would note that no person's rights are violated by another's verbal boasts or statements of threatened actions, until such actions are taken. The neighbor's rights are not violated until the tree falls on his house, and thus no debt is created by the action of his neighbor until it does. The notion that it is just forcefully to deprive others of their values or to violate their rights because they are likely in the future to act in a criminal manner is a basic distortion of the meaning of crime. It implies that a person attains criminal status before anyone is actually victimized, one of the assumptions common to many forms of what are called "victimless crimes," and to the excuse of future threat to the Aryan Race that Adolf Hitler employed so well to "justify" his campaign against the Jews.

A Case Study

Perhaps it would be instructive, in concluding this discussion, if we compared the manner in which an actual case of constitutional law was decided by the U.S. Supreme Court—unfortunately, the only judicial level where such issues seem permissible for argumentation today—with the application of natural law principles that might be applied in courts were legal positivism to be replaced by the alternative here proposed. For this purpose I shall use a case concerning issues closely related to many of the positions taken by the ACLU.

The case is *Shelly* v. *Kraemer* (334 U.S. 1). The Supreme Court of Missouri had reversed a judgment of a state trial court on the matters involved. The U.S. Supreme Court granted certiorari, hearing the case in January, 1948, and deciding it on May 3. The facts of the case are as follows.

On February 16, 1911, thirty out of a total of thirty-nine owners of property on both sides of a street in St. Louis signed an agreement that for fifty years no portion of the total property could be sold to or occupied by anyone other than a member of the Caucasian "race." These thirty persons owned forty-seven of the fifty-seven parcels of land described in the agreement, including the particular parcel involved in this case. Negroes owned five of the parcels of land and were apparently not informed of this agreement when it was made. Owners of seven of nine homes on the street failed to sign the agreement in 1911.

On October 9, 1945, owners of property on the street who were subject to the terms of the restrictive agreement brought suit in the Circuit Court of the city of St. Louis to prevent the Negro petitioners Shelley from occupying the parcel of property in question, which the petitioners had purchased two months earlier. The petitioners stated that they had no knowledge of the agreement when the purchase was made. The other property-owner respondents asked the Circuit Court to divest title to the property out of petitioners Shelley and revest it in the immediate grantor or in such other person as the court should direct. The trial court in St. Louis denied the requested relief on the ground that the relevant restrictive agreement had never become final and complete as intended by its parties because the signatures of all property owners in the district had never been obtained.

The Supreme Court of Missouri reversed this decision and directed the trial court to grant the request of the respondents. That court held the agreement to be effective and concluded that enforcement of its provisions violated no rights guaranteed to petitioners by the federal Constitution.

There were two primary issues in this case, according to the U.S. Supreme Court's decision. First, does a restrictive agreement voluntarily entered into by several persons and managed, conducted, and enforced by their private agreement and association, violate any portion of the federal Constitution, and specifically, the Fourteenth Amendment? The Court ruled no. Secondly, does a restrictive agreement voluntarily entered into by several persons and enforced by the courts of any state violate any portion of the federal Constitution, and specifically, the Fourteenth Amendment and its "equal protection" clause? On this question, the Court ruled yes. The judgment of the Supreme Court of Missouri was reversed, and this decision also reversed a similar case on the same grounds and issues, *McGhee* v. *Sipes,* on certiorari to the Supreme Court of Michigan.

The author of the Court's written decision, Mr. Chief Justice Vinson, first reviewed the facts of the two cases and the contentions of the petitioners and respondents. He noted that the U.S. Supreme Court had not previously been asked to determine if restrictive covenants based on race and enforced by state courts violated the "equal protection" clause of the Fourteenth Amendment. He recognized that the Fourteenth Amendment held no jurisdiction over private agreements made and executed voluntarily among individuals. He opined that the enforcement of such agreements by state courts abridged the property rights of the individuals involved in this case. He cited past cases in which state statutes that made or required enforcement of such restrictive agreements had been held by the Court to violate the Fourteenth Amendment. By reference to a number of cases and opinions, he contradicted the claim of the respondents in *Shelley* v. *Kraemer* that the state courts, by enforcing such an agreement, had not constituted positive action by the state to deprive citizens of "equal protection" under the law. He held that such actions by the judicial division of two states had deprived individuals of their rights. With this ruling, there were offered no dissenting or concurring opinions.

This case is famous as an example of the legal dichotomy that has resulted in recent years between the liberty of the use of one's property and the equality before the law of one's opportunity to acquire and own property. The decision reached by the Supreme Court was an attempt to defend the "equal protection" clause of the Fourteenth Amendment, which is understood generally to apply to state governments the same substantive legal restrictions imposed on Congress by the Bill of Rights. However, the result of this case was the encouragement of the notion that individuals' property rights are potentially adverse to one another, and consequently, a state government cannot enforce the property rights of one person in a transaction without violating those of another. From what we have discussed, it should be clear that the two courts which ruled against the respondents in this case, the St. Louis Circuit Court and the U.S. Supreme Court, did so not on the basis of any conceptual argument based on the nature of rights or criminal violations of same, but on grounds that are markedly positivist-empiricist. The St. Louis Circuit Court did not focus on whether or not a person's property rights had been violated, and what that would mean, but rather on the factual question of whether or not the restrictive agreement had been signed by all the property owners. The parcel of land that Shelley purchased was owned by one of the respondents, who had been a party to the agreement. Chief Justice Vinson likewise did not explore the issue of whether or not such an agreement had violated Shelley's rights on the basis of natural law or constitutionalist reasoning, but rather ruled against the respondents and their favorable interim ruling, with a positivist appeal to prior decisions. In doing so, both the legal validity of private contractual agreements and transactions, as well as the respondent's basic rights of property, were grossly violated.

A conceptualist argument on this case would reach a different conclusion by virtue of a fundamentally different approach. If one's right of private property includes not only the right to nominal ownership of what one has earned, but also to its free use, control, and disposal in any manner except that which would constitute its employment to violate the rights of others, then one should be free voluntarily to enter an agreement with one's neighbors who own adjacent property and to contract the conditions to govern its disposal. There is no reason why such a contract, until mutually dissolved, should not be enforced in all courts with the same objectivity given cases of personal default on payment for purchased items. The contract would only govern the land areas owned by those who signed it. The enforcement of such a contract against purchase of property by those excluded from doing so by it does not constitute a deprivation of their values, or, consequently, a violation of their rights. The parties to the contract simply withheld from the exchange of values desired by the excluded potential purchasers. The refused purchaser is still free to recover what he had paid, or, in other cases where payment had not already been made, take his money and purchase property elsewhere. In no way does enforcement of such an agreement based on private property rights deprive the refused purchaser of the values he already possessed. But in *Shelley* v. *Kraemer* two judicial bodies ruled as if it did. There is no logical explanation for this error and the injustice which resulted from it, except that the judges who made the decisions did so on the basis of something other than a rational understanding of human rights and natural law.

Of course, many might wonder if we should not be equally concerned over the fact that racist motivations were behind the respondents' refusal to sell property to Shelley. And they obviously were. I could make a good moral and philosophical case, and have tried to do so elsewhere, [6] that racism as a viewpoint is dreadfully irrational. But one's right to free thought and speech includes the right to irrational thought. And one's actions with regard to one's property can be predicated on the most nonsensical whim and still be legally just, as long as no action is taken to deprive another of his same values and rights. Those who are so morally committed to the refutation of irrational doctrine, such as racial collectivism, should be equally strict in attending to what is essential in the protection of an individual's rights to his values. And libertarian political theorists should be equally interested in promoting the influence of a rational morality. [7]

The situation in this case did not deprive Shelley of his tangible values. The fact that Shelley was not informed of the agreement when he purchased the property *may* be legal grounds for a separate suit to recover costs incurred during the aborted transaction, but that is clearly another matter, unrelated to the court rulings in this case. The decision forced the respondents to nullify their contract, and thus their contractual rights, after such had been upheld in the state, and it violated their right to agree mutually on the disposal of their property. All of this was done in the name of upholding another's "civil rights" and "equal protection" under the laws. And, as we shall see in the context of most recent issues, such is also the record of the American Civil Liberties Union.

5

ACLU Positions on Issues of Criminality, Due Process, and Equal Protection Under the Law

With some understanding established concerning the philosophy underlying American constitutionalism and of what has replaced it, we are now in a position to examine the statements of leading spokesmen for an organization that claims to uphold and defend individual rights. Our groundwork will enable us to discover if this organization is true to the principles that we have identified in our brief discussion of natural law and rights, or, on the other hand, if it is strongly influenced toward the positivist approach and away from justice. In this chapter and the next we shall examine positions taken by the American Civil Liberties Union on a broad range of issues, which I have for convenience, and perhaps a bit arbitrarily, divided into two categories. This chapter will deal with some positions in the fields of procedural due process of law and equal protection under the law, particularly in reference to the rights of those accused and convicted of criminal actions. The next chapter will discuss positions on substantive natural law issues, and primarily those dealing with various forms of "victimless crimes."

First Impressions of the ACLU

Due to the ACLU's organizational structure and the authority and policy relationships between its national board and local affiliates (to which we shall return in greater detail later), it should be recognized that not all the positions reviewed here may be *official* policies of the ACLU's leadership in New York. However, such positions have been clearly and openly associated with the Union by virtue of being either statements published in official literature of the National ACLU or its local affiliates, or published under the endorsement of the ACLU or written by those prominent among its leadership. The extent to which such sources of ACLU positions reflect national policy, especially in recent years, is quite substantial. Within the practical confines of a book such as this, it is not possible to review and discuss a complete listing of positions taken by the Union, say, in the past decade. We must therefore be selective and attend to major issues of current concern, which include such a variety of issues or assumptions as to serve as a representative gauge for measuring the organizations's tendency toward or away from the principles inherent in what it says it advocates. And for the sake of fairness, a desire to avoid reasonable objections, and the fact that this study amounts to an appeal to those sympathetic to the Union, in this section of our analysis we shall confine ourselves to positions taken in recent years.

In the revised constitution of the American Civil Liberties Union, adopted January 7, 1957, and amended through 1968, we read of its purpose:

Section 2. Objects

The objects of the American Civil Liberties Union shall be to maintain and advance civil liberties including the freedoms of associations, press, religion, and speech, and the rights to the franchise, to due process of law, and to equal protection of the laws for all people throughout the United States and its possessions. The Union's objects shall be sought wholly without political partisanship.[1]

In other official literature we read that the ACLU's only purpose "is the preservation and strengthening of the freedoms guaranteed to us under the Bill of Rights."[2] Because we understand the nature of those freedoms, resulting from the strict limitation of the national government's legislative power to the negative function of protecting individual rights, and the states likewise, we would initially respond that such objectives are our own. They *are* our rights as men, and what the vast majority of all men would want protected. The single arguable exception to that in the ACLU constitution is the assertion of suffrage as a right. This is a bit of definition by nonessentials, since men would not vote *naturally* and therefore possess no natural right to vote, unless a political state provided such an institution as suffrage as the only alternative means through which men could appoint their representatives. Thus, one's forced or arbitrated "right" to vote, to the extent it is a right, is a "right," or better still a privilege from the essential right to freedom. Still we would expect most Americans to praise an organization that supports their rights and the Constitution, which clearly most people favor.

Oddly enough, such is not the case. In pamphlets of the Union we read, alongside statements of its worthy goals, reprinted articles from the *National Observer*[3] and *Playboy*[4] in which we find that a chief characteristic of the group is

63

its widespread *unpopularity*. It seems that many Archie Bunkers out there forget that the ACLU has pledged itself to defending rights that "belong to all—*without exception.*"[5] Many Americans tend to forget this and get furious when the ACLU takes the case of a self-admitted rapist or murderer, or defends the free speech of an American Nazi, Black Panther, or Communist. The problem seems to be that such people "believe they have the right to decide who is or is not 'deserving.' "[6] Immediately we should note that you do have the right to decide such an issue for yourself, but the ACLU means that you do not have the right to force your notion upon someone whose rights have been violated. With all that in mind, let us examine some of the rights, for the defense of which the ACLU members "don't enter popularity contests."

The ACLU on "Rights"

Very little ACLU literature, especially that prepared for those other than its own membership, discusses the nature of human rights in themselves. The Union's publications primarily seem to assume that its readers all know or sense what rights are, and that it is only important to identify or discuss what rights you have, the fact that they are recognized by the Constitution, statutes, or court decisions, and are thus "civil rights" or "civil liberties," and what you can do under the law if they are violated by individuals in or out of government. One new publication does briefly discuss the nature of rights. It is the most recent in a series of ACLU "handbooks dealing with the rights of people." It is *The Rights of Hospital Patients*[7] by George J. Annas, an acknowledged academic authority on interdisciplinary subjects of law and medicine. Other books in this series concern the rights of mental patients, prisoners, servicemen, teachers, students, women, criminal suspects, the poor, reporters, and "gay" people. And in the preface that appears in each volume, we are informed by ACLU General Counsel Norman Dorsen and Executive Director Aryeh Neier that we can look forward to volumes in progress on the rights of "aliens, civil servants, veterans, and the aged" among others.[8] We might react to this by suspecting that the ACLU is not focusing upon characteristics common to all persons as the basis for their rights, but rather has adopted the positivist perspective of identifying one's "rights" on the basis of observable behavior, from one's discretion in bedside manner to one's occupation, or lack of same. But jumping to such a conclusion might be too hasty. We need to see the sort of statement on the nature of rights to which the Union is willing publicly to attach its name before we can be sure.

And, from George Annas, we have it in the question-and-answer format in which this series of books has been prepared:

> What is meant when a patient says "I have a legal right to 'X'?"
> . . . The statement "I have a right" performs several functions and has several

different meanings. Which function and which meaning are generally not made clear to the listener and may not even be clear to the person making the statement. Possible meanings include:

1. Because I am a citizen of this country, I possess "X" as a legal right created by the Constitution, by legislative action or by prior court determination.
2. Because of my relationship with another party, there is a strong possibility that a court of law would recognize "X" as my legal right.
3. I believe that "X" should be recognized as a right even though a court of law would probably not recognize it as such.

As the examples demonstrate, there is no single or absolute definition. To understand any definition, it is necessary to understand the purpose for which the definition is sought, the audience for which it is intended, and the identity of the definer. In regard to the concept of a right, it is most helpful to consider that a continuum exists.[9]

Annas elaborates by calling "probable meaning" number one a *legal right*, and we recognize the essence of legal positivism in this version. He calls the second example a *probable legal right*, which needs a court case as a test for it likely to become a *legal right*. This second meaning translates into a subjectivist view of law. At the whim of those who rule or legislate, it may become a positive or *legal right*. And, sounding increasingly like what we have been over before, he describes the third variety as a statement "of what the law ought to be, based on a political or philosophical conception of the nature and needs of man."[10] He calls it a *human right*, and states that he will concern himself with all three kinds of rights in his book. And then our hopeful expectations suddenly fall.

Just as soon as this ACLU authority seems to be talking about rights based on natural law, he proceeds utterly to disqualify his statements from that sphere. He begins this with the citation of sources for our reference to *human rights*, or natural law. He says, "The early civil rights movement provides numerous examples, as does the United Nations' Universal Declaration of Human Rights."[11] Because we are not told what aspects of "the early civil rights movement" are to be consulted, we are left with the terribly disappointing example of the UN Declaration, which, we have already noted, does not acknowledge any rights as inalienable human characteristics, as did our Founding Fathers, by virtue of the fact that it makes the protection of all enumerated "rights" vulnerable to whatever existing provisions there are in statutory law. Indeed, such an error is not unlikely from an author who accepts an essentially nominalist approach to the concept of rights. Observe that the meaning of the word *rights* for Annas is not in abstract characteristics of human nature, but rather in the use made of it in discussion or the function its use performs. For him, all definitions are judged, not on the basis of conceptual analysis, but on their particular utility, purpose of use, and the subjective consciousness peculiar to their user. With such a variety of definitions available for any concept on these grounds, the nominalist assumptions of many linguistic analysts, it is no surprise that he considers such a concept to exist as a "continuum." But, perhaps, Annas has not had a chance to study Aristotle's rules for objectively valid definitions. He does talk about one sense in which "rights" are related to "natural law." He even makes a passing reference to our rights of "life, liberty, and the pursuit of happiness"[12] as expressed in the Declaration of Independence. But on closer examination our disappointment heightens.

It seems that Annas sees that famous expression as unfulfilled or "made difficult without proper health care." He views one's right to life as "the right to health care," which is "specifically set out in documents of both the United Nations and the World Health Organization,"[13] but not so clearly in American documents. He allows that those persons receiving Medicare and Medicaid "enjoy a right to have some of their medical bills paid" although there is no "legal right" that allows one to demand such services. Annas seems to favor "the movement, now endorsed by both major political parties, toward some form of comprehensive national health insurance."[14] But he cautions us that the adoption of such a program would, "by itself, serve only to expand the payment right without addressing itself to the problem of access to services."[15] Perhaps national government control and distribution of all medical services would be the answer for guaranteeing a patient's rights?

From this we observe a particularly obvious example of the influence of legal positivism, resulting in the opposite of what the ACLU's authority may have intended. Annas makes crystal clear that, for him, one's rights in a medical context are to medical products and services. These products and services are produced by the competitive labor of other persons who, presumably, have the same rights. When Annas speaks of one's "payment right," he obviously avoids the question of who should be forced to *pay* for one's medical costs other than oneself. We might wonder if he also thinks individuals have a "payment right" in other aspects of their life that determine their survival such as the provision of their food, clothing, and shelter. Regardless of the extent to which he would apply his positivist approach to one's legally enforceable rights, we have already shown, by an understanding of the principles championed by the ACLU, that this author of one of the Union's "handbooks on the rights of people" is actually advocating the self-contradictory "right" to *enslave*.

In his *Rights of Hospital Patients,* Annas continues to make obvious his position that the owners of private hospitals have no property rights to them. We are told that "hospitals are not sovereign islands" and must function "within the framework of the law."[16] For Annas, this means a number of things. He sanctions state legislation under which *any* hospital must obtain a "certificate of need" before initiating any expansions or substantial changes in the services offered. The government would extend such permission if the hospital can satisfy them that there is "a public 'need' for such a change or expansion." Annas is still worrried because "this remains a 'brick and mortar' approach to health care in hospitals, with almost no attention being paid to the quality of care provided in the institutions." He notes that states have the power to regulate that quality, but have been "loathe to exercise it."[17] If all this were not enough, he continues by implying throughout his detailed review of hospital administration and the positive laws concerning it, that private owners of hospitals should not be free to decide with whom they will trade,[18] even if such decisions are not based on morally objectionable reasons, but on the most fundamental grounds of financial prudence necessary for the survival of a private hospital or any other private enterprise.[19] He further conveys his approval of a vast maze of government controls and enforced regulations with which all hospitals, including private ones, must comply.[20] These are actually initiations of forceful deprivation to which they must submit *in advance* of, and in *anticipation of,* their responsibility for any criminal actions. Annas introduces us to all this with the disclaimer that "is not the intention of this book, however, to castigate medical professions for occasional past misdeeds."[21]

But he would shackle the owners of private hospitals, and the private individuals who work in other hospitals, with the same violations of their rights that are built into the bureaucratic maze of socialist medical systems, the only medical systems that have brought their patients consistently worse medical care every year before their inevitable bankruptcies.[22] Indeed, such a system as Annas advocates, and which is rapidly forming in this country, would destroy whatever just semblance of a patient's right to the health care he has earned that is still freely obtainable, by making the availability of quality health care nonexistent, at any price. We shall return to Annas in other contexts, but we might conclude that his statements speak very poorly for himself and the ACLU on the subject of equal protection of individual rights.

"Due Process" and "Equal Protection" Positions

We will now try to find a favorable example of an ACLU position on matters of due process and equal protection under the laws. It should not surprise us that the vast majority of ACLU literature and lawsuits concern the group's intention to defend individuals from violation of their rights to unjust or inequitable enforcement of the laws on the books. It has rarely challenged the content of laws as being unconstitutional, unless their wording or enforcement amounted to a violation of one of the protections listed in the Bill of Rights. Obviously, a great deal of the Union's attention would be focused on the treatment of those arrested, accused, or convicted of criminal violations. It is reasonable to suspect that persons in these categories are more likely than others to experience violations of their rights. And we shall now turn to some of the Union's positions on these problems and their proposed solutions.

We should note that the ACLU publishes useful factual material dealing with the rights of persons under arrest or on their way to trial. A bilingual card in English and Spanish is available from the Union's Southern California affiliate, informing its owner about what to do if he is arrested.[23] Legal papers written in layman's language are issued from the national office. They deal with such subjects as one's rights before a grand jury and how and why that judicial institution functions differently, on such matters as admissable evidence, from a trial jury.[24] Available as a reprint from California ACLU affiliates is an interesting article[25] that *rightly* attacks the current excuse for sweeping judicial reform in order to make our court system more efficient and "run on time." Most of us who have been to court, for whatever reasons, have noticed that a case that takes a few moments may occupy us waiting in our uncomfortable seat all morning or afternoon, after we have grown a year older waiting for it to occur. To solve this problem some, including Chief Justice Warren Burger, have suggested a number of remedies to speed up the process. They include the holding of pretrial hearings by judges to determine which cases really need a jury trial, reducing the size of the jury in criminal cases, and limiting the right of defendants to raise objections on the basis of unlawful search and seizure. All of these suggestions constitute abridgment of due process of law, a guarantee of the U.S. Consitituion. Such abridgments also increase the positivist character of criminal proceedings. One's "right" to due process of law is a *derived* right from one's natural right to be free from forceful deprivation of one's values unless it is proven that one has acted to put oneself in commensurate debt. Denial or reduction of due process increases the likelihood that such unjust deprivations will occur. And the ACLU publication to which we refer here firmly opposes such measures. There is much reason for us to be pleased with this position, at least until we reach the final paragraphs containing the "alternatives for reform" to solve the problem of slow justice.

And this is where positivist assumptions really become amazing. The first "solution" involves "prosecutorial discretion" or screening of cases in advance of trial by judges at preliminary hearings. The purpose is "to evaluate realistically the ultimate disposition of a felony filing and, where appropriate, dispose of cases in the municipal court." If this sounds fine, it should perhaps be more carefully considered. If justice is not served by preventing the defendant in a criminal case from having access to all his available due process remedies, it is also not served by a judge ruling against the hearing of a criminal case and prompting its dismissal by the district attorney on the basis that it appears to the judge that the evidence is not sufficient for a jury's verdict. The only purpose this will serve is to protect the accused from the possibility of conviction by a jury.

The ACLU advocates who wrote this article obviously feel that reducing the size of juries or allowing cases to be arbitrated in omnibus pretrial hearings would constitute a loss of due process and an increase in the probability of arbitrary and unjust convictions. It is amazing that they do not recognize the same degree of arbitrary presumption of a judge's opinion over a jury's verdict in the solution they offer. They must be assuming that such a procedure would result in a positive goal, such as a less crowded docket. But the problem is, if an accused person escapes the conviction and commensurate punishment for an action he performed, but which is not as immediately apparent to a "screening" judge in a hearing as it might be to a jury moving slowly in its deliberations, then the result is the same injustice about which the Union has complained.

The next solution suggested for sluggish courts is the participation of judges in what is called plea-bargaining. This practice usually takes place between an accused or indicted defendant and the district attorney. In it, the district attorney bargains with the defendant because he knows that a trial on the original charges will consume a considerable amount of court time and expense. The DA agrees to reduce the charge to that of a different offense carrying a significantly lesser penalty if the defendant agrees to plead guilty to that lesser offense and accept the court's sentence of jail, fine, or parole. An example might be a case of a man who is to go on trial for rape. Due to its nature, proving guilt for that offense is often quite difficult, so the DA might seek a bargained plea of guilt for criminal assault, breaking and entering, or another lesser offense. In doing so, according to this publication of the ACLU, the congestion of our courts is reduced without measures resulting in unjust denials of due-process rights.

The fact that I spent so much of this book discussing the nature of justice and natural law allows me not to be required to spend much time now explaining why plea bargaining is a guarantee of injustice. If a person is guilty of the original offense for which he is charged and is not punished commensurately, but given a penalty appropriate for a less serious deprivation of values, justice is not done. If a person is actually not guilty of the original charge, although this is not apparent to a grand jury or judge, his panicked resort to pleading guilty to a lesser crime may condemn him to a guaranteed punishment for which he is equally unworthy. In either case, the avoidance of a jury trial on the original charge *for any purpose* and a dependence on plea bargaining *must* result in injustice and hardly could qualify as due process or equal protection under the laws. Such was recommended in this article as a solution for overcrowded courts, but that is just as much nonsense. Because we know so many persons accused or convicted of serious or violent crimes are multiple offenders, the practice of getting them shorter sentences through plea bargaining can only be expected to result in a later overload of the court when they return for repeated violations.

But the recommendations in this article become even more ludicrous as we continue. The ultimate example of legal fiction under a positivist tradition of law is illustrated in the next solution for clearing out our halls of justice. This one calls for judicial redefinition or reclassification of crimes from a category that requires a potentially lengthy trial to another that can be expedited more quickly. Although the result is the same, this differs from plea bargaining in that the defendant does not get involved in making the decision. The pamphlet states that:

> In Los Angeles, a policy was launched of filing marijuana possession cases as misdemeanors. As a result of this change, in 1971-72 there were some 10,000 fewer felony cases filed in Los Angeles than the previous year—a reduction of 25%. Criminal cases fell from 20% of the total filings in Los Angeles Superior Court to 16%.

Of course, few but the authors of this pamphlet would marvel over the fact that reclassification or redefinition of one criminal action into another category will result in a a reduction of items in the first category and an increase of inverse proportions in the second. But misdemeanor cases can be processed in the courts more rapidly. That is true, and they also carry lesser penalties because they are presumed to be punishments appropriate for less serious wrongs. Indeed, a person's unpleasant duration in court might justly be longer in a felony case than a misdemeanor because he stands the possibility of being convicted of a more serious crime. So the arbitrary redefinition of criminal charges to expedite court proceedings must bring injustice by a default on due process and equal protection under the boot of judicial fiat and the positivist distortion of reality.

The fact that this example of reclassification dealt with the "crime" of marijuana possession, which I agree with the ACLU is a victimless, or non-, crime, should not distract us from the fact that it was used as just one illustration in the article of this recommended practice. The authors were arguing for it, not merely on the basis of the injustice of the law against marijuana possession, but on the basis that its reclassification as a misdemeanor will help clear the courts. Indeed, they claim that "reform of the marijuana laws would have an overwhelming effect on the volume of criminal cases in the courts." If those in government are free to redefine at will the punishment which is appropriate for various crimes in order to make their jobs easier, what precedent would there be to prevent the reduction of first-degree murder to battery? And, just as in the case of plea bargaining, how would the cause of efficient jurisprudence be served by criminals exempt from full punishments frequently returning to the courts for more *injustice?*

In civil cases, which also clog the courts, the example of reforms in the Los Angeles Superior Court is pointed to as a solution. These involve "changes in calendaring procedures and continuance policies," which, the article boasts, "have already reduced the backlog of civil cases by 14%." It further states:

> In Los Angeles Municipal Court, the waiting time for civil suits to come to trial was reduced from 16 months to 4 months by simply allowing litigants no more than three continuances.

A continuance amounts to the decision of a judge to allow the trial of a case to be resumed at a date in the near future. The interim allows for one party's attorney to prepare a legal response to a motion introduced by the other party's attorney, or the raising of matters of fact or law that were not anticipated by one of the attorneys prior to the trial. This is usually necessary because argumentation must be on the basis of prior statutes and judicial precedents, particularly in civil cases. The attorney must research these in order to make a competent response for his client. Quite often it is only through such continuances that a defendant is able to make use of all the established due process remedies in a civil proceeding. The ACLU would apparently approve setting an arbitrary number of continuances as a limit on the use of such remedies. Again, this is advocated for the goal of efficient justice. But it could hardly be advocated for due process and equal protection under the laws.

Amazingly the one solution for reducing the load on our courts *without guaranteeing injustice* that the ACLU obviously does not consider is an end to the monopoly over the arbitration of civil and criminal law cases that is now held by government. If private arbitration companies were allowed to decide awards in cases of civil disputes and on the *verdicts* of criminal cases with the use of the same jury procedures employed in government courts for all disputing parties or defendants who were willing to submit to their decisions rather than await the government's creeping schedule, some genuine progress might be made. And, yes, the government would still justly enforce the criminal and civil verdicts of private "courts" against unwilling-to-comply losers.

Some defendants or disputing parties would surely opt for private arbitration because private "courts" would have to establish records of justice to compete successfully in a free market. Government courts could still prosecute private courts for acts of injustice, and such a verdict would be disastrous for its business reputation. There would consequently be built-in incentives and higher legal protections against injustice in private courts. And the competition might have many beneficent effects on the justice provided by government. The ACLU article discussed here agrees that our criminal justice system was designed for the purpose of justice, not for the purpose of running on time. But in addition to making recommendations which will destroy both purposes, the article fails to recognize that a major reason why the delivery of justice is so slow today is because government has that service function locked up.[26]

The "Rights" of the Accused

We will now examine a sampling of the ACLU's published positions on the "rights" of criminal suspects and convicted prisoners. In doing so, we unfortunately find that we are running into the same disregard for the natural law assumptions of American constitutionalism. The Union's most recent source on the subject of those questioned, detained, or arrested in law enforcement investigations is another of those handbooks on "the rights of people." It is called *The Rights of Suspects,* and is by Oliver Rosengart,[27] an attorney specialist in this field. He worked for the scandal-ridden Mobilization for Youth "antipoverty" program in Harlem, leaders of which were proven to have fomented the riots that occurred there in 1964 and were also shown to be quite adept at making vast amounts of taxpayers' money disappear. MFY was a prototype for the Office of Economic Opportunity, the so-called war on poverty, which fit the mold of its prototype quite well.[28] But we should conclude nothing from this about Rosengart. Nor should we do so on the basis of his work with the National Lawyers Guild, which was cited by a congressional investigating committee as "the foremost legal bulwark of the

Communist Party," U.S.A.[29] I mention Mr. Rosengart's background only because it will become apparent that ACLU medical "rights" expert George Annas was right, at least about the fact that one's view of rights has a lot to do with the "identity of the definer."

Information on a suspect's rights is important because of the many things which, according to Rosengart, police do to suspects that amount to violations of their rights. Indeed, he says, "Most of this conduct is obviously illegal, but police engage in so much of it so often that many people erroneously think it is authorized by law."[30] Rosengart spends the majority of his book instructing his readers on how to deal with law enforcement officials during all kinds of contacts one might have for questioning or investigation. He details the laws under which the rights of suspects are supposed to be protected and cautions those who would assert their rights under such circumstances or interject themselves into circumstances of someone else's unlawful arrest. This is important if a person wishes to avoid what "many policemen consider the sin of questioning a police officer's authority."[31] He also spotlights special circumstances in which abuses seem to be involved. He and the ACLU take the position that airport searches of passenger baggage to deter potential highjackers are unconstitutional. I would agree that such forceful action *on the part of government* amounts to an action taken on the anticipation of criminal conduct which has yet to occur, although Rosengart does not state this as his reason. We should also note that airline companies, still the titular property of individuals, have the right to include in their passenger contracts the stipulation that passengers will be searched, an imposition anyone can avoid by taking his business elsewhere, but unavoidable when government orders it for all companies and installs federal police in municipal airports to carry it out.[32]

Perhaps the most controversial portion of the subject matter Rosengart discusses is comprised of the Supreme Court decisions on a suspect's rights to be free of self-incrimination. He discusses them and obviously approves.[33] The major one is *Miranda* v. *Arizona* (384 U.S. 436). This 1966 ruling, actually a clarification of the 1964 ruling in *Escobedo* v. *Illinois* (378 U.S. 478), led to the so-called "exclusionary rule." This rule states that a suspect's confession of guilt in a criminal case, even if given voluntarily and without the pressures called "third degree methods," is not admissible in court unless the arresting officers can prove that the suspect was told of his right to remain silent, that anything he says may be used against him in court, and that he has a "right" to an attorney *free of charge* if he says he cannot provide one for himself. When the voluntary confession of a suspect in cases like this and *Mallory* v. *U.S.* (354 U.S. 449, 1957) is the only strong evidence available to secure conviction, its inadmissibility results in the defendant being released from any punishment. These decisions, as federal judicial precedents, not only freed the self-admitted criminals involved in these cases to return to the streets, and in several cases to commit crimes again, but also served to reverse many convictions of similar offenders in state courts, producing the same results. Particularly in the *Miranda* decision, where the defendant voluntar-

72

ily confessed to kidnapping and rape after being informed of all his rights except that he was entitled to a *free* attorney, the rulings of confessional evidence as being inadmissible and excluded have led many critics to conclude that the court was more concerned with the criminal's rights and not at all with the victim's.

And this is precisely correct. One's rights can be violated by the omission of most of the due process procedures listed in *Miranda* on the part of arresting officers, particularly the right to remain silent. However, there is no constitutional basis for the court's insistence that a defendant must be provided with an attorney free of charge. Once again, this entails the positivist notion of an "economic right," or the "right" to the forced labor of another without his consent. True, the court-appointed attorney may not object to his employment in such a case, but the taxpayer from whom his salary is being involuntarily extracted does. On this basis, grave injustice was done because a kidnapper and rapist was allowed to escape the punishment he had earned.

In the *Miranda* case, another principle is obvious, perhaps more so than in the other landmark exclusionary rulings. That is, by his voluntary confession, in which he declared in advance that he understood his rights, Miranda objectively waived his "right" to the "free" attorney that the court later "qualified" as being required to be present during that statement. It is rather clear that by volunteering to speak one waives one's right to remain silent. But notice the positivist implication that one's right to legal counsel means that an attorney *must* be physically present, not that one has a right to contact and engage the services of one. It might be objected that, in this and other such cases, obvious violations of suspects' due process rights did occur. Certainly the ruling judges thought so. But observe that the criminal status of the defendant, as a result of these cases and their lack of commensurate punishment, was predicted not on the quality of his actions, but solely on those of the arresting officers. By this approach, injustice was done in each and every case because the rulings amounted to incredible transfers of legal focus, or distortions of reality.

It might be suggested, as Rosengart does not, that a more just remedy for a situation in which a self-confessed criminal is deprived of due process rights would be to prosecute him for the crime to which he has confessed and, if convicted, punish him commensurately. Where such would not result in capital punishment, he could be free to sue the arresting officers for the violations of his civil rights and, if successful, receive either an award appropriate for such a violation or a number of years of reduction in his mandatory sentence, assuming that the civil rights violation carried a substantially lesser penalty than the original crime of which he was convicted. Where such is not the case, the convict's suit might earn him an award greater than the fine which he had to pay. But for such to be possible in many cases, his right to sue for rights violations, before or after his conviction on other charges, would have to be recognized, and there would have to be removed the immunity from prosecution that arresting officers at all levels of government currently enjoy. In the case of a person who has earned capital punishment, the proceeds of any suit he wins prior to his death would go into his estate for his family or any other beneficiary he might designate. The point is, one criminal wrong does not justly erase another.[34]

But why might a spokesman for the ACLU disagree? Oliver Rosengart makes his position easier to understand by writing that the source of a suspect's rights "are some Supreme Court decisions, state statutes, and local police department regulations, which vary greatly."[35] From such a positivist outlook on the sources of human rights, we might expect him to arrive at equally positivist conclusions.

The ACLU has had to defend its support of these Supreme Court decisions in response to objections by many that they benefit only criminals at the expense of the rights of their victims. Some critiques of these decisions have even come from leading authorities in law schools who are inclined to accept many positivist premises. The ACLU makes available academic answers to these protests over the results of such rulings. In an answer to one of these criticisms, the author makes this statement:

> To suggest, as Inbau does, that *Miranda* rules are "unnecessary for the protection of the innocent and they are not soundly derived as constitutional requirements," is to fail to recognize that *Miranda* is the product of a court which believes that society changes and the law must change with it. The alternative is atrophy, perhaps one similar to that which has withered the Congress.[36]

No clearer statement of a positivist and subjectivist theory of law is possible. And for those of us who understand that ACLU official Mel Wulf is correct when he says "the natural tendency of any government is to diminish the rights of the citizens and increase its own power,"[37] we would properly be against *Miranda* for the atrophy alone!

But what is the solution to protecting the rights of suspects, the long-range solution, proposed by the author of the ACLU's handbook on the subject? Let's see if he recommends reducing the size and power of government to a minimum:

> In the final analysis, the problem of police misconduct goes to the roots of our society. We live in a country with an enormous amount of crime on all socioeconomic levels; why should the police be different? Like most of society, the police are dissatisfied and alienated; they resent the lack of dignity in their work and the lack of respect society has for them. They resent much of the job they have been given, because part of it is to mop up the casualties of society's neglect of one quarter of the population, to contain the fifty million or so have-nots and to preserve the status quo for the haves. The authoritarian nature of the work attracts politically conservative individuals who oppose political change and political activism. It may be trite, but it must be said: that the only real answer to the problem of police misconduct is a more socially and economically just society.
>
> The instigation of some immediate changes would be a beginning, although they are politically very difficult to impose. These include: a system of psychological testing to

weed out the small number of authoritarian, repressed, policemen who are attracted to police work only because of the opportunities for violence and racism that the work offers; massive recruiting of minority-group people for the police force; and real community control of the people—that is, control by the local community where the police are working, not by the local municipality. And most importantly, the police need a great deal of education about the nature of society, why it is so badly split, why the resources are so unevenly distributed and why we have so much crime on all levels. Police should be taught the psychology of crime, how crime is often an adaptation to a horrible environment and to a feeling of powerlessness, as well as the psychological meaning of drug use, not just its behavior. And the police should be exposed to the life background and conditions of criminals, so that they might understand that except for luck the person the police officer arrests could be himself or you or me.[38]

There is certainly much to ponder over in these, the concluding words of Rosengart's book, especially since it is sanctioned sufficiently to be copyrighted by the ACLU. In this statement we get several messages. Our ethical and legal attention, and that of police officers, to the subject of crime should be focused not upon the voluntary actions of individuals, but upon the social and economic factors of our society that produce this phenomena. Criminals are not willing creators of victims, but rather *the victims of* the fact that our "resources are so unevenly distributed" because of society's neglect of the "have-nots" in order to protect the economic position of the "haves." To solve this problem, Rosengart is not advocating a free market, but rather government controls and forceful redistribution of resources, which are the earned values of individuals. We can be sure of this because "politically conservative individuals" among the "haves" are against such "political change," which is "very difficult to impose."

He thinks a number of things should be imposed. First, individuals should not have the right to seek employment in government police departments if they fail to pass a test designed by those in government to weed out repressed, authoritarian majority-group people who find violence and racism appealing. Since such a test would only reveal those problems through answers to questions or statements of opinion, Rosengart thinks it is necessary to deny equal protection under the Constitution, which says that no laws shall be made abridging freedom of thought, including the thoughts one has before joining a police department. But, you see, this is in anticipation that such thoughts will lead to actions of a criminal nature. He urges massive recruitment of minority-group people for police forces, apparently to replace those who have a liking for racism and violence. This is presumably because no minority-group people, as far as Rosengart is concerned, are very fond of racism and violence. When they get arrested for violent crimes, it is because they are mechanically reacting to a hostile environment. Only majority-group criminals fail to qualify for this excuse and should be fired. We must assume this thinking behind his recommendations, because otherwise we would have to assume that he thinks members of minority races, by their nature, somehow make better policemen than members of majority races, which would make Rosengart a racist.

Rosengart holds that police need to be controlled by the people of the community in which they work, but this is not the local city or county government. He seems to be recommending either a police review board sanctioned by the municipality to discipline or prosecute policemen or a separate system of government on the local level which would form a structure parallel to, but independent of, the municipality. If he is talking about a review board, it would be manned by the same people who are given no alternative by society but to commit crimes and who would regard any force used against a criminal as an attack on themselves. If he is recommending a system of parallel local governments, we might wonder how he would suggest that they be controlled and kept free of repressed, violent racists among those who are to control the uniformed repressed, violent racists.

Finally, we are told that policemen must be educated to understand the economic deprivation that forces people to be criminals. If such a policeman failed to realize these things after taking the course, he is obviously unfit for the job. And the best way for him to understand the causes of crime is to "be exposed to the life background and conditions of criminals," which apparently can only be done by giving into his own miserable feelings and becoming a criminal himself. Then he would really believe that the guy he arrests "could be himself." But this does not mean Rosengart believes good policemen should become criminals; it would be perfectly possible as an alternative to recruit good policemen from among experienced criminals. All of which is hellish nonsense derived from what Marx and his followers have done with positivism.

But we still should not assume that Rosengart is reflecting the ideology which we would simplistically expect from the National Lawyers Guild. Indeed, we might well bend over backwards to be fair and note another source of his inspiration. In his discussion of one's rights in the context of laws concerning loitering and vagrancy, Rosengart remembers:

When I was thirteen, I saw a very moving theatrical play and took a walk to think about it. A policeman stopped me and asked what I was doing. I replied that I was walking. He asked where to. I answered nowhere and he asked what I was doing. I again said walking and he said but what are you doing? I replied that I was thinking, and he then asked me if I had ever been in a mental institution.[39]

The "Rights" of Criminals

We might expect to find a better formulation available from the ACLU on the rights of those persons who have already been convicted, but such is not forthcoming. A recruiting flyer[40] from the New York office sets the pace by declaring, "The legitimate purposes of imprisonment are rehabilitation of the prisoner and protection of society." We note immediately that individuals can be rehabilitated, for instance, medically in hospitals and psychotherapy sessions, without necessarily being in prison. But, according to the ACLU, prisons are still legitimate for protecting society, which probably means all the individuals living in "society." But, still we wonder. Cannot a person be protected from criminals without having those criminals locked up? Such protection is offered by privately owned guns in one's home, providing one has become skillful in their use, or by hiring a bodyguard or private security force. Besides, why justify locking people up on the basis that they *might* harm someone else again in the future? But, such is apparently the Union's belief.

We have further confirmation of this from the author of the ACLU's official handbook on *The Rights of Prisoners*.[41] His name is David Rudovsky, obviously an expert in his field of law, and he practices in Philadelphia. As chance would have it, his book's first page informs us that he is staff counsel for the National Emergency Civil Liberties Committee, which, again as chance would have it, has been cited by congressional investigating committees as one of those Communist fronts which reaches "out far beyond the confines of the Communist Party itself."[42] But we should not bother with that too much, since we have learned that such says little necessarily about Rudovsky. And, besides, our concern is with the ACLU, not the NECLC.

On views toward prisons, other than those held by the ACLU, Rudovsky states:

> It was not until the nineteenth century that the use of prisons became widespread. Until the middle of the eighteenth century, European penology was motivated principally by punishment and retribution. Most crimes were dealt with by corporal punishment and a great many by execution. Imprisonment was thought to be a deterrent to criminal activity (an idea prevalent today although still not established through objective criteria) and was considered more humane than corporal punishment. Moreover, prisons were also built with the idea of reformation: the penitentiary was intended to serve as a place for reflection in solitude leading to repentance and redemption. But these prisons served in reality only to punish—physically and mentally. Supported by court-adopted theories that prisoners were in fact slaves of the state, prison administrators had absolutely free reign to abuse their inmates as they wished. There was no question of prisoners' "rights."[43]

And, we should add, about several of the facts in that description, although not for all of those reasons, rightly so. We might wonder about on just how firm a footing is any discussion of the "rights" of prisoners when it is only by forfeiting one's rights or indebting one's values that a person receives justice by becoming a prisoner.

Prisons may deter some potential criminals from their unlawful actions. Objective criteria for determining this come from asking a criminal how he would have felt before committing his crime if he knew that no possible jail term was in his future. Prisons may keep some criminals from harming other people. But these factors are consequences of their existence, not the reason for them. Prisons, like corporal punishment before them, simply serve the function of depriving criminals of the pursuit of most of their positive values and provide the discomfort of negative ones. And such provisions, when reasonably commensurate with the harm done by the criminal, the debt he established to his victim, the extent to which he equally forfeited his rights by violating those of others, provide justice. The fact that we would admit many prisons are dreadful places to be, and that frequently prisoners receive abuse which is, perhaps, not merited by the harm they did, still does not change the basic reason why they are just. And it does not change the nature of the same error in the ACLU's position.

The only question that such a problem as the abuse of prisoners might bring is whether or not government, once again, should have a monopoly over their maintenance. If there were private prisons competing for the business of government judicial branches at all levels, the available quality would have to improve. Such private institutions could be supported by the charity of individuals horrified with government prisons. Inmates could also work for the private prisons, producing manufactured goods that could be sold for a maximum profit. The possibilities are many, but before we continue, we should note that Rudovsky is apparently not interested in such an approach. He sees part of the problem in the fact that:

> Each level of government operates independently of the others in administering its prisons and correctional apparatus. Thus, the Federal Government has no control over state corrections; the states have responsibility for prisons but usually no control over county or city jails; and the rules and regulations vary substantially from penal institution to penal institution.[44]

Perhaps Rudovsky, in his lament that there is no federal control over all prisons and jails, has not learned that such a system of balance of power in our federalist framework was designed by our Founding Fathers to keep any one level from exercising, as ACLU's Mel Wulf has said, its "natural tendency . . . to diminish the rights of the citizens and increase its own power." Rudovsky might find such a conception difficult to understand, since he believes that

> The only source of law applicable to all prisons is the Constitution, which provides only a minimum standard for prisoners' rights.
> Ideally, state and federal statutes, and administrative rules and regulations could expand these rights, but except in a few instances, the Constitution continues to provide the most meaningful basis for assertion of prisoners' rights.[45]

Of course, such a view of the Constitution as a *source* of rights, or of the ability of statutes, rules, or regulations to "expand" one's rights, is rank legal positivism, which, as we have seen, is quite at home in the ACLU. But even if we assumed the Constitution, rather than the philosophy it communicates, was the source of one's rights, there are only two items that deal specifically with the context of a person after he has been convicted of a crime. The Fifth Amendment, in part, guarantees that no one shall "be deprived of life, liberty, or property, without due process of law," meaning that no one forfeits his right to those values he owns until he is proven to have violated the same rights of others. Further support for our overall view of crime is found in the Eighth Amendment's prohibition against excessive bail, excessive fines, and cruel or unusual punishments, which all implies that punishments must be fair and fines equitable by matching, as closely as possible, the harm done. Notice that neither says anything about the protection of specific rights *after* one has been justly deprived of rights or values by due process. Just how one's forfeited rights selectively become revalidated, after the harm is done but before the debt is virtually repaid, is not made clear by Rudovsky. But if our approach is correct, he could not make it clear anyway.

Let us examine what "rights" Rudovsky thinks are contained in those two sections of the Constitution, or should be "expanded" from them. He believes prisoners should enjoy all the due process remedies at prison disciplinary hearings that are enjoyed by citizens in courts before they are convicted.[46] He believes that "cruel and unusual punishment" prohibitions should be "expanded" to allow for all prisoners to enjoy conjugal visits.[47] He would support a prisoner's "right" to be free of all censorship on his mail, including letters written to present a false and libelous picture of conduct by prison employees, and letters to other persons involved, or suspected to be involved, in cooperating criminal maneuvers. Rudovsky attacks the idea that unlimited postal privacy would facilitate plans for escape or other criminal plottings. He says, "The likelihood of any of these dire predictions becoming reality is very slim indeed. The experience in jurisdictions which permit an unlimited right to communication indicates that there is, in fact, no support for these fears."[48] He adds that, with so many prisons allowing inmates the "right" to private visitations anyway, what purpose would mail censorship serve? Law enforcement agents who attempted to interrogate Charles Manson after his friend's attempt on the life of President Ford must not be privy to Rudovsky's data.

In addition to advocating the "right" of prisoners to wear the clothes they want and maintain the appearance they want, Rudovsky is all for their "right" to receive and distribute religious and political literature, particularly when such constitutes the practice of personal religious faith, even though the material may be highly inflammatory and advocate racial violence.[49]

But most amazing, he believes that prisoners have a "right" to the means with which they may institute suits in the courts over their treatment, as well as "up-to-date vocational and educational training, and psychological and medical treatment."[50]

We must insist that, if free men do not have the "right" to enslave others and receive their "free" services, then, most certainly, neither do those who have forfeited their rights by actions that justly qualify them for conditions of enslavement. The incredible fact is that, in Rudovsky's statements on behalf of the ACLU, our prisons are conceived as places where, not only would there be no punishment truly commensurate with the harm done by criminals, but also where criminals would enjoy many privileges that constitute a higher standard of living even than that possessed by many of the justly free men who are forced to provide it for those incarcerated. How could injustice be more supreme?

A reading of Rudovsky's book would convince many people that he would have criminals enjoying all the freedoms of other citizens, plus all those "free" privileges, with the single exception that they could not leave the premises unless, of course, they are paroled immediately after conviction. Unemployed people on welfare, outside of physical prisons, are similarly unfree, in that they are not supposed to have other significant sources of income. It is hard to tell how the two categories differ in Rudovsky's mind, except that the criminal must be given more, at *your* expense. For *your* rights, there is not much difference.

Because in publishing such material the ACLU has shown itself to be committed to a crudely positivist view of due process and equal protection under the laws, regardless of *their* inherent justice or injustice, we need now to examine more of the *substantial* issues relative to the laws that the Union and its misunderstanding idealists are determined equally to enforce on *us*.

6

ACLU Positions
on "Victimless Crimes"

The major distinction we can make fairly well between the issues discussed in this chapter and the last is that we have just been dealing with ACLU positions on the constitutionality of the manner in which positive laws are enforced and criminal punishments applied, and we shall now consider outstanding examples of laws on which the Union takes a stand regarding the constitutionality of the content of the statute or decision and how it relates to individual rights. Of course, this distinction often wears thin because criteria for both categories would be properly based on the same understanding of man's nature and rights, which are vulnerable to attack from substantive and procedural injustice alike.

Victimless "Crimes"

If we are dismayed by the inconsistencies with natural law constitutionalist thought as exhibited in the Union's positions on suspects' and prisoners' "rights," we should expect even more problems in the area of substantive legal questions that require for accuracy even finer understanding of the philosophical foundations we have reviewed, and are thus prone to be areas of greater ignorance and injustice in today's legal education and practice. The primary question we shall be dealing with is: What human actions are criminal by virtue of constituting the violation of individuals rights, or deprivation of values, and thus justify the use of force on the part of government or any concern of the law? Thus we need to keep in mind our understanding of values, rights, and crime.

In doing so we confront a wide spectrum of human activities that must be viewed from two properly separated perspectives. We may view a person's actions as alternatives that we hold are immoral because they are at odds with Divine commands, ethical positions, or just the physical or psychological well-being of the person involved. However, unless and until such actions include criminal violations of others' rights, they are not properly to be judged in a legal context. If actions that do not qualify for criminal appraisal are still legislated against, we can call them "victimless crimes." Such would include any thought or action not violating another's rights that is expressive of one's capacities for life, free thought, and action, and the exchange of tangible and intangible values among men, no matter how personally harmful these actions are to each individual as he carries them out. So we will discuss those actions arising directly from the most essential human capacities to the more consequential ones, and we shall compare our findings with the positions taken by the ACLU.

Implications of the Right to Live

As an individual's life is his most essential property, we must first deal with the Union's views on the subjects of suicide, euthanasia (or mercy killing), capital punishment, the individual's right to control the manner in which his life is protected by medical care, the right to be free from involuntary treatment, the alleged right of a mother to terminate the life of her unborn child, and the right of any person to own anything, including any means for self-protection, until such is used to violate the rights of another.

The most fundamental human right, derived from human nature, is the right to life itself. Because human beings exist as living creatures, they have the right to do so until that existence is terminated by age, illness, or accident. They must be free to live without the initiation of force aimed at their existence. In this clearly temporal context, each man is the master over his own life. That is, he can act justly in self-defense to preserve his life, even to the extent of taking the life of another who imperils his own. This would-be assailant virtually forfeits his right to life by physically attacking that of another.

Everyone also has the right in the face of natural law to terminate his own life. In this subject we encounter a matter with such strong emotional attachments that our understanding is easily misled if we are not careful. The only circumstances under which those in government would be justified in initiating force to prevent someone from committing suicide would be in a situation where the means of suicide that has been selected will unavoidably violate the rights of others. An example of this would be a man who chooses to end it all by setting off a bomb in an airplane in which he and a hundred other passengers are riding. The state would be justified in stopping him in this case. However, in the case of the miserable soul who opts for an overdose of sleeping pills in his home—and omitting any imaginable contingency that might result, such as the house burning down from appliances left running—any representative of government would be "trespassing" on his rights by using force to stop him.

For anyone who may have just concluded that I have no compassionate desire to save the life of a distraught person on the verge of self-destruction, allow me to develop my position on this issue a bit further before moving on to another issue. I have no desire to see anyone commit suicide, even if they should choose to do so. I consider the act *morally* abominable when it is performed by someone seeking to avoid the responsibility of temporarily overwhelming problems in life. I hold to religious convictions that such an act, for that reason, is an attack on God's creation and an affront to His Will. However, such an act also represents a confession, on the part of many who attempt it, that they are psychologically "at the end of their rope" and have no personal strength or reservoir of self-confidence to apply to the alternatives they face. There are tragedies and circumstances that can occur in a person's life that would convince the most compassionate advocate of forceful suicide prevention that the person may be quite justified in taking his life, or, at least, make such a course of action considerably less incomprehensible, if not less tragic.

A soldier captured by an enemy that is preparing to torture him could know very well that he would not be able to hold up under such treatment without revealing the information sought by his captors. If he chose, on his own, to value nonsubmission over his life, he would have some sort of moral justification for cheating his inquisitors. It is assumed that he would, perhaps, not end his life until he knew that there was no possibility of escape, that his enemy had no other source for the information (making his self-sacrifice futile), and that they were not bluffing. This is not an advocacy of suicide under these or other hypothetical circumstances, but merely an illustration of a situation in which a person might choose self-inflicted death with reason, for the purpose of depriving his captors of the information they were seeking.

In a free society, efforts toward suicide prevention would continue in much the same way they do today, except for the initiation of force to stop a person from committing suicide in a manner that would not harm others. Compassionate individuals would still talk suicidal persons back through windows into buildings or onto bridges. Government would not compete with this activity of individuals. However, special distress charity companies could be established and funded by the contributions of those interested especially in suicide prevention. Private insurance companies would have an interest in the suicidal problems of their clients holding life insurance, unless such policies were written with death benefits excluded in cases of suicide, a factor with perhaps insignificant influence as a deterrent on the suicidal person.

Although members of the ACLU would be unlikely to advocate criminal penalties for those who unsuccessfully attempt suicide, many would find acceptable a sort of "good samaritan" legal standard to protect those who used force to abort the effort, including some injury to the person whose life was saved or destruction of his property. Some states have laws like this to protect individuals who try to help injured motorists at the scene of an accident from suits for damages on further injuries incurred from the actions of the person who tried to help. In either case, if the government prohibited the surviving person from bringing suit against whoever used force against him, even for the "best" of motivations, his rights would be violated.

The right of a person to commit suicide in any manner that does not violate another's rights is an issue closely related to several others. Its validity is no sanction for the practice of euthanasia, or mercy killing. The reason for this should be obvious. A person slowly dying of a torturous disease possesses the right to life until he or she is dead. He has this right until he forfeits it by taking the life of another. He can justly take his own life, but he must do it himself. On the issue of euthanasia, representatives of the ACLU and other groups are not simply advocating the legal existence of well-managed suicide clinics such as those in Sweden, but rather they are calling for the legalization of someone else's decision to end the suffering patient's life.[1] The crucial problem of euthanasia lies in that fact. No doctor or family member has the right to end the life of the patient without such being murder, regardless of the entreaties of the patient for him to do so.

It is at this point that we should note how illusory is the distinction that advocates of legalized euthanasia make between so-called "active" and "passive" euthanasia. Active euthanasia would be legal if doctors or family members were free to decide if and when a patient's life could be terminated. Passive euthanasia denotes the legal ability of hospital personnel to receive permission from the patient to make the decision concerning if and when his life will be ended by the action of withholding further treatment.

Such legal passive euthanasia is supported by the ACLU. This is made clear by their patients' "rights" expert, George Annas, who notes that such a position is based on one's right of "self-determination,"[2] and further argues that

> A Harris poll taken in the spring of 1973 indicated that approximately 62 percent of Americans favored allowing the terminally ill patient to direct his doctor to "let him die rather than extend his life when no cure is in sight," and only 28 percent thought this practice was wrong.[3]

We should refrain from assuming that Annas necessarily thinks that truth in such matters is indicated by majority vote, but it would be helpful to consider some of the reasons why he or any number of others might lean toward this position.

One emotional consideration is the fact that it is excruciatingly painful for relatives to watch the daily deterioration of a loved one in the agonies of a terminal illness. This sort of situation is usually in the minds of those who would advocate the transfer of the function of terminating such a patient's life to someone else. The issue of the patient's inalienable right to life, and the fact that he is the only person who can forfeit it rightfully, and by his own action, is obviously overlooked. This justification for euthanasia misses the essential point concerning why it is a criminal act because the focus of the advocate is not on the essential concepts involved. An argument *against* euthanasia would be similarly nonessential if it were based on another reason, say, the possibility that a miracle cure may be discovered in time to save the patient if he is kept alive until all available supportive efforts fail.

The question of who should be required to pay for the terminal patient's extended care until he dies, including payment for care after the point where advocates of euthanasia would agree his life should be ended, is another question entirely from whether or not the action of withholding treatment, under any conditions, constitutes murder. Regardless of whether payment for the hospital's services comes from the patient's assets, his family, an insurance company, or a charitable institution, withholding care to terminate his life amounts to murder.

The absurdity of those who would advocate passive euthanasia by withholding treatment at the patient's request, but who would object to a doctor acting entirely on his own to administer gas or an injection to accomplish the same result, is clear if we consider transferring their perspective to ordinary homicide. Perhaps they would make such a distinction if a murder suspect testified, without any available testimony of witnesses to contradict him, that right before he pulled the trigger, the victim requested to be sent to his reward. In such a parallel situation the doctor performing passive euthanasia and the gunman would have something quite in common. There would be no contradictions from the victim concerning any last-second thoughts.[4]

But ACLU and author Annas seem to think that there are due process safeguards that a person who wants passive euthanasia could use to guarantee that his death would be brought about with "equal protection under the laws." Annas recommends that people have prepared a "living will" similar to one available from the Euthanasia Educational Council of New York. This is written as a legal testament to one's family, doctor, clergyman, and attorney, and instructs them to withhold further treatment should the person who writes it contract an illness that progresses to the point where there is "no reasonable expectation" of recovery. The problem is, according to Annas, that most people just will not follow such instructions. As a solution, he feels that

A state statute is thought to be necessary to make such a document legally binding on doctors and hospitals because such a statement might violate "public policy" against suicide or euthanasia.[5]

Of course, such a policy of government-enforced life-termination might apply to parental discretion over the fate of infants born with minimal chance of survival or severe physical handicaps or deformities. Annas notes the danger of such a practice extending the permissible time for life-termination considerably after birth, and reminds us that in Nazi Germany "the killing of 'defective' children continued, the age limit being raised from 3, to 8, to 12, and, in some cases, to 16 or 17."[6] But we should not worry about that fact of legal euthanasia, because

the United States is far different from prewar and World War II Germany, and sufficient safeguards could be built in to prevent such abuses. The purpose here is not to debate the merits of such a program but to outline the current status of the law.[7]

Some of us have less trust in any government than does Annas. But we should note that he has expressed a position for the ACLU that would not only legalize a doctor's decision to act toward ending a patient's life, such a decision being transferred from the only one rightly entitled to do so to the ultimate discretion of the doctor who carried it out, but also would give government the power to enforce such discretion. Nothing more than the essentials of such a law would be necessary to bring the United States to the legal perspective on euthanasia that existed in Nazi Germany.

And after reading the other arguments Annas presents, noting that the advocates of legalized euthanasia frequently dwell on nonessential issues with strong emotional overtones, we might be allowed to project that a laissez faire economy would encourage research in medical science far beyond its rate of advancement today. Medicine would be out of the hands of government. Those offering medical services would compete as actively as those offering cosmetic services, and there would be no government regulations on the development and testing of new therapies. Anyone harmed, or his relatives if he were killed, by the application of new treatments would be free to sue the physician responsible for their administration. Without any official seal of government sanction on new drugs and other therapies, doctors would be far more cautiously selective in their use of remedies to avoid the personal and career disaster that carelessness or negligence would surely bring. If such an economy did not succeed in significantly extending the average man's longevity and health by the development of new products in the health industries, we can be fairly sure that it would succeed in conquering most dread diseases and in alleviating far better than is presently done the discomforts of those that remained incurable. Certainly, many patients of modest means would have better access to such advanced and intensive care as a result of the tremendous purchasing power that would be reclaimed by citizens with the abolition of taxation, and which would be available for those interested in humanitarian charities that would, presumably, be run as profitable enterprises. They would provide the service of effective use of charity funds and recognition of the donors' beneficence, and they could compete quite realistically on this basis. A free society

86

would not be left with just the alternatives of either handing the terminal patient a gun in a bullet-proof room or devising execution machines that the patients themselves could activate.

Unfortunately, the benefits of an economically libertarian society are not among the solutions being sought by the ACLU. Indeed, as we have seen, its spokesman George Annas seems to favor total monopoly control over medical services in the hands of a central government, another feature we found accompanying legalized "mercy killing" in Nazi Germany.[8]

When Killing Is Not Murder

We need immediately to turn our attention to the fact that, while the ACLU favors the "decriminalization" of killing terminally ill people at their verbal or written request, it strongly opposes government putting any person, sick or well, to death for a capital crime.[9] The Union views the death penalty as "cruel and unusual punishment" for "any crime." They argue that it has been a chief weapon in society's campaign to deprive Negroes of their "equal protection" under the laws. This is because more Negroes convicted of capital crimes have been executed than whites convicted of capital crimes. They claim that capital punishment is ineffective as retribution because it is so rarely used, useless as a deterrent to serious crimes due to the same irregular use, and otherwise serves "no valid social purpose."[10] All of which, of course, has nothing to do with its justification and its justice. By taking this position for entirely nonessential reasons derived from recent Supreme Court opinions, the Union is actually saying that there are no capital *crimes,* that there are no criminal violations of rights for which the death penalty, even painlessly administered, would be an equitable and commensurate, if not merciful, punishment. And if I were to sum up the validity of this ACLU position, after all that we have discussed, and utter such as a single word in a small Bible-belt community, I would likely require the Union's services to defend my right of free speech. So much, then, for the ACLU's defense of a murderer's "right" to life, particularly after we have seen what they advocate regarding euthanasia and similar illogic in the position we must next examine.

"Abortion on Demand" As Murder

The one area in which the ACLU departs from an insistence on "equal protection" under the laws for all people is in the controversial matter that, by virtue of their sexual anatomy, only pertains to women. This is the issue of abortion, on which the Union fully supports the 1973 Supreme Court ruling that declared unconstitutional all state laws prohibiting abortion on demand up through the first trimester of pregnancy. The Court's and the ACLU's rationale for this timing is that no fetus born prematurely before this point and up to the twenty-fourth to twenty-eighth week has ever survived. The earliest recorded point at which a premature child has survived after birth is called by the court and the ACLU "viability." Until the unborn child passes the first trimester of development into a stage of potential viability, the Court and the ACLU believe that it is just a part of the mother's body.[11] As such, it is not a human being possessing the right to life, and the mother has an unqualified right to end its existence by having it removed from her body for any reason. After the fetus reaches viability, it somehow takes upon itself the right to life, although still unborn, and the Court, as well as most persons in ACLU, would allow states to prohibit abortions except where clearly necessary to save the life of the mother. Even though there are strong medical dangers to the woman undergoing the various methods of induced abortion, particularly as she gets closer to term,[12] the ACLU has published a paper advocating that the "right" to an abortion must be extended to minors, with or without the knowledge and consent of their parents.[13] One might wonder if the ACLU believes a father has the right to force his infant son out of the path of automobiles in the street that the child does not know would kill him.

But what about the Union's position on abortion for adults? We must first realize that a human being is a particular kind of living organism, a rational one, whose existence historically is a continual development from his conception. The fact that an embryo (or later, a fetus) is in a temporarily dependent relationship with another human being, its mother, for purposes of protection, nourishment, and assistance in the performance of vital life functions, does not change the fact that it is still a human being, a temporarily dependent one.[14]

We could conceive of a similar situation for a person after birth. A child or an adult could be stricken with a variety of infirmities that require him to be fed intravenously and breathed by an iron lung, while such vital organs as his heart and kidneys were stimulated or assisted by pacemakers and dialysis machines. A person in this terrible shape would be in a physically dependent relationship very much like that of an unborn child. If suddenly disconnected from that relationship, he, like the fetus during the first trimester, would not prove too "viable." But would we say that a person in this condition was no longer a human being, but merely a portion of the apparatus with which it was related? Would we say that he no longer possessed the right to life and allow someone legally to shut off the machines for some other reasons?

The focus by the Court and the ACLU on the "viability" of a fetus as the means for identifying the time at which it suddenly acquires the right to life confesses the fact that they both have ignored the origin of human rights in human characteristics and capacities, and have looked, as positivists might be expected to do, only at physical behavior, or the lack of same. The viability of a child at term is also quite limited. It is able usually to survive delivery, but is actually not fully viable until the doctor has gotten it to start breathing. Then it is hardly viable without constant care and attention. Of course, full or independent viability in another sense does not come until many years later, and seemingly, in the lives of some it never arrives. Clearly the ability to survive as a living organism by means of its own physiology and anatomy, or viability, is not at all what is meant by the characteristics or capacities of human life that give rise to rights for all men, the development of which is continuous from conception.

Some libertarians have taken a different position, defending a woman's "right" to abortion. They admit that a fetus is a living and developing organism from conception onward, but they hold it is not human until after birth, and thus has no rights of any kind until after that event. The rationalization for this position is as follows.[15] Man is an animal unique by virtue of his possession of a level of consciousness not shared by the lower animals. In addition to his sensory perceptual form of immediate awareness, man also is able to think on a conceptual level of ideas and abstractions. It is this faculty that makes him human and, with his related faculty of free will, in possession of rights. The unborn child does not function on such a conceptual level of consciousness, and it demonstrates no volitional control over its mental processes. Stated another way, because of where the fetus is, it has no sensory consciousness, because such implies the presence of something of which it is conscious.

It is such reasoning that has led some libertarians to advocate a mother's right to abortion on demand. The errors inherent in this excuse are, perhaps, more grave than those made under the ACLU's notion of "viability" because the persons who hold it are more likely to accept a rational understanding of man's nature and rights along conceptualist lines.

But the absence of human characteristics is not indicated by their incomplete utilization. A man still has the capacity for sight although he may not have seen anything during a period of isolation in a cave. The developing unborn child has, from conception to term, the physical structure of which all life processes are characteristics. The reason the unborn child is not functioning conceptually or volitionally is due to the limits on sensory input available to it and the restrictive nature of its physically dependent relationship. Such is *not* due to the unborn child's lack of the physical attributes that will generate mental processes once the child has come into the open environment.

It is even sillier to require a conceptual level of consciousness in a child as a requirement for humanity and rights when we realize that the child does not employ its potential for concept-formation until it begins to use language. By requiring the active use of a child's conceptual faculty—rather than the possession of that capacity prior to learning its use—for the child to be regarded as possessing the right to life, we might wonder if persons holding this position would not logically commit themselves to infant euthanasia.

I have no quarrel with those, including the ACLU, who approve the American tradition of legal abortions for mothers who could not possibly survive childbirth. In such a case, the mother's right to life can be weighed quite evenly with that of the unborn child. The same *might* be said to hold true for those rare pregnancies that result from rape, a crime doing potentially permanent damage to the victim. However, objections can be raised to abortions permitted for rape or incest, the latter being usually justified on the basis of probable deformity in the offspring. The problem is that, in the case of rape, although the mother's rights have been grossly violated, she will still remain alive following the childbirth. However, if she is allowed an abortion, such will not result in the punishment of the criminal rapist, but in the death of another passive victim, the unborn child who was not a volitional partner in the original violation of rights. In a case of incest, the child still retains the right to life, even if such is made miserable by a birth defect. The product of an incestuous union could rightly sue his parents for damages resulting from their negligence in an act that is known to produce a high degree of abnormal offspring. And if a child does not forfeit his right to life by being abnormal, a mother certainly has no right to terminate the life of her unborn child because its birth will cause her some problem short of losing her own life, including any resulting psychological problems that can potentially be solved later in life. No matter what their rationalizations are, civil libertarians, in or outside the ACLU, are advocating legalized murder when they support a woman's "right" to abortion on demand.

On the subject of the Union's lack of consistency, it should be mentioned at this point that there is an important assumption built into the Union's specious argument that a woman has the right to control her own body, and thus the "right" to destroy the life of another, temporarily dependent on her body. That assumption is that the law should reflect the physical or anatomical characteristics peculiar to women alone. Only women become pregnant; laws on abortions, one way or the other, reflect this unique difference between the sexes. However such a reflection of *any* physical or anatomical differences between the sexes—objective facts of reality—in the body of statutory law, is precisely what would be illegal under the terms of the proposed so-called Equal Rights Amendment, and such is perhaps the essential flaw in it.[16] If rights immediately result from human characteristics and capacities, on a physical level if not a mental level, then any statute declaring that all people have identical rights in the face of objective differences in physical characteristics between the sexes is a *legal fiction* of the first positivist calibre. And such a legal fiction, a potential source for more injustice, is not necessary in order to repeal what statutes do exist and support "rights" distinctions that are not based on objective characteristic differences between the sexes.

The Right to Self-Destruction

Of course, unless it serves as a false excuse for the taking of another's life, every person has a right to protect his own or violate it. The most widespread form of self-violation is probably the ingestion of harmful substances, some of which serve other purposes, including inducing temporary relaxation or serving as one of the many means by which we may neurotically escape unpleasant realities. As long as the ingestion of such substances constitutes harm only to oneself, harm of which one is reasonably aware in advance, this activity is one to which a person certainly has a right, and not at all one that is a just concern of government. In this context, we must first deal with the question of drug abuse, but we shall see that we are concerned with a number of other issues as well.

Among the organizations most vocal in advocating the decriminalization of marijuana sale, possession, and use, has been the ACLU.[17] There is no question but that such actions constitute no initiation of force or fraud to violate another's rights. Thus they are not crimes, nor the just concern of the law. The ACLU has said all this, and *rightly* so, in spite of the fact that it has been somewhat less than objective or honest concerning the potential physical and mental harm of the drug, which would be a basis for urging people to freely choose not to use it.

Have we found that long-sought-for area of consistency between what is meant and what is said by the ACLU? Before jumping to conclusions, let us examine their recommendations more carefully. The Union argues that after all criminal penalties for the use or possession of marijuana are abolished, government should institute "a system of regulation which would control, by means other than criminal sanction, such matters as prevention of adulteration, distribution to minors, etc. One reasonable model is the system used to license and regulate the sale of alcohol; many variations are possible."[18] Notice that the Union apparently wishes government to expand its monopoly control over another type of free value-exchange between individuals that many would call "vice." That such a system would necessarily produce violations of individual property rights *in advance of* specific criminal violations by those same individuals—on the assumption that regulations are necessary and sufficient to prevent criminal actions—is obviously ignored. Thus the Union effectively neutralizes its advocacy of individual freedom on the marijuana issue by calling for the forceful intrusion of monopoly government control into another area of the marketplace which they would "free."

In making this objection, I am being consistent with the Union's general policy of decriminalizing the ingestion of *any* substance, as well as its ownership. Unfortunately, the Union does not recognize that one's right to private property also includes the free sale or disposal of that which one has a right to own and use, providing such is not employed to harm others. This approach would not prevent criminal punishments for those convicted of selling harmful substances to persons unaware of what they are or on the basis of a claim of their not being harmful. This would cover sales to ignorant youths and fraudulent sales of adulterated or substituted substances to adults.

Also, in the case of hallucinogenic drugs that have the capacity to impair temporarily one's volitional control over one's actions, or to induce clinical psychosis, any person who sold such a substance to another person without making sure that the buyer understood its risks would be criminally liable with the buyer for any harm done by the buyer while under its influence. In such a situation, both the seller and the user would be parties to the criminal violation of rights resulting from the user's actions under the drug's influence. The seller's guilty action would be his misrepresenting a fraudulent sale of the substance, and the user's guilt would result from his ingestion of it without making sure he knew the likely consequences. He would be responsible legally for taking the drug that induced his psychosis.

Therapeutic Freedom of Choice

If a person has a right to own and use upon *himself only* any substance as long as such can be done without endangering others, then we must also conclude that he has a right to select and control substances or means of treatment, both medical and psychological, that are available for purchase as alternative aids in preserving his health. Such a position would logically prohibit the intrusion of government regulation and control over the manufacture, sale, and use of all foods and medicines in advance of any criminal violations committed by those engaged in these activities. But we have already seen that the ACLU favors the establishment of a government monopoly control over the sale of those drugs that are currently illegal for sale and use by private individuals. This unfortunately reflects the Union's support for virtually all government regulation of the exchange of tangible values among men, based on the assumption that such force is necessary in advance to "protect" consumers from the criminal abuses of businessmen in all fields. Oddly enough, businessmen are not viewed by the Union equally as consumers themselves, and we detect the veiled notion that such regulation is a deterrent against greedy businessmen selling spoiled or diseased food, which every smart capitalist knows is the way to stay in business. Although the Union assures us that capital punishment is no deterrent to violent crime, we get the message that government regulation and control over the sale of ingestible substances is a deterrent against unscrupulous commercial practices.

In recent years, a number of people, including a handful of competent American physicians, have challenged the federal government's control over the authorization of which drugs are legal for use in the prevention and treatment of such diseases as cancer.[19] They feel that it is as dangerous for government to arbitrate issues of scientific controversy as it is for the state to be empowered with the authority to decide what is "moral" or "obscene," for the "common good of all."

No one could seriously dispute that one's right to ingest any substance not inducing psychosis does not have serious implication for laws prohibiting the sale or use of medicines or treatments officially regarded as quackery. I believe that a person has a right to use a worthless remedy if he chooses to do so. The opponents of a "quack" product are free to publicize their doubt of its value as long as they can factually defend their position in court. The owners or promoters of that treatment have an equal right to promote what they think are its advantages. And anyone who suffers or dies as a result of either's false or fraudulent claim has experienced a violation that constitutes grounds for legal action against one side or the other, but only after such damage has been done. In spite of the widespread publicity of such cases, particularly over the promising agent for cancer control and prevention called laetrile, the ACLU has been conspicuously inactive or altogether silent.[20] Perhaps this is because those who are fighting for the freedom of a patient to decide with his doctor which treatment to use, how they will exercise his "right to control his own body," are advocating the absence of government control over the private ownership and exchange of medical goods and services, while the ACLU has only recommended a vastly more bureaucratic government control over these activities.

The Right to Be Sick

If it seems unfair to criticize the ACLU for issues on which it has *not* taken a specific position or gotten actively involved, we might turn to several other closely related issues that demonstrate the same regrettable betrayal of its own ideals, properly understood, in what the Union had advocated.

Two corollaries of a person's right to control what he receives as medical treatment are his right to be free from legally enforced medication and his right to be free from being forced to pay for anyone's medication other than his own or that of a family member for whom he has assumed such responsibilities voluntarily. We have already noted the ACLU's position, expressed in George Annas' *The Rights of Hospital Patients*, that one's right to life means one's right to the free availability of medical services, which would be best facilitated by some form of national health insurance.

But the Union, and especially some of its local affiliates, have expanded this "right" to include what they believe to be the satisfaction of one's "right" to free dental care: artificial fluoridation of government-controlled water supplies.[21] We can forget about the fact that such a position presupposes tacit approval of government monopoly over the provision of water. We can ignore the fact that the often touted alleged dental benefits of fluoridated water in the United States are still very much in doubt among specialists in this field.[22] We can put aside as irrelevant that fluoridation is always imposed on localities by those in government and never is put into effect by grass-roots initiative or voter approval. We can even avoid considering the fact that fluoridated water is dangerous to many persons with certain organic problems, who, like members of religious sects opposed to medication who wish to remain true to their beliefs, *must* purchase bottled water in fluoridated areas while still being forced to pay for the system that is hazardous to their health or offensive to their beliefs.[23] We simply should note that it is very wrong for anyone in the ACLU to support a program in which government mass-medicates you, and even if you avoid the dosage, does so with your confiscated values.[24]

The right to determine one's treatment implies the right to be free from involuntary treatment and involuntary confinement for treatment. This is most obvious as an issue in the context of legalized involuntary commitment of persons to mental hospitals by doctors or family members, on such grounds as personal incompetency, or on the basis of statements and behavior that have convinced those initiating involuntary commitment that the person to be committed is a *potential* threat to his own safety and that of others. This, of course, amounts to a huge unjust deprivation of the values and an unjust violation of the rights of the victim.

This is not the appropriate place to detail all the reasons why a determination of someone's "mental illness," with the varying degrees of validity concerning just what that means, does not constitute a forfeiture by that person of his rights. Detailed presentations of these reasons are available elsewhere.[25] However, we should note that in the positions of the ACLU, such is not universally recognized. In another one of the Union's handbooks on "the rights of people," *The Rights of Mental Patients,* authors Bruce Ennis and Loren Siegel personally affirm

> that involuntary hospitalization should be abolished. Completely. And if it cannot be abolished, we believe that prospective patients should be given so many rights and safeguards that it will be extraordinarily difficult to hospitalize anyone against his will. . . . Our quarrel is not with psychiatry, but with coercive, institutional pyschiatry.[26]

That this position is the personal opinion of the two authors and not at all consistent with the record of the Union on this issue is made clear by the fact that they spend the rest of this book detailing how the enslaved mental patient's life may be made more comfortable. Their suggestions represent a capitulation to the ACLU leadership's stand, which has viewed involuntary committment of noncriminals as a last and final resort, after all other methods of treatment or assistance have failed. If all else fails, the ACLU consensus has held, utterly violate the rights of the "mentally ill."[27] Authors Ennis and Siegel expand George Annas' "right to free treatment" to include the "right" to a free lawyer and the patient's right to free clothing and cash upon release.[28] Need I say more?

The Right to Own and Protect Any Property

The final issue vitally involved in one's right to life is one's right to defend oneself from an attack by someone bent on murder. That right of self-defense is observed in our courts today, and this protects a person who has killed someone in defense of his or another's life from prosecution for a criminal offense. However, the right of self-defense of one's life and possessions also implies the right to own any weapon useful or necessary in that self-protection as long as that weapon can be owned without necessarily endangering others (a vial of nitroglycerine or an atomic bomb might not qualify) and as long as it is not employed in a criminal initiation of force. We would expect the ACLU to take this position, which is logically presupposed by the right to life. We would expect them to agree that this right is recognized explicitly in the Second Amendment of the U.S. Constitution, and implicitly in the Ninth. However, holding out such expectations, we would once again be disappointed. The Union firmly opposes unregulated private ownership of all firearms by persons who have not used them to commit crimes.[29] The Union has been a strong advocate of federal gun registration and control. In taking this position it has sided with judges who ignore the obvious meaning of two sections of the Bill of Rights, particularly in the light of what we know from the writings of their "principal author."[30] The ACLU has not only perpetuated the logical fallacy that *guns,* rather than volitional criminals, cause violent crimes—by implying that crime could be reduced by controlling the one particular type of weapon most frequently used in criminal actions (which assumes that criminals would find others so unappealing that they would not use them)—but it has also offered another unique rationalization. It seems that the unregulated private ownership of firearms creates

> an atmosphere stifling to the enjoyment of civil liberties. . . . Our free society is rooted in the concept that social problems and differences can be debated and resolved in rational dialogue. Where armed citizens flaunt guns in the midst of race conflict, or labor-management controversies, or political turmoil, citizens who hold minority or unpopular opinions on these issues can be cowed into silence. In these instances violence—or the prospect of violence—becomes more powerful than the First Amendment.
>
> Moreover, in areas where halfway gun control measures exist, or where the laws are loosely enforced, certain parts of the population may be armed to the teeth, while the law is applied only to their intended victims. Unless strong gun control regulation is adopted, the freedoms associated with civilized society cannot be fully enjoyed.[31]

So we see that the ACLU's position in favor of strong gun controls is based on the belief that such will result in the protection of "the free and fearless debate on which our free society rests."[32]

It is not necessary to explain why guns are not responsible for criminal actions or a tendency to "kill free speech," as the Union suggests. Such would be an insult to the reader's intelligence. Anyone has the right to own anything that he has earned, so long as it can be owned safely, from a "Saturday-night special" to a World War II surplus tank, and the government has no just reason for interfering with that right, regardless of how eccentric a whim it is based upon. The Union is silent on the consequences of its proposal. While pointing to the growing legal repression in the United States against its best efforts, the ACLU is recommending one of the several most essential legal institutions necessary for the suppression of all civil liberties in Communist nations, a monopoly control of firearms in the hands of the state. And even if that were not a fact of reality, such a proposal would still amount to a severe violation of human rights according to the philosophy that is expressed in the U.S. Constitution.

First Amendment Freedoms and Voluntary Morality

Since the ACLU recommends police-state control over all guns on the basis of such protecting our rights of free speech and personal expression, we need to review briefly the group's major policies on our First Amendment freedoms.[33]

The right to free expression implies all uses of one's intellectual and material property to pursue one's values. Human beings have the right to free speech and the unregulated production or publication of their creative works. An individual's right to free action entails all possible exchanges of values among humans, from the expression of love to the sale of securities. As long as all such essential human activities are carried out with property earned and in such a manner as not to deprive others of their values or violate their rights, government has no proper or just reason to employ force. This is true even if the activities of free speech and action are quite immoral according to the standards held by the majority, or are obviously harmful to those participating in them. This means that there should be no laws passed against such morally objectionable activities as the creation, sale, and ownership of pornographic literature, the production of pornographic films and their commercial display, private establishment of nudist parks and beaches, prostitution, and all forms of private sexual activities between consenting adults, heterosexual or homosexual.

A situation in which all these activities were "decriminalized" is imagined by some to amount to a total downfall of law and order, to say nothing of an official encouragement of immorality. I should state that I feel capable of making a convincing argument to anyone concerning why practically all of these activities are evil, or immoral, by virtue of being either (1) against Judeo-Christian teachings and objectively prone to be self-destructive to the individuals engaged in them, usually because they feed neurotic problems, represent false perceptions of reality or inequitable development of both one's psychological and physical sexuality, or (2) exchanges of moral values for others which are hardly commensurate or altogether inappropriate. Although this is not the place for me to detail my moral objections to these activities, I wish to be understood as feeling quite competent to convince any reasonable person of their undesirable qualities.

All of this is additional to the fact that legal protections against the violation of human rights would still exist in a country that had no legally established victimless crimes. A theater could be sued for fraud by a patron who entered it out of interest in its family-program advertisement, only to be forced unavoidably to view something that is offensive to him. Prostitutes could be sued if they were found to carry venereal disease.

But a slightly different problem might arise if we apply what I have just said about the theater's guilt of fraud to a public beach or street. Suppose you went to the Los Angeles public beach. You do not approve of nude beaches. The city council has just set aside a strip of the beach for nude bathers. You enter an adjacent strip, but it is close enough so that you cannot look around freely without seeing some nudists nearby. Or suppose you are walking down a street with your child and you pass a newspaper vending machine that has a transparent front. Copies of a pornographic paper are in the machine, with a lurid cover in plain view. You are enraged that you and your son have been exposed to this. Or suppose you purchase a farm that has a freshwater creek running through the pasture. On your second visit to your property, you see and smell a sticky substance in the water that is building up on your embankments and killing your plants. You investigate and learn that the sludge is coming downriver from a leather tannery fifty miles away. The creek begins at the factory as a river on public land. It is used by the factory as a dumping ground for its wastes.

All three instances constitute violations of your rights and values. But little can be done by you to bring justice on these matters. In each case, the violation, at least partly, occurred on public property, that "property" belonging to everyone and controlled by the government. You can do nothing. You must ask, and hope, that government will take action on your behalf. But you will find that government officials have a strange opinion. They view you as just one individual complaining over what is done with that which belongs to all, specifically, complaining over the actions of others who also "own" that public property and pay taxes "to keep it up."

This should well illustrate how government ownership and control of property tends to war inevitably with First Amendment freedoms.[34] It should be obvious that you could sue the newsrack owner or the the street owner, or the beach owner, or the tannery or the river owner, for all the above violations *if* all that property were privately owned. Now let us see what the ACLU proposes as ways to protect our First Amendment freedoms, which, they agree with me, should be "decriminalized."

The American Civil Liberties Union believes in freedom of speech and assembly among all people meeting together *in person*. However, it sanctions the existing government monopoly control and regulation of the radio and television airwaves.[35] This is supposed to guarantee that their use will be in the "public interest," a necessity since radio waves are transmitted through the atmosphere, which is the common property of all. For the ACLU, the federal government's administration of the most advanced means for free expression may be at times inequitable, but it is still necessary to uphold the public property of the airwaves. Somehow forgotten is the private property that someone had to earn and that produces the radio waves that travel through the air. The rights of the owners of this property must be subordinated to the "public interest," according to the Union.[36] (By the same reasoning, we would conclude that anyone has the right to a sailboat, *regardless of whose it is,* because they wish to sail on the public waters that border their property!) Remember that the ACLU believes an important way to protect free expression is to put the arbitrary control of the most influential means of expression in the hands of those who run the government.

The ACLU recommends a publication on the issue of censorship that outlines their basic positions.[37] The Union is listed as one of a number of organizations supporting a person's right to read whatever he wishes[38] or view whatever he wants. This booklet denies any inherent immorality or harmfulness in pornographic materials, thus going beyond simply taking a legal position on the issue of rights in this context. In fact, it seems to convey something of a favorable moral appraisal of such material. The author's presentation of the views of those opposing restrictions on the free use of pornographic material is far better than his treatment of the moral rationalizations of those taking the opposite position, but he assures us that such supporters of its legalization as the ACLU "do not necessarily view or enjoy such materials themselves, but they do insist that those who wish to should be free to do so."[39]

What is the solution proposed in this article that is recommended and available from the Union? In the context of current laws and decisions, its author approves of court rulings that have allowed states to outlaw materials if they were judged "obscene" by virtue of being "utterly without redeeming social value" or lacking "serious literary, artistic, educational, political, entertainment, scientific or other social value."[40] Indeed, this ACLU-approved writer believes that "nothing less than a national standard to measure serious value" is a very compelling position.[41] And thus we see that those persons in the ACLU who sanction and distribute this article obviously wish arbitrary local government censorship violations of the human right to read and express oneself to be abolished. They want such local-level rights violations to be replaced with a national system of enforced censorship of an even more frightening variety. Perhaps a few local government officials have enforced censorship on the basis of some material "lacking any redeeming social value," a meaningless phrase they must have picked up from the Supreme Court. But do you think any local government officials could get away with dictating what constitutes "serious literary, artistic, educational, political, entertainment, or scientific value" in a work on trial? Obviously no local government has the police power to enforce such an incredible decree.[42] Perhaps the author of this article distributed by the ACLU thinks there is sufficient power in Washington to enforce his "compelling" recommendation.

The ACLU recognizes in the right to free expression the implied right to be free of forceful intrusion into or violation of expressive actions, or the right of privacy. On this issue, the Union displays some rather bizarre contradictions. First, we must note that each person has the right to be unobserved by others to the extent that he provides for himself and uses property that will accomplish that goal. One has a right to the privacy possible in his own home, but such is voluntarily forfeited when one goes out among other people, who have the right, derived from free speech, to observe, remember and make records of what they observed. This free action of keeping records of past events is an unqualified right, as long as one earns the information by one's own efforts. Only the forceful or fraudulent employment of such information against another person, such as the crime of libel, constitutes a deprivation of his values or a violation of his rights. Just collecting data does not, and is quite exemplary of freedom itself when performed by individuals, even if the information is gathered with the aid of sophisticated surveillance equipment that is somebody's private property. As long as observation and record-keeping about humans by other humans is done without force or fraud, and as long as the information is not harmfully used to *deprive* another unjustly of his values, no crime has been committed. But the ACLU does not see it this way.[43] The Union even thinks that it is wrong, or unnecessary, for law enforcement officers to keep records on the people they investigate, which records may be evidence building toward a case against a criminal or simply past records of court rulings and decisions that are useful or required for reference should a case ever be reopened.

In a separate book on this subject, Aryeh Neier, executive director of the ACLU, tells us:

> Nor do the records maintained by law enforcement agencies serve the investigative purpose claimed for them. They punish people, though the dossier compilers seldom admit this is the purpose or acknowledge that it is the consequence. Because they have such enormous punitive impact on their direct and indirect victims, I want to destroy the dossiers.[44]

Neier does not make clear whether he would like also to destroy records kept by private individuals outside of government, a practice about which he also complains vigorously in his book. Such a remedy would make the ACLU's work quite difficult, because all records of possible rights violations in the past would have to be destroyed. Neier tends to forget his assumptions as he continues:

> A frequent proposal for curbing the use of criminal conviction records is to seal them, after a period of seven years. . . . Examination of what happens to exconvicts suggests that sealing records after seven years would benefit very few.
> A FBI report on 18,567 offenders who had been released in 1963 showed that after three years . . . [45]

Perhaps Mr. Neier forgot that such statistical support for his argument against the legal keeping of dossiers on people would not be available were law enforcement officials and other individuals not free to keep dossiers.

He suggests, as a possible solution to the problems facing ex-cons, that "a law could prohibit the use of arrest records as a criterion for employment or continuing employment.''[46] He finds this "attractive," but admits it "would be hard to enforce." Remember that the executive director of the ACLU finds "attractive" a law that would prevent you from being free to refuse to hire someone for your private business because of a past criminal record. Make a note of that. So much for Neier's defense of our rights to privacy, but we might be understanding of his position if we keep a note on his admission concerning his feelings: "Over the years, I have accumulated my share of derogatory records."[47] We should not hold that against him. But we should resist mightily any attempt he makes to force us not to observe, remember, and record events, and act on the basis of that information in the free exchange of our values.

Although the ACLU does not support the right of private citizens and law enforcement officials to assemble and keep records on each other, it does seem to regard such activities when performed by news reporters as a separate category of "rights."[48] We know that freedom of the press means that any individual may publish his writings on any subject without government force being used against him unless he does so in a manner that libels another person, thus presenting a false picture of another person that results in the deprivation of his values, including his friends, reputation, or job. The Union views the reporting of the actions of those in government to be so important that it serves a "public need" or "right to know."[49] The problem is that information is not free. Someone must work to obtain it. It is therefore the property of the person who obtains it. He is free to benefit commercially by having done so as long as the information is not harmfully and unjustly used. However, the Union assumes that everyone has a "right" to information gathered on the subject of government, so it supports laws that make that information easily available to reporters, often in a manner that results in the expenditure of funds taken forcefully by government from those who have a "right to know."

This special status of the media also leads the Union to support the "right" of reporters to keep their sources confidential, even if this obviously prevents a proven criminal from being punished.[50] By taking this mistaken position, the ACLU is advocating transmuting the right of a reporter to publish the nonlibelous material he has earned by his labor, or the right of free press, into the "right" of a reporter to be a legally immune party to criminal conspiracy by allowing him to safeguard one of the three essential characteristics of any conspiracy: the identity, whereabouts, and actions of the criminal conspirators involved. He certainly is not responsible for the crime that the criminal committed. But he can, with the Union's blessing, be quite responsible for conspiring with the criminal to obstruct the application of justice. But, remember, such a privileged status of legal immunity allows the reporter to get you that information to which you have a "right," and allows him to do so legally at *your* expense.

Consequences of Group "Rights"

We now turn to an examination of a few of the Union's positions on the "rights" of "special people," discriminated against with regard to their "rights" on the basis of their sex, occupation, or lack of occupation. It has already been noted that the Union believes in free expression of everyone's views under government-controlled "guarantees." This extends to the field of education, where the ACLU has been especially active in working for the academic freedoms of teachers and students in government schools at all levels.[51] The Union's primary motive seems to be an overall defense of the growing near-monopoly that government has over the service function of education.[52] This is made clear in the ACLU's opposition to government aid to church schools, which they also object to on the grounds that it constitutes unconstitutional government establishment of religion.[53] Unfortunately, they do not object to it on the equally valid grounds that it constitutes unconstitutional government involvement in the business of education. A major reason why the Union opposes parochial aid is that it weakens our government education system, which is the only one that can provide everyone's "right" to a free *quality education,* the goal that they seem to think could never be provided by private schools.[54]

In government schools the ACLU would establish a system of due process, administrative procedures as legal requirements blocking the expulsion of teachers and students for most all conduct, in or out of school, short of violent crime.[55] The Union must favor the resulting phenomena of teachers and students being free from practically all restrictions on conduct that displeases those who are forced to provide the money to maintain the schools. But this is an inevitable consequence of another advocacy by the Union of government assuming control over the provision of freely exchangeable values between individuals. In spite of the fact that the ACLU falls short of urging that owners of private schools be forced to surrender *all* control over their assets to their employees and customers, no organization has been more vocal in urging that the rights of those unfortunately having to attend government schools be further violated by legal provisions on even voluntary prayer and Bible reading in classrooms,[56] as well as forced busing to achieve essentially racist government quotas of school integration, which the Union feels necessarily ensure quality education for all.[57]

On the subject of the "rights" of servicemen,[58] the Union utterly abandons the burden of logical consistency. Although the organization never held to the quite valid position that conscription *anytime* amounts to unconstitutional *involuntary servitude,*[59] now that the draft is temporarily a thing of the past, it takes the position that a serviceman who has voluntaily contracted for employment with a branch of the services, and has thus consented to submit himself to myriad procedural regulations and the requirements of the Uniform Code of Military Justice and the rather harsh discipline with which it is enforced, still is entitled to

101

the full due process procedures and equal protection under the laws that govern civilians.[60]

This position is blind to the fact that the volunteer serviceman consents to forfeit many of those procedural protections in order to obtain service employment. He subjects himself to an additional body of statutory law with a parallel judicial system of its own, which does not apply to others who have not placed themselves under its jurisdiction.

What the Union is actually objecting to as being truly wrong is the fact that many persons were placed under that other jurisdiction, and deprived of the procedural and substantive protections available to civilians, without voluntarily contracting to do so. That was called the draft, which the Union always hesitated to denounce as inherently unconstitutional. Further, the Union has pushed strongly for legal "amnesty" to be awarded to those guilty of violating statutes during their military service while the Vietnam War was underway.[61] It does this because it held with many servicemen and others that the war, although not the draft, was unconstitutional.[62] Unfortunately, legal amnesty for any statutory offense amounts to the same violations of the procedural "equal protection under the laws" in reverse as that which the Union rightly condemns, along with the Constitution, as ex post facto laws. If it is a violation of equal protection under the laws for the government to outlaw an action *after* it has been performed and then punish the actor, it is equally unconstitutional to decriminalize an action and prohibit *retroactively* punishment of actions which were statutory violations when committed, all of which is a valid *constitutional* objection regardless of the substantive justice of the content of the laws concerned.

When we consider the Union's policies on the "rights" unique to women[63] and "gays,"[64] we find that its "solution" extends beyond such legal *fictions* as those inherent in the so-called Equal Rights Amendment. Indeed, for the ACLU, after telling us all about "male chauvinism" and the "normalcy" of homosexual life,[65] the "rights" of these people, discriminated against on the basis of their sex and sexual preferences expand to the same legal enforcement of so-called equal-employment opportunities, which legally are binding on government and private hiring of racial and ethnic minorities, as well as similar "protections" over the use of private property defined as public accomodations.[66] All of these "rights" amount to the false notion of economic rights over the control and use of another's private property. Those who provide the means of employment and various public accommodations should be forced, according to the Union, to obey laws that prohibit their voluntary withholding from exchanges of economic values on the basis of such irrational, *but noncriminal,* whims as the distrust of women or the dislike of homosexuals. Such are the major concerns of the ACLU's spokespersons.

But none of these advocacies of the legal violation of private property rights match what is contained in the "looters' handbook" on the *Rights of the Poor* by the ACLU's expert on "welfare rights," Sylvia Law.[67] She includes in her presentation a detailed explication on "how to get yours" by means of government force, recognizing that

> Poor people have the right to receive welfare, free medical care, food stamps, and free or low-cost school lunches. These rights are discussed in this book. In addition, poor people have rights to: public housing, free legal services; go to court without paying court fees in some cases; day care and other social services; unemployment compensation; tuition reductions or scholarships; school breakfasts; and special food programs for the elderly. These rights are not discussed in this book because there is not enough space to talk about all of the rights of all of the poor.[68]

And, we might add, thank God! It will be of particular interest to the productive people who must be forced to provide these "rights" to the only people who qualify for them, those who are not similarly productive, that Sylvia Law deals with the problem of a poor person's "right" to know about all of this, and get all of it, by owning and reading a copy of her book:

> There is a disturbing irony in the commercial publication and sale of a book to the poor. If this is to be of any use to the people for whom it was intended, it will be because more affluent people and organizations buy copies and make them available without charge to poor people.[69]

So, all potential victims of the laws that Sylvia Law supports should race out to buy many copies of this manual of instructions on the forcible expropriation of their property and see that they get into the hands of those who do not know all the ways to get really into the business of expropriation with government as their partner. And, all the while, be assured that Sylvia Law will be willing to endure the "disturbing irony in the commercial publication and sale" of her manual on "legal plunder"—all the way to the bank.

Disillusionment in the End

We have examined thus far a number of very representative ACLU positions on current issues illustrating the group's attraction to causes beyond procedural and substantive safeguards of our rights. We have seen the Union advocate a most unsatisfactory variety of "economic rights,"[70] while failing to oppose the increasing economic power of our central government.[71] We must try to understand why this has taken place, something of proper interest to the ACLU's members, since the Union's leadership has taken a position inherently destructive of its own professed goals. I know my evaluation is not arbitrarily my own, since the positions taken by the ACLU against laws prohibiting many victimless crimes reflect the same natural law philosophy that I have outlined. However, I cannot find a single issue on which the Union takes an official position that is constitutionally or logically consistent *overall,* on both the problem and the suggested solution. This may be due to the fact that its leadership, with its large contingent of lawyers, is greatly influenced by the notions of positivist legal theory. We have certainly seen such reflected in their positions on most major issues of contemporary concern.

There is another possible explanation. That is that some of the ACLU's national and local leaders want the "solution" of more government control over individuals because they support a movement toward that end. We have not here examined all the policies of the ACLU, just enough of them to see the tragic trends unmistakably. Those policies are subject to change, and we hope that any changes will be for the better.

Because the policies of the ACLU represent views of the group's leaders —particularly those in the national office—and not necessarily all of its many sincere members, we need to examine the history of the national ACLU's connection to statist ideology and movements that have totalitarianism as their goal. It is known that subversive leaders of idealistic followers have promoted destructive ends in this country, while reassuring their supporters that all was being done in the name of a most noble cause.[72] With such a realization, we will now examine the history of subversive leadership in the American Civil Liberties Union.

Part II

History of the ACLU:
Inconsistency or Conspiracy?

7

Some Considerations
Prior to a Verdict

The ACLU's legal director, Melvin L. Wulf, has demonstrated his perceptivness on many issues. Consistent with his awareness that governments are always seeking to expand their power at the peril of individual rights, he also has observed that some people do indeed agree privately to undertake efforts that many regard as evil or destructive. In other words, he believes in conspiracies. Several years ago he described what seemed to be opposing conspiracies both in and outside our national government:

> The crimes which the government is committing in the name of law and order are far more grave than the so-called crimes committed by private citizens, for the latter "crimes" consist of a disorganized conspiracy to force the government out of a brutal, aggressive war in Viet Nam. . . .
> Another of the conspiracy's objectives is the improvement at home of the condition of the poor and non-white. That objective necessarily requires the reallocation of public and private resources, and it is in defense of the present inequitable *status quo* that the government commits its crimes.[1]

In spite of the fact that Wulf impresses one as taking sides with one bunch of would-be expropriating conspirators against another, and although he did not make clear what distinguishes a *disorganized* conspiracy from a plain old organized one, he obviously was telling us that some people really do intend the logical consequences of their actions. And Wulf's identification of Nixon, Agnew, and the rest of the creepy Palace Guard as persons engaged in conspiring against others rather than sincerely following stupid advice or mistaken judgements[2] was proven entirely correct by subsequent events. What is significant about all this is that he, quite out of step among his leading ACLU colleagues and outstanding luminaries elsewhere, recognized the existence of conspiracy in, and aimed at, high places while it was still just becoming permissible to do so.

Conspiracy Is a Household Word

Before Watergate climaxed with the downfall of Nixon after months of televised hearings, major preoccupations with conspiracy in government had been the monopoly of those "unfashionable" or "irresponsible" individuals with whom I have been pleased to associate, as well as adversaries holding similarity radical views at the other end of the ideological spectrum. But now, believers in political conspiracies have become altogether commonplace, if not academically "acceptable." Conspirational activity has become so obvious that even the most socially timid "conservative" spokesmen hesitate to deny it, and a leading academic "liberal" specialist on those who formerly had cornered the "conspiratorial theory" market has expressed concern that a major tragedy of the Watergate episode will be a widespread tendency for people to assume that those involved in significant historical events actually *intend* what they do![3]

The fact that the conspiratorial view of history is rapidly gaining implicit acceptance across the country does not by itself, enable us to apply it with the same almost prophetic success of Melvin Wulf. We must take pains to understand it better if we are to be consistent and make use of it in our overall judgment of the ACLU.

A Rational View of History

Very basically, as I have briefly stated elsewhere,[4] the conspiratorial view of history is just one variety of what we might call the volitional view of history. Such assumes that in any historical event involving human beings, we bring to our examination of the data the understanding that individuals, unless psychotic, possess free will, or volitional control of their actions. We recognize instances of the abstract concept *conspiracy* by identifying particular human actions. These must involve two or more persons working toward the same objectives without announcing their plans to others in advance. Also, the objectives sought must be clearly immoral, or criminal. Often conspirators follow a plan outlined in advance, keep in close contact during their voluntary conspiring, and form or join organizations to accomplish their goal. But all such mechanics or means of conspiring are optional; none are essential to the concept or required for its identification in any instance. All we must know is that, for a significant period of time, two or more people having been working in concert toward the same negative ends, and doing so without making clear, at least to their potential victims, that such was underway.

All this is quite incomprehensible to those who have found compelling such academic doctrines as linguistic analysis in philosophy, psychological determinism either internal or external, and the methodological empiricism of professional historians. These persons, however, find a volitional view easier to accept when they identify those engaged in benevolent actions as *philanthropists,* and perhaps this variety of activity is often easier to spot because it does not rely on others' disbelief of its existence for its success. I hope the reader does not share these problems, and with the recognition that *criminal* actions are evil actions, that he can apply the long-accepted legal definition of conspiracy and the corollary that a man is held to be responsible for the consequences of his actions to the subject of totalitarian influence over the leadership of the American Civil Liberties Union.

A Consistent Pattern of Inconsistency

At the outset of this study, I expressed my desire to avoid the repeated practice of past critics of the Union, the simple listing of Communist and Communist-front affiliations of its founders and leading members, which, by itself, leaves many questions unanswered. However, we must deal with related issues—indeed, closely related ones—in the group's history if we are to understand its accomplishments. For the multi-faceted problem of fundamental inconsistency between the Union's professed beliefs and its positions and work on specific issues is far from a phenomenon confined to the publications of recent years that we selectively reviewed in Part I. A huge quantity of similar inconsistencies could be cited throughout the ACLU's public record of over fifty years.[5] But to avoid arbitrary prejudgment in approaching a final explanation of why the Union has succeeded or failed to accomplish the fulfillment of its ideals, we must consider what alternative understandings are possible to derive from any detected failure (the issue would hardly arise if full success was recognized) and what are the requirements for justifying the reasonableness of one interpretation over the other. What this means is that, while we note other apparent philosophical inconsistencies in the Union's history, we must examine them in a context that will allow us to judge whether those inconsistencies resulted from philosophical sloppiness among its leadership or from a combination of that and the more detrimental influences of persons deliberately leading the organization toward aggregate failure because they were engaged in a conspiracy for entirely opposite goals from the ideals held by the vast majority of their followers.

Philosophical Incompetency
As an Unsatisfactory Explanation

If at this point the reader recoils with the expectation that this book will now lapse into an inquisitional attempt to label the ACLU as a Communist front or something similar, permit me to request a bit more patience. I need to clarify the approach I am about to take and explain how it differs from what I have sought to avoid.

It is unreasonable to assume, as a prejudgment, that the leaders of the ACLU have worked counter-productively to the organization's goals over the years simply because they did not understand the philosophy underlying American constitutionalism and civil liberties. Any such claim would fly in the face of objective facts There have been numerous occasions in which the group's leaders and members have expressed and litigated positions that were consistent with a goal of limited government. On such issues as actual victimless crimes, Union spokesmen have given as their reasons for taking their positions the same philosophical understanding of natural law that was examined in Part I. However, those cases of consistency have been erratic, the infrequent exception, rather than the rule. Another problem with the notion that the Union's failures result exclusively from intellectual bankruptcy is the fact that there has been widespread diversity of opinion among the ACLU leadership, both national and local, as well as among its members, now numbering in the tens of thousands. The ACLU has undergone fundamental changes in official policy; it can hardly be said to have been philosophically immune to, or isolated from, rational positions in accord with its objectives. And yet, it has "consistently" been inconsistent with them, as we shall see as we examine it over five decades. To introduce another possible explanation for, at least, a part of this problem, we must consider another context in which the ACLU has existed, both casual and consequent to the popularization and acceptance of philosophical positivism.

The Conspiratorial Context

Almost coincidentally with the establishment and growth of the American Civil Liberties Union, there has arisen a world-wide Communist movement, which by our understanding must be defined as a totalitarian criminal conspiracy. World communism has not been the only totalitarian criminal conspiracy in this century, but by virtue of the assistance it has received from so many productive souls among its willing collaborators and unwilling victims, it has obviously been the most devastatingly successful.[6] And since there is an inevitable inverse relationship between the success of any such conspiracy and the protection of human rights and values, the growth of world communism must be examined in relation to the ACLU. But what are the criteria for making any such comparisons?

We would first note that the Union *could be* an instrumentality of that conspiracy. No one doubts that numerous organizations have been established by the Communists to misuse the idealism of sincere members who knew not of the real, behind-the-scenes leadership they were following. Such Communist fronts have often expressed noble goals as their objectives: freedom, civil rights, peace. Many innocent people joined these organizations not knowing the real objectives of their leaders, which were often distinct from those of the noteworthy sponsors or endorsers whose names were borrowed by the front to attract the unwary.[7]

A front, or, originally, ad hoc committee, is a group organized to seek support for limited objectives from persons who may not agree with the organizers on other projects. But—unless the front is Communist inspired—the organizers are obvious, as are their other purposes. In a Communist front, these last two characteristics are conspicuously absent, or deliberately denied. And it is because of this that critical appraisal of groups that have existed as Communist fronts must be reserved for the knowing leadership that is intentionally acting "inconsistently." Misled or philosophically naive members cannot fairly be subject to the same sort of criticism unless they continue in the group, and thereby give it their sanction, after reasonable evidence has been made available to them that they have been victims of fraud.

Characteristics of Communist-Front Activity

How might we recognize leaders in a group fronting for communism, as distinguished from "making mistakes," so-called *honest* mistakes, in pursuit of ideals at odds with communism, rather than what we would call, in another sense, the *mistake* of conspiring *for* communism? There are many clues.

If a group's controlling leadership has been infiltrated, partly or entirely, by persons under the discipline of a totalitarian conspiracry, then it effectively becomes a front for that conspiracy to the extent that the infiltrators influence its policies. This control can be exercised by conspirators either serving as leaders of the group or contributing to it funds with the private understanding that certain performances are expected. The amount of infiltrated leadership necessary to control a group over the wishes of nonconspirators also at the helm may vary according to the organizational structure of each group. An organization may be monolithic and under the management of one person or only a few. Another may have its policies set by a board of persons who meet together solely for this purpose. If diverse viewpoints have equal voting power on the board, it would be harder for any one faction to remain in control—if, of course, when the board is not present and meeting, the group's administrators are actually conducting its day-to-day affairs according to the board's policy decisions. A conspirator in charge of an organization's daily management can easily usurp control from any board of policy by selective application of its policies. Keeping this point in mind as we examine the ACLU, we must remember to note when significant changes occur in both the policy and administrative leadership of the group.

A group professedly committed to freedom also becomes suspect of inconsistent or conspiratorial leadership if it accepts money from persons or organizations with a record of service to totalitarian goals. If such a group contributes money or labor to persons or movements obviously under conspiratorial control, then it is likewise suspect, regardless of the temporary purpose or activity in which both groups are engaged. If much of the time a group works to accomplish ends that result in positive aid to totalitarian movements against their antagonists, it becomes worthy of closer examination. If, in the great majority of instances when a group advocates things or works in a manner consistent with its beliefs, it also facilitates results that, for entirely different reasons, are helpful to totalitarian progress, we may wonder if its peculiarly selective "consistencies" are not accidental successes.

If an organization has specific purposes, but diversifies to make statements or do work that is really nonessential to those purposes, and in doing so its leadership promotes propaganda or efforts to accomplish objectives sought by political conspiracies, then we are justified to wonder whose purposes are really being served.

And if an organization, during any part of its history, does all of these things, its actions are virtually indistinguishable from a totally controlled front for a conspiratorial movement. The traditional conception of a Communist front group held by most official government investigating bodies is that of an organization whose leadership is under continual, disciplined control by the Communist conspiracy, or that portion of the conspiratorial movement with a known address, the Communist Party. Communists can exercise control over groups and individuals without any actual party affiliations, and I shall not be so lenient as to make any such distinctions between the *practical results* of a stereotyped Communist front and any other organization that has continually fronted for the Communists. The concept of conspiracy is equally applicable in either case, and we shall apply it with equal measure as we examine the notably "inconsistent" history of the ACLU. The ultimate judgement rests with you.

8

1920-1929: Origins of the ACLU and Struggle Between Warring Collectivists

Never before in American history were the forces of reaction so completely in control of our political and economic life. Never before were the civil rights guaranteed by constitutional provision so generally ignored and violated. The revolutionary changes brought about by the war and industrial conflict are nowhere more apparent than in the new machinery for the suppression of opinion and of traditional minority and individual rights. . . .

Behind this machinery stand the property interests of the country, so completely in control of our political life as to establish what is in effect a class government, a government by and for business. Political democracy as conceived by many of America's greatest leaders, does not exist, except in a few communities. This condition is not yet understood by the public at large. They are drugged by propaganda and blinded by a press necessarily subservient to property interests. Dazed by the kaleidoscopic changes of the past few years, the rank and file citizens accept the dictatorship of property in the name of patriotism.

The only groups of the American people conscious of this condition and capable of outspoken resistance to it are the radicals, the more aggressive wings of the labor and farmer movements, and a few influential liberal journals, organizations and individuals in public life. Among other classes more or less conscious of the condition but incapable of outspoken resistance are the Negroes, many foreign-born groups and the tenant farmers of the west and south.

Resistance to reaction has two aspects, first, activities looking toward a reorganization of our economic and political life, and second the demand for 'rights' of those minorities and individuals attacked by the forces of reaction. The demand for 'rights' is couched usually in an appeal to free speech traditions and constitutional guarantees, though behind that, lies the historic insistence on the 'natural right' of the advocates of any cause to agitate, - a right prior to and independent of constitutions. In the long run causes get that natural right in proportion to their power to take and hold it. Or legal 'rights' securing it will be freely exercised when no class conflict threatens the existing order.[1]

With these angry words began the first *Annual Report* of the American Civil Liberties Union, published in September, 1921. The compiler of the report, the Union's reputed founder and executive director for thirty years, had much to be angry about. He had only been released from prison slightly over two years earlier, after serving most of a one-year sentence for draft resistance. After his education at Harvard and a teaching and social service career in St. Louis, Roger Nash Baldwin began his lifelong crusade by taking up the cause of consciencious objectors, experiencing the response of an official government policy totally insensitive to the individual's life. He was not motivated by any consistent libertarian position on the issue of conscription, but had long held to the ideology of the class struggle that he expressed in the 1921 report.

In that statement we note that the "new machinery" suppressing "opinion" and "rights" consists of the "property interests of the country" who have established a "class government" for the interests of "business," a "dictatorship of property in the name of patriotism." This condition will persist, he believes, until either the somewhat unknowing victims of oppression exercise their "power to take and hold" their "natural right," a concept that Baldwin seems to have long struggled, quite unsuccessfully, to understand, or when these "rights" are made "legal" as a result of the absence of "class conflict."

Simply stated, Roger Baldwin was claiming that our rights were being denied by the power and influence of super-rich capitalists in control of our country at the time he wrote. Presumably he meant such giants as the Rockefeller, Morgan, and Carnegie empires, since practically everyone owned *some* property, including himself, but the vast majority of property owners were not those exercising the "dictatorship." As we review Baldwin's work and associations in this chapter, remember that he saw these Wall Street interests as the enemy.

As a consequence of this outlook, Baldwin looked for a society free of class conflict, which must mean a society free of class distinctions, or the ultimate idealistic goal in Marxist theory. His frequent waverings between advocacy of anarchy and a government-controlled economy have made his ideological position hard to define. Certainly it changed somewhat over the years. One of the earliest influences on his thinking was the American anarchist Emma Goldman, who was often in league with other anarchists in support of the Bolshevik cause. Although

Baldwin often professed the goal of the abolition of the state, he welcomed the Marxist-Leninist movement as the road toward that objective. But it remained for Emma Goldman to awaken his interest in the "class struggle" at a time when he had already become "discouraged" with the social work and municipal reform efforts he had tried in St. Louis.[2]

Early Organizational Roots

The American Civil Liberties Union was created by Roger Baldwin and others as a result of a split in an older organization. To understand the early orientation of the ACLU, we must briefly trace that lineage.

The year 1914 brought not only a tragically unnecessary and avoidable war to Europe, but the beginning of a massive campaign of military preparedness to the United States. The extent to which this official U.S. policy was made to conform to the Morgan-Rockefeller Wall Street interests, who saw the war as an immense source of business for their industrial holdings, would only be proven after the war ended in 1918.[3]

In response to this campaign and the media propaganda against Germany, a number of wealthy and prominent leaders of the settlement house movement, such as Jane Addams and Lillian Wald, began to hold informal discussions on the domestic effects of the war. These gatherings resulted in a formal antiwar and anticonscription declaration in March, 1915, and, the following December, formation, under Wald's chairmanship, of what was finally called the American Union Against Militarism. Public concern was soon raised over the nobility of this group's purposes, as a result of its directors including German and Bolshevik sympathizers, as well as the wealthy altruists who were also represented. Several of the more disturbing officers included Louis P. Lochner, Max Eastman, and his sister Crystal. The concern was well-founded, since less than two years later, Lochner (along with others, including David Starr Jordan) would head the People's Council of America, the official American branch of the Russian Bolshevik faction. Max and Crystal Eastman would also be active in the People's Council, along with Morris Hillquit and Socialist candidate and self-avowed Bolshevik, Eugene V. Debs. Max Eastman was already making his position known in the pages of the *Masses* and would continue doing so later in the *Liberator*. He later saw through the socialist fallacies that had held his youthful devotion, and wrote of his outlook at this time as having been that of a staunch supporter and defender of Leninism.[4]

Other members of the committee (most of them political collectivists) included: Adolph A. Berle, Sr., Rev. Herbert S. Bigelow, Sophonisba Breckinridge, Francis King Carey, John Lovejoy Elliott, Mrs. Glendower Evans, Zona Gale, Charles T. Hallinan, Scott Nearing, Owen Lovejoy, Frederick Lynch, James H. Maurer, Henry S. Mussey, Amos Pinchot, Paul Kellogg, Alfred S. Scattergood, Rudolph

Spreckels, Norman Thomas, Oswald Garrison Villard, and James P. Warbasse. Some of these people were located away from the committee's office in New York, so the actual work was primarily done by Wald, Kellogg, Eastman, Thomas, and others who were more accessible. The group's educational activities were supplemented by Washington lobbying on the part of Hallinan.[5]

It was into this staff operation in New York that Roger Baldwin entered in April, 1917, coming from his AUAM activities in St. Louis to assist the ailing Crystal Eastman.[6] Two events occurred in 1917 that overwhelmingly influenced the course and public image of the AUAM. The first was the carefully contrived entry of the United States into the war in April, the second the Bolshevik Revolution in Russia that fall. The consequences and entangling alliances rapidly became complex.

With America's involvement in the European war came legal measures aimed at anyone engaged in propaganda on behalf of Germany or active in resisting conscription. The consequences were dreadful for religious groups like the pacifist Jehovah's Witnesses. They were far more complex for those in the American Union Against Militarism. Many of their leaders were openly sympathetic or in league with the Bolsheviks who seized power in Russia. About the same time it became known that the German General Staff had assisted Lenin in carrying out his coup, the connection between leaders of AUAM, the new Communist People's Council of America, and the German espionage and sabotage networks in Great Britain and the United States was revealed. Much was made of this connection in the press and government investigations of such groups as the AUAM through 1919, but it was not until after the war that evidence began to come to light indicating a far more intricate opposition of forces.[7]

The Strange Internationalist Alliance

Roger Baldwin recalls his association with the leaders of the AUAM during the war, whom he said "represented an influential leadership with easy access to the highest officials from the White House down."[8] In view of the revolutionary anarchist or Bolshevik views of many of these leaders, we should stop to examine how they were so influential, especially at this time, and why they had such access to the White House and elsewhere.

Before being elected President in 1912, Woodrow Wilson had been greatly influenced by the Fabian socialist movement at Princeton.[9] In 1905, this British-based group organized the Intercollegiate Socialist Society, which had as members most of the early founders of the AUAM and the ACLU.[10] Woodrow Wilson, while President, was virtually captive of the influence of his close adviser, Colonel Edward Mandell House, who had been so instrumental in securing his election victory. House was responsible for originating most of Wilson's policies in domestic and foreign affairs throughout his two terms in office.[11] And House's

116

dominance over Wilson was another factor that made the White House receptive to the AUAM. Intercollegiate Socialist Society members such as Norman Thomas had well established contacts with other ISS members like Walter Lippman, who served among House's assistants. During the Versailles conference after the war, Thomas, with Lippman and others,served as an assistant to House. This group comprised "the Inquiry" and was instrumental in helping to draft the harsh terms of the "peace treaty" that would help guarantee another war.[12] It was not at all unlike House, with all his Wall Street ties, to have assistants and asociates such as these. House himself was an advocate of Marxian socialism, a fact that he admitted in a thinly veiled, anonymously written autobiographical novel in 1912, *Phillip Dru: Administrator*.[13] In this novel, House outlined a number of statist institutions that he would help install in America during the Wilson years. These included the graduated personal income tax, The Federal Reserve System, and the Federal Trade Commission. *Phillip Dru* served as something of a guideline for programs instituted by a later political protegee of House, Franklin Delano Roosevelt.[14]

But Colonel House was not the only sympathetic contact the AUAM had in high places. Louis P. Lochner, prior to the time he established the Communist People's Council, had been the assistant to industrialist Henry Ford, and was personally in charge of the old man's unsuccessful and somewhat laughable Peace Mission.[15] The question naturally arises as to why prominent capitalists would have employed leading revolutionists to agitate against a war that was making millions for the so-called robber barons. To answer this we must look further.

The result of the Ford Peace Mission was the establishment at The Hague in 1915 of an international committee of women for permanent peace, organized in New York as the Women's International League. At a meeting of this early manifestation of "women's lib" on November 28 of that year, the distribution of a pamphlet by Louis Fraina, "Bolshevism Conquers," produced a riot on the part of some unattached soldiers in attendance who did not seem to appreciate the connection.[16] After the war was underway, more of these antiwar activities came to public attention and were widely criticized by virtue of their obviously pro-Communist or pro-German orientations. The odd fact was that much of the money for these groups, including the AUAM, was coming not from Germany, but from the source of vital assistance to the Bolsheviks, Wall Street.[17]

In 1903 there was organized in New York a club of wealthy socialists (the "X" club) who shared the same dreams of world union that, years earlier, had motivated Cecil Rhodes and Lord Alfred Milner to found the Round Table groups in Great Britain.[18] The New York clique included Communist Lincoln Steffens, Communist Morris Hillquit, and socialist-pragmatist philosopher John Dewey. All of these men would become active in the antiwar movements slightly more than a decade later, as well as numerous other left-wing organizations, and, later, the ACLU. The club also included New York Life Insurance Company Vice-President Rufus Weeks, Charles Edward Russell, and another future assistant of Colonel House, James T. Shotwell. Hillquit found his association with these elite

117

businessmen quite helpful, especially when he was permitted to address the New York Economic Club in 1908, which was then presided over by Chase National Bank President A. Barton Hepburn.[19] Obviously Colonel House was far from being unique in his time.

The other leading light active in promoting revolutionary causes among the black tie set was Andrew Carnegie. Indeed, he paid for the establishment and maintenance of a number of organizations that formed the backbone of the antiwar, pacifist, and socialist movements during the first two decades of this century. His efforts were part of a world-wide drive, exemplified in America by Theodore Marburg's work, to unite wealthy capitalists and collectivist movements in a plan to form a world order that would eliminate the threat of war. Contrary to conclusions expressed elsewhere[20]—that such efforts as those of Carnegie and the Morgan-Rockefeller interests in promoting pacifist and Bolshevik movements were motivated by a desire to monopolize world markets in those areas where the virus would be spread—is the clear evidence that Carnegie and others were idealistically hopeful for a world government as a *political* goal.[21]

Jennings Wise wrote of the forces at work with the author-publicist Marburg:

> The Internationalists now formed the Conciliation Internationale in Paris with many of the leading statesmen, financiers and Socialists of France, including Leon Bourgeois and Baron d'Estournelles de Constant, (members of the Permanent Court of Arbitration) on its council: while in England the Fabian Society took up the work of conciliation. Marburg hurried home to found the Maryland Peace Society, and the American Association for International Conciliation, with himself as President, and with Secretary Root, Knox, Bryan, Carnegie, Nicholas Murray Butler, Lyman Abbott, Charles Eliot, Daniel Smiley, Cardinal Gibbons, Rabbi Wise, Oscar Straus, Paul Warburg, Otto Kahn, Bernard Baruch, Clarence Mackay and numerous other statesmen, scholars, philanthropists, and internatuonal bankers on its council.[22]

At this time, about 1906, Marburg and his elite associates saw Woodrow Wilson as the ideal candidate to back in 1912, a candidate who would willingly promote the world government plans that were in the making. To popularize these schemes, Marburg wrote a number of books, including *Toward An Enduring Peace,* around the time the Maryland Peace Society was established.[23] We read of his later work:

> Having founded the Maryland Peace Society since the Second Hague Peace Conference, Marburg next set about the formation of the American Society for the Judicial Settlement of International Disputes, as an agency through which to popularize the idea of a World Court. . . . Finally, in the *Peace Movement Practical* which Marburg now published, he showed himself to be behind all the Internationist declarations.[24]

This takes us up to 1910, about the time that Edward Ginn of Boston endowed the International School of Peace, which then became the World Peace Foundation. As the evidence indicates, virtually all of the elements of the American faction of the world-wide peace and world government movement were established prior to 1914 by representatives of Carnegie, Morgan, and Rockefeller interests, with those wealthy internationalists providing the funding for these activities and for the grooming of chosen politicians. And a leading organization of this movement in America from 1914 onward was the American Union Against Militarism, which after the war became the ACLU.[25]

The relationship between the Wall Street crowd and the peace and world government movements would, of course, continue after World War I and the failure of that first attempt at world government, the League of Nations, in enlisting the full support and participation of the United States. As we shall see, some of Marburg's associates who belonged to the AUAM separated themselves from that group when its active leaders widened the scope of its concerns toward the end of the war to form the ACLU. In later years, the AUAM "purists" continued their efforts in the Foreign Policy Association,[26] which was closely associated with, and supported by, leaders of the internationalist Council on Foreign Relations, formed in 1919 by Colonel House and others to spread their gospel among those in positions of power.[27]

The fascinating apparent contradiction in all this stems from the fact that it has been known for several decades that the same Wall Street interests who financed the establishment of the peace movement—a portion of which would become the ACLU—were not only instrumental in guaranteeing the success of the Bolshevik revolution,[28] but also responsible for pushing America into the European war in 1917.[29] Some of the elite obviously saw this war as attractive because of their own potential for Allied business. Others, including Andrew Carnegie, saw it as important to the plan for world order. On February 14, 1917, he wrote to President Wilson that Germany was

beyond reason. . . . Today she shows herself completely insane. No wonder the Cabinet . . . shows restlessness. Were I in your place there would soon be an end of this. There is only one straight way to settlement. You should proclaim war against her, however reluctantly, and then settlement would soon come. Germany sought peace recently because she knew her weakness. Britain and France co-operating with us, would ensure peace promptly beyond question, and at next meeting at the Hague we would abolish war forever.[30]

Just as it was clear to Carnegie that this war would fulfill its objective as "a war to end all wars" by leading to the establishment of an authority powerful enough to "abolish war forever," it became equally obvious that Wilson was listening carefully to his advisers.

This should help the reader understand why Carnegie would promote an unnecessary policy of American intervention in Europe's war after he had substantially established, through his representative Marburg, a nation-wide network of organizations agitating for pacifism and against military preparedness. Only one

119

question remains: why were these groups, especially the AUAM, allowed to function under the leadership of persons such as Hillquit, the Eastmans, and others so openly identified with "radical" political and labor movements internationally affiliated with the defeatist strategy of the German General Staff? The only rational conclusion that can be derived from these facts is that Carnegie and Morgan-Rockefeller interests saw these leftist movements as providing two key benefits for their plans. Such groups as the AUAM before the war and the CFR after the war would disseminate on different stratas of society propaganda that would condition Americans to accept some form of world order to prevent future wars. This is obvious from the statements of those involved. Another function that these groups served, although certainly unknowingly until after it was accomplished, was the provision of protective coloration for the influential tycoons and financiers who had pressured this nation into the war for their own purposes. With only identified leftists active in the public eye against the war preparedness effort, including those with pro-German affiliations, the prowar policies of Wall Street's White House would appear in contrast as the height of patriotism, when distinguished in the pages of a kept press.

Since all of this was known, at least to the Wall Street interests involved in it, we can reasonably apply the legal principle that one of their associates, in later years, found satisfactory.[31] We can assume they intended the logical consequences of their actions. But such does not apply to much of the leadership and virtually all of the membership in these organizations. In other words, when Roger Baldwin was railing against the "property interests" in 1921, we can be fairly sure that he did not know he was heading an organization that had grown out of part of a movement established by the elite class he so hated. We should assume that he did not know for what, or for whose other purposes, he was really laboring. Let us examine, however how hard he worked to play his intended role.

A Parting of the Ways

As a New York officer of the American Union Against Militarism, Roger Baldwin in 1917 found his time being almost exclusively taken up with cases of conscientious objectors who were victims of civil liberties violations. This was the rule after the Selective Service law was signed on May 18, 1917. Baldwin's preoccupation with assisting those charged under the conscription and espionage laws continued even after some members of the AUAM forced a showdown.

Some of the group's earliest leaders were so concerned about the Union's increasing work on behalf of COs that they suggested Baldwin's work should be separated from the AUAM and continued under the name of a new organization. These persons included Wald, Addams, Lewisohn, Gale, Kellogg, and Mussey. Baldwin and other more "radical" members naturally urged that the activities remain consolidated, Crystal Eastman being the most vocal member of this

120

faction. Lillian Wald wrote to Eastman that, if the Union continued on it present path, it would "drift into being a *party of opposition to the government.*"[32] Consistent with the views of the Fabian Society, Wald felt that her social objectives could be accomplished peacefully.

The crisis heightened when the AUAM voted to send representatives to a Minneapolis conference of the Communist-dominated People's Council. Wald threatened to resign if this were done, since a public association between the two groups would, she feared, destroy the AUAM's image as "a group of reflective liberals."[33] Her worry was well reasoned, since Crystal Eastman was already prominent in the People's Council and that Communist organization shared the same New York address with the AUAM and other groups.[34] By September, 1917, a decision had to be made.

A meeting was held on September 13, in which Max Eastman, Emily Green Balch, and Communist People's Council Chairman Scott Nearing, by this time a rather inactive member of the AUAM, represented the most extreme left-wing position. Wald and others spoke for those who, by comparison, might be called the conservatives. The various alternatives were examined, and finally the group decided to disband so that everyone would be free to pursue their own goals. The AUAM remained in existence until January, 1922, later becoming the Carnegie-financed Foreign Policy Association.[35]

On October 1, the radical faction formed the National Civil Liberties Bureau, with Roger Baldwin remaining as director. This new organization, the immediate predecessor of the ACLU, continued to host among its officers and leading members many of those who were so personally interested in the success of the coup that would take place in Russia within a month. The leadership included, from 1917 until January, 1920: Chairman L. Hollingsworth Wood, Vice-Chairman Norman Thomas, Treasurer Helen Phelps Stokes, Counsel Walter Nelles, and Albert De Silver, who would briefly stand in for Baldwin as director. A "Directing Committee" had as members: Crystal Eastman (when her health permitted), John Lovejoy Elliott, Reverend John Haynes Holmes (who had also been active in the AUAM), Agnes Brown Leach, Judah Leon Magnes, John Nevin Sayre, James P. Warbasse (until late 1918), Edmund Evans, William M. Fincke, and John Codman.[36] Although many of these names are no longer well known to the public, at that time, and for several decades after, they included some of the most active supporters of Communist and pro-Communist activities in the United States. However, there were those like Norman Thomas, who would insist that their advocacy of "democratic socialism" made them determined anti-Communists in later years. But during these early years, the coming disillusionment many would feel with the failure of the Soviet "experiment" was still in the future. The NCLB included the most influential pro-Bolsheviks in America, such as the Eastmans and Stokes.[37] But one's attention should not be on just the record of Communist affiliations that these leaders of the NCLB had accumulated or would accumulate in later years, but also on the work the Bureau undertook during these years when it almost unvaryingly expressed the positions held by Roger Baldwin.[38]

The Radicalization of Roger Baldwin

The fact that between 1917 and 1920 Baldwin would awaken to the "class struggle" in America and shift the focus of his major concern, particularly after the war, from the civil liberties of conscientious objectors to the struggle for the state ownership and redistribution of all commercial property, as expressed by Communist labor movement leaders, did not prevent him, with all his zeal, from appreciating a strategy of self-protection. It was not only his year sentence of imprisonment for resisting service induction in 1917 that had made him conscious of potential dangers. He seemed to favor a policy of appearing "innocent" in public as early as August, 1917, when he advised Louis Lochner concerning the People's Council:

> Do steer away from making it look like a Socialist enterprise. Too many people have already gotten the idea that it is nine-tenths a Socialist movement. You can, of course, avoid this by bringing to the front people like Senator Works, Miss Addams, and others, who are known as substantial Democrats. . . . I think it would be an error to get the public thinking that we are launching a political party in Minneapolis. To be sure, we are launching a political movement, but that is quite a different matter from a political point. . . .
> We want also to look like patriots in everything we do. We want to get a lot of good flags, talk a good deal about the Constitution and what our forefathers wanted to make of this country, and to show that we are the folks that really stand for the spirit of our institutions.[39]

Lochner replied later that month to Baldwin's advice to keep the "radical socialists" in the Communist People's Council out of the public eye by stating, "I agree with you that we should keep proclaiming our loyalty and patriotism. I will see to it that we have flags and similar paraphernalia."[40]

In attempting fairly to understand what was in Baldwin's mind at this time, we must contrast his advice to Lochner with the fact that he was not at this time attempting to hide his own radical views, as well as the fact that he had joined the major Communist-dominated labor movement in America to be prosecuted during and after the war, the Industrial Workers of the World.[41] Friends of Baldwin published a leaflet in November, 1918, which contained his statement to the court at the time he was sentenced for illegal draft resistance:

> Though, at the moment, I am of a tiny minority, I feel myself just one protest in a great revolt surging up from among the people—the struggle of the masses against the rule of the world by the few—profoundly intensified by the war. It is a struggle against the political state itself, against exploitation, imperialism, authority in all forms. It is a

122

struggle to break in full force only after the war. Russia already stands in the vanguard, beset by her enemies in the camps of both belligerents—the central empires break asunder from within, the labor movement gathers revolutionary forces in Britain—and in our own country the Non-Partisan League, radical labor and the Socialist Party hold the germs of the new social order. Their protest is my protest.[42]

This sort of statement could not easily be forgotten in the years ahead, in spite of the circumstances under which it was issued, because it was made by the man who really *was* the active force behind the ACLU for over thirty years.

But a disparity between Baldwin's statements and his advice to Lochner still remains. He wanted his organization and the other Communist groups to be separate and distinct, lest the public concluded correctly "that the same little bunch is running all these organizations."[43] However, he made no effort to conceal his avowed solidarity with the early American Communist movement, including the violent IWW "Wobblies." Was he simply being inconsistent, or was there a purpose to be served? The National Civil Liberties Bureau continued its work on behalf of pacifists who had fallen afoul of Selective Service and defended numerous persons charged under the Espionage Act, including German-Americans and organizers of the IWW involved in labor disturbances across the nation. The work continued until Baldwin, a model prisoner like Eugene Debs,[44] was released early from his sentence and persuaded by Norman Thomas and others to resume work in 1920 as director of his organization, under the revised name of the American Civil Liberties Union. It was not until August 22, 1922, that there came to light evidence indicating that someone else's purposes might be served by Baldwin's policy of public "patriot"–private revolutionist.

The Years of "Scared Reds"

The heat that American leftists felt during the war was over in 1919. Many of them looked forward to less opposition against their plans after the war, but such hopes were quickly dashed. In 1919 and 1920 such federal and state investigations as those of the Senate Overman Committee and the New York Lusk Committee exposed the coordinated network of subversive movements that had been established during the war years. Investigative raids on headquarters of subversive organizations, led in 1919 by the Radical Division of the Justice Department under Attorney General A. Mitchell Palmer, led to the arrest and deportation to Russia of a number of alien extremists, including the anarchist Emma Goldman.[45] Organizations like the American Protective League were stronger than ever, with widespread public concern over radicalism swelling their ranks. The campaign against subversion had official government support and a very cooperative press, and it brought with it many unfortunate abuses, including the growth of a dangerous and powerful counter-conspiracy, the revived Ku Klux Klan.[46] By 1920 the public had also tired of the flowery idealism that had characterized the Wilson Administration, which had resulted in an end to America's rather proud policy of isolationism. The election of President Warren G. Harding in that year was a manifestation of this change in political climate, a change that would initiate a battle to the death between the American "radicals" in and out of government and the new administration.

Contrary to the mythology that has become official American "history," Harding and his attorney general, Harry Daugherty, entered office as rather patriotic conservatives with a most tolerant attitude of sympathy toward such wartime prisoners as Eugene Debs,[47] and with no predetermined plan to unleash a wave of legal terror against the Left. The Palmer raids and subsequent deportations were over. The policy of the Justice Department was one of surveillance, but not prosecution, until the new head of the Bureau of Investigation, esteemed private detective William J. Burns, led a raid at Bridgman, Michigan.

To bring us up to the time of that raid, we should first note that the National Civil Liberties Bureau became the American Civil Liberties Union in January, 1920. Baldwin remained director, with Albert DeSilver, who had been director during Baldwin's jail term, as his assistant. In addition to the board members remaining from the AUAM and NCLB, there were added to the new organization: Reverend Harry F. Ward, Chairman; Duncan McDonald and Jeannette Rankin, Vice-Chairmen; Lucille B. Milner, Field Secretary; and Louis F. Budenz, Publicity Director.[48] Additions to the 1917 NCLB Board included: Jane Addams, Norman Hapgood, Arthur Garfield Hays, Morris Hillquit, B. W. Huebsch, James Weldon Johnson, Helen Keller, Henry P. Linville, Robert Morss Lovett, A.J. Muste, Elizabeth Gurley Flynn, Scott Nearing, William H. Pickens, Amos Pinchot, Vida D. Scuddder, Oswald Garrison Villard, B. Charney Vladeck, and Bishop Charles D. Williams. An examination of the records of these people, as prominent as many of them were, will reveal how strong was the pro-Communist influence on the organization,[49] in addition to its day-to-day guidance under its director.

The first two years of the Union's work were dominated by the defense of aliens arrested under the authority of Palmer's investigations and activists in the IWW. It is not only significant that an organization like the ACLU was overwhelmingly preoccupied with defending agents of the Communist apparatus, segments of which were so well represented by the affiliations of many of its officers and board. The fact that this was done while the ACLU was presented to the public as a civil liberatarian organization, distinct from the groups it was defending, followed all too closely a pattern that would soon come to light.

"Civil Liberties" As a Facade for Subversion

On August 22, 1922, Justice Department investigators under the leadership of William J. Burns raided a secret U.S. Communist Party meeting at Bridgman,

Michigan. William Z. Foster and all other early Communist Party leaders were present at this convention conducted under stringent security, although some escaped arrest. Two barrels full of documents were seized, providing a fairly complete record of the proceedings. These documents were later published and used as the basis for further investigations and prosecutions by the Justice Department. The Harding Administration had on its hands a problem that amounted to an underground conspiracy of nation-wide scope.[50]

The captured documents revealed a careful plan.[51] Because the Communist Party had been made effectively illegal under the espionage legislation, the Red leadership decided to continue its operation as a secret underground movement called Number One, which would control and use a public movement as a front for its activities. The front was a political organization called the Workers' Party, which was to promote itself as independent of the Soviet Union, but which would be a captive pawn. In this manner, the Workers' Party would succeed the People's Council as the first major Communist-front organization in America. As a political party, the Workers' Party could be used to promote the violent Communist strategy, but could remain protected from prosecution

> By taking advantage of the pretenses of "democratic forms" which the capitalistic state is obliged to maintain. By this means the Communists can maintain themselves in the open with a restricted program while establishing themselves with mass support.[52]

Apparently the Communists, like Roger Baldwin, saw the success of their Workers' Party (or Number Two) resulting from their effort "to look like patriots in everything we do." To the extent they were successful until being uncovered, they probably owed some of their wisdom to the cautioning advice given Louis Lochner by Roger Baldwin. And, for the decade of the 1920s, if not longer, the Communist Party, One and Two, owed much of of its success in resisting the efforts toward its exposure and destruction to the ACLU's work.

We need now to briefly survey the landmark cases that highlighted the work of the Union during the 1920s. It would be helpful to note and pass over those cases that actually involve valid civil liberties issues with little or no political influence even possibly involved. The best example of this was the first in what would be a long series of cases involving the sect of Jehovah's Witnesses, whose religious doctrines forbid their members to participate in patriotic activities, including flag salutes and recitations of the pledge to the flag. The Union took the case of a Washington State youth who had been taken from his parents by a juvenile court because of his refusal to salute the flag in school. The Union went to court and returned the boy to his parents.[53] This case exemplifies what was largely the outstanding exception to the variety of issues that concerned Roger Baldwin and his associates during this first decade.

In spite of the individual amnesties for wartime law offenders issued by President Harding during 1921 and 1922, the public alarm and Justice Department actions that commenced after the Bridgman raid discoveries led to a wave of local legal actions against various left-wing groups, and more causes célèbre for the ACLU.[54] One such antisubversive legal measure in Los Angeles was aimed at suppressing the IWW in 1923. Protests were waged in the city against this firm restriction of the Wobblies, who had been implicated in many incidents of labor violence. The socialist novelist Upton Sinclair, whose *Jungle* served well as influential propaganda for statist controls, was arrested at a rally held to protest the anti-IWW measures. The Los Angeles cadre was thus given a martyr whose cause drew crowds estimated by the Union at 15,000. This agitation led to the establishment of one of the first ACLU local affiliates—today still among the largest and most left-wing—the Southern California branch, with Reverend Clinton J. Taft as director.[55]

Nineteen twenty-four was a banner year for the Union in many respects. Since 1921 it had been pleased to report that government actions against subversion were lessening, and thus the civil liberties climate was improving, in spite of the growth of the klans and other groups.[56] However, after 1922 the Justice Department widely publicized the facts concerning the conspiracy that had been uncovered at Bridgman. Information from the investigations appeared in such books as Whitney's *Reds in America*. And if Washington was not cracking the whip on Number Two and its affiliates, local and state authorities certainly were. The Union once again, to protect its philosophical allies and probably a few of its leaders, had its hands full.[57] But by now it had the assistance of influential men in both houses of Congress, whose ties to those on Wall Street brought them into the suddenly materializing campaign to "Get Daugherty." The Harding Administration, especially the attorney general's office, was in opposition to many of the policies sought by the Morgan-Rockefeller-Carnegie crowd. And it would soon pay the price for being out of step.[58]

Just as incredible as the truth is concerning the coordinated smear campaign and frame-up that was engineered to destroy Harding and Daugherty—a basket of eels as complex as Watergate—the ACLU was in the forefront of a crusade which began in April, 1920, and ended with the electrocution of Sacco and Vanzetti seven years later, a case which has since assumed such legendary proportions as to make public understanding of the subject almost immune to the truth.[59]

Fortunately, it has been conclusively established that these two anarchists of foreign extraction received punishment commensurate with their crime (the murder of two men in a bank robbery) after a fair trial. They got justice in spite of the remaining myth to the contrary.[60] It is also known that the Union saw this case as just what it would become, a tremendous case of potential martyrdom for the subversive underground already organized. By February 19, 1921, Baldwin and his friends had taken up the cause, assuming in advance of the record—which would prove otherwise—that the two defendants were not going to receive a fair trial, but were going to be punished merely for their views or ethnic background.[61]

The ACLU maintained its efforts on their behalf until 1927, the year they were given justice.

It is interesting that Baldwin maintained the strategy of "looking like patriots in everything we do." His policy was continued in 1926 and 1927, while he was travelling in Europe and Russia, by acting Director Forrest Bailey, who wrote:

> The Civil Liberties Union has been connected with the Sacco and Vanzetti matter, but has *hidden* its participation under various *false fronts*. We are at present *instigating* a nation-wide movement among lawyers in the various university faculties to join as signatories . . . for a review of the case de novo. This work is being done *behind the name* of a group of lawyers at Columbia: Karl Llewellyn is the chief promoter.[62]

Another would be Felix Frankfurter, Harvard Law School professor and later an associate justice of the U.S. Supreme Court, a longtime National Committeeman of the ACLU.[63] For anyone who may wonder why any particular significance is attached to the Forrest Bailey statement that the Union was employing false fronts to agitate for Sacco and Vanzetti, it may be more than a coincidence that a person in a position to know has identified Bailey as a secret Communist during this time.[64]

One of the most important of such ACLU fronts was the American Fund for Public Service, or the Garland Fund, organized in 1922, with Roger Baldwin as secretary. The Fund actually allocated over $2 million during its first decade, financing virtually every left-wing movement of significance, including heavy assistance to the IWW and the ACLU. Baldwin's influence as the Fund's secretary was not the only reason for its heavy subsidies to all major ACLU projects. It just so happened that eight out of thirteen of the Fund's officers and directors were influential in the Union by 1921, including Nearing, Flynn, and William Z. Foster (exposed by evidence seized at Bridgman), all of whom would later make crystal clear that they were part of Number One.[65] Another front used by Baldwin was the Communist-dominated International Labor Defense, of which he was a member. This organization served as a transmission belt for money and membership into the Communist Party. It fronted for the ACLU by assisting in cases, such as the Gastonia, North Carolina, textile strike in 1929, in which the clear issue was defending Communists from interference with their subversion and attacks on private property, and where the pretense of civil liberties was obviously secondary, if not transparent.[66] It was quite convenient for Baldwin to get the Garland Fund to finance the ILD, which would then take on cases that might not allow the Union, if handling them alone and publicly, to "look like patriots in everything we do." Baldwin could always make known the distinction between the Union and the ILD, if such became necessary to avoid suspicions that "the same little bunch" was running the whole show. He would later find this quite an item of utility, for it would be possible to finance the ILD for its objectives and, simultaneously, withdraw the ACLU from any cooperative efforts, establishing the non-

Communist identity of the Union. Such energetic operations make the harsh and intolerant attitudes of government investigators just a little easier to understand.

But the case during the 1920s that has remained foremost in the public mind across the years is unquestionably the 1925 Scopes "monkey trial" in Tennessee. The Union itself did not take this case, but was represented by a member, Clarence Darrow, who led the famous defense against William Jennings Bryan. Darrow, who had already shown his willingness to get paid for hopeless cases, [67] gained a long-range victory for his agnostic viewpoint in spite of the fact he lost the case. The publicity that the trial received effectively discouraged Tennessee from enforcing the unjust law prohibiting teaching of the Darwinian theory. We can note in passing that the Union saw this case as a victory within a defeat, very much like that of Sacco and Vanzetti, because of its future effects. [68] The Union contribution to the case did nothing to solve the root cause of the controversy: compulsory education by government, which has the power to reinforce any views it so chooses at the expense of people who do not agree. [69] In any event, the participation of famous legal personalities like Darrow, Frankfurter, Samuel Untermyer, [70] and Louis Marshall [71] in the cases promoted by the Union's work during the twenties did as much as anything else to promote the organization's growth and gradual acquisition of an image of respectability.

An interesting statement was allegedly made by Louis Marshall in 1928, at the time he was connected in business with Otto Kahn and others among the Wall Street crowd we discussed in reference to the financing of the peace movements out of which the ACLU developed. His statement, if authentic, may express in summary the larger scheme in which Roger Baldwin and his comrades may have been unknowing tools in their efforts at facilitating Bolshevism in America. Looking down on New York from his Wall Street window, Marshall reportedly said, "Look what we can do for a country we love, in Russia we have shown the world what we can do to a country we hate." [72]

The next year those in high government and banking circles, like Louis Marshall, would show their "love" for the United States through credit-market manipulations that produced a stock market crash and a depression that lasted a decade. [73]

9

1930-1939: Depression Years and the United Front

Looking back on his half century of leadership activities with the ACLU, Roger Baldwin wrote in 1970 of a "problem" that faced the groups's integrity, its reputation for taking up the cause of all whose rights were denied, regardless of their views. The Union's elder statesman lamented:

> It is quite true that the reality of impartiality has not been matched by its appearance. It could hardly be, because publicity emphasizes the unusual or the dramatic and so our concerns sometimes seemed to be with the "reds," and "pinks" and the extremists —always good copy for the press. It is also true that some of us in the leadership contributed to this impression in the 1930's by our personal associations with united fronts for good causes in which Communists and Socialists and other "disreputables" took part. The opposition never let us forget it even after we had long since abandoned such associations. The opposition of right-wing advocates of repression was able to mislead and confuse the uninformed, but it was unable to influence officialdom and the press into questioning the Union's good faith.[1]

What is "Guilt by Association"?

Because I make no attempt to hide the fact that I am a "right-wing advocate"— though I believe I am a more consistent libertarian opponent of government repression than most ACLU spokesmen—and because Roger Baldwin admits to having contributed to his own bad reputation, we can be sure he will not mind if we do not let him forget it all just yet.

Before we examine the "good causes" that Baldwin and so many other ACLU leaders joined in the 1930s, we should pause to discuss two issues. The fact that an individual associates with other persons guilty of certain memberships or activities does not constitute proof of any similar guilt on his part. Maintaining otherwise would be the sort of irrational "guilt by association" that is illustrated in blaming guns for violent crimes because they happen to be "accompanying" many violent criminals. However, since everyone's actions express their personal values, or lack of same, and because different people can be parties to the same conspiracy for different personal motivations though promoting the same general objectives, there is a sort of valid guilt by association. This does not necessarily equate the motivations of those associating in common activities, and it might be best termed "value identification by collaboration." This idea is related to one portion of Supreme Court Justice Robert H. Jackson's May, 1950, opinion on the Taft-Hartley Act:

> The conspiracy principle has traditionally been employed to protect society against all "ganging-up" or concerted action in violation of its laws. No term passes that the Court does not sustain convictions based on that doctrine for violations of the antitrust laws or other statutes. However, there has recently entered the dialectic of politics a cliche used to condemn application of the conspiracy principle to Communists.
>
> "Guilt by Association" is an epithet frequently used and little explained, except that it is generally accompanied by another slogan, "guilt is personal." Of course it is; but personal guilt may be incurred by joining a conspiracy. That act of association makes one responsible for acts of others commited in pursuance of the association.[2]

In other words, just as one's values are expressed by one's actions, similarly one's guilt in sanctioning or promoting criminal or conspiratorial activities is recognized in one's consistent associations with criminals or conspirators in pursuance of their objectives.

The Importance of the Executive Director

But, it may be asked, why should such a record of associations to which Baldwin admitted be considered relevant to evaluating an organization like the ACLU? This question would naturally arise from the structure of the Union, made known in its official publications, a structure in which the administrative staff does not control the policy-making function. Roger Baldwin has insisted that the Union, particularly during his three decades as executive director, was never a staff-controlled group.[3] He claims, and with the facts obviously on his side, that he was only carrying out the policies voted on by the Board. He says he agreed with the vast majority of those policies and was able to execute them, with a few rare exceptions, in good faith. He attended Board meetings and responded, with advice or opinion when such was requested. Of course, he did work to change or affect Board policies when he felt strongly on an issue. This situation, which has existed from the Union's earliest years to the present, has apparently escaped the notice of some of the Union's anti-Communist critics. It would seem to require that we examine the members of the Board to detect only ideological partisanship, a subject which is certainly worth investigation.[4]

Yet we find that across the years, and especially since 1940, the Board has not included any significant representation of identified Communists, and has included a number of staunch anti-Communists. More of this will be examined in a following chapter, but we are here concerned with the decade in which, continuing the tradition of the 1920s, many of the policy-making Board members held the same views and affiliations as their executive director. We should also be critical enough to realize that our primary source of information concerning how well the staff of the ACLU reflected its Board's policies, particularly in the earlier decades, is the surviving chief-of-staff himself. And Roger Baldwin could easily be forgiven for administering the Board's general policies in a manner sufficiently selective and discriminating with regard to case and issue selection as to satisfy fully what he knows were his own noble ideals.

After all, his admirers have said he was the daily spirit of the organization. The Board members met regularly, but were involved in their own professional activities on the other days of the week. What got done between eight and five was what Baldwin and his staff workers wanted done. From the earliest years, Baldwin was in charge, handling most of the Union's correspondence and experiencing "power in manipulating people,"

in being the *eminence grise;* this was for many years practically the monopoly of Roger Baldwin, Richelieu to the public, Brother Joseph *vis a vis* the Board. . . . Roger Baldwin was certainly a strong executive, and while he had many admirers within the organization, he also had those who believed him too strong, I have tried to show that the extreme which views him as an absolute dictator is wrong; and also that the formal, external, technical picture of the organization as a functioning, representative corporation is wrong. Baldwin was a strong executive, partly by knowledge, partly due to the fact that he "chose" many of his associates and those technically his superiors, or chose the ones who chose them, partly by manipulation, but mainly by force of personality, fecundity of ideas, and charm of manner.[5]

The author of these conclusions, an obvious admirer of Baldwin, goes on to point out (correctly) that such administrative control is commonplace in many organizations and businesses. But in this case, whether or not the cats on the Board were away, the charming mouse seemed free to play.

131

It is because Roger Baldwin had so much influence over the daily work of the Union for at least thirty years, as well as over those who made the policies he was supposed merely to execute, that we must examine the ideology that he held at this time. Only such an examination will make it possible to assess accurately the accomplishment of *his* movement.

Mr. Baldwin's Convincing Performance

By 1930 Baldwin had not only made clear that "the cause we now serve is labor"[6] à la IWW, but he had taken a firm stand on the central issue on the Left, support for Soviet Russia. He had a problem with this position. Soviet Russia was a totalitarian dictatorship in which no civil liberties were protected. How could Baldwin defend the USSR and still manage to posture as a defender of American freedoms? As usual, he had an answer. In his 1928 book *Liberty Under the Soviets* he wrote:

> Such an attitude as I express toward the relation of economic to civil liberty may easily be construed as condoning in Russia repressions which I condemn in capitalist countries. It is true that I feel differently about them, because I regard them as unlike. Repressions in Western democracies are violations of professed constitutional liberties and I condemn them as such. Repressions in Soviet Russia are weapons of struggle in a transition period to Socialism.[7]

While acknowledging that dictatorship was somehow less objectionable if used to approach socialism, Baldwin was expressing his long-held view that "economic rights" were of equal or greater significance than individual rights. And, remembering our earlier discussion of the "right to enslave" that is essential to all talk about "economic rights," we must agree with Baldwin that the system he defended has accomplished its inherent goal.

Roger Baldwin repeated his favorable outlook on Stalin's police state in the article "Freedom in the U.S.A. and the U.S.S.R.," which appeared in the September, 1934, issue of *Soviet Russia Today*. The article "took a 'class position' and minimized defects in the USSR."[8] He had already elaborated on "economic democracy" in a letter written to the *New York Times* of April 11, 1933, concerning a story that had discussed a Communist-sponsored meeting:

> In "Topics of the Times" you called attention to my comment at a public meeting that "political democracy is moribund." You very properly ask why anyone who thinks democracy moribund should continue to be interested in civil liberties.
> Civil liberties like democracy are useful only as tools for social change. Political democracy as such a tool is obviously bankrupt throughout the world. Dictatorship in one form or another is rapidly replacing it. Harold Laski, expert in democracy, in a recent book comes to the conclusion that political democracy without economic democ-

racy is wholly unworkable. While civil liberties, too, have gone out of fashion, I am interested to maintain such freedom of agitation as can be won, not primarily as a political principle, but as a means of resolving economic conflict with a minimum of violence.[9]

This statement made publicly in the *New York Times* reveals much about Baldwin's motivations at the time. We see that he was influenced by Fabian Socialist Harold Laski[10] to a position of viewing individual freedom as valuable only to the extent it could be taken advantage of to promote coercive redistribution of property by the state. We may assume that his goals have changed since 1933, but there is no mistaking his own admission that, at least at that time, he saw civil liberties exactly as did the Communists who met at Bridgman, Michigan, eleven years earlier: a weapon to be used to institute Marxian socialism "with a minimum of violence."

Could it be that Baldwin had accepted the Marxian notion that a classless society was inevitable, believing that civil liberties simply would make the fated transition more pleasant for everyone? Or, did he, like Max Eastman, look forward to the violent revolution that Lenin instructed would be led by the dedicated cadre? Was he in favor of such an upheaval? In *Socialism of Our Times* he proclaimed:

I would rather see violent revolution than none at all. . . . Even the terrible cost of bloody revolution is a cheaper price to humanity than the continued exploitation and wreck of human life under the settled violence of the present system.[11]

In spite of these statements and the official Communist meetings he was attending in the early 1930s, Baldwin's desire to keep the ACLU separate in the public mind from the American Communist movement occasionally produced some misunderstandings with his less pragmatic comrades. As we have already noted, the Union was working with, and financing, the Communist-dominated International Labor Defense in joint projects aimed at defending Communist agitators arrested during labor disturbances. The ACLU attempted to keep publicly clear of these violent activities and assist indirectly through the ILD. In 1931 this policy produced some unpleasant rumblings from the ILD, which Baldwin discussed in a letter to the ILD's Louis Engdahl on October 13 of that year:

Dear Louis:

We note in the October number of the "Labor Defender" a center page article by you on the class war prisoners, in which you make the following statement:

"This campaign shall clarify more than ever our working class defense policies from the anti-working class programs and, therefore, the betrayals of the General Defense Committee, the American Civil Liberties Union, and similar organizations."

Since you do not specify these betrayals for which this organization is responsible, we would like to hear about them. We are not aware in our years of cooperation with the I.L.D. in working-class defense that any responsible official of the organization has ever [used] such strong language. We are at a loss to understand what prompts you to use it, particularly in the light of the facts that your office and ours are in daily cooperation on a score of matters, that we are jointly responsible for various cases and that you only recently requested us to take over a case which funds did not permit you to handle. Is this betrayal of the workingclass [sic]?

If you refer to our general point-of-view, which is not like the I.L.D.'s a class viewpoint, the language, it seems to us could have been better chosen. We have never taken any exception to characterization of our viewpoint as bourgeois, or to specific criticism of a line of conduct with which our critics may disagree. We are subject to making errors, like all the rest. But "betrayals" is a strong word, and in the interest of our common work we would like to know what it means.[12]

It was particularly such "common work" that led to the ACLU being cited along with the Communist-controlled ILD in the report of Congressman Hamilton Fish III's Special Committee to Investigate Communist Activities in the United States, released in 1931. That report correctly concluded "that the main function of the ACLU is to attempt to protect the communists in their advocacy of force and violence to overthrow the Government. . . ."[13] As we have seen, Baldwin was just as interested, if not more so, in the advocacy as he was in the protection.

His public statements and affiliations after 1931 reveal no desire to avoid such reasonable criticism, which would again come from federal and state investigative bodies.[14] In an article appearing in the *Harvard Class Book* of 1935, spotlighting Baldwin's class of 1905 on its thirtieth anniversary, he was quoted as saying:

I have continued directing the unpopular fight for the rights of agitation, as Director of the American Civil Liberties Union on the side of engaging in many efforts to aid working class causes. I have been to Europe several times, mostly in connection with international radical activities, chiefly against war, fascism and imperialism; and have traveled constantly in the United States to areas of conflict over worker's rights to strike and organize. . . .

My chief aversion is the system of greed, private profit, privilege and violence which makes up the control of the world today, and which has brought it to the tragic crisis of unprecedented hunger and unemployment. I am opposed to the New Deal because it strives to strengthen and prolong production for private profit. At bottom I am for conserving the full powers of every person on earth by expanding them to their individual limits.

Therefore, I am for Socialism, disarmament, and ultimately for abolishing the State itself as an instrument of violence and compulsion.

I seek the social ownership of property, the abolition of the propertied class and sole control by those who produce wealth. Communism is, of course, the goal. It all sums up into one single purpose—the abolition of the system of dog-eat-dog under which we live, and the substitution by the most effective non-violence possible of a system of cooperative ownership and use of all wealth.[15]

If such was needed, this statement makes even clearer the position of solidarity Baldwin held with the Communists in 1935. His consistent opposition to economic fascism, as represented by the New Deal, derived from the fact that Washington was only controlling, rather than owning major industries. This opposition vanished as the Roosevelt welfare state blossomed. Baldwin's long attraction to the welfare state led him to favor the same measures of statist control that were in 1935 being practiced in Fascist Italy and Nazi Germany.[16]

But Baldwin did not spend the 1930s just making pro-Communist statements when his work load at the Union would permit the time. In addition to his promotion of the Communists' legal objectives, he became one of the most active, well-known participants in the galaxy of Communist-front organizations that was established throughout the world as the Popular or United Front, in America as a network with Sidney Hillman's CIO National Citizens Political Action Committee at its center.[17]

The Entangling Alliances

It is difficult to talk of the history of the Communist fronts established during this time, or of the thousands of prominent Americans who joined them, without having to meet some objections at the outset. Because these organizations were Communist fronts, established by party members and under their control, they postured as serving idealistic causes and attracted many innocent people as nominal sponsors and members, most of whom were undoubtedly unaware of the actual Communist influence or control. Thus, a person's membership in such a group, unless continued well after the group was factually and publicly exposed as Communist, would mean nothing concerning their position of loyalty. But Roger Baldwin and many of his fellow ACLU leaders, notably Reverend Harry Ward[18] and Reverend John Haynes Holmes,[19] were in a position to know about the Communist influence in such groups from considerable prior experience. We have already seen that Baldwin understood the position of the ILD's leadership. We have seen that he expressed interest openly in the objectives secretly held by those who controlled these fronts. For Baldwin a lengthy record of Communist-front affiliations during this decade is just more evidence that he was being consistent by means of his maximum participation in the conspiratorial strategy the Communists were using to enlist the aid of idealistic dupes for the promotion of their plans.

And his record was indeed lengthy.[20] The "good causes" with which he was associated, by designation of the Special Committee on Un-American Activities, included early activities in the Labor Defense Council and later the International Labor Defense, both Communist-dominated organizations in the vanguard of the Mooney-Billings case.[21] We have also already mentioned his work as an officer of the American Fund for Public Service, or the Garland Fund, a major source of support for Communist Party projects and publications.[22]

In a number of Communist fronts, Baldwin was joined by other ACLU National Committee or Board members. In 1928 he served with Clarence Darrow, Scott Nearing, William Z. Foster, Louis Budenz, Robert W. Dunn, Robert Morss Lovett, and Arthur Garfield Hays on the National Committee of the "Communist-controlled" All-America Anti-Imperialist League.[23] Ten years later Baldwin was on the Executive Committee of the "Communist-front" American Friends of Spanish Democracy, along with Communist ACLU Board member Corliss Lamont. John Dewey was vice-chairman and Holmes, Lovett, Wise, Archibald Mac-Leish, and Oswald Garrison Villard, were among present or future ACLU leaders on its committee and that of its Medical Bureau.[24] Baldwin, Ward, and Lovett were active in 1938 as members of the front that called itself the American League for Peace and Democracy, a positive-sounding mirror image of the earlier American League Against War and Fascism that J.B. Matthews and Ward had directed with the assistance of such Communists as Lincoln Steffens and Earl Browder.[25] Lovett, Baldwin, Darrow, Hays, Holmes, David Starr Jordan, Norman Thomas, and Jane Addams had served together as early as 1926 on the Advisory Board of Russian Reconstruction Farms, Inc.[26]

Roger Baldwin served on both the Advisory Board and the Sponsoring Committee of the Communist American Student Union in 1937-38, along with ACLU leaders Dunn, Thomas, Lovett, Osmond Fraenkel, and a professor who, although leftist, would prove a sincere opponent of those who make wars, Harry Elmer Barnes.[27] During the same years, a similar Communist front, the American Youth Congress, not only boasted of Baldwin, Barnes, Lovett, and MacLeish, but also included earlier Union figures Lillian Wald and Communist Rose Schneiderman on its National Advisory Committee, or Board.[28]

Communists Robert Dunn and Corliss Lamont served on the Editorial Board of the Communist book club called Book Union, Inc.; Baldwin, Huebsch, and Lovett served on its Advisory Board.[29] The monthly selections in 1937 and 1938 were just what might be expected. Although this effort was obviously peripheral to civil liberties, the campaign to defend Earl Browder, in which the same gentlemen participated, may not have been.[30]

Certainly the identified Communist "transmission belt" called the Consumers National Federation represented a predictable sort of concern with *some* economic issues in the mind of one of its sponsors, Roger Baldwin, who was thus able to get in on the early Communist-controlled infancy of organizations that have developed into today's "consumerism" movement.[31]

In 1933 Baldwin, Ward, Lovett, Holmes, and Lamont joined with some of America's leading Communists as endorsers of the Communist-front Friends of the Soviet Union, which also presented a reception committee to welcome a group of visiting Soviet airmen. The committee included Budenz; Margaret DeSilver, widow of Albert, who died after serving alongside Baldwin until 1924; Hays; Holmes; and Lillian Wald.[32]

Other Communist fronts that enlisted the support of, sought the assistance of, or

136

otherwise made use of Roger Baldwin and other ACLU officials were the 1936 Joint Committee for the Defense of the Brazilian People[33] and, by 1940, both the League of Young Southerners[34] and the Greater New York Emergency Conference on Inalienable Rights.[35]

Tribute was paid in 1936 to veteran American Communist Ella Reeve ("Mother") Bloor at a banquet sponsored by Baldwin, Budenz, Dunn, Nearing, and another earlier ACLU National Committeeperson, Communist Anna Rochester. Baldwin and Budenz were joined by Lovett, Upton Sinclair, and Communist Elizabeth Gurley Flynn of the ACLU Board, in establishing the Mother Bloor Celebration Committee for the dear old lady's seventy-fifth birthday.[36]

Efforts to suppress Clifford Odets' "Communist play," *Waiting for Lefty* in 1935 provided ample excuse for the creation of a National Committee Against Censorship of the Theater Arts, which had official ACLU assistance.[37] And the endorsement of Baldwin and Lamont was given that year to a Communist front promoting "economic democracy" as the National Congress for Unemployment and Social Insurance,[38] an outfit closely related to the New York Professional Workers Conference on Social Insurance.[39]

Numerous Communists fronts were formed during this period to champion cases of specific criminal defendants. In 1935 Baldwin met with Lamont for the Political Prisoners Bail Fund Committee,[40] and with Schneiderman shortly thereafter in the Committee to Aid the Striking Fleischer Artists.[41]

Outstanding Crusades

Two of the most famous cases of the 1930s were the Scottsboro Boys case in 1931 and the Bonus Army march on Washington the following year. In the first case, nine Negro boys were charged with the rape of two white women near Scottsboro, Alabama. In addition to the racist emotionalism that threatened to obscure the process of a fair trial for the youths, the testimony of the alleged victims was clouded by attempts on the part of the defense to make the most of their somewhat questionable backgrounds and behavior at the time of the original state trial. That defense was handled by representatives of the ACLU and the Communist ILD, which soon parlayed the case into a nation-wide cause for recruiting interested sympathizers into Communist ranks. A special Communist front was organized in 1933 to promote the case. Baldwin and J.B. Matthews, representing the Fellowship of Reconciliation, were among a host of Communists and pro-Communists serving on its Executive Committee. For what injustices may have been constituted in the original convictions, this campaign managed not only to fan flames of racial hatred that were to explode in places as far away as Harlem, but it also was successful in saving from capital punishment the seven boys who were convicted. They instead served substantial sentences after their final appeals.[42]

In the second incident, a number of World War I veterans decided in 1932 to organize a march on Washington to force Congress to pass legislation that would award them immediately a bonus due to be paid in 1945. As with the Scottsboro Boys case, the Communists saw this as an ideal project to infiltrate until it was fully under their control. The opposition was their outstanding target, President Hoover. By June 8 the Communists had taken control of the effort and led 11,000 veterans in a march down Pennsylvania Avenue. Violence was engineered as Hoover used force to evict the assembly. The Communists tried to escalate the turmoil into a military takeover of the nation's capital city, actually succeeding in capturing a number of government office buildings. United States Army detachments, under command of General Douglas MacArthur, firmly retaliated, and the activists, as well as their victimized dupes, were driven from the area. This response served marvelously as an excuse for much protest by, and through, the Union.[43]

These affiliations and cases—promoted primarily by the Union through Baldwin's work—use of ACLU funds, and the ACLU long-time practice of dealing with cases by official protests to the government and the submission of friend-of-the-court briefs, with rarer instances of courtroom pleading by its better attorneys, illustrate well the unmistakable pro-Communist trend of the "Red Decade" with which the ACLU was quite in step. Other famous cases were taken during this decade. These include more attempts to protect the First Amendment rights of Jehovah's Witnesses and the famous anticensorship ruling that ACLU attorney Morris Ernst won in the case of James Joyce's "novel" *Ulysses*. The Union opened up the domains of local dictocrats in Alabama and New Jersey to the practice of free speech and assembly, though it missed the point made earlier in this book that the ability of local governments to impose such restrictions resulted from the fact that one of Baldwin's goals was in force in those cities: government owned some of the land, providing the excuse for arbitrary permissions over those wishing to use it for political purposes, or as Mayor ("I Am the Law") Hague might have echoed Baldwin, in Jersey City there was something of a "system of cooperative ownership and use of all wealth." The only major case in which the Union stood in opposition to the New Deal was its 1937 defense of the Ford Motor Company's right to disseminate antiunion material against prohibitions on such activities by the NLRB. Why they chose this case involving Ford from among the thousands of other violations of property rights which were then occuring is anyone's guess. Could it be that Ford's intensive campaign of technical assistance to the Soviet Union had influenced the decision?[44]

The record we have examined is only partially illustrative of the orientation of Baldwin and the other ACLU National Board members and committeemen whose names were given above. Exhaustive study of the United Front in the thirties will reveal to anyone that these ACLU officials formed an elite cadre of activists not only in the Union, but in virtually every major organization that the Communists established. Although Roger Baldwin, in effective administrative control of the ACLU, gave every impression that "he planned it that way," he still maintained a significant enough distinction between his and his fellow's multitude of extracurricular activities and the official work projects of the ACLU for the Dies Committee to find any evaluation of the Union in 1939 as a Communist front still inconclusive without further investigation.[45]

Shockwaves from the War

But in 1939 something happened in the world that paralysed the American Left and separated the sincere anti-Fascists from those who had used the banner of "antifascism" as a cloak for promoting whatever Stalin decreed. It was not just the outbreak of the European war. The struggle against "war and fascism" remained the struggle for "peace and democracy," although it would be some time before such ACLU scholars as Harry Elmer Barnes learned the degree to which the new war and America's entry in 1941 had been engineered by high-ranking conspirators on the model of the World War I pattern.[46] But the "nonaggression" alliance for conquest that was signed in that year between Stalin and Hitler was the stunning blow that, according to the best authorities, more than anything else set the stage for a dividing of pro-Communist ranks and determined the course of the ACLU for the next twenty years.

10

1940-1959: The Stalin-Hitler Pact and the ACLU's Temporary "Anticommunism"

After 1936, ACLU Chairman Harry Ward continued to lead the American left's crusade against war and fascism. The anti-Communist revolt in Spain and the German occupation of Czechoslovakia were the major events exciting their concerns. However, in 1939, the alliance Stalin formed with Hitler prior to their joint division of Poland soon parted the "Red Sea" of fellow travelers. Hitler had proven that, without foreign assistance, he could not provide sufficient excuse for another world war.

By the end of 1938, something of a faction had formed on the ACLU National Board as a result of concern over the degree of Communist influence in the Union, or, at least, how public knowledge of this problem was adversely affecting the group's respectability. Far from being anticollectivist, the opposition to the Communists included: Morris Ernst, Roger Riis, Elmer Rice, Anti-Communist Socialist Norman Thomas, and to some extent, John Haynes Holmes. The Board also contained a strongly pro-Communist faction, which included Communist Robert Dunn, Corliss Lamont, Nathan Greene, Abraham Isserman, William P. Spofford, Mary Van Kleeck, and, on most occasions, Osmond Fraenkel. This leftist group also included Harry Ward, who, as chairman of the Union, was a prime object of contention. Other Board members, including Arthur Garfield Hays, apparently avoided siding with either faction. When the Soviet Union signed its nonaggression alliance with Nazi Germany and both together began dividing up Poland, the issue of the Board having Ward as its chairman, or "recent" Communist recruit Elizabeth Gurley Flynn in its ranks, came to an inevitable head.[1]

The Move Toward a Consistent Leadership

Although members of the Board had been unsuccessful in getting passed even a weak antitotalitarian resolution during early 1939, the response was so strong after the pact was signed in the fall that in October Roger Baldwin resigned from Ward's American League for Peace and Democracy. Considering his apparent blindness to the mounting facts of Soviet brutality and internal repression prior to that year, Baldwin's action indicates that things must have been getting hot.

A crisis soon developed over the division that existed on the Board. The pro-Communists and Communists there refused to waver from the Red switch to support of an alliance with Hitler, just as Stalin ordered. Roger Baldwin, throughout the crisis that lasted well over a year, rode the fence amid pleas by his friends on both sides to champion their cause. Once again he found the issue of civil liberties on a world scale less important for him to champion when he felt it was more important to do everything he could as ACLU executive director to hold the organization together.

In October, 1939, Margaret De Silver, Riis, Thomas, and Holmes started appealing to Baldwin for Ward's resignation. Although he had requested not to be considered for chairmanship again in 1940, Ward appealed for his own case. In a series of rather abusive letters aimed at his critics, Ward exhibited a propensity for inconsistency of the Baldwin magnitude. He pointed out that only one member of the National Committee, Andrew Furuseth, had been expelled. This was not because Furuseth had joined the Ku Klux Klan, but because, according to Ward, he had *taken the action* of advocating wider application of criminal syndicalism laws. Ward's record obviously contained no *actions,* only opinions and statements.

In January, 1940, there was an attempt by the Board to placate the "anti-Communists" with a resolution that, along with other actions of the Board, amounted to nothing. About this time Baldwin conceived of a more clever way to solve the dispute. He recommended that the warring members of the Board be appointed to head special committees on broad issues relating to the Union's concern, adding that these committee heads should not also serve on the Board. Communists Dunn and Flynn, along with Isserman and Van Kleeck, were asked to serve on the Committee on Civil Rights in Labor Relations. Baldwin figured that this would avoid the unpleasant necessity of an expulsion resolution, keeping the pro-Communists happy, but he said a statement on the issues would have to be made for public consumption. This deceptive compromise was challenged by

Norman Thomas, who threatened to expose it if not remedied. It was Thomas' act of calling Baldwin's hand that left the Board with no recourse but to pass on February 1 a resolution barring believers in totalitarianism from the National Board, National Committee, and the staff of the ACLU.[2]

Ward resigned on February 26, but Flynn, learning quickly the tactics of her "recent" comrades, refused to cooperate and decided to test the resolution. Her decision to stay soon led to expressed doubts concerning whether or not the Union meant business. The result was her hearing, or "trial," on the turbulent evening of May 7. The situation was made more difficult for members of the board because some respected her record of work with the Union and other causes, even those who realized she had to go. A tie vote on the matter of her Communist affiliation was broken by Holmes, and she was "convicted" by a larger majority of the issue of having authored a series of attacks on the Union for the Communist press. In her corner throughout the voting remained those who comprised the pro-Communist faction, along with Dorothy Kenyon and Jonathan Bingham. The issue was decided: Flynn was out. In spite of this, most of those who had sided with her continued their work with the Union, with Margaret De Silver and John Dos Passos resigning from the Union. (Both later rejoined.) Others, with perhaps more partisan interest in the issues of the case, chose not to let others forget it, even into the late 1960s.[3]

But, at least the Board, as distinct from Baldwin, had taken a nominal position consistent with its principles in response to glaring world events. And this fact made the ACLU more interesting and attractive to many liberal intellectuals in all fields, most of whom were not interested in joining a Communist front.

Contributions of New Personalities

It was into this newly "anti-Communist" civil liberties organization, in the first year of Baldwin's third decade as executive director, that Clifford Forster was invited to take the place of Staff Counsel Jerome Britchie, who was being inducted into the Army.

For the sake of the Union, Baldwin's choice of Forster proved a wise decision. The Yale law graduate from New York had a deeply profound and, for the period, remarkably consistent libertarian outlook. His intellectual curiosity had grown and matured as a result of his European travels, and by 1938 he had organized a discussion group called the Open Mind, which was devoted to a free and balanced airing of all views on leading issues. In spite of his idealistic libertarian outlook, he had avoided falling prey to the United Front of the 1930s by being fortunate enough to marry someone who had witnessed the truth about communism in Russia during 1928 and 1929. Forster's anticommunism contributed to the staff an influence that, along with that exerted by a few Board members, allowed the Union to maintain some semblance of consistency during the years he was there. And next to Roger

Baldwin himself, who has made clear his own resistance to the facts, Clifford Forster knows more about the daily national office work of the Union from 1941 to 1954 than anyone else.[4]

Although Forster would eventually leave the Union as part of a minority of Board and staff members, we can be sure that his perspective was not unlike that of members of the Board who, over those years, would only meet together an average of ninety minutes a week. One former Board member, attorney C. Dickerman Williams of New York, has essentially the same recollections.[5]

A Majority Maintains Old Policies

The most dramatic result of the new antitotalitarian policy was the accelerating growth of the Union membership and the number of influential people who joined the Board, Committee and staff. Among the officers there remained Baldwin as director, Holmes as the new chairman of the Board, with Hays and Ernst remaining as general counsels. One National Committee vice-chairman was authoress Pearl Buck.

Corliss Lamont remained on the Board (though probably with less influence than before),[6] along with Ernst, Fraenkel, Hays, Thomas, and Huebsch, who served also as treasurer. To Thomas' ranks were added two staunch anti-Communists, Merlyn S. Pitzele and C. Dickerman Williams.

Among the many famous, though generally leftist, personalities who remained on or joined the National Committee during the 1940s were Melvyn Douglas, Harry Emerson Fosdick, Robert M. Hutchins, Max Lerner, Robert Morss Lovett, Archibald MacLeish, Francis J. McConnell, A.J. Muste, J. Robert Oppenheimer, G. Bromley Oxnam, A. Philip Randolph, Will Rogers, Jr., Arthur M. Schlesinger, Jr., and Aubrey Williams.[7] Their influence was apparently sufficient to keep the Union concentrating on the same issues and kinds of cases that had monopolized Baldwin's time before, in spite of the fact that they were now officially *opposed to the beneficiaries of their assistance* in so many of those cases. A review of the leading ones, against the background of simultaneous major events, will help set the stage for consideration of the Union's ultimate compromise.

Conscription Rears Its Ugly Head

Nineteen forty-one brought not only Hitler's fateful invasion of Russia, which produced instant enthusiasm for war in the hearts of pro-Communist stalwarts like Lamont, but also the event which intellectuals across the spectrum worked so hard to prevent: America's entry into another world war. The year's conscription act reintroduced the issue of rights for conscientious objectors, and the Union established a national committee for that cause, under the leadership of Ernest Angell of New York. A member of the American Legion, which would remain a continual foe of the Union, Angell assisted in the cases of hundreds of resistors during the war. With the leftist orientation being stronger in Washington during the New Deal than even that which had existed during the Wilson Administration, the handling of this category of cases proved encouragingly successful.[8]

Free Speech for Communists Only

On the domestic scene, the war had increased interest in the subject of subversive propaganda activities by both Communists and Fascists. The Dies Committee became the permanent House Committee on Un-American Activities. And in 1940 there was passed the Smith Act which, among other things, made criminal advocacy of the violent overthrow of the United States government. Those states that did not already have their own sedition or criminal syndicalism laws followed suit, many of them by passing what amounted to mini–Smith Acts. The Union, which, as early as 1931, had published its position that anyone had the right to *advocate* acts of violence as long as no action was taken to carry them out,[9] was plunged into a long series of cases to restore their position. It should be noted that although the Union's work, commencing in 1941, on behalf of Communists prosecuted under the Smith Act was enormously helpful and welcome interference from the Communist viewpoint, it was still undertaken by *some* ACLU leaders for distinctly anti-Communist, libertarian reasons.[10] The Smith Act cases and others under similar laws passed after 1950, led to the Supreme Court's evolving doctrine of "clear and present danger," or an imminent danger of violence resulting from any mere advocacy, which must be proven before anyone is deprived of their First Amendment freedoms. Union Board members and counsel did not object to the legislation that was passed requiring propaganda by foreign agents to be published with an identification of its source. Though this seems a bit inconsistent since the publication of such material violates no one's rights, ACLU officials, like Morris Ernst, supported the law because they felt it contributed somewhat to more free and better-informed public discussion.[11]

Whatever can be said in favor the Union's criticisms of the Smith Act and the misbehavior of congressional investigators, its brief record of ideological consistency was seriously marred by what amounted to partisanship concerning which persons should be defended from Smith Act prosecutions. That there was still a very strong pro-Communist faction on the Board, in addition to the leadership remaining under Baldwin and Holmes, was revealed in the relative paucity of expressed concern over Soviet imperialism during the "war against fascism."[12] If it was not obvious prior to 1944, it manifested embarrassingly during the Mass Sedition, or Conspiracy, Trial of 1944.[13]

In that episode, the federal government attempted to prosecute for sedition a number of citizens, some of German and Russian descent, who had been leading spokesmen for viewpoints ranging from Charles Lindbergh's isolationist America First Committee to claims about the "Zionist-Jew conspiracy" that was imagined to be behind Communism to outright solidarity with Nazi Germany. The group included Gerald Winrod, Elizabeth Dilling, William Dudley Pelley of the occult Silver Shirts, and American fascist Lawrence Dennis. The trial bore a strong resemblance to the harrassment of outspoken Britons of similar mixed opinions that began in 1939.[14]

Roger Baldwin looks back upon this incident as one of his rare disappointments with the Union's integrity.[15] Clifford Forster also felt that the Union should have applied its opposition to the Smith Act provisions inherent as issues in this case. But because a number of the defendants were pro-Nazi, and others slightly confused anti-Communists *who had attacked the Union,* some Board members responded by preventing the Union from getting actively involved in the case, although they stated that they would watch its proceedings for any violations of due process. A number of Board members thought that some of the defendants were paid agents of Germany, not just sympathetic propagandists for Hitler. (They exhibited no similar doubts during later Smith Act prosecutions of the leaders of the Moscow-financed Communist apparatus in America.) Of course, this was a mere pretense for leaving the case alone, as was made clear in a book published by the National Civil Rights Committee, a front established to support the defendants:

Not one whit of such evidence was ever promised in the prosecutor's opening statement or produced in seven and a half months of trial, except as to four defendants, and it was a very minor part of the case against them. This shallow pretext served to mask the true reasons for the refusal of the American Civil Liberties Union to take an interest in the number one civil liberties case of the war—a trial in which any impartial lawyer studying the indictment and the known historical record must have concluded that there was something wrong with the government's case. For the American Civil Liberties Union to have said anything about German money in connection with this trial, while it was either in preparation or in course, was utterly indefensible, since it would not have made the slightest difference whether any defendants had received German money or not so far as proving the charge of the indictment was concerned. One of the defendants, George Sylvester Viereck, had unquestionably been in the pay of the German Government before Pearl Harbor as a registered German agent. The charge, as the legal staff of the American Civil Liberties Union knew perfectly well, was not that the accused had been German agents. The charge was that they had conspired to cause insubordination in the armed forces.[16]

Other Wartime Issues

Other domestic issues, relating both to the war and New Deal policies, exhibited a precarious mixture of a little consistency with the usual "selective" aid and

145

comfort to those whose First Amendment freedoms were threatened. The Union and some local affiliates tried in 1942 to make a test case out of the protest that was rising against the Roosevelt Administration's police-state repressions of Japanese in California, most of whom were second-generation Americans. [17] A number of factors, including the hesitancy on the part of some in the ACLU to press the matter too hard with their leftist friends in Washington and Sacramento, served to keep the disgraceful program in effect. Its victims, whose property had been seized, would not see justice done until a quarter of a century later. The national ACLU and its California affiliates at least exhausted every avenue of legal defense available in their overall unsuccessful effort to defend the rights of Japanese-Americans.

Although it was effective in gaining more protections for the rights of Jehovah's Witnesses in a procession of flag salute cases, the Union accumulated a very poor record on the issue of the fascist economic system which FDR was using to his political advantage.[18] It is true that, after New Deal laws had given labor unions virtually a legal monopoly over labor in many industries, the Union realized in 1943 that the new legalized private concentrations of market power were ripe for criticism because they lacked adequate internal due process in their proceedings.[19] The fact that the Union did not recognize that the abusive essence of the issue was the compulsory legal status of unions across the country was exemplary of a tendency that led to ACLU support of the Fair Employment Practices Act and its cooperation in 1943 with the federal commission it created. The totalitarian implications of this and other "protective" economic measures at the time were, however, obvious to certain ACLU staff and Board members.[20]

Other national test cases were fought over policies of state and local legal segregation.[21] But by 1945 and the war's end, the interests would loom large on the Union's horizon until the end of the decade were international, despite the continued effort to posture as being opposed to communism *and* the House Committee on Un-American Activities.[22]

Internationalist Idealism and Blindness

A new opportunity for expanded work appeared with the Allied "denazification" of the postwar world and the establishment of that dream-come-true for Roger Baldwin, the institution that the First World War failed to produce, the United Nations. Though some ACLU Board members expressed concern over the near monopoly of pro-Communists, most of whom were later identified as Communists, and fellow travelers who were the American "founding fathers" of the UN,[23] the Union was represented by Baldwin at the 1948 Paris meeting of the UN General Assembly, which adopted the so-called Universal Declaration of Human Rights. Baldwin, Hays, and Board member Norman Cousins assisted General Lucius Clay in the administration of the Allied occupation of Germany in 1948,[24] but only after the executive director had returned from a trip to Japan and Korea in 1947, a mission to assist with civil liberties protections there at the request of General Douglas MacArthur.[25] Although MacArthur had been the Union's target in 1932 for his conduct of the Bonus March eviction, his request for Baldwin's aid had been granted as, if nothing else, a wise move of strategy that would later discourage the light of congressional inquiries into the Union's record.

As the Union moved to operate on an international scale, it quickly lost its civil liberties objectivity there, too, in a manner which reflected the policy on the Sedition Trial. The Union had always held that, regardless of the type of crimes with which a person was being charged, he deserved a fair trial replete with all protections of due process. A fair trial meant one in which the defendants were not tried by their accusers. It implied that the prosecutors, if guilty of the same kind of offenses, would also be tried and punished. It also implied that objective legal principles, not the arbitrary whims of the prosecution, would govern the entire proceedings. The ACLU upheld all of these standards, at least by giving lip service to them, until there occurred the greatest violation of substantive and procedural due process in any legal case of this century: the Nuremberg War Crimes Trials. The ACLU's silence on this massive injustice, which was obvious to a number of leading jurists and some Union staff and Board members, surely dwarfs their inaction on the Sedition Trial.[26]

With the record in on the 1940s, the Union had demonstrated very little change in the highly selective application of its principles to outstanding events and issues, a consequence that meant that its official "anticommunism" had had little or no effect in altering the practical *results* of a majority of these efforts, which were as pleasing to the left-wing collectivists in Washington and Moscow as ever before.

The Union's departure from any substantial anticommunism would become increasingly apparent in the 1950s. Although the years of Senator Joseph McCarthy's notoriety would make a crisis of the problem of lingering procommunism among ACLU leaders, the radicalism of major local affiliates of the Union during the prior decade had already become a widely publicized problem for the national office.[27]

The "Departure" of Roger Baldwin

In 1950 a major staff change occurred. After thirty years of service,[28] during which he had gained the friendship and respect of his coworkers, including those who often differed with him,[29] Roger Baldwin retired from his post as executive director. The man who took Baldwin's place was a wealthy Quaker internationalist and former economics professor at Swarthmore College, Patrick Murphy Malin.[30] Some who have written on the ACLU have made a point of the fact that Malin arrived on the job with no record of past affiliations more subversive than the International YMCA. Some saw his appointment as a reconfirmation of the

147

Union's 1940 resolution and another reason why the heat of the congressional investigations of subversive activities, which were well underway, was not turned on the Union. Yet, in spite of Malin's lack of Baldwin credentials, he was known to hold the same interest in world government schemes that would, to this day, occupy the man he replaced in something called the International League for the Rights of Man, the major link between the ACLU and UN.[31] In fact, Malin had some credentials that Baldwin was never wealthy enough to possess: more direct access to the elite of the nation's financial, political, educational, and philanthropic establishment, as well as membership in the Council on Foreign Relations.[32]

The Nexus in the New Director

Malin fairly completed the circuit of influence that we examined as having existed since the founding of the Union: the relationship between super-rich collectivists, their foundations, and domestic and foreign movements that caused or encouraged "problems" that made more acceptable as "solutions" growing central government control at home and over the entire world.[33] He was not the only ACLU leader belonging to the CFR, not all members of which necessarily agreed with the collectivist policies they met *secretly* to discuss. Malin's CFR membership would indicate little or nothing, had not other CFR members joined him at the ACLU: Union Board members Richard S. Childs and Norman Cousins; Union National Committee members J. Robert Oppenheimer, Elmo Roper, Arthur M. Schlesinger, Jr., Palmer Hoyt, Jr., and William F. Butler. Corliss Lamont never made the CFR, but he was well represented there by his multimillionaire father, Thomas, who was so helpful with the rise of Bolshevism as a Morgan man.[34]

The War Against Anti-Communists

Because the Union as an organization was not an object of Senator Joseph McCarthy's investigations, although a member of the staff and a member of the Board were criticized by him,[35] the ACLU concerned itself with taking related cases arising from the Government's loyalty review programs,[36] as well as carrying the torch against the campaign of voluntary "blacklisting" that was developed in the private communications and entertainment media.[37]

Some members of the Board supported the purposes of McCarthy's investigations, not only because they knew he was on firm ground despite any personal limitations on his part or on the part of some persons on whom he unfortunately was relying,[38] but also because his investigations threatened so mightily the international conspiracy that the Union's 1940 resolution had condemned. Because the Union had no grounds for others hostile to McCarthy to use in making test cases out of his work, it primarily continued to talk about everything unfavorable to civil liberties, never concentrating on an appraisal of the evidence that supported McCarthy's charges.[39]

It was in this propaganda campaign, which led to the contrived Senate Watkins Committee's 1954 censure recommendation, that one saw the participation of the Union in the largely CFR-populated assault on McCarthy, so reminiscent of the attacks that had disgraced Harry Daugherty in 1924. The Council and its major financial source, the Rockefeller Foundation, had proven their determination to "rewrite" history and frustrate anyone who might attempt to call their hand.[40] The seemingly eternal mythmaking about the period of "McCarthyism" remains as the outstanding propaganda achievement of leading representatives of the CFR and the Rockefeller foundation. And, for the Union in 1952, the censure recommendation against Senator McCarthy was "one of the greatest milestones in the history of American civil liberties."[41]

A close associate of the Union and the CFR in this anti-anti-Communist crusade was the Ford Foundation's Fund for the Republic.[42] In 1955 the Fund embarked on a project that would present the debate over the alleged abuses by congressional investigating committees of individuals' Fifth Amendment right to be free from "self-incrimination." In addition to a selection of anti-anti-Communist books, the Fund distributed Harvard Law School Dean Erwin Griswold's *The Fifth Amendment Today* and C. Dickerman Williams' *Problems of the Fifth Amendment,* which presented a much narrower view of the Fifth Amendment than the Griswold article. The Williams article also specifically answered Griswold's arguments with respect to the use of the Fifth Amendment in congressional investigations under the law as it then stood.

The Fund was very fair, it appeared, in bringing both viewpoints to the public's attention, at least until it was exposed as having distributed thirty-five times as many copies of Griswold's work than that of Williams, as well as not having distributed copies of a later attack on Griswold by *Marxist* Sidney Hook.[43]

Why did the Fund do these things? In response to that question in December, 1953, Ford Foundation President Rowan Gaither had told Reece Committee investigator Norman Dodd that

Most of us here were, at one time or another, active in either the O.S.S., the State Department, or the European Economic Administration. During those times, and without exception, we operated under directives issued by the White House, the substance of which was to the effect that we should make every effort to so alter life in the United States as to make possible a comfortable merger with the Soviet Union . . . . We are continuing to be guided by just such directives.[44]

Having appropriately responded to this disclosure, Dodd was destined to become as popular with the Left, including the ACLU, as had been Dr. William Wirt. The ACLU did not merely complement the campaign of anti-anticommunism waged by the Fund for the Republic. The collaboration included mass distribution of an ACLU annual report by the Fund and the Fund's bankrolling of a book on civil rights that portrayed the Union in a very favorable light. But the reader may well wonder how the Union came to cooperate with an outfit such as the Fund for the Republic in matters of great importance to the Communists but of little substantive relation to civil liberties. What about the 1940 resolution that McCarthy could not have better phrased? What about the presence of such outspoken anti-Communists as Clifford Forster, Dickerman Williams, Mel Pitzele, and Irving Ferman[45] in the Union's leadership? Why were their efforts now becoming the object of the Union's attacks? The answer is that, by 1955, they had recognized the collectivist recapture of the Union under Patrick Murphy Malin, and they were gone for good.

Exodus of the Uncompromisers

The dispute that resulted in this exodus is not very well known outside the ranks of those who were involved. It never received the publicity attention given to the 1940 crisis, perhaps because it signaled the Union's formal departure from that position of short-lived "anticommunism," a return to the orientation of the pre-1940 years that would increasingly show itself into the 1960s. It was, however, as pivotal an event in the ACLU's history of left-wing affiliation in the 1950s as had been the Stalin-Hitler pact in 1939. We cannot conclude our survey of this period without defining it.

The ACLU Board debated and finally adopted a number of resolutions between September, 1952, and February, 1954, dealing with major issues raised in connection with Communist Party membership. Three of these were obviously the most important and were adopted by the Board in revised form by May 4, 1953.[46] Board and staff members were clearly divided on the issues. Clifford Forster and Merlyn Pitzele were anxious for the resolutions to take as firm and realistic an anti-Communist position as possible. Corliss Lamont opposed everything about them, from original drafts to the revisions that were suggested. Even the superficial antitotalitarian tone and wording of the resolutions were too much for him. The majority of the Board supported the resolutions, leading to another clear division of factions in the New York headquarters. Forster recalls that his faction, and the oposition's, met often during those months to discuss the resolutions and prepare arguments. At least his group did, and he can only assume that the others did likewise, since they always seemed to arrive at Board meetings with prepared drafts.

The first resolution repeated the tone of the 1940 and 1949 resolutions in that it condemned all totalitarian ideologies and all organizations upholding them. It implied that the Communist Party, U.S.A. was part of a "world-wide revolutionary movement'' dominated by the Soviet Union. However, the statement went on to say that ''the ACLU does not hold that all persons who submit to the Communist Party's rigid totalitarian discipline (whether formal members or not), are engaged in illegal secret conspiracy or illegal acts.'' Although the Union recognized that some employment circumstances would justify a consideration of a person's Communist affiliations, ''it will defend those rights regardless of the associations of individuals to whom they may be denied.''

In this proposal the Union was assuming that the Communist apparatus in America functioned as two distinct and separate parts: an obnoxious but actual political party and an underground subversion and espionage network. This assumption was clearly unrealistic on the basis of the evidence that had been collected by the government for espionage prosecutions in years immediately prior to this. In fact, it reflected adherence to exactly the Communist line that was discovered during the 1922 Bridgman raid. The Communists would pretend that their illegal Number One was unrelated to their legal party, Number Two. But One would control Two and accomplish its work through its members, with full protection of our ''democratic'' processes.[47] The ACLU's resolution provided aid and comfort to this strategy.

The second resolution opposed any ban on teachers belonging to the Communist Party, a position which also assumed ignorance of the facts concerning the use of all disciplined Communists for conspiratorial purposes. Norman Thomas opposed this resolution at the time, although he supported the Union's position that the ''conspiratorial'' Communist Party was still a party and could not be outlawed. Those like Clifford Forster, who were familiar with the evidence that the Party was functioning as a criminal espionage apparatus, thoroughly disagreed. The second resolution also opposed any control of hiring of Americans as UN personnel, but stated that any valid UN security programs should be administered ''by the United Nations as a whole,'' which would mean that they would be administered exactly as the Communists desired.[48]

The third resolution criticized hasty employment decisions on the basis of individuals having Communist affiliations or having taken the Fifth Amendment when questioned by government investigators about such affiliations. The Union admitted there might be some circumstances of employment in which these matters would be revelant concerns. But the resolution supported, not only one's ''right'' to be free of ''self-incrimination'' before a purely investigative body, but urged that no such inquiries be made by investigators on activities or associations that were not prohibited by law. Under such a rule, the House Committee on Un-American Activities could not have collected evidence to help prepare a bill to outlaw the Communist Party, since the party's existence was a matter not already illegal.

The disappointment Clifford Forster felt with the adoption of these resolutions, the full import of which was not clear to all who had voted on them, made him conclude that he could no longer continue in the Union, for it had reversed whatever position of opposition it ever had to the real Communist threat. He resigned, and was followed by Ferman of the Washington office, C. Dickerman Williams, and others. Since Pitzele and Lamont were equally unhappy about the resolutions, but for opposite reasons, it was agreed that they would both resign. Lamont soon established a Communist front called the Emergency Civil Liberties Committee to pursue his interest in "civil liberties" while making sure he never disappionted his comrades.[49] Although Lamont left the ACLU, the financial support of his family did not. In fact, it may be more than a coincidence that the Union received at this time "a magnificent $25,000 bequest from the estate of the late Mrs. Thomas W. Lamont."[50]

Norman Thomas had led the opposition to the weak and compromising resolutions, personally conducting the meetings of the anti-Communist faction in his apartment. Clifford Forster was surprised when Thomas was not among those who resigned after the passage of the resolutions. Thomas said he thought he should stay because he had been a founder of the ACLU.

A Conspiracy Against Consistency

Although the Union did not formally reverse its 1940 ban on totalitarians among its leadership until more than a decade later (by means of a policy statement that opened its doors once again to *anyone* who professed a "democratic" faith), the adoption of these resolutions marked the point at which the Union seemed to start on its long path back to being just another left-wing pressure group, much of whose work would be virtually identical with that of identified Communist fronts.[51] There may have been some excuse for sincere and consistent libertarians to have worked for the Union since 1940, despite its disturbingly overt anti-anti-Communism on matters of fact, but all such excuses vanished in 1954, and with them went what little record the ACLU may have accumulated in holding true to its professed ideals. The 1954 resolutions ended whatever conservative influence had existed during the decade and a half of the Union's history that is remembered by modern-day Corliss Lamonts in the group's leadership as its most embarrassingly inactive period.[52]

By the end of the 1950s things were augering in the new direction. In 1970 Roger Baldwin, who had expressed his pleasure over a decline in anti-Communist sentiment and activity,[53] looked back on the complex oppositions within the Union during the two decades we have just discussed and wrote:

> An examination of the record would reveal what might be reasonably expected in failures to takes some cases and issues or mistakes in taking others. There were matters which at the moment seemed worthy but which later hindsight proved otherwise. Integrity does not require consistency. . . .[54]

Integrity does not *guarantee* a record of consistency, but honesty requires us to recognize that "inconsistency" later admitted is a most convenient excuse for collaboration—by those who have every reason to know what they are doing —with an international conspiracy for *prerequisites* necessary to the successful accomplishment of its criminal objectives, despite the fact that the motives of all those parties to the overall conspiracy may differ.

11

1960-1975: "Civil Liberties" Become Leftist Activism

The ACLU's fortieth anniversary was surely an occasion for celebrating past successes. Joseph McCarthy had been dead and "officially" discredited for three years. For six years there had been no congressional investigations of subversive activities in government. It seems that employees of federal agencies were not permitted to testify before legislative panels without the permission of their superiors. This resulted from President Eisenhower's decree of "executive privilege" in May, 1954.[1] A most welcome measure to those in the ACLU interested in stopping McCarthy, it somehow lost its charm when it was again made use of in 1973 to withhold some tapes. But in 1960, there was elected a new liberal Democratic administration, which would be staffed with members and friends of the Union and would accelerate the growth of powerful Washington bureaucracy that had mushroomed under Eisenhower. The Union had many reasons for rejoicing at the end of its fourth decade, yet there was much unfinished work to be done.

Renewed Anti-Anticommunism on New Fronts

The first problem to be tackled was the remaining activity of government and private agencies investigating and exposing subversive activities. Although in

154

1959 the Union had protested an Air Reserve Center Training Manual that contained information on Communist infiltration of American society,[2] particularly in religious circles, the major targets for at least two years would be the House Committee on Un-American Activities[3] and the John Birch Society.[4]

It was not surprising that the ACLU sprang to the forefront of this renewed anti-anti-Communist crusade. The Union's Northern California affiliate had led protests, in league with the Communist-front National Committee to Abolish HUAC, against the Committee's hearings on Communist influence in academic circles, held in San Francisco in spring, 1960. When Communists present agitated their dupes into four days of rioting, the Union was quick to help with the defense of those arrested. When the House Committee had produced and made available for sale the documentary film *Operation Abolition,* which showed the obstructionism and agitation unleashed by identified Communists, the ACLU and its allies in the anti-"HUAC" brigade almost evaporated.[5] Strangely they never seem to have been angered by any other of the many self-serving documentary films produced by federal government agencies. This one, intended to disseminate widely, as it did, the investigative facts uncovered by the Committee in pursuance of its functions, triggered an ever-louder smear campaign to destroy the Committee, the Senate Internal Security Subcommittee, the Subversive Activities Control Board, the Attorney-General's List of Subversive Organizations, and such state investigative bodies as the California Senate Fact-Finding Subcommittee on Un-American Activities. The ACLU, in terms of both influence and support, led these efforts[6] both nationally and locally. As a result of this campaign, only the SISS exists today. Before this success was achieved, the Union advanced a number of strange positions on the work of these bodies, while supporting the increasing trend of Supreme Court eradication of state and federal laws designed to restrict the Communist conspiracy.[7]

The ACLU was evaluated at length by the California Senate Subcommittee in 1961,[8] the final major report on the Union by this now extinct body. Quite uncharacteristically, the Union requested the inquiry. In spite of the strong criticisms contained in its report, the Subcommittee decided to amend its 1943 judgment and declare that there was not sufficient evidence to indicate the group was under disciplined Communist control. The Union was more than eager to publicize this inquisitorial finding. Yet, when Robert Welch requested the Subcommittee, composed largely of Democrats, to investigate the John Birch Society at that time, the Union protested this step.[9] The Society wanted the investigation to clear it of the smears it had received, which the Committee's reports in 1961 and 1965 did accomplish. However, the Union opposed this procedure, the findings of which in their own case they welcomed, and claimed to be defending the civil liberties of the JBS. While it is true that local affiliates of the Union took several cases involving Birchers and other conservatives in the early 1960s,[10] the ultimate effect of this served primarily to counter arguments that the organization was obsessed with helping criminals and leftists.

The Selective Assault of "Impartiality"

Significantly, the ACLU also opposed investigations of, as well as restrictions on, obnoxious racists like the late *agent provocateur,* Nazi George Lincoln Rockwell.[11] It supported the various Ku Klux Klans in an attempt to prevent the 1966 investigation of the hooded orders by the HCUA. This is interesting in view of the fact that the investigation was part of an effective, though competitive, drive to destroy the klans on the part of the FBI and the HCUA. And the violence that unusual *agents provocateur* led those klans to accomplish provided more excuses for the campaign waged by the Union and others to pass the 1964 Civil Rights Act and the 1965 Voting Rights Act, both of which enormously increased central government powers, made criminal matters of purely voluntary association and exchange, and opened the door for an utter violation of private property. The klans and the Union applied pressure on Congress from two directions to pass such legislation. And, with regard to the leadership of the most violent klan group, we know such legislation was its hidden objective.[12]

In 1972, as we have noted, *The Rights of Servicemen* expressed the Union's position that members of the armed services still have their First Amendment freedoms of speech and association, which they should be free to exercise during the course of their service-related duties. This policy was a response to attempts of various service personnel to discourage the dissemination of left-wing literature on Army property, as well as resisting attempts to establish leftist political and labor organizations at various bases. The transparency of the Union's posture of impartiality in these cases is clear when one remembers that they saw no civil liberties issue involved when in the late 1950s and early 1960s servicemen stationed in Germany were prevented fron attending an anticommunism course presented under the sponsorship of Major General Edwin A. Walker, who was criticized for presenting his personal views as part of a military training program. The Union fully supported the left-wing muzzling of the military,[13] but in 1975 it sent out recruitment literature warning that our freedoms are imperiled because former CIA employee Vincent Marchetti was not permitted to print everything he wanted to include in his book on the Agency, including material of a validly confidential nature—an abridgement of his ''right'' to do something Walker could not, and in the case of Marchetti, probably something in violation of existing laws.[14]

More important, as the Union tried to promote its official ''impartiality'' by taking cases of a few anti-Communists, in 1962 it was quite prompt in joining the left-wing chorus of world-wide attacks aimed at a small educational group that had been made terribly controversial because of the rapid growth and influence it had developed in just four years. By 1962, the John Birch Society and its founder, Robert Welch, were bearing the brunt of a massive smear campaign throughout much of the nation's media, an incredible parade of honest and not-so-honest misunderstandings, villifications, and distortions that manifested a renewed world-wide Communist assault on anti-Communist movements.[15] This crusade against the Society, in which the ACLU, nationally and locally, had continued to participate irrespective of whether any criticism was related to a matter of civil liberties, peaked in 1964, after the Society had survived a likely extinction in late 1963. In spite of the efforts of Earl Warren and others to place blame for the assassination of President John F. Kennedy on the "right wing," which meant the Birchers, the Society weathered the storm when it was shown that Lee Harvey Oswald had no connection with the JBS, although now it seems he did have some connection with the FBI. Nonetheless, the anti-Birch crusade was not abandoned, not even when it became known that Oswald was a member of both the Fair Play for Cuba Committee and the ACLU.[16]

Making It Official

The degree to which the national leadership of the Union was approaching the more determined procommunism of its leading affiliates is indicated by the fact that the California and Washington locals voted to revoke the 1940 antitotalitarian resolution in 1965, while the headquarters in New York waited until 1968 to make things official.[17] On the other hand, it can be said that there were some diehards in New York. They never voted to follow the suggestion of George Slaff, board president of the Southern California affiliate in Los Angeles, who, in 1969, was desperately pleading that the Union "right an old wrong" and adopt Corliss Lamont's request that the late Communist Elizabeth Gurley Flynn be posthumously reinstated on the National Board.[18] The time was not yet right for National to follow Lamont's procommunism beyond the grave.

"Free Speech" at Whose Expense?

The concern the Union showed in landmark cases on pornography censorship and restrictions during the past fifteen years, though defensible on libertarian grounds, did not suffice to undo their policy of implying that, in the overwhelming majority of cases, free speech rights apply primarily to those who are seeking violently to persuade those in government to make laws that will install a dictatorship. As an illustration of this, the Union firmly stood against local "textbook review committees" composed of citizens who thought their rights might be violated by questionable textbook materials, which they were forced to purchase for the compulsory "edification" of their children. The Union asserted that "laymen" were unqualified to make such determinations without violating the academic freedom of the real "experts," the professional government educators who were also financed by the involuntary dole.[19]

Similarly, the ACLU's participation in heralding and enforcing the Supreme

Court's ruling banning prayer and Bible reading in government schools was conducted in a manner quite contrary to the spirit of any valid civil liberties issue. Surely it was unconstitutional for the government of any state to *require* attendance and participation in such activities at school. But when such were voluntary, as was the rule, and any child was free not to participate, no issue of "establishment of religion" was involved. But the Union and others did not see it this way. They took the decision as a mandate for intimidating local school boards in advance of any evidence of wrongful conduct, and some local ACLU affiliates went about this, and related issues, with a heavy-handed vengeance.[20]

In the course of the "civil rights" movement of the 1960s, prominent members and leaders of the Union on the national and local levels cooperated with the movement that would so greatly increase racial tensions by forming new or renewing old affiliations with the handful of leading organizations active among black Americans, most of which had similar histories of pro-Communist leadership, some dating back further than the ACLU. The Union's annual reports during the sixties chronicle this participation in the overall movement that accomplished so many Communist objectives in America in accord with some who certainly planned it that way.[21] In addition to the major pieces of federal legislation that were passed in this field in 1964, 1965, and 1968, so greatly advancing that "economic democracy" that we have learned to define, the ACLU pioneered in the earlier stages of harrassment of local police forces, primarily through the not-always-successful program to establish so-called "police review boards" composed of "experts" of the calibre of those recommended to pass judgments on school textbooks.[22] This was before 1968, about the time the Union got on the bandwagons for government gun controls and federal authority over local police departments.

The numerous cases of press censorship, which through Watergate allowed the ACLU to stand as the nation's champion defender of the freedom of the press, all amount to a gigantic mirage when viewed against the positions that the Union took in support of the gradually tightening control of radio and television programming by the Federal Communications Commission. The Union saw no issue of freedom here, but declared that the media of the airwaves were "public utilities," and should thus be nationalized with regard to control of what they broadcast, so that everyone will have easier access to expressing their views! Not only did this support for the FCC demonstrate an amazing trust in a bureaucracy's willingness to be impartial in the application of arbitrary power, it helped silence some of its intended targets: conservative radio commentators whose *paid* broadcasts would be henceforth transmitted at the peril of the station, and often at additional expense for providing *free* time to opposing views.[23]

The question naturally arises: If the ACLU is supported by the wealthy, elite Left of the Council on Foreign Relations and related foundations, why would it favor turning over the captive electronic forums of these establishmentarians to arbitrary bureaucratic control? The only answer must be that the same crowd is

,highly influential in Washington. And the record is quite lengthy that the CFR and organizations closely related to the ACLU in the Fabian socialist orbit here at home formed the pool from which most of the leading figures were selected to staff the top positions of the Kennedy, Johnson, Nixon, and Ford administrations. Why should one CFR member worry about FCC control over the major television network of which he is chairman of the board when the FCC answers to another, or several other, CFR associates?

Council on Foreign Relations member Ramsey Clark, U.S. attorney general under Lyndon Johnson, has become the "chairperson" of the ACLU's National Advisory Council, formerly the National Committee. Arthur Schlesinger Jr., and Walter T. Fisher continue to serve, along with such leftist stalwarts of the learned and artistic professions as General Counsel Osmond Fraenkel and Board activist Philip Hirschkop, both of whom have been active in the Communist National Lawyer's Guild; actors Melvyn Douglas and Burt Lancaster; former Cabinet member Willard Wirtz; and well-known pro-Communists Carey McWilliams, Max Lerner, William Kunstler, and Stuart Chase. Politicians Philip Hart, Albert Gore, Shirley Chisholm, Patsy Mink, and Robert Drinan also serve, as do civil rights and labor functionaries Julian Bond, Fannie Lou Hammer, Aaron Henry, A. Philip Randolph, and James G. Patton. The academy is well represented by historian Henry Steele Commager; and of course, there is *still* Roger Baldwin.[24]

New Leaders and Old

The Union has reached its present position with 275,000 members under the leadership of two executive directors since the retirement of Patrick Malin in 1962, followed shortly thereafter by his untimely death. The immediate successor was another Quaker, John de J. Pemberton, Jr. A Harvard-educated attorney, he has a somewhat milder manner than his two predecessors, but lacks none of their interest in carrying the torch against all who would expose and destroy collectivist conspiracy. By the time Pemberton was succeeded by the present executive director, Aryeh Neier, the Union had already officially reversed its 1940 policy of excluding totalitarians from its leadership. And from the emotional problems that we have seen Neier having over dossiers, we should not be too concerned with seriously examining at length his meditations on human liberty. If he does not make use of the Union to promote Communist objectives, the door has been opened for seven years to anyone else who might be interested in the effort.[25]

And, yet, in spite of his advancing years, Roger Baldwin remains ahead of this leadership crowd in pointing the way to the future. From his international work on behalf of the Union, he has, at least verbally, supported the UN throughout every crisis or event in which it opposed demon colonialism and advanced Communist slavery around the world,[26] usually with Americans paying most of the bills. Baldwin, although still expressing skepticism on the efficacy of governments, has promoted every measure to make the United States "interdependent" in and subservient to a world government,[27] while expressing the hope that such a world authority "might make the efforts of a private citizen organization unnecessary."[28] It is more than disquieting that Baldwin would entertain the idea of a collectivist world government, under which any respect for civil liberties would be a thing of the past. But perhaps he is just continuing to be consistent.

A Wiser Perspective on the Union Today

In two earlier chapters I reviewed the Union's policies and publications on a broad range of issues. These policies provide a fair picture of the Union's position today, but most were direct continuations or variations of policies and projects of the late 1950s and the 1960s. The earlier consideration of those current policies was in the context of measuring the ideas underlying them against the meaning of American constitutionalism and human liberties, or rights. I was not there concerned with any question of motivation, content only to demonstrate to sincere members or friends of the ACLU that it was promoting, for *some* reason, generally the opposite of its professed goals. In the isolated theoretical discussion presented, it was quite reasonable to assume that the pattern of errors observed resulted from an inept understanding of their concerns on the part of the Union's leaders, matched only by the zeal with which the mistakes were made.

And this is certainly the explanation for the support given the Union by the vast majority of its members. If they understood how much the Union is working at odds with the goals they seek, they would leave it alone. A number of ACLU staff and Board members departed in the mid-1950s because they were sincere, and sincerely disappointed. All those who remained accepted tacitly the fact that their support was sanction of, if not conviction favoring, the Union's orientation. We could have assumed that the Union's policies in very recent years derived from a common misunderstanding in the minds of all its leaders. From that it would be easy to explain ACLU support for a government-controlled economy, laws to establish a monopoly of guns in the hands of the state, a national police force, and other distinctly totalitarian objectives at home and internationally as the consequences of a group led by men with bankrupt philosophy. From that conclusion, an individualist, also interested in civil liberties, might want to stay in the Union and fight for the acceptance of a rational concept of rights, or, failing in that, be content to leave it alone and tend to his own consistency of thought.

All of this would be reasonable, based on what was partially reviewed in the first part of this book. But having completed an examination of representative and important items in the ACLU's history and a scrutiny of its influential leadership, it cannot be avoided that the Union's record of "inconsistency" could have been the result of, *rather than merely resulting in,* the great degree of directing influence on the Union by persons who, throughout its history, were primarily interested in "civil liberties" for promoting the growth of statism, specifically, the world-wide aggrandizement of Communist tyranny.

That this could have been the objective that produced the Union's philosophical betrayal of natural-law constitutionalism is very clear from the earliest days of the group's record. Roger Baldwin never made any attempt to hide his primary motivations, as few other leftists in the ACLU leadership did, over the thirty years during which he used the Union as an effective adjunct for protecting and supporting the Communists' United Front. In spite of the respectability the group earned —largely from those in sympathy with it who had also become "respectable"— regardless of the turmoil resulting from world events and disputes by long-departed anti-Communists in a minority among its officials, and despite the different motives held by those officials who remained, the Union seemed to function remarkably *consistently* in support of Communist objectives.

De Jure or De Facto?

From our understanding of the concept, as earlier discussed, was not the Union functioning rather well as a *de facto* Communist front, virtually indistinguishable in its work from any of the organizations under *formal* Communist control? They also find helpful for their public relations the performance of deeds that are worthwhile, and occasionally, after Lenin,[29] even a few that appear to reflect a hostility to communism. If the reader can grasp the concept of a *de facto* Communist front, the question of the existence at any time of formal and disciplined Communist control over the group's leadership becomes purely academic, indeed wholly unnecessary for one's decision as to whether it should be supported or opposed.

However, if the reader recognizes the substantial Communist influence that has existed over the Union's most influential officials for surely better than three quarters of its duration and knows that the primary Communist objective, officially stated since the end of World War II, has been to support the concentration of power on the national level of countries not formally under police-state control, then another verdict may be indicated. For the individualist interested in promoting his freedom, and that necessarily requires opposition to those who would destroy it, two courses of action are open.

One can attempt to communicate the errors in Union policies and their rational alternatives to concerned members of the ACLU. This will, if properly done, result in the defection of many sincere people from the Union as long as it continues on its current course. This is a worthy project, but probably a futile one. There are far too many young people being indoctrinated with fashionable notions supporting the Union's positions. They exit colleges and law schools by the thousands yearly, having their misunderstandings reinforced daily by that great body of ACLU sympathizers in the mass media, meaning those who influence its major institutions and their policies. The libertarian striking out on a campaign of purely ideological debate against the ACLU may be hopelessly outnumbered before he starts. And with the current rate of accelerating government controls over us, he has not the time to recruit a philosophical corps of sufficient size to assist him. The disaster would arrive too soon. There are very few measures necessary for the imposition of a police state after *national* wage, price, gun, and police controls are instituted. The individualist must recognize the imminence of this threat and the obvious plan behind it. The Senate's televised circus in which we all heard Sam Ervin, another ACLU favorite, scold the measly "Watergators" for trampling on the Fourth Amendment, led to pundits suggesting that we were once again concerned with the abuse of government power. Once the old crowd was partially replaced by the new, it was easy to forget that what was temporarily delayed was the progression of the United States toward a "perpetual Presidency."[30]

Any such effort could also be fought by what may be the only action to which it is vulnerable, the measure it opposes at all cost: an exposure of the record of its activities. If the American Civil Liberties Union has, in the overwhelming majority of its work, seemed to function *in effect* as a vitally necessary adjunct in the Communist conspiracy's required attempt to conceal its activities, it should be opposed, if one means not to waste time, by exposing it as a party to that conspiracy. That does not mean passing any law to prohibit its existence, or even that of the Communist Party or any other department of the conspiracy it serves.

If enough Americans are informed of the ACLU's overall record and how it compares with the history and strategy of the international conspiracy that stretches from Wall Street and Washington to Moscow and Peking, both would collapse from a cessation of support by those productive people who have paid for their successes, either voluntarily without realizing what they were doing, or involuntarily via the IRS. At such a time nothing would be more important to the future of freedom in the world than a voluntary dissemination of rational philosophy to encourage widespread understanding as an investment for a better future.

But we may not have that opportunity to build a better world until the current threat of a police state is averted by an exposure of those who are building it. Such exposure of conspiracy is not necessary for those living in Communist countries. Anyone who studies a bit of history and visits the Soviet Union will discover that those people know they are enslaved. They no longer have the opportunity to expose the criminals who are their officially recognized government, because once the "dictatorship of the proletariat" is in place, "democratic" institutions and "civil liberties" have served their intended strategic purpose. And totalitarians in power are not interested in debating philosophy.

162

Your Response Would Be the Same

If you are serious in your desire to promote human freedom, you must first prevent the rapid expansion of a world-wide police state. You should oppose it by exposure of its activities, whether or not it amounts to a conspiracy in which people have participated for a variety of motives. It should be opposed on the basis of its probable nature, rather than what we might in advance wish it to be. This will require a wide study of the activities and personalities in the constellation of organizations, from the CFR to the SDS, among which the ACLU has been so influential. A further study of the ACLU from the evidence here presented will only shed more light on the question of the degrees of philosophical inconsistency or leadership conspiracy that have produced the Union's record. We have only begun to examine that evidence. Further research would undoubtedly make a stronger case either way, although the time for free decisions is growing shorter daily. From the evidence presented here and that which the reader is encouraged to find on his own, the question of the ACLU's relationship with a conspiracy to build an international police state remains. The verdict, or answer to that question, and the response to that evidence are *yours*.

Appendix

Excerpts from
Major State and Federal
Investigative Reports
Concerning the ACLU

Excerpts from the Overman Report, 1919[1]

Maj. Humes. Could you prepare a brief summary, and put it into the record, of those organizations and their activities?

Mr. Bielaski. [A. Bruce Bielaski was testifying as a representative of U.S. Attorney General T.W. Gregory, December 6, 1918.] Yes; there were a number of them. The one which continued the most active and lived the longest was this organization of Roger Baldwin's, the National Civil Liberties Bureau. That organization continued right up until Baldwin's arrest and imprisonment, and, to a limited degree, still lives, though it is not in any way active.

The same people that were in that organization were in these other organizations. To a large extent it was the same bunch of pacifists, conscientious objectors, and pro-German people who made up all of these organizations, although they changed their names frequently.

Senator Overman. Did you have any estimate of how many there were?

[1]U.S. Congress, Senate, Subcommittee on the Judiciary, *Brewing and Liquor Interests and German and Bolshevik Propaganda,* 66th Congress, 1st session, 1919, vol. 2, pp. 2254–2256, 2707–2717, 2729–2735, 2782–2785.

Mr. Bielaski. You mean in point of numbers?

Senator Overman. Yes.

Mr. Bielaski. I think they were comparatively small, indeed. There were not very many. They would announce a tremendous meeting at Cleveland to organize, and they would have seven or eight people there, and they would be the same people that were in the People's Council, or something of that kind. They were almost always the same radical pro-German or pacifist type of people.

Maj. Humes. Was the People's Council of Peace and Democracy one of these organizations?

Mr. Bielaski. Yes.

Maj. Humes. What was that organization?

Mr. Bielaski. The People's Council for Democracy and Terms of Peace, or something of that kind, was an effort to unite into one organization all of the radical pacifist and socialistic organizations. They expected to bring into their organization the I.W.W., the Socialist Party, all the pacifist organizations, and to get support from the German-American societies. They were to be modeled after some of the people's councils in Russia. They met with practically no success, because each one of these organizations that they wanted to bring in wanted to run the thing their own way. They did not amalgamate at all.

Maj. Humes. Do you know who inspired that organization?

Mr. Bielaski. Who inspired it?

Maj. Humes. Yes.

Mr. Bielaski. No; I do not know who inspired it.

Maj. Humes. Was Roger Baldwin active in that organization?

Mr. Bielaski. He was very active; yes. There was a group of, I guess, 8 or 10 who came down here. According to my recollection, the first meeting was in Washington, the preliminary meeting to their organization, and some 8 or 10 people were present.

Maj. Humes. Do you remember who attended?

Mr. Bielaski. No; I do not, offhand. I know that they hoped to bring into that organization in some way some of our leading public men who had, they thought, shown pacifist tendencies, etc.; but I do not think they were successful in that at all.

Senator Overman. Where is Baldwin from?

Mr. Bielaski. Baldwin is a Harvard graduate, I think. That is one of the things I have always had to mention to Mr. O'Brien when the case comes up. He was a very intelligent, likeable sort of fellow. He, however, was, I think, in addition to taking the position that he was following his conscience, actively disloyal and opposed to the conduct of the war. He lived, I think, in the Middle West for a while, and then lived in New York. He was a member or sympathizer or director or an officer in from 40 to 50 of these various organizations. Some of them, I think, had little more than a letterhead and officers.

Senator Overman. He was one of these "jiners"?

Mr. Bielaski. Yes; he was decidedly a jiner and an organizer.

Eventually he went to jail for failing to comply with the provisions of the conscription act. I do not know whether there have been indictments returned against him, but he has been involved in specific instances of trying to get other people to become conscientious objectors who had not properly come within that class under the act.

Maj. Humes. He also arranged, did he not, for an organization over the country that would locally represent conscientious objectors in the various communities?

Mr. Bielaski. He did. He said his associates endeavored to perfect a sort of legal aid association to conscientious objectors, also providing radical speakers, and all that sort of thing.

Our trouble with him was not that he was a conscientious objector, but that he was a man who was trying to create conscientious objectors, and to really interfere with the conduct of the war.

Senator Wolcott. Was Prof. Scott Nearing tied in with that organization?

Mr. Bielaski. Oh, yes. Scott Nearing was one of the men who was associated with Baldwin. I think he was also deliberately opposing the successful conduct of the war.

Senator Wolcott. He was arrested, too, was he not?

Mr. Bielaski. Yes; he is under indictment awaiting trial.

Maj. Humes. Have you in your files a record of the officers of the various organizations?

Mr. Bielaski. I think so; yes.

Maj. Humes. Can you furnish us with a memorandum of who they are and their location?

Mr. Bielaski. Yes. If you do not object, I will ask Mr. Allen to get that up. It is all a matter of record.

Maj. Humes. Do you remember who the officers of the People's Council for Peace and Democracy were?

Mr. Bielaski. No; I do not remember, offhand. I remember Theodore Lunde was the most active man from Chicago. He had been an especially active pro-German. The same group of principals made up most of the officers in all these organizations.

Senator Overman. Were they financed by the German Government?

Mr. Bielaski. I think not; no, sir.

Senator Overman. Did you say David Starr Jordan was treasurer of this concern?

Maj. Humes. Yes.

Mr. Bielaski. He was treasurer of the organizing committee of the People's Council.

Maj. Humes. He was treasurer of the organizing committee of the People's Council for Peace and Democracy. . . .

BREWING AND LIQUOR INTERESTS AND GERMAN PROPAGANDA
Wednesday, January 22, 1919

United States Senate,

Subcommittee of the Committee on the Judiciary,

Washington, D.C.

The subcommittee met, pursuant to adjournment, at 10:45 o'clock a.m., in room 226, Senate Office Building, Senator William H. King presiding.

Present: Senators King, Wolcott, and Nelson.

Senator King. The committee will be in order. Proceed, Maj. Humes.

Maj. Humes. I will ask Mr. Stevenson to proceed with the analysis he was making yesterday.

TESTIMONY OF MR. ARCHIBALD E. STEVENSON
—Resumed

Mr. Stevenson. [Stevenson was an expert investigator of subversive propaganda for the Justice Department's Bureau of Investigation and U.S. Military Intelligence. He was also a New York attorney.] At yesterday's hearing we had just mentioned the first of a series of pacifist organizations, the American League to Limit Armaments. This organization had in its membership men of conservatism with pacifist leanings, as well as some of the men who have since developed into violent radicals.

Senator Nelson. This American League to Limit Armaments was distinct from the matter of the embargo on the shipment of arms, was it not? It embraced a different subject?

Mr. Stevenson. They participated in that, however.

Senator Nelson. But this arose before?

Mr. Stevenson. Yes; this arose in December, 1914.

Senator Nelson. Yes. It was in opposition to any increase in our Army or our Navy?

Mr. Stevenson. Precisely.

Senator King. Of course, there were connected with that, however, many who were strongly anti-German.

Mr. Stevenson. Oh, yes. Some of the men who were in that movement have since become extremely chauvinistic and have entirely changed their point of view. For that reason it does not seem wise to name the membership in the old committee.

Senator Nelson. We came to the conclusion yesterday, I want to say, that we would not give the names of all, but only of those who continued to be vicious.

Senator King. Is the claim made, Mr. Witness, that Germany, directly or indirectly, was responsible for this organization?

Mr. Stevenson. There were some members of this organization who were connected with the German propaganda and had written for propaganda sheets.

The claim is made that propaganda, being a peculiar instrument, can direct a movement by inspiring a sentiment in the country, and that will bring to that movement people who are not in any way connected with the propagandist. That has been shown in all the analyses that we have made. In other words, that is the fruit of the propaganda.

I did mention, however, as being members of this organization, Mr. L. Hollingsworth Wood, a lawyer in New York, because of his subsequent connections with most of these organizations, and also Mr. Oswald Garrison Villard, for the same reason, and Mr. Morris Hillquit.

Senator Nelson. A noted socialist?

Mr. Stevenson. A noted socialist; and John Haynes Holmes.

The members of the executive committee of this organization felt that the scope was not wide enough, and therefore the antipreparedness committee was formed, which later became the American Union Against Militarism, with headquarters at 70 Fifth Avenue, New York City, and offices in the Munsey Building in Washington.

The American Union Against Militarism was a national organization, having branches in various cities, and which maintains an office in Washington. It was engaged in issuing propaganda literature, in circulating petitions, and in attempting to influence Members of Congress on the subject of preparedness and antiwar.

Senator Nelson. They were against war?

Mr. Stevenson. They were absolutely against war.

Senator Nelson. Under any circumstances?

Mr. Stevenson. Under any circumstances.

Senator Nelson. And against any increase in our Army and Navy?

Mr. Stevenson. Precisely. That was during the period of our neutrality. They continued after we entered the war and opposed conscription and issued literature calculated to discourage recruiting.

Senator Wolcott. Were they ever arrested for that?

Mr. Stevenson. No.

Senator Nelson. This was before we padded our spy law. It was during the period of neutrality?

Mr. Stevenson. No; but after that also.

Senator Wolcott. After we got into the war, the witness said they issued literature which was designed to discourage recruiting.

Mr. Stevenson. Yes.

Senator Wolcott. Did they keep that up after the espionage act was passed?

Mr. Stevenson. Yes.

Senator Wolcott. Yet they were never arrested for it.?

Maj. Humes. That is the organization that Roger Baldwin was connected with?

Mr. Stevenson. Yes.

Maj. Humes. Roger Baldwin has been convicted.

Mr. Stevenson. Yes; but on another count.

Maj. Humes. But he was convicted because of his antiwar activities—

Mr. Stevenson. No.

Maj. Hunes. It may not have been that this particular charge was in the indictment.

Mr. Stevenson. He was convicted on his own confession, or on his refusal to submit to physical examination when he was drafted under the selective-service law.

Senator Wolcott. After we got into the war, did they continue to agitate against war?

Mr. Stevenson. Yes.

Senator Wolcott. And also, at the same time, agitated against recruiting, or against conscription?

Mr. Stevenson. Yes. I will mention also the following: As one of the men connected with this organization who has since been connected with a large number of other organizations of a similar nature, Amos Pinchot; Max Eastman, who has been indicted several times for violation of the espionage act, but the jury disagreed—that was in connection with the *Masses* case in New York City; Roger Baldwin, who is now serving sentence for violation of the selective-service act; L. Hollingsworth Wood, whom I have previously mentioned as one of the executive committee of the American League to Limit Armaments; Scott Nearing, who is now under indictment for violation of the espionage act; Oswald Garrison Villard; Max Eastman, who is the brother of Crystal Eastman, and the editor of the *Masses,* which is now known as the *Liberator,* and continues publication along the same line; Rev. John Haynes Holmes; Rev. Frederick Lynch; Prof. Emily Greene Balch, of Wellesley—I believe she was dropped from Wellesley on account of her activities in these organizations.

The executive committee of this union then organized a separate bureau which was entitled "The civil liberties bureau".

Senator Nelson. Let me ask you, there, is that the organization that is looking after these conscientious objectors?

Mr. Stevenson. That was the original organization that began to do that.

Senator Nelson. There is an organization now, because I have been getting some literature from them lately.

Mr. Stevenson. I will mention that in just a moment.

Senator Nelson. All right.

Mr. Stevenson. Because that was a development from this civil liberties bureau, the American Union Against Militarism.

Senator Nelson. Yes.

Mr. Stevenson. In this civil liberties bureau Roger Baldwin was the director; L. Hollingsworth Wood, Norman Thomas, a minister in New York, Amos Pinchot, and Rev. John Haynes Holmes, were on the directing committee, among other people.

They continued an agitation against the draft, encouraged conscientious objectors, and issued a considerable amount of pacifist literature.

Senator King. Amos Pinchot was quite conspicuous in that propaganda, was he not?

Mr. Stevenson. He was, and still is, in regard to similar propaganda.

They found that the demands on their organization became so great that they organized a separate organization known as the National Civil Liberties Bureau, and that is the bureau to which Senator Nelson refers.

Senator Nelson. That is now looking after the conscientious objectors?

Mr. Stevenson. Precisely.

I might say that this National Civil Liberties Bureau was a national organization and had attorneys representing them in all parts of the country. They agitated against the conscription act.

Senator King. Even after it had become a law?

Mr. Stevenson. After it was passed.

Senator King. Did they not arrest some of them?

Mr. Stevenson. You mean—

Senator King. For trying to prevent the execution of the law and conspiring to defeat the execution of valid laws of the Government?

Mr. Stevenson. Their offices have been raided, and their documents seized by the Department of Justice, and the matter, I believe, is now pending in the United States attorney's office.

Senator Nelson. They have prosecuted some of them.

Senator Wolcott. What matter is pending—some indictment, or the legality of the seizure of the papers?

Mr. Stevenson. No; the legality of the seizure is not questioned, I think.

Maj. Humes. You mean that the investigation is still pending?

Mr. Stevenson. Yes; they have the papers still and, so far as I am personally acquainted with it, I do not know that any indictment has been brought in.

Senator Nelson. I know of a case in Minnesota where they have tried a man and convicted him, and given him four years, and his case is before the Supreme Court today to be argued.

Senator King. If Mr. Pinchot, or this organization, tried to obstruct the draft law and the proper execution of the laws of Congress, I do not see any reason why they should not be prosecuted the same as other people have been prosecuted. Is there any reason?

Mr. Stevenson. Our bureau, Senator King, has been confined solely to the examination of the papers and the preparation of the relationship of these various organizations. We, ourselves, have not looked into the motive of any of these people and have had nothing to do with the preparation of any cases.

171

Senator King. Indeed, there would be less excuse for men of intelligence to obstruct the execution of the laws of Congress, which laws were passed for the purpose of saving our Nation and civilization, than for ignorant men to do so.

Mr. Stevenson. The National Civil Liberties Bureau not only undertook this matter, but attempted to assist any violators of the acts passed by Congress or the various States relative to the war. They took a very active part in assisting at the trial of the I.W.W.'s in Chicago.

Senator Wolcott. On the defense side, of course?

Mr. Stevenson. On the defense side; yes. They issued a large amount of propaganda in the form of articles, leaflets, and booklets to justify the position and activities of the I.W.W.

Senator King. Who were the chief officers of the organization you are now describing? Were they the same persons whose names you mentioned a few moments ago?

Mr. Stevenson. Practically. I will give you those.

In November, 1917, the officers were: L. Hollingsworth Wood, chairman—you can see the line coming together as the thing develops—the Rev. Norman Thomas; Helen Phelps Stokes, who is the sister-in-law of Rose Pastor Stokes; Albert De Silver, a lawyer in New York; William G. Simpson; and Walter Nelles, counsel.

On the directing committee we find Rev. John Haynes Holmes and Judah L. Magnes.

By the way, it is rather interesting to note that Judah L. Magnes was mentioned by Von Bernstorff in one of his aerograms to the foreign office dated 9th month, 8th day, 1916; and the aerogram was No. 381, eastbound, saying that "Magnes belongs to circles very friendly to us."

That may have no particular bearing on the proposition, but it is interesting in this connection.

Crystal Eastman was also a member of the directing committee.

This was after Baldwin had been sentenced to one year in prison.

To give an illustration of the sentiments entertained by the members of this committee, I have personally talked with a number of them, and if you will permit me to quote from the statement of Roger Baldwin himself to the trial judge at the time of his sentence—

Senator Wolcott. He was sentenced, then, for declining to perform military service, was he not?

Mr. Stevenson. Yes. He says:

Though at the moment I am of a tiny minority, I feel myself just one protest in a great revolt surging up from among the people, the struggle of the masses against the rule of the world by the few, profoundly intensified by the war. It is a struggle against the political state itself; against exploitation, militarism, imperialism, authority in all forms.

That is pure anarchy. (Continuing reading:)

It is a struggle to break in full force only after the war. Russia already stands in the vanguard, beset by her enemies in the camps of both belligerents. The central empires break asunder from within. The labor movement gathers revolutionary force in Britain; and in our own country the nonpartisan league, radical labor, and the Socialist Party hold the germs of a new social order. Their protest is my protest.

The American Union Against Militarism organized another organization known as the Collegiate Anti-Militarism League, which had representatives from all the universities and colleges in the United States and worked for the same purpose.

Senator Nelson. When was that organized?

Mr. Stevenson. That was organized in the fall of 1915 and continued active up until a few months ago.

Senator King. Let me interrupt you for a moment. Have you discovered that in many of these universities of the United States there were professors who subscribed to these dangerous and destructive and anarchistic sentiments?

Mr. Stevenson. A very large number.

Senator King. And participated in this class of revolutionary and bolshevik meetings and organizations?

Mr. Stevenson. Quite a large number of them, mostly among professors of sociology, economics and history.

Senator King. It seems to me this is a good time for the States and those who control the universities to look into that matter.

Senator Nelson. I should like to get a list of those professors.

Mr. Stevenson. I have here a "Who's Who", that I prepared, giving a brief biographical sketch of them.

Senator Nelson. When you get to them, give it to us. I think the American people ought to know those professors.

Senator King. It is a remarkable thing, Senator—I have made some investigation myself, and it is a remarkable thing—that in these universities there has been a festering mass of pure atheism and the grossest kind of materialism, and teachings destructive to our form of government and the civilization which a Christian nation recognizes.

Mr. Stevenson. An examination of the records, Senator King, shows that that is very widespread.

Senator King. We ought to weed it out and drive out of the universities these pernicious teachers.

Mr. Stevenson. These national organizations were cooperated with by local organizations in different places. In New York there was the New York Bureau of Legal First Aid, which later changed its name to the Bureau of Legal Advice. The purpose of this bureau was to assist draft evaders and men who were conscientious objectors, or those opposed to doing military service.

Senator Nelson. They called themselves "first aid", using a medical term?

Mr. Stevenson. Yes; in Chicago they had an organization known as the American Liberty Defense League. In Boston, they had the League of Democratic Control. A separate group which was very closely identified with these movements consisted of such organizations claiming a religious attitude. One of these was the Fellowship of Reconciliation, which was a branch of an organization of a similar name in England, and was established in this country by the Rev. H.D. Hodgins, of Devonshire House, London.

Senator Wolcott. Were these organizations of which you were just speaking organizations with some past history, some years of life behind them, or were they mushroom things that were nurtured by the war, and the prospect of having to go into the military service?

Mr. Stevenson. I am not at all familiar with the English branch of the Fellowship of Reconciliation, but there was never such a thing in this country before the war; and this same group of people who were active in these other organizations were the ones who developed it here.

Senator Wolcott. What did they call it?

Mr. Stevenson. The Fellowship of Reconciliation.

Senator Wolcott. I wonder how they hit on that name?

Mr. Stevenson. It is beyond me, Senator. They published a paper entitled "The World To-morrow", which is still being published. It is an extremely radical sheet. It was opposed to militarism; opposed to conscription; opposed to war; and is now taking up the economic questions of the day along similar lines.

Senator Nelson. Is it still carrying on its propaganda?

Mr. Stevenson. Yes. I have with me some of the copies of the paper, which will perhaps give you an idea of what sort of a sheet it is, in case you should like to look at it afterwards.

Roger Baldwin was connected with this; Norman Thomas, Oswald Garrison Villard, John Haynes Holmes, Helen Phelps Stokes, and I could go down the list; they are practically the same people—

Senator Nelson. The same outfit that was in these other concerns?

Mr. Stevenson. Yes; the same group of people.

The Church Peace Union, which is an organization founded by Andrew Carnegie, and, I believe, a very conservative and excellent organization, was used by its secretary to gather information for the use of the National Civil Liberties Bureau on the question of pacifism and the question of conscription; in other words, the secretary of that Church Peace Union issued letters to the pastors and rectors and clergy asking them to express their opinions on the question of conscription and conscientious objection; and the results of that canvas were turned over for the use of the National Civil Liberties Bureau in their propaganda literature.

The socialists, gaining some strength among certain of the clergy, have organized two organizations known as Christian Socialists; one is the Christian Socialist Fellowship, which was organized in Louisville, Kentucky, in 1906, and the Church Socialist League in America, which was organized in 1911.

Senator Nelson. All that would imply that there are heathen socialists, too?

174

Mr. Stevenson. Yes. They took a very strong position on the question of the war, and a good many of their officers—

Senator Wolcott. What do you mean by ''the war''? Do you mean the European war—

Mr. Stevenson. No; our war. A number of their officers also participated in these other organizations that I have mentioned.

Senator Wolcott. You employ the pronoun ''they''. By that do you mean the socialists that were identified with these two organizations?

Mr. Stevenson. Yes.

Senator Wolcott. And only those socialists?

Mr. Stevenson. That is all I am speaking of at the present moment.

Senator Wolcott. As I recall, there was quite a violent split amongst the socialists over our war?

Mr. Stevenson. I will bring that out in the political parties that participated in the pacifist movement. I have tried to separate these things.

Senator King. Is it your contention, Mr. Stevenson, that all of these organizations to which you have referred, and others to which you may refer, were controlled more or less by or in association with Germany?

Mr. Stevenson. Not exactly, Senator. What I do contend is that they were encouraged by the Germans. They were hailed with enthusiasm by all of the German propaganda sheets, and given publicity.

Senator King. Is there anything to show that they knew that their propaganda was regarded by Germany as helpful to Germany and its interests and hurtful to the United States and its interests?

Mr. Stevenson. That would require a deduction, Senator. We have, for instance, in the *Issues and Events,* which was a distinctly German propaganda magazine, created by the Germans for the purpose of influencing public opinion in this country, a continuous series of articles giving publicity to the activities and approving in every way of the activities of these organizations.

Senator King. What I have in mind is this: We can conceive of a person doing an act which is treasonable, and yet, because of his lack of intelligence, or because of some peculiar mental quirk, he does not conceive it to be treasonable, and we can conceive of another person who might do the same act with an intent to do a treasonable act.

Mr. Stevenson. We have tried to treat propaganda as a separate and distinct subject. The Germans launched the attack, creating public opinion, and the consequence of that attack is the fruit of it. The success of it depends upon whether they have encouraged a certain sentiment in the people of the United States.

During the early period of the war we found a concerted attack on the question of pacifism engineered by German agents—mass meetings, and thousands of articles in newspapers, thousands of booklets and pamphlets.

From that we find a strong pacifist movement growing up in the United States, carrying out exactly what the Germans wished, although we do not say what the motives of the people are; we do not know. But we believe that an analysis of the situation would convince anyone that it was the result of German propaganda.

Senator King. Can there be any question but what the activities of these organizations to which you have referred contributed to the cause of Germany, and was harmful to the United States and the morale of the American people?

Mr. Stevenson. I think there can be no question of that.

Senator King. And is it apparent from the records which you have, and from the examination which you have made, that the members of these organizations of this sort, who were conspicious in them, were cognizant of the fact that they were helping Germany and hurting the United States, and perhaps affecting the morale of some of the people in the United States?

Mr. Stevenson. Well, Senator, that would call for a conclusion. I think that a reasonable man is supposed to know what are the reasonable consequences of his acts.

Senator King. That is the implication of the law, that a man is presumed to know the consequences of his act.

Mr. Stevenson. I have been very careful to emphasize, throughout this whole proposition, that we are not going into the motives of anybody who has participated in the propaganda campaign. We have tried to confine ourselves solely to the facts, and let the facts speak for themselves.

Senator King. When your country is at war, fighting a nation that is determined to destroy your country and civilization, there is only one conclusion that I can draw from the activities of any person if those activities in any degree help the enemy and hurt their own country, and that is that they are enemies to their country. Proceed.

Mr. Stevenson. In connection with this, the American Friends Service Committee, of Philadelphia, which was made up wholly of Quakers, participated in the pacifist propaganda, and some of their members assisted the National Civil Liberties Bureau in the particular work in which it was engaged, which was a little beyond what the Society of Friends would ordinarily have done. . . .

A very interesting phase of the pacifist movement was initiated with the Ford peace mission, and is particularly interesting because that commission was really inspired by Rosika Schwimmer, who was undoubtedly a German agent.

Senator Nelson. Where was she living?

Mr. Stevenson. She was an Austrian journalist.

Senator Nelson. Where was she living?

Mr. Stevenson. She just came over here, I believe, to start this movement, and she did not come back to the United States after she went over.

The result of that is interesting. Mr. Ford's peace secretary at that time was Louis P. Lochner, and it is interesting to bear his name in mind, because it continues over into the radical movement of today.

Mr. Benjamin W. Huebsch, a publisher in New York City, was also one of the members of the party, and Rebecca Shelley.

Huebsch was connected with the German propagandists in this country, and has published a large number of books on pacifism and antimilitary subjects, and has been connected with a number of pacifist organizations.

Prior to the entrance of the United States into the war, and subsequent to the Ford peace commission, there was organized a national association entitled the Emergency Peace Federation, of which the most prominent members were Mrs. Henry Villard, who was the mother of Oswald Garrison Villard, Emily Greene Balch, and Louis P. Lochner.

Senator Nelson. The same men you referred to before?

Mr. Stevenson. The same men that I mentioned before.

Lella Faye Secor I will speak of later; also Rev. Frederick Lynch, who was connected with the Church Peace Union; Rebecca Shelley, and a number of others who were, in one way or another, connected with the other organizations.

This organization was designed to start propaganda to bring about peace at the time. It was after one of the German peace balloons went up that this organization was formed.

Another organization, participated in by a number of these people, was the American Neutral Conference Committee.

In this committee there were a number of prominent men. A good many of them were educated in German universities, and undoubtedly had German leanings at that time, which it was no crime to have prior to the entrance of the United States into the war; but it is interesting to note, in connection with the other movement, that we find this Prof. Emily Greene Balch again, George W. Kirchwey, of Columbia University, Rebecca Shelley—she was the secretary—and the Rev. John Haynes Holmes, the publisher Benjamin W. Huebsch, Rev. Frederick Lynch, Lella Faye Secor, and others.

Senator Wolcott. How were all of these organizations financed? These people seem to have done more in the way of forming committees, bureaus, and so forth, than anything else.

Mr. Stevenson. They published a large number of pamphlets, and this organization also issued petitions, and so on.

Senator Wolcott. But it takes money to run all these things, and it takes money to print. How did they get their money?

Mr. Stevenson. That is a phase of the matter, Senator, which I have not gone into.

Our committee has simply been studying the phases of the propaganda. We have not gone into the financial side at all. That is something that it may yet be found wise to investigate.

Senator King. It may have been done by other branches of the Government.

Mr. Stevenson. It may have, though I am inclined to doubt it. I am not sure.

Senator King. How late were those organizations of which you have been speaking actively engaged in their work or propaganda?

Mr. Stevenson. The Emergency Peace Federation and the American Neutral Conference Committee are both defunct, and became defunct before the United States entered into the war.

Senator King. Did any of them continue their activities after we went into the war, and were any of them organized after our country went into the war?

Mr. Stevenson. I am coming to some that were organized afterwards. The American Union Against Militarism continued after we entered the war, and the Fellowship of Reconciliation is still continuing. The National Civil Liberties Bureau is still continuing and has continued during our participation in the war.

Senator Nelson. Yes; that is the one that is nursing the conscientious objectors.

Senator Wolcott. What is the place of residence of all of these organizations? Where is their habitat—in New York City?

Mr. Stevenson. The American Union Against Militarism's habitat now is the Munsey Building, I believe, in Washington here.

The National Civil Liberties Bureau is now located at 41 Union Square, New York City.

The Fellowship of Reconciliation headquarters is 118 East Twenty-eighth Street, New York City.

Senator Wolcott. Were not any of them located at 70 Fifth Avenue?

Mr. Stevenson. Most of them were, until the owner of the building evicted them.

Senator Wolcott. They had a very expensive layout there, did they not, in the way of offices?

Mr. Stevenson. Oh, yes—well, they were sufficient for their need.

Senator Wolcott. The rent, I should think, would be pretty high there. Did they subsequently buy any property?

Mr. Stevenson. Not that I know of, Senator.

Senator Wolcott. The Y.W.C.A. in New York City—where is that located; on Fifteenth Street, I believe?

Mr. Stevenson. No; the Y.M.C.A. building—

Senator Wolcott. The Y.W.C.A. building.

Mr. Stevenson. I do not know, Senator.

Senator Wolcott. You do not know about that at all?

Mr. Stevenson. No; I do not know about that.

With the declaration of war by the United States the raison d'etre for the Emergency Peace Federation and the American Neutral Conference Committee ceased to exist, and they became defunct.

However, the movement continued to become more radical, and on August 4, 1917, the People's Council of America for Democracy and Peace was organized, with offices at 2 West Thirteenth Street, New York City.

Among the officers and executive committee are found Louis P. Lochner, Lella

Faye Secor, Rebecca Shelley, Scott Nearing, Jacob Panken—who, by the way, is an extremely radical speaker, and a judge of the municipal court in New York City; Algernon Lee, socialist alderman, New York City; Max Eastman; Emily Greene Balch; Judah L. Magnes; Morris Hillquit; Eugene V. Debs, who is now serving a sentence for violation of the espionage act; Irving St. John Tucker, who was just convicted with Victor Berger for violation of the same act; and the treasurer of this organization is David Starr Jordan.

The advent of this organization was hailed with enthusiasm by the German propagandists, and wide publicity was given to it in the German organs, such as *Issues and Events, The Fatherland,* etc.

The object, of course, was to discourage the military activities of the United States and to bring about peace.

In a telegram which was sent by Lella Faye Secor to President Wilson they stated that their membership is 1,800,000.

Senator Nelson. Evidently these organizations were all in opposition to Gen. Pershing's organization over in France?

Mr. Stevenson. That is certainly the impression that one might get, Senator. This telegram to President Wilson states:

> The organizing committee of the People's Council of America, now representing 1,800,000 constituents, believe that a combination of world events makes it imperative that Congress speak in no uncertain terms on the question of peace and war.

Senator Wolcott. What is the date of that telegram?

Mr. Stevenson. This was in August, 1917.

Senator Nelson. After we entered the war?

Senator Wolcott. After Congress had spoken.

Senator Nelson. Yes; we spoke in April, did we not?

Senator Wolcott. Yes.

Mr. Stevenson (continuing reading:)

> The eminent position of our country among the allies and the democratic members of our Government, and the lives and the future happiness of the young manhood of our Nation all demand that Congress should no longer remain silent and inactive on what is now the supreme interest of mankind, The Russian people are united for peace, based on the formula which is gaining acceptance everywhere: No forcible annexations, no punitive indemnities, and free development for all nationalities.

Senator Wolcott. They might also have added: "And victory for Germany"?

Mr. Stevenson (continuing reading:)

> Thus we have the representative assemblies of Russia, Germany, and England debating peace terms while only the American Congress remains silent in this fateful war.

Forward-looking men and women throughout the world are looking expectantly to Congress. Democracy is shamed by your silence.

That was a telegram addressed by this organization to President Wilson personally. This organization is still in operation, and they held a dinner last Monday evening in New York City, at which Scott Nearing presided, and they determined to flood the country with handbill propaganda, because their literature has been denied the use of the mails.

Senator Wolcott. What have they in mind now? What is the nature of their propaganda now?

Mr. Stevenson. They are taking up the league of nations. They are seeking the amnesty of all political prisoners. They do not want any military establishment here. It is a very mixed type of propaganda. I do not know exactly what they are doing.

Senator King. It is practically the overthrow of our republican form of government, and the establishment of a—

Senator Nelson. Bolsehevik government?

Senator King. Yes.

Mr. Stevenson. There are a large number of persons connected with this organization that sympathize with the Bolshevik and Soviet form of government.

Senator King. Class government is what they want.

Mr. Stevenson. I think we shall have to wait until we see their propaganda before we know exactly what they are doing.

Senator Wolcott. There is no telling what they are going to do?

Mr. Stevenson. I do not think so.

The outgrowth of this People's Council was the Liberty Defense Union, with offices at 138 West Thirteenth Street, New York City, in which there is a curious mixture of intelligentsia and anarchists, radical socialists and—

Senator Wolcott. What do you mean by "intelligentsia"—intellectuals?

Mr. Stevenson. Intellectuals.

Senator Nelson. Senator, it means those anarchists who confine their operations to brain storms and not to physical force.

Mr. Stevenson. Among the members of this organization were the Rev. John Haynes Holmes; Scott Nearing; Elizabeth Gurley Flinn, who is well known as an I.W.W.; Max Eastman; Kate Richards O'Hare—and, by the way, there is an extremely interesting connection. Kate Richards O'Hare is now serving a sentence for violation of the espionage act, but she was an associate of Nicholas Lenine in the International Bureau, the People's House, in Brussels before the war, in 1914.

Senator Wolcott. This question has been running through my mind, Mr. Stevenson: Is it not a fact that these people, after all their efforts and agitation and the expenditure of a great deal of labor and emotional energy, after all did not make any kind of an impression at all on the plain, common-sense American people —speaking by and large, I mean; they did not make any dents, did they?

Mr. Stevenson. I think if you really mean the American people, I should say no, Senator.

Senator Wolcott. That is what I mean. I mean the ordinary American citizen.

Mr. Stevenson. But it is a fact that—

Senator Wolcott. Of course, they can make some trouble here and there in spots; but, taking the great body of the American people, were they not too level headed to be influenced by this outfit?

Mr. Stevenson. We must remember, Senator, that the American people—and by that I mean really American people—are not present in very large numbers in our industrial centers. They have made a very great impression on the foreign element, which we will develop in the progress of the radical movement.

I have brought in this pacifist movement in this way because of its direct connection with the subsequent radical movement, which is the thing which is of most importance before the country today.

In connection with this Liberty Defense Union, Amos Pinchot was also a member; Eugene V. Debs; Henry Wadsworth Dana, a late professor of Columbia University; David Starr Jordan; Abram Shiplacoff, a Socialist assemblyman in New York; James H. Maurer, of the Pennsylvania Federation of Labor; and a large number of other persons of similar character.

The result of the Ford peace mission was the establishment of an international committee of women for permanent peace, which was organized at The Hague in 1915. They organized a special branch for the United States and that branch had a subsidiary in New York City, which is now known as the Women's International League.

It is rather interesting to note that at a meeting held on the 28th of November in New York City by this league, among the other literature which was disseminated was a pamphlet by a man known as Louis T. Fraina, entitled "Bolshevism Conquers", and the meeting resulted in a riot by some unattached soldiers that did not like the general tenor of the meeting.

Senator Nelson. They broke it up?

Mr. Stevenson. Mrs. Henry Villard, the mother of Oswald Garrison Villard, was the honorary chairman; Crystal Eastman was the chairman; and Prof. Emily Greene Balch was also a member of that organization. . . .

Mr. Stevenson. The corollary of the propaganda which was mentioned this morning, and in which a large number of the persons engaged in the pacifist organizations have taken part and now take part, is what may be generally classified as the radical movement, which is developing sympathy for the Bolsheviki movement, and which in many quarters constitutes a revolutionary movement among the radical element in this country.

Senator King. Your contention is that this is the result of German propaganda, had its orgin in Germany, and therefore would be properly investigated under the resolution of this committee?

Mr. Stevenson. Yes. The Bolsheviki movement is a branch of the revolutionary socialism of Germany. It had its origin in the philosophy of Marx and its leaders were Germans.

Senator King. And is this German socialism of this country and Bolshevism of this country the product of or taught by these organizations to which you referred this morning, in part?

Mr. Stevenson. The membership of those organizations was in large part made up of persons either members of the Socialist Party or in sympathy with it.

Senator Nelson. You mean that the German socialism was imported into this country by these men?

Mr. Stevenson. By some of these men.

Senator Nelson. That is what I mean.

Mr. Stevenson. Yes.

In order to have a clear conception, however, of the radical movement, I might say that there are three principal currents of thought that go to make it up, one of which is the syndicalist, which is represented in this country by the I.W.W., and the Socialist Labor Party—

Senator Nelson. They are in favor of what I would call sabotage?

Mr. Stevenson. Yes. If you will permit me to read briefly a little memorandum that I have here, I will read it more rapidly.

The word "syndicate" is the French equivlent of our trade-union, but syndicalism has a decidedly revolutionary flavor, and must therefore be understood to mean revolutionary trade-unionism. This does not mean, however, that syndicalism is merely a fighting trade-unionism, although it originated from the cooperative or trade-union movement. It goes much further, and demands that wealth, productive and distributive, be controlled by the various trade unions to the exclusion of the capitalists and the State. It believes that the railways should be controlled and operated by the miners' union, etc. Capitalists have no place in this scheme, save that experts in finance, engineering, and technology may be hired by the union. No central authority is contemplated, and national industry must be carried on by agreements made between various groups of workmen. This form of economic program has accordingly been termed "group anarchism". With syndicalism is coupled "propaganda by deed" or "direct action"; that is, the tactics of general strike and sabotage.

Senator Overman. Are they in favor of legislative bodies?

Mr. Stevenson. No.

Senator Overman. Or executive officers?

Mr. Stevenson. No.

Senator Overman. They are in favor of a sort of mob rule?

Mr. Stevenson. It is group anarchism.

Senator Nelson. Each group of workmen, for instance—in the case of miners, each group of miners—is a law unto itself, a government to itself, and each group of railroad men would run the railroads, and so on?

Mr. Stevenson. The syndicalists believe society is divided into two sharply defined groups, the producers, usually interpreted as manual laborers, and non-producers; and among the latter are capitalists and employers.

Between the exploited—namely, the workers—and their exploiters—namely, the employers—the syndicalist recognizes a state of continuous warfare, which is known as class struggle.

Syndicalism was developed in France in comparatively recent times.

Trade-unionism in France was not permitted until 1884, and, as in Russia, the workmen had to organize in secret. This made them law-breakers and developed their antagonism to the government authorities.

The propaganda of socialists, anarchists, and other revolutionary bodies stimulated their revolutionary principles, and the employment of the regular armed forces of the French Government to break up strikes developed among some of these French trade-unions a pronounced militarist and antipatriotic character.

This attitude was aggravated through the propaganda of Gustav Herve and others, who skillfully exploited the circumstances surrounding the strike of Longwy in 1905.

Senator Overman. Do you know to what extent these groups have gone in the different nations—England and Italy and our other allies?

Mr. Stevenson. They were quite extensive, only with varied forms. Each country modifies rather the theories of the different groups, but almost identical with the French syndicalist is the I.W.W. in the United States.

The I.W.W., because of its activities—

Senator Overman. I do not know but I have seen it in the record, but I will ask you to state now just what you mean by the I.W.W.

Mr. Stevenson. Industrial Workers of the World.

The Industrial Workers of the World, which, because of its activity, has attracted wide attention, has been the subject of various prosecutions for violations of the Federal and State laws and has aroused the sympathy and engaged the support of a large number of organizations and individuals who have acted against the interests of the United States during the war. For instance, the National Civil Liberties Bureau, which was mentioned this morning, cooperated very extensively in the preparation of propaganda to justify the existence and tactics of the I.W.W. and raised funds for their defense and in every way cooperated to assist in their defense. They procured bail for William D. Haywood and, I believe, one or two others of those indicted in Chicago.

Senator Nelson. That bail went glimmering when they tried to blow up the courthouse.

Mr. Stevenson. The I.W.W. movement began in the fall of 1904, and at a secret conference in Chicago, Illinois, on January 2, 1905, the industrial union manifesto calling for a convention to be held in Chicago on June 22, 1905, was drawn for the purpose of launching an organization in accordance with the principles set forth in the manifesto, which were distinctly syndicalist.

183

The work of circulating the manifesto was handled by the executive committee of this conference, the American Labor Union, and the Western Federation of Miners.

After several modifications, the preamble of the I.W.W., which is now in force—that is, the preamble of their constitution—was adopted at their fourth convention and is as follows:

The working class and the employing class have nothing in common. There can be no peace so long as hunger and want are found among working people, and the few who make up the employing class have all the good things in life.

Between these two classes a struggle must go on until the workers of the world organize as a class, take possession of the earth and the machinery of production, and abolish the wage system.

We find that the centering of the management of industries into fewer and fewer hands makes the trade unions unable to cope with the ever growing power of the employing class. The trade unions foster a state of affairs which allows one set of workers to be pitted against another set of workers in the same industry, thereby helping to defeat one another in wage war. Moreover, the trade unions aid the employing class to mislead the workers into the belief that the working class have interests in common with their employers.

These conditions can be changed and the interest of the working class upheld only by an organization formed in such a way that all its members in any one industry, or in all industries if necessary, cease work whenever a strike or lockout is on in any department thereof, thus making an injury to one an injury to all.

Instead of the conservative motto "a fair day's wages for a fair day's work", we must inscribe on our banner the revolutionary watchword "abolition of the wage system".

It is the historic mission of the working class to do away with capitalism. The army of production must be organized, not only for the every day struggle with the capitalists, but also to carry on production when capitalism shall have been overthrown. By organizing industrially we are forming the structure of the new society within the shell of the old.

The methods employed by the I.W.W. to carry out their purposes are described by Vincent St. John, who was one of the defendants in the Chicago trial. In a pamphlet entitled "The I.W.W., Its History, Structure, and Methods", published by the I.W.W. Publishing Bureau, 112 Hamilton Avenue, Cleveland, Ohio, we find the following statement of their methods and tactics:

As a revolutionary organization, the Industrial Workers of the World aims to use any and all tactics that will get the results sought with the least expenditure of time and energy. The tactics used are determined solely by the power of the organization to make good in their use. The question of "right" and "wrong" does not concern us.

No terms made with an employer are final. All peace so long as the wage system lasts is but an armed truce. At any favorable opportunity the struggle for more control of industry is renewed. . . . No part of the organization is allowed to enter into time contracts with the employers. Where strikes are used, it aims to paralyze all branches of the industry involved, when the employers can least afford a cessation of work—during the busy season and when there are rush orders to be filled. . . . Failing to force concessions from the employers by the strike, work is resumed and sabotage is used to force the employers to concede the demands of the workers. The great progress made in machine productions results in an ever increasing army of unemployed. To counteract this the I.W.W. aims to establish the shorter working day and to slow up the working pace, thus compelling the employment of more and more workers. . . . Interference by the government is resented by open violation of the government's orders, going to jail en masse, causing expense to the tax payers—which is but another name for the employing class.

In short, the I.W.W. advocates the use of "militant direct action" tactics, to the full extent of our power to make good.

That is their own statement of their methods of action.

Shall I refer to some of the matters that were spoken of in the executive session, Mr. Chairman?

Senator Overman. Yes; those connected with this propaganda ought to be mentioned.

Mr. Stevenson. I mean in reference to the attempt to quash the indictment in the case of the United States against William D. Haywood et al.

Senator Nelson. Those connected with the I.W.W.

Senator Overman. Yes.

Mr. Stevenson. The indictment of the I.W.W. leaders and their subsequent trial in Chicago, namely, the case of the United States against William D. Haywood et al., attracted wide attention. Defense committees were organized for the purpose of raising money to carry on the expense of the defense and to issue propaganda designed to lead the public to believe that the I.W.W. was a labor organization whose sole purpose was to better working conditions.

One of the organizations most active in assisting the defense committee, both in the matter of raising funds and securing bail for William D. Haywood and in carrying on a widespread publicity campaign, was the National Civil Liberties Bureau, of 70 Fifth Avenue, New York City.

A very careful examination was made of the files of the National Civil Liberties Bureau relating to the I.W.W.

Mr. Roger N. Baldwin, director of the National Civil Liberties Bureau, in a letter to Justin Ebert, 223 Richmond Street, Brooklyn, dated November 8, 1917, speaks of the proposed pamphlets against "The silly and outrageous indictments against the I.W.W."

Senator Overman. Is that organization now existing in New York?

Mr. Stevenson. Yes.

Senator Overman. Is Baldwin still president of it?

Mr. Stevenson. No. Baldwin is now in jail.

A further examination of these files indicates that a movement was set on foot about this time to exert influence upon officials and others to quash the indictments in this case, and on December 26, 1917, Mr. Frank P. Walsh, at that time cochairman with ex-President William H. Taft, of the Industrial Relations Commission, addressed a letter to the National Civil Liberties Bureau, introducing J.A. Law and L.T. Chumley, both members of the defense council of the I.W.W. Thereafter Mr. Chumley took up his offices with the National Civil Liberties Bureau and worked with them in the plans for raising funds for the I.W.W. defense and in putting out propaganda literature justifying the position of the I.W.W.

Senator Wolcott. Was either of those men among the I.W.W. defendants?

Mr. Stevenson. Jack Law was.

On January 11 Mr. Baldwin sent to Clarence Darrow, at 140 North Dearborn Street, Chicago, Ill., a copy of the minutes held in Washington relative to the I.W.W.'s on January 12, 1918. Copies of this report were sent to Gilbert E. Rowe, George B. West, Jack Law, Lawrence Todd, and others. The report says: "No action taken in the absence of Messrs. Walsh and Darrow".

A letter was received from L.T. Chumley, of 1001 West Madison Street, Chicago, Ill., by the National Civil Liberties Bureau, sending material for a pamphlet under separate cover and saying: "Frank P. Walsh will do the same", and asks suggestions as to how to raise $25,000 bail for Haywood.

As an illustration of the type of propaganda put out by the National Civil Liberties Bureau, I offer as an exhibit this pamphlet, "The Truth About the I.W.W."

Senator Wolcott. That is an I.W.W. pamphlet?

Mr. Stevenson. No; that is a pamphlet justifying the I.W.W. by the National Civil Liberties Bureau.

Senator Wolcott. I mean the National Civil Liberties Bureau put out this pamphlet, which is really I.W.W. propaganda?

Mr. Stevenson. Yes; it is propaganda, precisely.

The mailing list of the National Civil Liberties Bureau was put at the disposal of Wm. D. Haywood, who, in a letter, addressed to them on May 21, says that he has engaged Harrison George to write letters to be sent to the National Civil Liberties Bureau mailing list.

Senator Wolcott. Is that one of the organizations—that National Civil Liberties Bureau—whose officers you were going to enumerate later on, or not?

Mr. Stevenson. We enumerated the principal ones this morning, Senator.

Senator Wolcott. That had slipped my mind.

Mr. Stevenson. Yes.

Scott Nearing assisted in the preparation of material for the defense and Mr. Charles W. Erving, 440 Pearl Street, New York City, Socialist candidate for governor at the last election in New York, received $400 for reporting the I.W.W. trial.

The danger of the sympathy which was raised by the I.W.W. is illustrated by an advertisement which appeared in the *New Republic* on June 22, 1918.

Senator Nelson. Where is that published?

Mr. Stevenson. That is published in New York. It is a magazine.

Senator Nelson. Is it a monthly magazine?

Mr. Stevenson. No. It is a weekly magazine.

Senator Nelson. Who are the publishers of it?

Mr. Stevenson. Mr. Walter E. Weyl is the editor of it.

Senator Nelson. But who owns it?

Mr. Stevenson. I think the main backer of it was Willard D. Straight. This advertisement appeared on June 22.

Senator Nelson. This last June?

Mr. Stevenson. Yes; June, 1918. (Reading:)

Never mind what you think about the I.W.W. They are at least entitled to a fair trial and an open-minded public hearing. That is a primary American right.

One hundred and ten of their leaders are now before the Federal Court at Chicago, charged with conspiring to obstruct the war. But the trial involves essentially the activities of the I.W.W. as a labor organization.

The I.W.W. are entitled to the best legal defense they can make. They must bring scores of witnesses long distances. The trial will probably last months.

The Department of Justice, the Court, and the jury can be relied upon to deal effectually with any criminal acts that may be disclosed. It is for American liberals to make it financially possible for the defense to present fully the industrial evils underlying the I.W.W. revolt against intolerable conditions of labor.

Such a labor trial is of necessity enormously expensive. It will cost over $100,000. Of this about $50,000 has already been raised from the membership alone. But it is impossible to raise the entire fund from the members.

The whole sum needed cannot be secured without the liberal financial support of those Americans who believe in the right of a fair trial, even for the I.W.W.

The undersigned therefore appeal to all liberals for financial help. Checks should be made out to Albert DeSilver, treasurer, 2 West 13th St., New York City.

Robert W. Bruere	Hellen Keller
John Dewey	Jas. Harvey Robinson
John A. Fitch	Thorstein Veblen
Percy Stickney Grant	George P. West
Carlton J. H. Hayes	Walter E. Weyl
Inez Haynes Irwin	

By the way, Albert De Silver was a member of the directing committee of the National Civil Liberties Bureau.

Mr. George P. West is the editor of *The Public,* a magazine.

Mr. Veblen is one of the editors of *The Dial.*

Mr. John A. Fitch is the industrial editor of *The Survey*—all of them rather liberal magazines.

Mr. Walter E. Weyl is the editor of the *New Republic*.

I might call attention to one of the newspapers issued by the I.W.W., entitled "The Labor Defender, an organ of revolutionary unionism".

There appears on the back page a rather inconspicuous cartoon. This is the issue of December 15, 1918. The title of this cartoon is:

Every strike is a small revolution and a dress rehearsal for the big one.

Here is the paper, if any of you gentlemen would like to look at it.

Senator Wolcott. Mr. Stevenson, my recollection is that the National Civil Liberties Bureau was organized primarily to protect conscientious objectors from service in the Army and to oppose the idea of fighting. Is that correct?

Mr. Stevenson. The National Civil Liberties Bureau was the outgrowth of the Civil Liberties Bureau of the American Union Against Militarism, made up of persons in sympathy with the pacifist movement. It then branched out into the protection of civil liberties in war time; in other words, the right of free speech, the right of peaceful assembly, "liberty of conscience and freedom from unlawful search and seizure".

Senator Wolcott. That is, the right of a conscientious objector not to serve.

Mr. Stevenson. That was one of the main features.

Senator Wolcott. Did I, in the main, correctly describe its purposes as twofold, first, against fighting, and, as a corollary to that, to protect everybody in all his activities of a nature designed to promote the idea of opposition to fighting?

Mr. Stevenson. The literature issued by that bureau was calculated to instruct a man how to be a conscientious objector, if he did not know what a conscientious objector was.

Senator Overman. It was a suggestion to him to keep from fighting.

Mr. Stevenson. It can be so construed.

Senator Wolcott. Is that general description that I have given there fairly accurate?

Mr. Stevenson. Fairly accurate, yes; but they also attempted to protect everybody who was indicted under the act of Congress or of the various States.

Senator Wolcott. I am just coming now to this thought: This organization, which seems to be animated by a very violent opposition to the idea of fighting, at the same time, from what you have just been saying, seems to have been quite in love with fighting as that idea was applied to these I.W.W.'s, because it was rendering assistance to them in their defense and was circulating their pamphlets?

Mr. Stevenson. While they did not say that they justified the ends or methods of the I.W.W., yet they claimed that civil liberties were being infringed upon by that prosecution.

Senator Wolcott. But they also circulated a pamphlet by the I.W.W. laying out its propaganda?

Mr. Stevenson. They did.

Senator Wolcott. That I.W.W., as I understand it, is an organization which recognizes as one of the legitimate weapons the institution of revolution—violence?

Mr. Stevenson. They certainly recognize violence.

Senator Wolcott. But this peaceful and pacific organization which was called the National Civil Liberties Bureau found violence as applied by the I.W.W. quite acceptable to them; whereas violence as applied by the armies of a free people was unacceptable to them? Is that correct?

Mr. Stevenson. Apparently, that would be the conclusion. . . .

(The list of names mentioned and submitted by Mr. Stevenson is here printed in full in the record, as follows:)

Jane Addams: Chairman, Woman's Peace Party; vice chairman, Amer. Neutral Confer. Committee; exec. comm. Amer. Un. Ag. Militarism; Council of Fellowship of Reconciliation; Amer. League to Limit Armaments.

James J. Bagley: President of Franklin Union, No. 23, Inc., New York City; member org. comm. People's Council; exec. comm. Peace Without Victory League; speaker at conference of Young Democracy, May 1918; exec. comm. Young Democracy.

Henry J. Cadbury: Professor Univ. of Penna.; exec. comm. Young Democracy; Amer. Friends Service Comm.; Fellowship of Reconciliation.

Edmund C. Evans: Architect, Philadelphia; org. comm. People's Council; exec. comm. Fellowship of Reconciliation; exec. comm. Nat'l. Civil Lib. Bur.; active in Young Democracy.

Harold Evans: Lawyer, Philadelphia; atty. for Civil Lib. Bureau of Am. Un. Ag. Mil.; gen. comm. Liberty Defense Union; exec. comm. Fellowship of Reconciliation; Amer. Friends Service Comm.; exec. comm. Young Democracy.

Kuno Francke: One time prof. Harvard; Amer. Neutral Conf. Comm.; Intercol. Socialist Soc.; Knight Royal Order Prussian Red Eagle and Order of Crown.

Prof. William F. Bade: Berkeley, California. Studied University of Berlin 1905–06; prof. at University of California 1902; member of Intercollegiate Socialist Society.

Prof. Emily Greene Balch: Economist; studied with Profs. Schmoller and Wagner; prof. of political economy and social science Wellesley; American Neutral Conference Committee; People's Council of America; Liberty Defense Union; Woman's Peace Party of New York City; Emergency Peace Federation; American Union Against Militarism; Collegiate Anti-Militarism League; Woman's International League; Intercollegiate Socialist Society.

Roger N. Baldwin: Now serving sentence for violation of Selective Service Act; former instructor sociology at Washington University, St. Louis; member of National Civil Liberties Bureau, American Union Against Militarism, Liberty Defense Union, Collegiate Anti-Militarism League, Fellowship of Reconciliation,

Bureau of Legal Advice, League for the Amnesty of Political Prisoners, National Conference of Labor, Socialist and Radical Movements.

Prof. Charles A. Beard: Formerly of Columbia University; Member of Intercollegiate Socialist Society; Lecturer at Rand School of Social Science.

Prof. Sophonisba P. Breckinridge: Asst. Prof. of Household Administration, University of Chicago since 1908; American Union Against Militarism; Woman's Peace Party.

Prof. Frederick A. Bushee: Studied in Berlin; Prof. at Colorado College; Member of Intercollegiate Socialist Society.

Evans Clark: Formerly Instructor of Economics at Princeton University in Economics: Head of Bureau of Research and Lecturer at Rand School of Social Science; Member of Intercollegiate Socialist Society.

Lindsay T. Damon: Prof. at Brown University; Member of Intercollegiate Socialist Society.

Henry W.L. Dana: Former Prof. of English at Columbia University; member People's Council of America, Collegiate Anti-Militarism League, Young Democracy, Nation Conference of Labor, Socialist and Radical Movements.

John Lovejoy Elliott: Educator; Ph.D. from Halle University, Germany; Member American Union Against Militarism; Liberty Defense Union, Bureau Legal Advice, National Civil Liberties Bureau.

Elizabeth Freeman: Born in England; exec. sec'y Peoples Council; advisory board League for Amnesty of Political Prisoners; comm. League of Small and Subject Nationalities.

Elizabeth Gurley Flynn: I.W.W. for last 10 years; under indictment for violation espionage act; exec comm. Liberty Defense Union.

Thomas C. Hall: Professor and theologian, studied in Germany, connected with Union Theological Seminary; member Intercollegiate Socialist Society; on Reception Comm. Friends of Peace; org. Comm. of German Univ. League in this country; wrote many articles for *Fatherland*; decorated by Kaiser with the Order of the Crown. Now living in Germany.

Morris Hillquit (originally Morris Hilkowist): Born in Russia; org. comm. People's Council; atty. cooperating with Nat'l. Civil Liberties Bureau; Amer. League to Limit Armaments.

John Haynes Holmes: Clergyman; exec. comm. Amer. Neutral Conf. Comm.; exec. com. Amer. Union Ag. Mil.; Civil Liberties Bureau; dir. comm. Nat'l. Civil Liberties Bureau; vice-pres. Liberty Defense Union; edit. board "World Tomorrow"; of Fellowship of Reconciliation; Amer. League to Limit Armaments.

Frederick C. Howe: Lawyer, Commissioner of Immigration at New York; studied in Germany; gen. comm. Amer. Neutral Conference Comm.; pres. League of Small and Subject Nationalities; Member of League of Free Nations Ass'n. advisory board Brown Open Forum.

Jessie W. Hughan: professor, Barnard College; adv. board, Collegiate Anti-

190

Militarism League; council, Fellowship of Reconciliation; exec. board, Woman's International League; sec'y. N.Y. State Branch of Woman's Peace Party; exec. comm. Intercollegiate Socialist Society; member, League of Conscientious Objectors.

William I. Hull: professor Swarthmore; studied in Germany; gen'l. comm. Amer. Mutual Conf. Comm., member council, Fellowship of Reconciliation.

Paul Jones: bishop; org. comm. People's Council; council, Fellowship of Reconciliation; interested in Young Democracy.

Rufus H. Jones: professor, Haverford College; on editorial board, "World Tomorrow"; council, Fellowship of Reconciliation; Amer. Friends Service Comm.

David Starr Jordan: chancellor, Stanford Univ.; Amer. Mutual Conference Comm.; exec. comm. Amer. Un. Ag. Militarism; gen'l. comm. Liberty Defense Union; adv. comm. Collegiate Anti-Mil. League; comm. Amer. League to Limit Armaments, People's Council of Amer.

Lindley M. Keasbey: professor, Univ. of Texas; studied in Germany; member org. comm. People's Council of Amer. & in charge of org. work in southern states.

Geo. W. Kirchwey: formerly dean of Columbia Law School; Amer. Neutral Conf. Comm.; member Civic Club of N.Y., a meeting place of radicals; member adv. board Brown Open Forum.

Edward Krehbiel: professor, Stanford Univ.; member League to Enforce Peace; gen. comm. Amer. Neutral Conference Comm.; Civil Liberties Bureau of Amer. Union Ag. Militarism; member League of Free Nations Ass'n.

Agnes Brown Leach, of New York: exec. board Woman's International League; treas. N.Y. State Branch of Woman's Peace Party; treas. Woman's Peace Party of N.Y. City; exec. com. Amer. Union Ag. Mil.; dir. comm. Nat'l. Civil Liberties Bureau; interested in Young Democracy; member Civic Club of N.Y.

Louis P. Lochner: pers. representative of Henry Ford on Ford Peace Mission; exec. sec'y. People's Council of Amer.; member Liberty Defense Union; org. comm. Nat'l. Conference of Labor, Socialist & Radical Movements.

Frederick Lynch: clergyman exec. comm. Amer. Neutral Conference Comm., treas. Emergency Peace Federation; exec. comm. Amer. Union Ag. Militarism; interested in Nat'l. Civil Liberties Bureau; connected with Leagues of Small & Subject Nationalities.

Judah L. Magnes: rabbi; org. comm. People's Council of Amer.; dir. comm. Nat'l Civic Liberties Bureau.

Theresa T. Malkiel, of New York: exec. board Woman's Internat'l. League; member, N.Y. State Branch of Woman's Peace Party; exec. com. Liberty Defense Union.

James H. Mamer: pres. Penn. Federation of Labor; org. com. People's Council of Amer.; exec. com. Amer. Union Ag. Mil., gen'l. comm. Liberty Defense Union.

Miss Tracy Mygatt, of New York: Member Overflow Meeting Comm. of Friends of Peace; exec. comm. Bureau of Legal First Aid; assoc. editor for *Young Democracy*.

Scott Nearing: Formerly asst. professor of Univ. of Penna.; exec, comm. Amer. Union Ag. Mil.; Liberty Defense Union; org. comm. People's Council of Amer.; Intercollegiate Socialist Society; indicted under espionage act.

Kate Richards O'Hare: Was chairman of comm. on War and Militarism at nat'l. convention of Socialist Party held in St. Louis, Mo., Apr. 7/14, 1917, which reported the antiwar resolution; represented Amer. in Intern'l. Socialist Bureau at People's House in Brussels; member of exec. comm. Liberty Defense Union; now serving term of imprisonment for violation espionage act.

James P. Warbasse, M.D.; Brooklyn N.Y.: Member American Union Against Militarism, National Civil Liberties Bureau, Peace Without Victory League.

Harry F. Ward, Union Theological Seminary, New York: Member of Collegiate Anti-Militarism League, Fellowship of Reconciliation, Liberty Defiance Union.

Donald Winston of New York: Member National Committee of Collegiate Anti-Militarism League, Executive Committee Fellowship of Reconciliation; Active in organization of Young Democracy; Connected with Union Theological Seminary.

L. Hollingsworth Wood: Lawyer, New York City; Treas. of American Union Against Militarism; Chairman National Civil Liberties Bureau; Treas. Fellowship of Reconciliation.

Eugene V. Debs: Socialist; Now serving sentence for violation of Espionage Act; Member Organizing Committee, People's Council of America, General Committee Liberty Defense Union; Member of National Conference of Labor, Socialist and Radical Movements.

Prof. Harry A. Overstreet: Prof. in College of City of New York, Philosophy; Member of Emergency Peace Federation, Collegiate Anti-Militarism League, Intercollegiate Socialist Society, League of Free Nation's Association.

Judge Jacob Panken: Judge Municipal Court, New York City; Pres. of "Forward", radical Jewish Newspaper; Member of People's Council of America, National Conference of Labor, Socialist, and Radical Movement.

Elsie Clews Parsons (Mrs. Herbert), of New York: Member People's Council of America, American League to Limit Armaments.

Amos R.E. Pinchot: Lawyer; Member American Neutral Conference Committee, American Union Against Militarism, Liberty Defense Union, National Civil Liberties Bureau.

Gilbert E. Roe: Lawyer, New York City; Atty. for National Civil Liberties Bureau; interested in People's Council of America.

Rev. Harold L. Rotzel, Boston, Mass.: Member of League of Democratic Control, Fellowship of Reconciliation, League for Permanent Peace; interested in defense of I.W.W.; connected with National Civil Liberties Bureau.

Rev. John N. Sayre, Suffern, N.Y.: Member of Fellowship of Reconciliation, National Civil Liberties Bureau.

Joseph Schlossberg: Sec'y. of Amalgamated Clothing Workers of America; member People's Council of America, Liberty Defense Union, National Conference of Labor, Socialist and Radical Movements, Young Democracy.

Nathaniel Schmidt: Prof. Cornell University; studied in Germany; member of Intercollegiate Socialist Society.

Vida D. Scudder: Prof. at Wellesley College; member American Neutral Conference Committee Intercollegiate Socialist Society; writer on Socialism and Literature.

Prof. Clarence R. Skinner: Prof. Tufts University; member of Collegiate Anti-Militarism League; on Editorial Staff *Young Democracy*.

Helen Phelps Stokes, of New York: Treas. National Civil Liberties Bureau; Vice Chairman Liberty Defense Union; member of Council of Fellowship of Reconciliation; Executive Committee Intercollegiate Socialist Society.

Rev. Sidney String, Seattle, Washington: Member of People's Council of America, Liberty Defense Union, Fellowship of Reconciliation.

Rev. Norman M. Thomas, of New York: Member American Union Against Militarism, National Civil Liberties Bureau, Liberty Defense Union, Fellowship of Reconciliation; Editor, *World Tomorrow;* National Conference of Labor, Socialist and Radical Movements.

Alexander Trachtenberg, of New York: Member of Collegiate Anti-Militarism League; Director of Dept. of Labor Research Rand School of Social Science; contributor to *The Liberator,* successor to *The Masses*.

Rev. Irwin St. John Tucker: Clergyman and Editor, Chicago, Ill.; Managing Editor "Christian Socialist"; member of People's Council of America; Chairman Peoples Council of Chicago; convicted of violation of Espionage Act.

Oswald Garrison Villard: Born in Germany; Editor of *The Nation;* member American Neutral Conference Comm., American Union Against Militarism, American League to Limit Armaments, Fellowship of Reconciliation; interested in National Civil Liberties Bureau.

Lillian D. Wald: Sociologist, of New York; member American Neutral Conference Committee American Union Against Militarism, Civil Liberties Bureau, American League to Limit Armaments, Woman's Peace Party of New York.

Excerpts from the Lusk Committee Report, 1920[1]

The moving spirit of the organizing activities of the National Civil Liberties Bureau was its Director Roger N. Baldwin; and there can be no better example of

[1]*Revolutionary Radicalism, Its History, Purpose and Tactics* (Albany, N.Y.: J.B. Lyon, 1920), vol. I, pp. 1087–1100; vol. II, pp. 1983–1984.

his type of mind than to quote again from his advisory letter of August, 1917, to Louis Lochner, in reference to organizing the People's Council Convention:

"Do steer away from making it look like a Socialist enterprise. Too many people have already gotten the idea that it is nine-tenths a Socialist movement. You can, of course, avoid this by bringing to the front people like Senator Works, Miss Addams, and others, who are known as substantial Democrats. . . . I think it would be an error to get the public thinking that we are launching a political party in Minneapolis. To be sure we are launching a political movement, but that is quite a different matter from a political point. . . .

"We want also to look like patriots in everything we do. We want to get a good lot of flags, talk a good deal about the Constitution and what our forefathers wanted to make of this country, and to show that we are really the folks that really stand for the spirit of our institutions".

The advice to have plenty of flags and to seem patriotic in everything was particularly characteristic of Baldwin, to the naked eye a charming, well-bred liberal, of good American stock and traditions, in reality a radical to the very bone, with a strong leaning towards the I.W.W. According to the sworn testimony of Norman Thomas, Baldwin was a philosophical anarchist. His point of view is also illustrated by the statement to the Court at the time he was sentenced for a violation of the Selective Service Act, as follows:

" Though, at the moment, I am of a tiny minority, I feel myself just one protest in a great revolt surging up from among the people—the struggle of the masses against the rule of the world by the few—profoundly intensified by the war. It is a struggle against the political state itself, against exploitation, militarism, imperialism, authority in all forms. It is a struggle to break in full force only after the war. Russia already stands in the vanguard, beset by her enemies in the camps of both belligerents—the central empires break asunder from within, the labor movement gathers revolutionary forces in Britain—and in our own country the Non-Partisan League, radical labor and the Socialist Party hold the germs of a new social order. Their protest is my protest." (Quoted from a leaflet issued by friends of Roger Baldwin, November, 1918.)

After the conviction of Roger Baldwin above referred to, the National Civil Liberties Bureau continued its activities; and on November 18, 1918, its officers were as follows:

L. Hollingsworth Wood, chairman; Norman M. Thomas, vice-chairman; Helen Phelps Stokes, treasurer; Albert De Silver, director; William G. Simpson, associate director; Walter Nelles, counsel.

The directing committee was John S. Codman, John Lovejoy Elliott, Walter W. Haviland, Agnes Brown Leach, Crystal Eastman, Edmund C. Evans, John Haynes Holmes, Judah L. Magnes, and John Nevin Sayre.

An examination of the various accounts for the formation of the bureau from

October, 1917, to August 31, 1918, showed a turnover of $17,000. Of this amount, about $10,000 was received from the following subscribers:

Eliza Cope, William P. Bancroft, Sarah J. Eddy, Mrs. J. Sargent Cram, A.G. Scattergood, Harold A. Hatch, Mary McMurtrie, Alexander Fleischer, Edith Borg, Albert De Silver, Agnes Brown Leach, Helen Phelps Stokes, John Nevin Sayre, James H. Post and Mrs. Maurice Lowenstein.

One of the principal activities of the National Civil Liberties Bureau, as will be disclosed in this chapter, was to create sympathy for the Industrial Workers of the World, commonly known as the I.W.W. In order to be acquainted with the precise character of the I.W.W., Part I, Sec. 2, Sub-sec. 3, Chapter I of this report, should be read. There will be found a statement of the purposes, objects, methods and tactics of the I.W.W. as defined by its own membership.

Perhaps the one organization which was most active in assisting the defense committees of the I. W. W., both in the matter of raising funds and securing bail for William D. Haywood and in carrying on a widespread publicity campaign to create sympathy for the I.W.W., was the National Civil Liberties Bureau.

In a letter of Baldwin to Justin Ebert, 233 Richmond Street, Brooklyn, dated November 8, 1917, he speaks of proposed pamphlets against "the silly and outrageous indictments against the I.W.W." In preparing the proposed pamphlet on the I.W.W. (which was issued as a bulletin of the National Civil Liberties Bureau) he discussed its contents first on November 13, 1917, with the secretary of the I.W.W., C.E. Payne, of 19 South La Salle Street, Chicago, receiving Payne's approval on November 17, 1917.

A further examination of the National Civil Liberties Bureau's files indicates that a movement was set on foot about this time to exert influence upon officials to quash the indictment in the I.W.W. cases; and on December 26, 1917, Mr. Frank P. Walsh, at that time co-chairman with ex-President William H. Taft, of the War Labor Board, addressed a letter to the National Civil Liberties Bureau, introducing J.A. Law, and L.S. Chumley, both of the Defense Council of the I.W.W. Thereafter Mr. Chumley took up his offices with the National Civil Liberties Bureau, working with them in the plans for raising funds for the I.W.W. defense, and in putting out propaganda literature justifying the position of the I.W.W. Chumley is now the organizer of the I.W.W. in New York, and editor of the "Rebel Worker".

Presently a conference was proposed to take place in Washington on January 10, 1918, for the purpose of taking certain action in regard to the I.W.W. trial. On January 7th, Mr. George Creel, chairman of the Committee on Public Information, addressed a letter to the National Civil Liberties Bureau, in regard to the I.W.W., as follows:

"Please omit my name from any lists that you send out, and be at particular pains not to give the impression that I am a part of your organization or connected with it in any way. I will see Mr. Walsh when he comes."

Mr. Baldwin's reply to Mr. Creel, on January 8, 1918, states that he appreciates Mr. Creel's position and says Mr. Walsh wants Creel at the meeting, "in the interests of a harmonious handling of a matter of such great public merit".

On January 11th, Roger Baldwin sent to Clarence Darrow at 140 North Dearborn Street, Chicago, a copy of the report of the I.W.W. meeting in Washington on January 9, 1918. Further copies of this report were sent to Gilbert E. Roe, George P. West, Charles Merz, Jack Law, Laurence Todd, Ned Cochran, Basil Manly. The report says in effect:

> No action taken in the absence of Messrs. Walsh and Darrow. (Clearly Walsh and Darrow were unable to be present.)

In reference to the sending of material for the I.W.W. pamphlet under separate cover, L.S. Chumley wrote about the same date in part to Baldwin: that Frank P. Walsh would do the same, and asked for suggestions how to raise the $25,000 bail for Haywood.

In answer to this telegram Mr. Baldwin on the 22d of January wired:

> "Wiring Carlton Parker about having Haywood's bail reduced."

There are a number of other examples to illustrate that the relation between the National Civil Liberties Bureau and the I.W.W. was intimate. For instance, the mailing list of the bureau was put at the disposal of William D. Haywood, who, in a letter of May 28, 1918, said that he had engaged Harrison George to write letters to be sent to the National Civil Liberties Bureau mailing list. Assistance was also given by the bureau in gathering material to help the I. W. W. trial.

Again on June 18, 1918, Mr. Baldwin wrote to Prof. Irving Fisher, at 460 Prospect Street, Chicago, asking him to give him information on material for "social extravagance", this to be used by the defense in the I.W.W. trial. It is also on record that Professor Fisher gave the required information.

Other co-operation between the National Civil Liberties Bureau in regard to the I.W.W. trial itself was as follows:

(1) A letter from George F. Vandeveer, on June 22, 1918, referring to Scott Nearing's "Social Extravagance", which he enclosed for Baldwin's benefit. Much further correspondence between Baldwin and Vandeveer about various books on social extravagance. (Emphasis to be placed upon this phase of capitalism for the I.W.W. trial.)

(2) A letter from Baldwin, June 25, 1918, to Charles W. Ervin, present editor of the New York "Call", and later candidate for governor on the Socialist ticket in this State. In this letter Baldwin confirmed the arrangement to pay the "Call" $400 for reporting the I.W.W. trial, it being understood that David Karsner, Chicago representative of the "Call", would write an article once a week about the trial for the National Civil Liberties Bureau.

(3) Vincent St. John, convicted as one of the I.W.W. defendants, on July 9, 1918, writing from Chicago, acknowledged receipt from the National Civil Liberties Bureau of $1,167, and on July 13th of an additional $1,021, which payment seems to have been made for publicity, etc., concerning the I.W.W. trial.

(4) A letter from the I.W.W. defense committee to Baldwin:

"Vanderveer advises us of your offer to handle all I.W.W. cases where the right to agitate and organize is concerned."

(5) Paul Hanna, publicity agent for the I.W.W., outlined to Baldwin a "side door plan" to make the public sympathetic to the I.W.W. "The front door to fair publicity on the I.W.W. trial is shut and closed. But the side door stands wide open".

It was this idea of creating sympathy on the part of the public for the I.W.W. that was perhaps, after all, the most important contribution that the National Civil Liberties Bureau gave to "The Cause", for just at the psychological moment there was issued a pamphlet called "The Truth About the I.W.W.", published by the National Civil Liberties Bureau. On the first page of this pamphlet the following quotations from the reports of the President's Mediation Committee was printed:

"The I.W.W. has exercised its strongest hold in those industries and communities where employers have most resisted the trade movement and where some form of protest against unjust treatment was inevitable."

The object of the pamphlet, as stated in the introductory paragraph was:

"To furnish interested citizens with a fair statement about the I.W.W. by unprejudiced observers. This is necessary in view of the flood of unfounded and partisan 'information' constantly given to the public."

The most important contributor to the pamphlet was Mr. John Graham Brooks, of Cambridge, Mass., whose high standing as a writer among the scholars and intellectuals of the country naturally went far toward commanding some strong, if sentimental, sympathy for the I.W.W. All the while Brooks was co-operating with both Baldwin and Judge George Anderson (in Washington, D.C.), in preparing I.W.W. pamphlets. It must be admitted that he went to no end of trouble in preparing the pamphlet, traveling to New York several times in order to consult with Baldwin and his other collaborators.

Among these was Prof. Carlton Parker, of the University of Washington, a young professor who, though a radical, had been given a position by the government as a special agent of the War Department in dealing with the I.W.W. of the Northwest.

Prof. Parker, who had previously published an equivocal article in the "Atlantic

Monthly'' on the I.W.W., was considered more or less of an authority on the subject. It is, therefore, interesting to note that during the time he was serving the government as a mediator, he was collaborating in the writing of the pamphlet in question, urging sympathy for the I.W.W. As a matter of fact, this idea seems to have occurred to Prof. Parker himself (as it happened just before he died in 1918), for there are on file several urgent telegrams and letters from him to Baldwin, insisting that his name be not signed to that portion of the pamphlet which he (Parker) composed. (I.W.W., Vol. II, pp. 183-214.)

Perhaps the most striking of these messages from Parker to Baldwin is as follows, dated January 17, 1918:

"Developments here make it highly inadvisable to use my name in pamphlet. You can naturally use any of material I have sent on. I.W.W. are striking and rioting in the camps in which I have obtained for them all their demands, and this is compromising my position as Government Mediator and makes it impossible to join officially in pamphlet publicity. Extremely sorry." (I.W.W., Vol. II, p. 203.)

Baldwin, who apparently received other urgent telegrams from Parker in the meantime wrote him on March 12, 1918:

". . . You may be dead sure we won't refer to you as special agent of the War Department. . . ." (I.W.W., Vol. II, p. 212.)

Among other contributors or men helpful in the publication of the I.W.W. pamphlet were: Robert W. Bruere; Harold Callender, of Detroit, Mich., special investigator for Frank P. Walsh into the labor situation during the war in industries where the I.W.W. were strong; John A. Fitch, industrial editor of "The Survey"; Prof. Thorstein Veblen, of the School of Social Research in New York, and George P. West, of New York City.

Each of these men was an apologist for the I.W.W., and the whole pamphlet was an attempt to represent favorably the position of the I.W.W. and to throw great blame upon employers.

John Graham Brooks even went so far as to suggest to Baldwin how he might co-operate with "the Stokers' I.W.W., and other more recent organizations for propaganda purposes".

Another characteristic co-operative effort on the part of the National Civil Liberties Bureau in coloring or confusing public opinion concerning the I.W.W. was the placing of an advertisement in the "New Republic," June 22, 1918, of which the following is a copy:

"Never mind what you think about the I.W.W. they are at least entitled to a fair trial and an open minded public hearing. That is a primary American right.

"One hundred and ten of their leaders are now before the Federal Court at Chicago, charged with conspiring to obstruct the war, but the trial involves essentially the activities of the I.W.W. as a labor organization.

"The I.W.W. are entitled to the best legal defense they can make. They must bring scores of witnesses long distances. The trial will probably last months.

"The Department of Justice, the court and the jury can be relied upon to deal effectually with any criminal acts that may be disclosed. It is for American liberals to make it financially possible for the defense to present fully the industrial evils underlying the I.W.W. revolt against intolerable conditions of labor.

"Such a labor trial is, of necessity, enormously expensive. It will cost over $100,000. Of this about $50,000 has already been raised from the membership alone. But it is impossible to raise the entire fund from the members. The whole sum needed cannot be secured without the liberal financial support of those Americans who believe in the right of a fair trial, even for the I.W.W.

"The undersigned, therefore, appeal to all liberals for financial help. Checks should be made out to Albert De Silver, Treasurer, 2 West 13th Street, New York City.

"Robert W. Bruere,	"John Dewey,
"John A. Fitch,	"Percy Stickney Grant,
"Carlton J.H. Hayes,	"Inez Haynes Irwin,
"Helen Keller,	"James Harvey Robinson,
"Thorstein Veblen,	"George P. West."
"Walter E. Weyl,	

In this connection it is interesting to note the endeavors of the League for Democratic Control of Boston (one of the co-operating organizations of the National Civil Liberties Bureau) to raise money for the I.W.W. defense. A letter from Harold L. Rotzel, organizing secretary (who once signed himself "Yours for Bolshevik democracy"), on July 29, 1918, reads:

"My Dear Baldwin: . . . Our appeal for the I.W.W. among the supposedly liberal members of the Twentieth Century Club, to whom we had sent the pamphlet "The I.W.W." fell flat. . . . I made bold to use them as an illustration in a sermon in a Quaker church yesterday. . . . I think that a regular murderer would have a higher standing in the eyes of most people than an I.W.W. But of such is the Kingdom of War."

It is worth noting further that the National Civil Liberties Bureau, under its new name of the American Civil Liberties Bureau, today is as active as ever working up sympathy for revolutionaries, influencing public opinion, and generally spreading subversive propaganda.

One of the most subtle of the weapons used by these radicals is the discrediting of any conservative force intent on exposing them. For instance, one of the leaflets published lately by the National Civil Liberties Bureau, entitled "Memorandum Regarding the Persecution of the Radical Labor Movement in the United States", tries to discredit the Department of Justice for its raids from September 5, 1917, on. As a result, there has been a tremendous amount of sentimental indignation created against these raids, which have, in effect, protected the very people complaining against them.

Another instance on the part of the National Civil Liberties Bureau forces and their more openly radical allies, the I.W.W., etc., to undermine the American Federation of Labor, may be illustrated by Baldwin's letter to Mr. John Haynes Holmes, in May, 1917, concerning the proposed Conference for Democracy and Terms of Peace:

> "I am hoping that the conference will at least serve the useful purpose of a new radical attack on the hidebound leadership of the American Federation of Labor."

Still another method of Baldwin and his friends may be set forth by the following excerpt from Baldwin's letter to Wm. Hard, June 13, 1918:

> "We wonder whether you would not be willing to let us send you exclusive material from time to time, with the understanding that you would be willing to look it over, with the idea of using such of it as appeals to you. We are particularly anxious to see that the case is constantly and vigorously stated by pro-war liberals and radicals whose motive is above question." . . .

Hard, who was supposed to be a "pro-war liberal", answered June 21, 1918:

> ". . . I think I see my way perfectly clear now to writing something about free speech in general and about the Post Office dep't in particular." . . . (General, Vol. II, pp. 175 and 176.)

Again, in writing to George Vandeveer, Baldwin suggests that unorganized labor could work against the American Federation of Labor "with a view to staging a revolution".

Other instances of this "boring-from-within" policy of Baldwin will be found in:

(1) Letters from Baldwin in regard to influencing and spreading propaganda in churches. (C.O. General, Vol. IV, pp. 2147, 2148.)

(2) Arthur W. Calhoun, of Clark University, offers to organize a branch of the National Civil Liberties Bureau in Worcester with "Ministers, Friends, radicals and Socialists co-operating" (C.O. States, Vol. III, p. 780), and on page 781 Mr. Calhoun gets specific directions from Baldwin as to how to go about this organization process.

The National Civil Liberties Bureau, though leaving no stone unturned to hamper the military strength of the United States Government during the war, was at the same time forehanded enough to look toward an after-the-war program, which should be altogether along the same lines. In this connection it should be remembered that when the American Union against Militarism withdrew from the active field of propaganda, this was only in order to conserve its forces for an after-the-war drive against military protection.

One of the chief members of the American Union, Miss Lillian Wald, followed this line of thought when, in October, 1917, she resigned from the executive board, not only of the American Union, but also of the National Civil Liberties Bureau. In writing to Baldwin, explaining her resignation, she ended by saying, "I am not at all out of the movement, even though I am not on the committee".

Baldwin, in answering this letter, said, in part:

> " It is a comfort to know that we can call on you with such assurance of response in any emergency."

Again, when Baldwin sent Chumley, Collector for the I.W.W., with the suggestion that Miss Wald introduce him "to Miss Lewisohn, Col. Thompson and Mrs. Willard Straight", Miss Wald replied:

> ". . . I believe it would be a great deal better for you to introduce him to the people you mention. If I have the opportunity I will be glad to say the encouraging word." (I.W.W., Vol. II, p. 96.)

Other instances suggesting after-the-war plans of both the American Union against Militarism and the National Civil Liberties Bureau are as follows:

(1) From Laurence Todd, Baldwin's "inside information" newspaper man in Washington, to Baldwin in 1917:

> "A million employees on the railroad are going to stand together to get democratic consideration of their demands, and they in turn are going to give the postal employees and other big groups their help in securing the same treatment. We are on the way to a big liberalization of industrial relations."

(2) Baldwin, August 20, 1918, addressing F.S. Fash, a conscientious objector, at Fort Worth:

> "It is men like you . . . who will be the centers of influence in the reconstruction of democracy which is bound to follow the war." (Legal Defense, Vol. VIII, p. 101.)

(3) Baldwin, in General, Vol. III, page 3:

> " Villard is saving himself for a program of agitation for disarmament and against universal military service after the war."

(4) Baldwin, in writing to Kenneth Darling, a "conscientious objector" (in

regard to court martial sentences of conscientious objectors), that he judges from what he hears from the War Department "that the men will all be freed as soon as the war is over."

At this point it may be interesting to note some of the general tactics, aside from that with conscientious objectors, employed by Baldwin in accomplishing his ends:

(1) Baldwin to Sugarman, of Detroit:

" We have found it best to use plain envelopes . . . without any indication of our identity." (Legal Defense, Vol. IV, p. 1405.)

(2) John Haynes Holmes, writing to Baldwin, May 6, 1918:

" There is nothing in the past that has pleased me more or more deeply stirred my admiration than the fine co-operation which you established between our bureau and the two Departments of War and Justice." (General, Vol. II, p. 114.)

(3) From Laurence Todd to Baldwin:

" I'm informed on good authority in G.C.'s bureau, that the Colonel House influence is now being thrown in favor of democratic liberties. . . . People's Council will henceforth be free to do as it pleases. Labor revolt is brewing. . . . Socialists and radicals are to be welcome in respectable official circles." (General, Vol. I, p. 144.)

(4) Baldwin to Harold Evans, Philadelphia (April 13, 1918):

" While the administration is full of liberals, they unfortunately are not in the two departments which enforce this war legislation, namely, the Post Office Department and Department of Justice". (General, Vol. I, p. 59.)

(5) Wire from Baldwin to Liberty Defense League, soliciting letters of complaint from drafted conscientious objectors to Secretary Baker at once:

"Administration plan depends on number and kind of such letters received before Tuesday." (C.O. General, Vol. III, p. 122.)

(6) Baldwin to Herbert Bigelow, in regard to proposed protest meeting, November, 1917:

" We will endeavor to get all of the pro-war men who still stand for constitutional rights, and if we can't get many of them we will put up the least objectionable among the radicals and the so-called pacifists. Men, for instance, like Amos Pinchot, John Haynes Holmes, Mr. Villard . . . and, very likely, Jane Addams." (Legal Defense, Vol. IV, p. 1165.)

(7) A letter from Mrs. Agnes Brown Leach to Baldwin, in praise of Baldwin and mentioning $500 given by her to People's Council, November 6, 1917:

" The radical who is going to help the people's cause most is not the unconventional freak, . . . but . . . engaging gentleman, like yourself, who will bring things to pass.'' (General, Vol. II, p. 66.)

(8) From Laurence Todd to B.W. Nelles, (May 14, 1918):

"Its strategy. . . . (The Non-Partisan League) is first to get the legislative and administrative power, and then quietly remove the autocrats and inciters of mob violence from the places of influence they have held. . . .'' (General, Vol. I, p. 180.)

(9) Mr. Charles Zueblin, declining to serve on a committee, to Baldwin, January 8, 1918:

" I think lobbying in Washington much more valuable. (than mass meetings.) Round up congressmen and senators, as suffragists and prohibitionists. . . . I believe in unrestricted free speech, but nationalization of railways and mines is more important.'' (Conferences, p. 103.)

(10) Baldwin writes to advise Kenneth Darling, conscientious objector and a radical Socialist, to apply for work in the Department of Justice, as German translator. He advises Darling to write to Mr. Keppel. (Darling never achieved this end.) (C.O. Camps, Vol. VI, p. 269.)

(11) From Alice Park, suffragist, on staff of "Votes for Women'', to Baldwin, congratulating him on his I.W.W. pamphlets and protesting against the activities of the home defense leagues of California against seditious activities. (Legal Defense, Vol. I, p. 395.)

General, Vol. I, page 88—Baldwin writes to Rabbi Judah Magnes:

" We need you, your point of view and your connections in building up an increasingly effective movement.''

General, Vol. I, page 115—Baldwin to James Warbasse:

". . . We are trying to preserve the fundamental rights of agitation, so that those who oppose war or who advocate peace may have a chance to talk more freely . . .'' (November 10, 1917.)

General, Vol. I, page 32—from Baldwin to George Nasmyth:

". . . This work is only half with objectors, half directly with freedom of expression as regards labor and radical movements.'' (August, 1918.)

From "Novy Mir", the Russian Socialist newspaper, to Baldwin, March 12, 1918:

"Your address was given us by Comrade Charles Ervin, secretary of the newly organized American Liberty Union, having for its purpose the protection of free speech in this country and giving aid to those caught in the net." (Legal Defense, Vol. VI, p. 138; on p. 139, Baldwin answers in a co-operative spirit.)

In Legal Defense, Vol. VII, page 60, Baldwin explains regretfully why he could not oppose Liberty Bond drives, etc.:

" Our main job is to help keep people's mouths open and their printing presses free. Our business is to see that all those who want to get any ideas across are protected in their rights."

It remains, in recording this history of the pacifist-Socialist movement in this country, to bring the National Civil Liberties Bureau up to date under its lately acquired name of the American Civil Liberties Union and to follow the achievements of some of the chief organizers of the movement to the present day.

A late bulletin (March, 1920) of the American Civil Liberties Union, representing the American Freedom Foundation, 1541 Unity Building, Chicago, Ill.; the Labor Defense League, 230 Russ Building, San Francisco, Cal.; the League for Democratic Control, 2 Park Square, Boston, Mass.; the Workers' Defense Building, San Francisco, Cal., and the Workers' Defense Union, 7 East 15th Street, New York City, discloses as its officers:

Harry F. Ward, chairman; Duncan McDonald, Illinois, and Jeanette Rankin, of Montana, as vice-chairmen; Helen Phelps Stokes, treasurer; Albert De Silver and Roger N. Baldwin, directors; Walter Nelles, counsel. Lucille B. Lowenstein, field secretary; and Louis F. Budenz, publicity director.

NATIONAL COMMITTEE:
Jane Addams, Chicago, Ill.
Herbert S. Bigelow, Cincinnati, Ohio
Sophonisba P. Breckenridge, Chicago, Ill.
Robert M. Buck, Chicago, Ill.
John S. Codman, Boston, Mass.
Lincoln Colcord, Washington, D.C.
James H. Dillard
Crystal Eastman, New York City
John Lovejoy Elliott, New York City
Edmund C. Evans, Philadelphia, Pa.
Edward W. Evans, Philadelphia, Pa.
William M. Fincke, Katonah, N.Y.
John A. Fitch, New York City
Elizabeth Gurley Flynn, New York City

Felix Frankfurter, Harvard
William Z. Foster
Paul J. Furnas, New York City
Zona Gale, Portage, Wis.
A.B. Gilbert, St. Paul, Minn.
Arthur Garfield Hays, New York City
Morris Hillquit, New York City
John Haynes Holmes, New York City
Frederic C. Howe, Washington, D.C.
James Weldon Johnson, New York City
Helen Keller, Forest Hills, L.I.
Harold J. Laski, Cambridge, Mass.
Agnes Brown Leach, New York City
Arthur Le Sueur, St. Paul, Minn.
Henry R. Linville, New York City
Robert Morss Lovett, Chicago, Ill.
Allen McCurdy, New York City
Grenville S. MacFarland, Boston, Mass.
Oscar Maddaus, Manhasset, L.I.
Judah L. Magnes, New York City
James H. Maurer, Reading, Pa.
A.J. Muste, New York City
George W. Nasmyth, New York City
Scott Nearing, New York City
Julia O'Connor, Boston, Mass.
William H. Pickens, Baltimore, Md.
William Marion Reedy, St. Louis, Mo.
John Nevin Sayre, Katonah, N.Y.
Rose Schneidemann, New York City
Vida D. Scudder, Wellesley, Mass.
Norman M. Thomas, New York City
Oswald Garrison Villard, New York City
L. Hollingsworth Wood, New York City
George P. West, Oakland, Cal.

These names will nearly all be familiar to anyone who has read the preceding chapters of this section; and the association here of women like Jane Addams and Helen Keller with extreme radicals like Elizabeth Gurley Flynn and leaders of the Socialist movement in America will explain, in large measure, the Socialist tendencies which manifest themselves in many so-called liberal papers and in some collegiate settlement and religious circles.

The National Civil Liberties Bureau has lately issued some fifteen pamphlets, among which are "Your Amish Mennonite", by William Hard, reprinted from the "New Republic", which is described in a foreword as "The following striking story of the conscientious objector in America''; ''Why Freedom Matters'', by Norman Angell; and ''Amnesty for Political Prisoners'', by Judah L. Magnes.

Under its new title, the American Civil Liberties Union has, as far as our knowledge goes, issued four pamphlets:

(1) ''General Amnesty'', by Dr. Frank Crane, of the New York ''Globe'', ending: ''I am in favor of a general amnesty for all political prisoners''.

(2) ''The Old America and the New'', by Judah L. Magnes, ending, ''Let us uphold the ideals of internationalism in the name of the old America that was free and is now dead, and in the name of the New America which is now being born.''

(3) ''Do We Need More Sedition Laws?''

(4) ''The issues in the Centralia Murder Trial'', an attempted defense of the Centralia I.W.W. murderers of American soldiers.

The Bureau has also issued the reprint copy of an article from the January 31, 1920, issue of the ''New Republic'', called ''The Force and Violence Joker''.

This includes more or less open attacks on Attorney-General Palmer, Mr. Lansing, the House Immigration Committee, the New York ''Times'', Senator Fall, this Committee, etc. It also quotes the dissenting opinions in the Abrams case, of Justices Holmes and Brandeis, and ends by making light of the danger of revolution in America.

This belittling of the very real danger to the institutions of this country, as well as the attempted discrediting of any investigating group (or individual), has become thoroughly characteristic of our ''Parlor-Bolshevik'' or ''Intelligentsia.''

Concerning the present status of some of these:

As we have seen, Roger Baldwin, though he spent a year in prison for his ''conscientious objector beliefs'', is now again one of the directors of the American Civil Liberties Union.

Many of the original organizers of the American Union against Militarism are at present on the list of officers or members of committees of the American Civil Liberties Union.

During the period which has been described, there were a large number of organizations co-operating with those described in the preceding chapter (in many cases having interlocking directorates), starting in the beginning with anti-militarism as their objective, but in nearly all cases winding up in the closest possible contact with extreme radicals and revolutionaries. The Committee feels that anyone who has followed closely the progress of the movement described in this and preceding chapters will recognize the influences which have been at play on public opinion and the efforts which have been exerted to stimulate the radical movement among persons of means and education.

(NOTE: The quotations from letters to and from the National Civil Liberties Bureau and allied organizations in this chapter, containing citations to various volumes, refer to the volumes of bound correspondence subpoenaed from the National Civil Liberties Bureau by this Committee, from which this data is gathered.)

Document I—"The Challenge"
Leaflet issued by American Civil Liberties Union. . . .

The struggle for freedom today centers in the fight of labor for increasing control of industry. Everywhere that struggle involves the issues of free speech, free press and peaceful assemblage. Everywhere the powers of organized business challenge the right of workers to organize, unionize, strike and picket. The hysterical attacks on "red" propaganda, on radical opinion of all sorts, are in substance a single masked attack on the growing revolt of labor and the farmers against industrial tyranny.

The hysteria aroused by the war, with its machinery for crushing dissenting opinion, is now directed against the advocates of industrial freedom. States vie with one another in the passage of laws against "criminal syndicalism", "criminal anarchy" and "sedition". Even cities enact such laws. A wholesale campaign is on to deny the right to strike, by compulsory arbitration and by injunction. The nation-wide open-shop crusade is a colossal attempt to destroy all organization of labor.

Patrioteering societies, vigilantes, "citizens' committees", strike-breaking State Constabularies and the hired gunmen of private corporations contend with the Attorney-General and zealous local prosecutors in demonstrating their own brands of "law and order". Meetings of workers and farmers are prohibited and broken up, speakers are mobbed and prosecuted. Picketing is made unlawful or prohibited by injunction in a score of states, and hundreds of cities. Searches are instituted without thought of warrant. Scores of persons are arrested without warrant and held in prohibitive bail for months without trial. Teachers suspected of liberal or radical views are dismissed from schools and colleges. Hundreds of aliens are held for deportation simply for membership in a political or industrial organization. The right of duly elected representatives to sit in a state legislature is denied, solely because of their opinions. Legislation pretending to be aimed only at the overthrow of the government by "force and violence", as a matter of fact is construed to punish the advocacy of political and economical change by any method.

OUR SERVICE

This menace to American tradition and the ideals of liberty can be met only by uniting those forces which will fight for orderly progress through freedom of opinion. The reaction to long-continued suppression is violent revolution. This organization is dedicated to the principle of progress by orderly methods. We hold no brief for any particular cause. We are not identified with any "ism". We fight for all those whose liberties are at stake.

We are attempting to meet the present crisis:

(1) By sending free speech organizers and speakers into areas of conflict to dramatize the issue of civil liberty, and where necessary, to fight them out in the courts.

(2) By opposing all legislation restricting freedom of speech, press and assemblage and by endeavoring to secure amnesty for political and industrial prisoners.

(3) By securing nation-wide publicity on all important civil liberty issues.

(4) By organizing legal defense throughout the country.

(5) By organizing a campaign to offset the "terrorism" in our schools.

We have a national press clipping service that brings the information about the case. We seek to get in touch at once with every person or group attacked. We recommend local counsel, and endeavor to secure financial aid and publicity. From district organization offices, we can get speakers, investigators and lawyers out on short notice wherever serious trouble arises.

We welcome the co-operation of correspondents, attorneys, speakers, writers and investigators anywhere in the United States. Any citizen willing to help in the publicity campaigns by writing letters to newspapers or public officials is urged to enlist. Any person will be put on the mailing list for all publications for $1.00 a year.

The Union is supported solely by voluntary contributions. Any contributions, monthly or annual, are warmly appreciated.

Excerpts from the Fish Committee Report, 1931[1]

The American Civil Liberties Union is closely affillated with the Communist movement in the United States, and fully 90 percent of its efforts are on behalf of Communists who have come into conflict with the law. It claims to stand for free speech, free press, and free assembly; but it is quite apparent that the main function of the A.C.L.U. is to attempt to protect the Communists in their advocacy of force and violence to overthrow the Government, replacing the American flag by a red flag and erecting a Soviet Government in place of the republican form of government guaranteed to each State by the Federal Constitution.

Roger N. Baldwin, its guiding spirit, makes no attempt to hide his friendship for the Communists and their principles. He was formerly a member of the I.W.W. and served a term in prison as a draft dodger during the war. This is the same Roger N. Baldwin that has recently issued a statement "that in the next session of Congress our job is to organize the opposition to the recommendations of the Congressional committee investigating Communism". In his testimony before the

[1]U.S. Congress, House, Special Committee to Investigate Communist Activities in the United States, *Investigation of Communist Propaganda, Report,* 71st Congress, 3rd session, 1931, pp. 56–57.

committee he admitted having said at a dinner held in Chicago that "The Fish Committee recommendations will be buried in the Senate". Testifying on force and violence, murder, etc., the following is quoted:

The Chairman: Does your organization uphold the right of a citizen or alien—it does not make any difference which—to advocate murder?

Mr. Baldwin: Yes.

The Chairman: Or Assassination?

Mr. Baldwin: Yes.

The Chairman: Does your organization uphold the right of an American citizen to advocate force and violence for the overthrow of the Government?

Mr. Baldwin: Certainly; in so far as mere advocacy is concerned.

The Chairman: Does it uphold the right of an alien in this country to urge the overthrow and advocate the overthrow of the Government by force and violence?

Mr. Baldwin: Precisely on the same basis as any citizen.

The Chairman: You do uphold the right of an alien to advocate the overthrow of the Government by force and violence?

Mr. Baldwin: Sure, certainly. It is the healthiest kind of thing for a country, of course, to have free speech—unlimited.

The American Civil Liberties Union has received large sums from the Garland Fund, of which Roger N. Baldwin is one of the directors. During the trial of the Communists at Gastonia, not for freedom of speech, of the press, or assembly, but for a conspiracy to kill the chief of Police, of which seven defendants were convicted, the A.C.L.U. provided bail for five of the defendants, amounting to $28,500, which it secured from the Garland Fund. All of the defendants convicted jumped their bail and are reported to be in Russia. The $28,500 bail was forfeited, including $9,000 more advanced by the International Labor Defense.

A committee of the New York State Legislature, back in 1928, reached the following conclusion in regard to the American Civil Liberties Union:

The American Civil Liberties Union, in the last analysis, is a supporter of all subversive movements, its propaganda is detrimental to the interests of the State. It attempts not only to protect crime but to encourage attacks upon our institutions in every form.

Your committee concurs with the above findings.

The principles of free speech, free press, and free assembly are worthy of an organization that stands for our republican form of government, guaranteed by the Constitution, and for the ideals of Washington, Jefferson, and Lincoln, instead of an organization whose main work is to uphold the Communists in spreading revolutionary propaganda and inciting revolutionary activities to undermine our American institutions and overthrow our Federal Government.

Excerpts from the Special Committee on Un-American Activities Report, 1938[1]

Naval Intelligence Accuses American Civil Liberties Union

In a report prepared by the Naval Intelligence, appearing in the September 10, 1935, edition of The Congressional Record, the following statement is made: "Organizations which while not openly advocating the 'forces and violence' principles of the Communists, give aid and comfort to the Communist movement and party. Among the strongest of these organizations are:

(a) American Civil Liberties Union. This organization is too well known to need description. The larger part of the work carried on by it and its various branches does undoubtedly materially aid Communist objectives.

American Civil Liberties Union Report Shows Defense For Communists, Industrial Workers of the World, Etc.

The reports of the American Civil Liberties Union over a period of years shows their continuous defense of Communists, Industrial Workers of the World, Socialists, Radical Pacifists, and other types of revolutionaries, as well as a continental attack on the efforts of Congress or State Legislatures to enact laws of protection from aliens, Communists and radicals. The Union has fought oath of allegiance laws as strongly as attempts to prosecute or deport or give citizenship or prevent entry within our country for any type of undesirables.

Red Financial Hook-Up of American Civil Liberties Union

Not only does the American Civil Liberties Union admit its open defense of Communists and other types of radicals in what it calls their "legal defense", but it also admits that it has loaned considerable money to the International Labor Defense, a Communist movement, which is a branch of the "Red" International Aid of Russia. It also admits having lost $40,000 in bails which it surrendered in the Gastonia riot cases after the Communists involved had escaped to Russia. Only a short time ago the Union received a refund for bails which it had furnished for the Bridgman (Mich.) Communists. The trial was abandoned by the government because of the death of the main witness in the case. The Union likewise admits that it has received funds from the Garland Fund.

[1]U.S. Congress, House, Special Committee on Un-American Activities, *Investigation of Un-American Propaganda Activities,* 75th Congress, 3rd session, 1938, pp. 533–34.

Excerpts from the Massachusetts Special Commission Report, 1938[1]

It is characterisitic of the American Civil Liberties Union, as well as of its Massachussets branch, the Civil Liberites Committee of Massachusetts, to insist on full license for the Left-Wing movements which these organizations defend and (belying the name of the organization) to fight for suppression of liberty, civil or otherwise, for any movement opposed by the officials leadership of the American Civil Liberties Union.

For many years Roger Baldwin, a former member of the I.W.W., had been and now is the national executive head of the American Civil Liberties Union. Among its other officials there have been and are well known Communist functionaries. This is not to imply, however, that the thousands of members contributing to the American Civil Liberties Union are all Communists. But the propaganda of this organization is dictated and dominated by Communists and Communist supporters. . . .

Throughout its existence, I.L.D. [International Labor Defense] has had as inseparable allies two other Communist controlled organizations. They are the American Civil Liberties Union and the Garland Fund, so called. The American Civil Liberties Union, with its "front" of respectability and with its large membership of sincere worthy citizens, has provided important legal talent and a camouflage of decency behind which Communists forces have agitated and promoted their campaigns.

Excerpts from the Special Committee on Un-American Activities Report, 1939[2]

The committee heard testimony with reference to the Civil Liberties Union. Some witnesses listed this organization as Communistic while other witnesses denied that it was Communistic. We received in evidence a number of official pamphlets distributed by the Civil Liberties Union, which speak for themselves. From the evidence before us, we are not in a position to definitely state whether or not this organization can properly be classed as a Communist organization. In this connection it is interesting to note the report of the United Mine Workers filed in 1924, wherein the following was said about the Civil Liberties Union:

[1]Massachusetts State Legislature, House, Special Commission to Investigate the Activities Within This Commonwealth of Communistic, Fascist, Nazi and Other Subversive Organizations, So Called, *Report*, House, No. 2100, 1938, pp. 56, 204.

[2]U.S. Congress, House, Special Committee on Un-American Activities, *Investigation of Un-American Activities and Propaganda, Report*, 75th Congress, 3rd session, 1939, pp. 82—83.

There are 200 organizations in the United States actively engaged in or sympathetic with the Communist revolutionary movement as directed and conducted by the Communist Party of America. Some of them are local in their scope and work; others are Nation-wide. Forty-five of organizations of either "pink" or radical structure are engaged in the Communist effort to seize control of the labor unions in this country and convert them to the revolutionary movement. In virtually every instance these organizations have direct contact, through the mechanism of interlocking directorates, with the central committee of the Communist Party of America, or with its "legal" branch, the Workers Party of America.

Illustrative of this arrangement is the executive committee and the national committee of the American Civil Liberties Union, at New York, posing as the champion of free speech and civil liberties but serving as a forerunner and trail blazer for the active and insidious activities of the Communist, among labor organizations. Harry F. Ward born in London in 1873, and chancellor of the Union Theological Seminary, is chairman of this organization. The managing director is Robert [sic] Baldwin who served a term as a draft evader in the Essex County jail in New Jersey in 1918 and 1919.

This statement of the United Mine Workers is borne out by the evidence we have heard thus far and we strongly urge this organization be thoroughly investigated.

The following are the officers of the Union:

> Chairman: Harry F. Ward
> Vice-Chairman: Rt. Rev. Edward L. Parsons
> Vice-Chairman: Dr. Mary E. Woolley
> Vice-Chairman: Dean Lloyd K. Garrison
> Treasurer: B. W. Huebsch
> Director: Roger N. Baldwin
> Secretary: Lucile B. Milner
> Counsel: Arthur Garfield Hayes
> Counsel: Morris L. Ernst

Mr. Roger N. Baldwin, National Director of the Civil Liberties Union, testified before a congressional committee as follows:

The Chairman: Mr. Baldwin, does your organization uphold the right of an American citizen to advocate force and violence for the overthrow of the Government?

Mr. Baldwin: Certainly, insofar as mere advocacy is concerned.

The Chairman: Does it uphold the right of an alien in this country to urge the overthrow and advocate the overthrow of the Government by force and violence?

Mr. Baldwin: Precisely on the same basis as any citizen.

The Chairman: That is not your personal opinion?

Mr. Baldwin: That is the organization's position. . . .

The Chairman: Does your organization uphold the right of a citizen or an alien—it does not make any difference which—to advocate murder?

Mr. Baldwin: To advocate murder?

The Chairman: Yes.

Mr. Baldwin: If it is mere advocacy?

The Chairman: Yes.

Mr. Baldwin: Surely.

The Chairman: Or assassination?

Mr. Baldwin: Of course.

In the printed leaflet issued by the Civil Liberties Union and called "Campaigns for Civil Liberty—1938", we find that among other things listed for their work is—

Aid in campaigns for the release of political prisioners, and against all prosecutions under sedition and criminal syndicalism laws.

****Changes in the immigration and deportation laws to end all restrictions merely because of political opinions; to admit and protect genuine political refugees; and in citizenship proceedings to remove tests of aliens' views not imposed on citizens.

Excerpts from the California Senate Fact-Finding Subcommittee on Un-American Activities Report, 1961[1]

Before the resignation of Executive Director Roger Baldwin, and particularly during the first decade of the organization's existence, it exhibited a far greater tolerance toward the Communist Party and Communist activities in general—this sort of predominant activity for the relief of the Communist Party and its satellite front organizations, together with the fact that a great many officers and staff members of the organization in Southern California had formidable front records themselves, led this Committee to describe the A.C.L.U. in its 1943 report as a Communist front organization, and a transmission belt for Communism in the following language:

"The American Civil Liberties Union may be definitely classed as a Communist front or 'transmission belt' organization. At least 90% of its efforts are expended on behalf of Communists who come into conflict with the law. While it professes to stand for free speech, a free press, and free assembly, it is quite obvious that its main function is to protect Communists in their activities of force and violence in their program to overthrow the government."

In our 1948 report we also devoted considerable attention to the American Civil Liberties Union, as follows:

"During the Stalin-Hitler pact, the American Civil Liberties Union suddenly

[1]California State Legislature, Senate, Fact-Finding Subcommittee on Un-American Activities, *Eleventh Report* (Sacramento: State of California, 1961), pp. 161–173.

took the position that persons who support 'totalitarian dictatorship' in any country can give nothing more than a tongue-in-cheek allegiance to civil liberties in the United States. Although the American Civil Liberties Union was organized in 1920 and has been defending Communists for over twenty years while the 'totalitarian dictatorship' was in ruthless operation denying elementary rights to the citizens of Russia, it took the Stalin-Hitler pact to awaken the organization.

"The resolution adopted by the American Civil Liberties Union, however, was discouraging to the California Legislative Committee Investigating Un-American Activities in California. While its philosophy and its activities plus its Communist and Communist Party traveling membership placed the organization indisputably in the Stalinite solar system, the action of 1940, on the surface, indicated that the loyal element within the American Civil Liberties Union was about to capture the organization for American purposes. The *Daily Worker* for March 19, 1940, carried the text of a letter signed by 17 alleged 'liberal leaders' addressed to the American Civil Liberties Union. These alleged 'liberal leaders' asked some embarrassing and pertinent questions: 'The phrasing of the resolution is dangerous', declared the 17. 'Its context is worse. The Civil Liberties Union was founded in 1920. The Soviet Union was established in 1917, and with it the 'dictatorship of the proletariat'. We are told that Communists are to be barred from office or employment in the Civil Liberties Union because, while fighting for civil liberties in America, they accept their suppression in Russia. Why then, did the Civil Liberties Union wait until 1940 before seeking to bar them?' The letter goes on to state: 'But civil liberties within the Soviet Union were no different before the pact than after. One could not print an opposition paper in Moscow in August, 1939, before the pact, or after it, in September, 1939.'

"When it is remembered that the U.S. Communists under directive of the Kremlin were vigorously supporting the Stalin-Hitler Pact while Hitler and Stalin were looting Europe, The Communist character of the Seventeen 'liberal leaders' becomes obvious. Their letter continues: 'Could it be that the majority of the national committee and board of directors of the Civil Liberties Union is taking sides in the developing of European conflict? Is their real objection an objection to the position of the Soviet Union in that conflict? Has that question anything to do with the need for defending civil liberties in America? . . . The Civil Liberties Union was formed in 1920 to fight post-war hysteria. It would be a great pity if it were now to be a victim of prewar hysteria.'

"Among the seventeen 'liberal leaders' signing this letter were two high officials in the executive branch of the United States Government, namely Robert Morss Lovett and Henry T. Hunt, both of whom were employees of the Department of Interior. I.F. Stone and James Wechsler were connected with the Washington bureau of Marshall Field's leftwing newspaper *P.M.* William F. Cochran, also a signer of the letter, is a millionaire real estate operator in Baltimore. All of the seventeen signers have been constant supporters of the

Communist Party, its leaders, and various front organizations. John T. Bernard, Prof. Franz Boas, Howard Costigan, Theodore Dreiser, Prof. Henry Pratt Fairchild, Prof. Robert S. Lynd, Carey McWilliams, Rev. Dr. A.T. Mollegan, Prof. C. Fayette Taylor, Charles S. Ascher, Gardner Jackson, and Maxwell S. Stewart.

"Undoubtedly the American Civil Liberties Union was resorting to drastic Communist strategy in retreating during the Stalin-Hitler pact. This fact is strongly indicated by the personnel of the National Committee and the Board of Directors in 1946. On the letter of the American Civil Liberties Union signed by A.A. Heist for September, 1946, we find many of the seventeen so-called 'liberal leaders' listed."

In 1948 the committee found no reason to disagree with the findings that had been made in 1943. It concluded its statement concerning the A.C.L.U. as follows:

"The Senate Fact-Finding Committee on Un-American Activities reiterates the findings of former legislative committees concerning the Communist character of the American Civil Liberties Union. The International Labor Defense, called 'the legal arm of the Communist party' by former Attorney General Francis Biddle, has not established a better Communist record than this thinly-disguised organization that devotes its energies to the defense of enemies of the United States.

"The Committee has stated in previous reports that all Communist fronts are characterized by the fact that many of the individuals attracted to such organizations are not necessarily Communists, and, in many cases, the membership of a Communist front organization will be composed, for the greater part, of non-Communists. This same finding applies, of course, to the American Civil Liberties Union. Ernest Besig, the director of the Northern California Branch of the American Civil Liberties Union, appears to be a sincere, conscientious American, whose reasoning leads him to the defense of most anyone, regardless of the accusation. Ernest Besig, however, has, on several occasions, expressed himself concerning Communists and Communism. He testified before a sub-committee of the Senate Committee on Un-American Activities in Fairfax, October 23, 1947. He identified the official organ of the Northern Branch of the American Civil Liberties Union for February and March, 1941, in which he had unequivocally stamped the Northern California Council for Academic Freedom and Civil Liberties a Communist front. He orally reiterated his written statement. His testimony, in part, is as follows:

"Q. (Mr. Combs) . . . The American Civil Liberties Union publishes a number of papers. I am speaking of the branch of the organization of which you are a member.

"A. That's correct.

"Q. What is the name of that publication?

"A. The American Civil Liberties Union *News*.

"Q. Did you publish such a paper in February, 1941?

"A. Yes. It's in its twelfth year, so we must have.

"Q. (Mr. Combs): Now in connection with the issues for February, 1941, and March, 1941, there are some statements concerning one of the organizations I mentioned a while ago, the Northern California Council for Academic Freedom and Civil Liberties I believe.

"A. Do you want to know what I think of that organization?

"Q. I know what you think of it. You said so in your paper.

"A. I said so not only in the paper but in speeches, and as a result the chairman of this group (Northern California Council for Academic Freedom and Civil Liberties) sent a protest to my committee.

"Q. Well, you think the organization was definitely a Communist front?

"A. Undoubtedly; and undoubtedly also, it got a lot of innocent people involved in it.

"Q. As Communist fronts are set up to do.

"A. Correct.

"Q. Now, how did you arrive at the conclusion that this particular organization was a Communist front?

"A. Well, after you've been in this business of civil liberties for the number of years that I have been in it, you come across certain individuals who, as you indicated with Mr. Flaxer, get involved in first one organization and then another. That was true of the Committee on Academic Freedom. Louise Branston had been connected with a number of front organizations and seemed to shift around."

This testimony from the director of the American Civil Liberties Union in Northern California, and who is still serving in that capacity, provides a pretty good test of a Communist front organization. We applied that test in 1943 and 1948 to the officers, staff members and announced policies of the American Civil Liberties Union in California and decided that it was under Communist domination. That was before Patrick Malin assumed control, and before the national organization reaffirmed its opposition to totalitarianism whether on the extreme right or extreme left, and bolstered up its 1940 resolution against permitting members of the Communist Party or its supporters from serving the A.C.L.U. in any official capacity. Prior to 1950 the publications of the American Civil Liberties Union in Southern California were little different than propaganda sheets similar to those issued by the Communist Party itself. Since that time there has been a marked improvement, and in 1959, without any solicitation from any source, we had this to say:

"In previous reports we have traced the origin and development of the American Civil Liberties Union as a national organization. We have also, from time to time, discussed the activities of its branches in San Francisco and Los Angeles. During the middle thirties and for a short period in 1946 and 1947, we received evidence that we believed justified the statements appearing in our 1943 and 1948 reports to the effect that the American Civil Liberties Union in California had become a transmission belt for the dissemination of Communist propaganda. We do not believe that the American Civil Liberties Union nationally is in any sense subversive; a part of its function is the protection of civil liberties of all people, regardless of the fact that some of them may be members of the Communist Party or other subversive organizations. The American Civil Liberties Union has also defended the right of Gerald L.K. Smith to make public addresses, and during the last war it performed similar services in defending the rights of members of the German-American Bund, especially on the Pacific Coast and particularly in California. The Southern California Chapter of this organization has, however, devoted an unusually large part of its time and energies to the protection and defense of Communist Party members and to the support of Communist organizations and fronts.

"It is difficult to make a firm and permanent evaluation of an organization like the Southern California Chapter of the American Civil Liberties Union. As its personnel fluctuates, so does the ideological character of the institution itself. The national organization has a policy that no member of the Communist Party can hold an office. This move, obviously motivated because of a realization that the Communist Party is a subversive organization and that it poses a constant and deadly menace to the preservation of all of our cherished institutions, has not been reflected by the activities of its Southern California branch in recent years. We make no criticism, of course, because the Los Angeles Chapter, like the other chapters of the American Civil Liberties Union, protects the civil rights of Communists as well as other people. It is a fact, however, that in addition to carrying out the regular functions of the organization, some of its representatives and some of its officers have presistently attended Communist front meetings, have joined many Communits fronts, and have participated at banquets and receptions honoring some of the leading Communists of the United States. Such activities are hardly in conformity with the anti-Communist policy of the national organization and most of its chapters throughout the United States.

"Several years ago a school teacher in the Northern part of the State was accused of being subversive by a radio commentator whose broadcast alleged that she was a member of the United World Federalists, which he described as a Communist-dominated organization. As a result of these broadcasts and criticism the teacher was discharged. She brought a suit for reinstatement and for damages against the commentator and the radio station that employed him, and a representative of this Committee went to San Francisco as an expert witness. He testified that we had never listed the United World Federalists as a subversive organization, had no evidence that it was Communist-controlled, and that we did have evidence that it was *not* a Communist front. Such an organization is an obvious target for Communist infiltration, but by the same token, so is the American Civil Liberties Union, because it espouses the defense of unpopular causes and members of unpopular organizations; and so is every trade union because through control of industry a country can be paralyzed; and so is every educational institution because they are lush fields for indoctrination and recruiting and provide further intellectual leadership for the Communist Party. Some chapters of the national organization may be penetrated at one time or another to such an extent that they become transmission belts for the Communist Party line; at the same time, other chapters of the same organization may be militantly anti-Communist. One of the most militantly anti-Communist chapters of the American Civil Liberties Union, indeed, is situated in Washington, D.C., and the National Director of the A.C.L.U., Mr. Patrick Murphy Malin, is certainly no friend of Communism. The Los Angeles Chapter of the American Civil Liberties Union, by permitting its officers and official representatives to participate in Communist front meetings and propaganda activities, is hardly being objective; and if it resents charges of partiality toward the extreme Left, those criticisms are generated by its own activities and it has no one to blame but itself.''

The A.C.L.U. in California Since 1948

We have previously stated that for a short period in 1946 and 1947 the Los Angeles A.C.L.U. was under powerful Communist influence. The Party had reached its greatest strength at this time, with a national roster of formal members mounting to between 85,000 and 100,000 persons and with many times that number of fellow travelers and sympathizers. The front organizations were flourishing, and the Communists were bold and active. The Party's influence on the A.C.L.U. in Southern California continued until after the retirement of Roger Baldwin and the election of Patrick Malin as National Director. Since that time the Commmunist influence in the southern California A.C.L.U. has diminished. . . .

We also point out, although the situation should be apparent, that since 1956 the numerical strength of the Communist Party in the United States has greatly diminished. As we explained in our last report, this does not mean that the influence of the Party has diminished or that its efforts at infiltration and propaganda have abated. Due to years of persistent exposure by investigating committees and the United States Department of Justice, Communist front organizations have largely disappeared; the Party has been compelled to operate from underground positions with only a few of its publicly known activists permitted to emerge above the surface when the occasion demands. We have seen instances of this in San Francisco during the demonstrations against the House Committee in May of 1960 when Mickey Lima, Saul Wachter, Archie Brown, and Merle Brodsky staged a typical Communist propaganda and agitation show, abetted by the Emergency Civil Liberties Committee and the Citizens Committee to Preserve American Freedoms, both represented by Frank Wilkinson, who was exposed as a Communist by this Committee in connection with its investigation of infiltration in the Los Angeles City Housing Authority in 1952. This absence of overt activity on the part of the Communist Party and its front organizations has not provided the A.C.L.U. with the same abundance of civil rights matters involving Communism that concerned it a few years ago.

The influence of Director Patrick Murphy Malin has been felt by every A.C.L.U. local organization in the country. The chairman of this committee, Senator Burns, and its counsel, R.E. Combs, conferred with Mr. Malin some time ago and found him to be a forthright, courageous, sincere man who left no room for the slightest doubt concerning his positive opposition to Communism and his concern about Communist efforts to infiltrate the A.C.L.U. . . .

We have devoted a considerable portion of our report to the A.C.L.U., both national and state, because it has long been a subject of controversy and we have received innumerable letters of inquiry concerning its status. We are not aware that any official organization has undertaken to set forth the history, objectives, organizational structure, operational techniques, and other detailed matter concerning the organization to such an extent, and we are glad to render this service at the specific request of the A.C.L.U. in California. The organization now has twenty-eight chapters in twenty-four states and a total membership of approximately 50,000 people. It seeks to exclude Communists from holding any office or serving on its staff—yet it permits them to become members and appears unconcerned about its representatives belonging to Communist fronts.

It operates a self-perpetuating directorate in its local chapters, the members being allowed no opportunity to vote for their own representatives. They are permitted to suggest candidates for official positions to a nominating committee—but the incumbent officers select the nominating committee and choose their own successors. This peculiarly un-democratic device certainly operates to make for an exceptionally tight control by a small group, that could elect each other indefinitely. It is a curious plan for an organization that advocates freedom and civil rights for all; but, as the new Chairman of the Communist Party pointed out, the A.C.L.U. was the first unofficial group in the country to adopt what the Communists term a "red-baiting" provision barring Party members from office. Perhaps this device was employed for the purpose of implementing the non-Communist resolution of 1940 and the resolution of 1954.

So far as the national A.C.L.U. is concerned, charges that it was a tool of the Communist Party have been made for many years, and we believe it appropriate at this place to include statements by Martin Dies, the first chairman of the House Committee on Un-American Activities and by Mr. Richard Arens, present staff director of that committee. On October 23, 1939, Congressman Dies declared: "This committee found last year, in its report, that there was not any evidence that the American Civil Liberties Union was a Communist organization."

On April 23, 1960, Mr. Richard Arens, present staff director for the House Committee, delivered an address at the University of Illinois. On that occasion and in response to a question, he said, "The American Civil Liberties Union, A.C.L.U., has never been investigated by the Committee on Un-American Activities, nor has it been found to be a Communist front by the Committee on Un-American Activities, or, so far as I know, by any governmental agency."

We greatly disagree with many things that the A.C.L.U. California chapters do, but we do not believe that any of them are so infiltrated by Communists or fellow-travelers at the present time to justify us in characterizing any of them as a Communist front.

Notes

Preface

1. Apart from official literature, collected essays by members, and autobiographical accounts of leaders—to all of which we shall eventually refer—there is a relative scarcity of book-length treatments of the ACLU. The best academic study by a partisan of the organization is considerably dated and was never published: Barton Bean, "Pressure for Freedom: The American Civil Liberties Union" (Cornell University doctoral dissertation, February, 1955; Doctoral Dissertation Series, Publication Number 11,893; available from University Microfilms, Ann Arbor, Michigan). I have used Bean's study as a major source of factual data for the historical portion of this volume and, for that purpose, recommend it highly. An example of the popular and polemical literature in tribute to the Union is Barbara Habenstreit, *Eternal Vigilance: The American Civil Liberties Union in Action* (New York: Julian Messner, 1971). Although at the time of writing this volume is the only recent book on the Union in print, it is written as propaganda for the high school level and is not a serious study of the organization even for the satisfaction of its supporters. Apart from the government reports on the ACLU from a critical internal security perspective, an essay representative of the anti-Communist attacks on the group is David Emerson Gumaer, "The ACLU: Lawyers Playing the Red Game," *American Opinion*, September, 1969, pp. 57–90. Also see Franklin V. York, "The ACLU Con Game," *Review of the News*, August 13, 1975, pp. 31–40. I mave hade very little use of another book about the ACLU: Charles Lam Markmann, *The Noblest Cry: A History of the American Civil Liberties Union*, (New York: St. Martin's Press, 1965). This is because, in addition to it being an undocumented polemic like Habenstreit's work, it is so full of the author's unsupported claims and opinions having little or nothing to do with his subject that it has been a bit of an embarrassment to the Union's leadership. In addition, without citing specific references, Markmann, in between his tangential remarks, relies heavily on Bean's unpublished study, which I have used. The ACLU should not be held responsible for Markmann's

221

vented frustrations, and the reader will recognize why they should be carefully distinguished if he will note Markmann's smear of anti-Communists by association with racists and fascists (p. vi), his repudiation of American federalism (p. 4), and his incredible attack on Christendom (p. 67). Also see Victor Lasky, "American Civil Liberties Union Should Repudiate New Smear Book," *Human Events*, December 25, 1965, and Aryeh Neier and Thomas S. Szasz, "The ACLU & Involuntary Commitment: Response and Reply," *Reason*, April, 1974, p. 28.

Chapter 1: The Philosophical Foundations of the Natural Law Tradition

1. This is not to say that we cannot abstract an accurate overall appraisal of the actions taken by the ACLU's influential personnel. This is possible after a review of the Union's record, as long as we avoid what is clearly nonessential to the subject at hand—and as long as we remember that we are evaluating the thoughts and actions of individuals, not equating those thoughts and actions necessarily with their potential or character.

2. Further inquiry into the varying motives of the ACLU representatives I shall discuss is not particularly relevant for the purpose of this book's first part. In this part, I am concerned with measuring the Union's consistency, or lack of same, with its professed principles. If I show that the Union has, for any reason, betrayed those principles in the majority of its work, the response of the sincere and idealistic ACLU member should be obvious. He will want no part of the Union under such circumstances, regardless of the motivations behind the betrayal.

3. For a grounding in the epistemological orientation of the author see Ayn Rand, *An Introduction to Objectivist Epistemology* (New York: The Objectivist, Inc., 1967). One rather technical work that deals with the confusions resulting from talking about concepts like "society" as if they were physical concretes is Ernst Gellner, *Cause and Meaning in the Social Sciences* (London: Routledge and Kegan Paul, 1973), pp. 1–17.

4. For a discussion of the problems resulting in political science from a lack of clarity in the meanings of constitutional topics, and the consequences, see Giovanni Sartori's linguistic article "Constitutionalism: A Preliminary Discussion," *American Political Science Review* LVI (1962): 853–64. This article deals well with the distinctions between authentic and facade constitutions. Sartiori's point is well expressed on p. 859; "I am only saying that terminological clarity is a basic requirement for any science, and that political scientists in particular have to take stock of the fact that the vocabulary of politics tends to be used for the purpose of beguiling the listener."

5. An excellent and very readable summary of some of these problems is Richard Taylor, *Metaphysics* (Englewood Cliffs, N.J.: Prentice-Hall, 1963). An older work on one area of metaphysics is also recommended as a foundation for conceptualist natural law theory: P. Coffey, *Ontology or The Theory of Being* (London: Longmans, Green, and Co., 1914).

6. On epistemology in general and the problem of universals in particular see Brand Blanshard, *The Nature of Thought*, 2 vol. (London: George Allen and Unwin, 1939) and H.W.B. Joseph, *An Introduction to Logic* (Oxford: Clarendon Press, 1950). These two outstanding older works were earlier sources for much of Ayn Rand's writings on epistemology, including her theories of axiomatic concepts, concept formation, and causality. (The reader may wish to review one critic of Joseph's Aristotelian defense of the law of identity: John Wisdom, *Foundations of Inference in Natural Science*, [London: Methuen, 1952], pp. 120–29.) Also of interest are Brand Blanshard, *Reason and Analysis* (La Salle, Illinois: Open Court, 1964), pp. 382–421 (on universals) and Henry B. Veatch, *Realism and Nominalism Revisited* (Milwaukee: Marquette University Press, 1954).

7. Unfortunately, since the end of the eighteenth century, most philosophers have consented to Kant's view that ethical statements cannot be logically derived from factual ones. According to this notion (which is well criticized in P. Coffey, *Epistemology or the Theory of Knowledge*, 2 vol. [London: Longmans, Green, and Co., 1917]), "Jones is being coerced" and "Jones ought to be free of coercion" are in separate categories and incapable of logical connection because of their forms, one being a statement of what *is* and the other a claim about what *ought* to be. With this stumbling block and others, Kant drastically influenced almost two centuries of followers in many

fields to believe that no claims about what ought or ought not to be, in other words, about morality, were rationally provable. For better or worse, this left all such claims with the status of subjective emotional whim. That Kant was greatly influenced by clandestine personalities of his time, with whom he was associated and who had as their goal the popular repudiation of any belief in absolute moral truths, is strongly indicated in Abbe' Augustin Barruel, *Memoirs Illustrating the History of Jacobinism*, 4 vol. (London: T. Burton, 1798), 4:523–28. The solution to the supposed nonrational origin of ethical statements is indicated in the argument of unpacking the characteristics of a concept's definition, as used in Leonard Peikoff, "The Analytic-Synthetic Dichotomy," *The Objectivist*, May-September, 1967. By this argument, "Jones ought to be free of coercion" translates into "Jones, a man possessing the faculty of free will as a part of his nature, is best left to live in accord with that nature, or free from coercion." The reader should also consult such works as Ayn Rand's *Virtue of Selfishness*, Henry B. Veatch's *Rational Man*, and Brand Blanshard's *Reason and Goodness* for further examinations of ethical concepts and their applications.

8. An excellent recent critique of psychological determinism is Tibor R. Machan, *The Pseudo-Science of B.F. Skinner* (New Rochelle, New York: Arlington House, 1974). Other leading accounts include Blanshard, *The Nature of Thought*, vol. 1; Nathaniel Branden, *The Psychology of Self-Esteem* (Los Angeles: Nash Publishing, 1969), pp. 54–59; J. R. Lucas, *The Freedom of the Will* (Oxford: Clarendon Press, 1970), pp. 114–116; and M.R. Ayers, *The Refutation of Determinism: An Essay in Philosophical Logic* (London: Methuen and Company, 1968).

9. John Locke, *An Essay Concerning Human Understanding, Selections* (Chicago: Regnery-Gateway, 1956), pp. 75–77.

10. Thomas Hobbes, *Leviathan, Parts I and II* (Indianapolis: Bobbs-Merrill Company, 1958), p. 59. Perhaps predictably, some traditionalist conservative advocates of government-enforced moral alternatives have attempted to deny Locke's strong influence on Madison and other American Founding Fathers. An example of this, which argues that Madison was a political medievalist, is Alexander Landi, "Was the American Founding a Lockean Enterprise? The Case of James Madison," *Intercollegiate Review*, Spring, 1975, pp. 95–105. Landi could have avoided his unfortunate characterization of Locke's moral ideals as base and low by a careful reading of Locke's defense of our ability to know universal truths (Locke, *An Essay Concerning Human Understanding*, pp. 268–94). This truly non-empiricist presentation would have been helpful. In the next chapter we shall examine the identity between Locke's theory of natural law and that of our Founding Fathers.

11. Hobbes, *Leviathan*.

12. Blanshard, *Reason and Analysis*, pp. 382–421. An excellent review of the problem of universals and a proposed solution consistent with Objectivist epistemology is found in Harry Binswanger, "The Metaphysics of Universals," *Enquiry*, February, and June, 1967.

13. Blanshard, *Reason and Analysis*, pp. 406–7.

14. Ayn Rand, "Introduction to Objectivist Epistemology," *The Objectivist*, July, 1966, pp. 5–11. This essay has been reprinted in book form, see footnote 3 above.

15. Binswanger, "Metaphysics."

16. Blanshard, *Reason and Analysis*, pp. 407–8.

17. For a discussion of the application of nominalism to logic see Henry B. Veatch, *Two Logics: The Conflict between Classical and Neo-Analytic Philosophy* (Evanston, Ill.: Northwestern University Press, 1969). See also C.W.K. Mundle, *A Critique of Linguistic Philosophy* (Oxford: Clarendon Press, 1970), pp. 110–119.

18. That the resulting nominalist philosophies of empiricism and positivism were adopted and promoted by those seeking political power in the nineteenth century is indicated, with the contents of footnote 7, above, in Mildred J. Headings, *French Freemasonry Under the Third Republic* (Baltimore: Johns Hopkins University Press, 1949), pp. 39–65. A typical political example of an event which carries with it a lesson in the various theories of universals, and is also tragically ludicrous, is the conviction of Indian Prime Minister Indira Ghandi on a number of criminal violations in 1975. After imposing a formal police state, arresting most of her opponents, and imposing press censorship, this champion of "democracy" proceeded to force the Indian legislature to repeal retroactively the laws that she violated. The resulting question concerning whether there exists any legality in India today resolves into a choice between realist or nominalist theories of universals. And with Indira ordaining what is law, past, present, and future, there is nothing objective or essential about it. Law in India is merely the words she chooses to use in her language.

Chapter 2: Constitutionalism and the Rise of Nominalist-Positivist "Law"

1. In anyone's writing on the history of ideas there are pitfalls that could be carefully avoided but seldom are. It should be recognized that much distortion and myth-making stems from several popular approaches to comparative quotations of great thinkers of the past. It is unfair to blame a theorist at one point in time for failing in some respect to do something that we might have liked but that he may have had no intention of doing. It is also risky to assume that he necessarily intended the tradition of what has been done with his ideas since his time unless he clearly expressed such a desire. We should also avoid straining to iron out inconsistencies that may really be inconsistencies and should shy away from searching for the thinker's secret message hidden between his lines. In tracing a principle, such as limited government or constitutionalism or natural law, throughout its long history of varied commentary, it is very important to make sure that the same meaning or context is indicated by the separate authors employing the same words. This is not to say that we cannot compare and relate an ancient's conception of a subject with a modern's. All conceptual knowledge is cumulative, and a man will still be a man in the future even if we discover that after year X in that future he suddenly begins to have a new essential characteristic that is not common to any other animals. We must keep in mind that, while we can critically compare medicine of two centuries ago with today's, we cannot blame doctors of two centuries ago for not being able to cure dread diseases with wonder drugs discovered in recent decades. On the history of constitutionalism and the philosophy of law in general, among many useful texts, are the following: Carl J. Friedrich, *The Philosophy of Law in Historical Perspective* (Chicago: University of Chicago Press, 1963) and M.J.C. Vile, *Constitutionalism and the Separation of Powers* (Oxford: Clarendon Press, 1967). An informative summary from which I have selected a number of quotations, is C. Perry Patterson, "The Evolution of Constitutionalism," *Minnesota Law Review*, vol. 32, no. 5 (April, 1948), pp. 427–57.

2. From: Aristotle, *Rhetoric,* as quoted in Patterson, "Evolution," p. 429. See also John Herman Randall, Jr., *Aristotle* (New York: Columbia University Press, 1960), p. 283.

3. Cicero, *De Republica*, as quoted in Patterson, "Evolution," p. 430.

4. *Ibid.*

5. St. Thomas Aquinas, *Summa Theologica*, as quoted in: *Ibid.*, p. 431. See also M.C. D'Arcy, ed., *Selected Writings of St. Thomas Aquinas* (New York: E.P. Dutton, 1950), pp. 75–88.

6. Some of these problems in the natural law tradition are outlined in Paul E. Sigmund, *Natural Law in Political Thought* (Cambridge, Mass.: Winthrop Publishing Company, 1971).

7. Patterson, "Evolution," p. 433. Original sources are cited in his notes.

8. *Ibid.*

9. *Ibid.*, pp. 433–34.

10. *Ibid.*, pp. 434–35.

11. *Ibid.*, p. 434.

12. *Ibid.*, p. 435, for both quotes here presented together. One conservative writer, L. Brent Bozell, in an otherwise largely laudable demonstration of the manner in which the U.S. Supreme Court has in recent years perverted the doctrine of judicial review to the purpose of actually claiming to declare what is both statutory and constitutional (natural) law, unfortunately makes a mistaken effort to repudiate judicial review as a position Coke took in substance. Bozell makes this error by assuming that judicial review must denote the institution of a national judiciary that passes on the higher legality of particular statutes. Beyond an attempt to belittle the meaning, use, and influence of Coke's statement in Dr. Bonham's Case, Bozell briefly argues that there was no basis in English constitutional history for the Supreme Court's judicial review doctrine as it has developed in the United States. Bozell's confusion lies in the fact that he is attacking his own strawman. In English history back to the Magna Carta, the function of articulating the natural law and the correspondence to it, or lack of same, in all particular statutes or executive decrees belonged, to the extent that it was successful in limiting arbitrary legislative and executive power, to the members of the local common-law courts, juries composed of commoners, not tribunals conducted by judges or lawyers. (See L. Brent Bozell, *The Warren Revolution* [New Rochelle, New York: Arlington House, 1966], pp. 123–36, in this connection. For a detailed discussion of the true English

tradition of judicial review see Lysander Spooner, "An Essay on the Trial by Jury," *Let's Abolish Government* [New York: Arno Press and the *New York Times,* 1972], pp. 1–224.) Bozell further argues that there is no precedent in the early history of the United States for the doctrine of judicial review by a national judiciary. This is not difficult to argue since the modern version of "judicial review" associated with the Supreme Court in recent years was not the judicial review tradition we inherited from England. However, there are precedents in early cases for the determination of natural law by local and state court juries of citizens. In the February term of 1974, the Supreme Court conducted a jury trial in the case of *The State of Georgia* v. *Brailsford et al* (3.Dall.1). The essence of justice was well enunciated in the charge to the jury by Chief Justice John Jay, who said, among other things: "It may not be amiss, here, gentlemen, to remind you of the good old rule, that on questions of fact, it is the province of the jury, on questions of law, it is the province of the court, to decide. But it must be observed that by the same law, which recognizes this reasonable distribution of jurisdiction, you have nevertheless a right to take upon yourselves to judge of both, and to determine the law as well as the fact in controversy. On this, and on every other occasion, however, we have no doubt, you will pay that respect, which is due to the opinion of the court. For, as on the one hand, it is presumed, that juries are the best judges of fact; it is, on the other hand, presumable, that the courts are the best judges of law. But still both objects are lawfully, within the power of your decision."

13. Patterson, "Evolution," p. 437.
14. *Ibid.,* pp. 437–38.
15. *Ibid.,* p. 439.
16. *Ibid.,* p. 457, quoting from John Locke, *Two Treatises on Civil Government,* chapter XI, section 135.
17. *Ibid.,* p. 439, quoting from John Locke, *Two Treatises on Civil Government,* chapter XI, section 135.
18. *Ibid.,* pp. 439–40.
19. *Ibid.,* pp. 444–45.
20. *Ibid.,* p. 446.
21. *Ibid.,* p. 449.
22. *Ibid.,* pp. 451–52.
23. *Ibid.,* p. 449.
24. *Ibid.,* pp. 449–50.
25. *Ibid.,* pp. 446–57.
26. *Ibid.,* pp. 440–44. Brent Bozell attempts to deny that Blackstone's predominant advocacy of legislative supremacy is contrary to the natural law tradition of Coke and Locke. (See Bozell, *Warren Revolution,* pp. 150–53 in particular.) In doing this, Bozell fails to mention the numerous errors and contradictions in Blackstone's *Commentaries* that are so frequently referred to by other scholars. Because of this Bozell is able to cite passages from Blackstone that acknowledge natural law, alongside the declaration of unlimited legislative power that we have quoted. It is rather clear to Patterson, in the pages cited, that Blackstone's inconsistent advocacy resulted from his mistake in interpreting Coke's doctrine of the supremacy of Parliament *as a natural law court* as the supremacy of Parliament as a legislative body. So much for Bozell's attempt to explain away the disastrous turn that legal theory took as Blackstone's work became the standard reference in its field.
27. Lon L. Fuller, *The Morality of Law* (New Haven, Conn.: Yale University Press, 1969), p. 101.
28. Blanshard, *Reason and Analysis,* pp. 25–92.
29. *Ibid.,* pp. 93–126. See also Fuller, *Morality,* pp. 106–18, 145–51. An outstanding individualist essay on the history of constitutionalism that surveys the positivist trend is F.A. Hayek, *The Constitution of Liberty* (Chicago: University of Chicago Press, 1960), pp. 234–49.
30. Fuller, *Morality,* pp. 226–27.
31. *Ibid.,* pp. 187–242. See also Friedrich, *Philosophy of Law,* pp. 165–77.
32. Fuller, *Morality,* p. 123. See Chapter 1, footnote 18 above in connection with this quote. Fuller's work is the leading and very well reasoned critique of positivist legal theory. As such it is the best critical material available from academic circles against the nominalist influence in the philosophy of law. Unfortunately, I think, what Fuller advocates as his alternative falls far short of its potential. He has outlined what he calls an "internal" morality of law or natural law. This is

distinguished from substantive natural law, the advocates of which, including myself, hold as containing the principles derived from reality that govern the content and subject matter of particular law on the basis of individual natural rights. Fuller unfortunately consents that such cannot be defined as logical and based on objective reality. He does try to defend what we might call a procedural natural law governing a number of matters concerning the possibility of obedience and enforcement of statutes as well as issues of "due process": statutes must be clear in meaning, must not apply retroactively, must not contain contradictions or require the impossible, must be enforced consistently over time, with the enforcement in reality matching the written prescription. Fuller defends these principles on the basis of their individual merits as being sensible or practical, not necessarily as properly conforming to a defended theory of human nature. In spite of these disappointing limitations, the book is strongly recommended as an excellent critique of much of what is the rule of "law" today.

Chapter 3: Alternatives in the Philosophy of Law in Today's Legal Education and Practice

1. The model referred to is "The Problem of the Grudge Informer" presented in Lon L. Fuller, *The Morality of Law* (New Haven, Conn.: Yale University Press, 1969), pp. 245–53. Fuller certainly bears no responsibility for my imitation and should not be assumed to be in agreement with whatever I have done with his model, correctly or incorrectly.

2. An excellent example of the influence of positivism in this respect is the facade constitution of the USSR. That document states that the people of the USSR have certain rights, including "rights" to tangible products and services produced by others, and that these rights cannot be abridged "except as provided by law." This qualification nullifies a "right" as being inalienable. Because the Soviet state is viewed, in a very positivist perspective, as the grantor of "rights" (actually privileges), it is equally able to take them away at will. The concept of inalienable rights, as held by Madison and Jefferson, implies that individual rights existed as characteristics of living individual men. Just as one's weight or height (in general, not a particular weight or height) cannot be taken away, neither can one's rights be deprived by anyone. One's rights can only be violated, not separated from one while one is alive. This philosophical distinction is obviously not apparent to those who try to compare the enumeration of certain rights in the U.S. Constitution with superficially similar language in the USSR constitution and its positivist companion, the UN Declaration of Human Rights. In my discussion of positivism and empiricism in legal philosophy, I have no desire to attack a "strawman," as some may characterize the positions I have described. Not all positivists or empiricists agree on specific conclusions to problems. Advocates of legal positivism might disagree with a number of the positions held by the leading academic positivist philosophers. It really is a matter of how consistently they apply those assumptions on which most of them do agree to the issues we have discussed. Strict positivists might refuse any discussion of rights at all. Legal positivists, those who accept a positivist approach to the law, are more likely to hold some general ideas about the relationship of rights to the law. If I have misrepresented any positivist's position, it is because I have had to present positivist assumptions rather strictly in a concrete example to show clearly the inevitable results. I do recognize that not all positivists want to be so consistent.

3. The best recent example of Americans losing valid constitutional arguments in court because of the inadmissibility of natural law pleading is the series of cases in recent decades that has come to be called the "tax rebellion" or "tax strike" movement. Discussion of these cases, the arguments made by those involved against the constitutionality of the personal income tax and the issuance of fiat paper money by the Federal Reserve System, as well as the results of those attempts can be found in Vivien Kellems, *Toil, Taxes and Trouble* (New York: E.P. Dutton, 1952); William Campbell Douglass, *The William Campbell Douglass Letters* (Freeport, New York: Patriot Press, 1968); Martin A. Larson, *Tax Revolt: U.S.A.!* (Washington, D.C.: Liberty Lobby, 1973); Marvin L. Cooley, *The Big Bluff* (Mesa, Ariz.: published by the author, 1972); Jerome Daly, "Judgment at Credit River," *The Daly Eagle* (Savage, Minn.), May 1, 1971; Don K. Hoate (Rolland A.

Vandegrift), *How to Fight a Windmill (How to Protest Property Tax Assessments)* (Magalia, Calif.: Dogtown Research Institute, 1972); and Henry J. Hohenstein, *The IRS Conspiracy* (Los Angeles: Nash, 1974). Most of these people have lost, or are losing, their attempts to represent themselves before the IRS tax courts or in federal district courts in their efforts to abolish an unjust and unnecessary tax. The weight of natural law and constitutional arguments are overwhelmingly on their side. But they find that when they go into court, all the judge will allow to be discussed is the factual determination of their income and whether they have failed to meet the statutory requirements of the Federal Tax Code. All efforts to raise the sort of philosophical arguments on constitutional points fall on deaf ears or are explicitly and firmly forbidden. Juries are instructed that they are to determine the facts of the case only. They are not to decide any point of the law. They are merely to decide if the defendant qualifies for its punitive application. With this hopelessly futile situation, all such cases are doomed to eventual defeat. But these heroic souls, with right clearly on their side, take comfort in the growing strength of their numbers, assuming "they won't be able to put everybody in jail." (Persons in the USSR might disagree.) The tax strikers rejoice over every favorable interim ruling they receive on grounds of due process and every procedural delay and remedy they can legally exercise among the myriad mechanics of our court system. They become arrogantly self-confident amateur attorneys, exhausting every recourse until they are finally convicted of violating the literal statute whose validity they were never permitted legally to question. One can admire their bravery, appreciate their tremendous sacrifices for right principles, and wish them well. But one cannot easily admire the blindness with which they frequently refuse to recognize the institutionalized futility of their proposed solution. After seeing that blindness, one cannot have much sympathy when they finally succeed in bringing on themselves the boot of the tyrant, who will quite effectively preoccupy or detain them from any promising program of activity aimed at public education and exposure of the reasons why our judicial system has become immune to justice. Until such a campaign of education brings a swing toward justice in our legal system, all who attempt to attack in court unjust statutory laws of all kinds—particularly those passed on a national level—will continue to be sheep leading themselves to a useless slaughter.

Chapter 4: Basic Foundations
for a Libertarian-Conceptualist Theory of Law

1. For what degree of understanding I have applied in this chapter, I am thankful for the ideas presented by a number of authors, most notably Ayn Rand in *Atlas Shrugged;* Ayn Rand *et al.*, *Capitalism: The Unknown Ideal* (New York: New American Library, 1966), particularly pp. 286–303; John Hospers, *Libertarianism: A Political Philosophy for Tomorrow* (Los Angeles: Nash, 1971), pp. 49–94; Murray N. Rothbard, *For a New Liberty* (New York: Macmillan, 1973), pp. 23–46; and Nathaniel Branden, "Free Will, Moral Responsibility, and the Law," in Tibor Machan, ed., *The Libertarian Alternative* (Chicago: Nelson–Hall, 1974). The principles of rational definition were well presented in Barbara Branden, *Principles of Efficient Thinking* (Los Angeles: Academic Associates Recordings, 1969), album no. 7. My understanding of the application of these ideas to law was greatly aided by their development in Howard Hood, "Law and Ayn Rand's Concept of Justice," *Enquiry,* February, 1967, pp. 1–9. A critical discussion of the conclusions from legal positivism is Ronald Dworkin, "Philosophy and the Critique of Law," in Robert Paul Wolff, ed., *The Rule of Law* (New York: Simon and Schuster, 1971). In the same volume, see also Lon L. Fuller, "Human Interaction and the Law," which is an interesting discussion of the roots of contract, or civil, law in the characteristics of human interactions and individual exchanges of values. Legal positivism and its results are also briefly discussed in Ludwig von Mises, *Theory and History: An Interpretation of Social and Economic Evolution* (New Haven, Conn.: Yale University Press, 1957), pp. 47–48. The discussion of law in this chapter does not pretend to be a comprehensive presentation or defense of the alternative being offered. It is merely an attempt to lay some groundwork for that task, which, I hope, I and others will be able to develop in the future.
2. Rand *et al.*, *Capitalism*, pp. 290–94. The fact that so much of positivist philosophy was promoted

by political collectivists since the French Revolution makes it quite reasonable to suppose that some saw it as a weapon of conquest. An additional item on this, pertaining to Condorcet's advocacy of the methodology of modern "social science," is contained in Helmut Schoeck and James W. Wiggins, ed., *Scientism and Values* (New York: Arno Press and the *New York Times*, 1972), p. 205.

3. Jacques Maritain, *The Rights of Man and Natural Law* (New York: Charles Scribner's Sons, 1943), pp. 64–68.

4. Some advocates of individualist anarchy, or "anarcho-capitalism," have discussed the need for arbitrary determination of amounts for the purpose of reparations for values that cannot physically be returned to the victim of a criminal act. For example, see Morris and Linda Tannehill, "The Market for Liberty," in *Society Without Government* (New York: Arno Press and the *New York Times*, 1972), pp. 96–100. The presentation of this anarchist view makes fascinating and stimulating reading. There are serious problems with the anarchists' advocacy of private arbitration companies to decide criminal cases and with competing private "law" enforcement companies. The central unsolved problem is the manner in which a society that has no agency with a monopoly on the just forceful deprivation of values, no government, would bring justice to a case in which two disputing parties agreed to private arbitration but the one who lost decided not to pay up. Conceivably his debt to his opponent could remain unpaid as long as he could hold the opponent off with superior private protection services. I think some of these inconsistencies in anarchist thought result from the fact that the anarchists tend to think of government in a manner that reflects the concrete-concept fallacy. That is, they fail to recognize that government is composed of individuals performing actions that can be identical to those performed by other individuals privately. If the actions are just, such as enforcement of laws against criminal actions, then it really is a matter of little controversy as to whether those actions are performed by individuals in or out of government. Only criminal–law enforcement and national defense seem to be natural monopolies for a government designed for justice. If private individuals are free to compete in the provision of all other goods and services, there only remains the challenge to keep government limited to the essential function of protecting individual rights. There is little else seriously worth debating, at least until we succeed in reducing our government to that scale. There also seems to be a strongly subjectivist strain of moral and legal philosophy in the writings of some individualist anarchists, including a denial of much of what I would call an objectively knowable natural law appropriate to the context of all men's lives. See Benjamin R. Tucker, *Instead of a Book: By A Man Too Busy to Write One* (New York: Arno Press and the *New York Times*), pp. 57, 132, 169.

5. Spooner, *Let's Abolish Government*.

6. See my *Klandestine: The Untold Story of Delmar Dennis and His Role in the F.B.I.'s War Against the Ku Klux Klan* (New Rochelle, New York: Arlington House, 1975).

7. I have observed that many libertarians and traditionalist conservatives share a common tendency toward inconsistency in these areas of the moral versus the legal. Many traditionalist conservatives are advocates of laws against some actions that I would define as "victimless crimes," or not crimes at all, such as personal drug abuse, the manufacture and purchase of pornography, and prostitution. They take this position because of religious, moral, or philosophical reasons, but they fail to realize that such actions ordinarily do not constitute force of fraud to deprive anyone of their values or to violate anyone's rights. Indeed, the forceful compulsion of alternative noncriminal actions strikes essentially at the nature of their inherent moral context. On the other hand, many libertarians, who would argue that such actions are, by definition, outside the scope of just law, seem to have little or no similar enthusiasm for advocating, as persuasively as possible, the reasons why most of the actions wrongly legislated against as victimless crimes, are inherently immoral by an objective standard based on what is necessary for the physiological and psychological health and happiness of all human beings. As a libertarian, I want to stress that I am just as interested in explaining my philosophical, factual, and religious reasons why such actions should be voluntarily avoided by my fellow men as I am in insisting that, in most contexts, they have no business being the subject of restrictive statutes. One could assert easily on that basis that all who do not apply their reason to the subject matter of both moral and legal perspectives on human actions are responsible for the same essential inconsistency, which, if widespread enough, will result in the same sort of tragic consequences for our civilization.

Chapter 5: ACLU Positions on Issues of Criminality, Due Process, and Equal Protection under the Law

1. Constitution of the American Civil Liberties Union, as revised January 7, 1957; March, 1963; March, 1965; July, 1967; and April, 1968.
2. "What Are Your Rights?," an ACLU recruitment flyer, no date. Another leaflet published by the Union contains the text of the Bill of Rights and excerpts from the other amendments and the original text of the Constitution dealing with civil liberties. It also contains this declaration: "The purpose for which the American Civil Liberties Union was founded in 1920 (as stated in its Charter): *To maintain throughout the United States and its possessions, the rights of free speech, free press, free assemblage and other civil rights, and to take all legitimate action in furtherance of such purpose.*"
3. Daniel St. Albin Greene, " 'We Don't Enter Popularity Contests' ACLU Takes on All Comers in Battle for Civil Liberties," *National Observer*, March 2, 1970, reprinted by the ACLU as a recruitment pamphlet.
4. Peter Andrews, "A.C.L.U.—Let There Be Law," *Playboy*, October, 1971, reprinted for distribution by the ACLU.
5. ACLU, "What Are Your Rights?"
6. *Ibid.*
7. George J. Annas, *The Rights of Hospital Patients: The Basic ACLU Guide to a Hospital Patient's Rights* (New York: Avon Books, 1975). The book is copyrighted by the ACLU.
8. *Ibid.*, p. ix.
9. *Ibid.*, pp. 4–5. In his footnote 2 (p. 8), Annas refers his readers to theorists on the subject of law. The leading one he recommends is John Austin, a positivist advocate of the "command theory" of law, that law is the command of the sovereign.
10. *Ibid.*, p. 6.
11. *Ibid.* The later Universal Covenant on Human Rights expressed the positivist philosophy even more consistently and blatantly.
12. *Ibid.*
13. *Ibid.*
14. *Ibid.*, p. 4.
15. *Ibid.*, p. 6.
16. *Ibid.*, p. 21.
17. *Ibid.*, p. 22.
18. *Ibid.*, pp. 23–24, 48.
19. *Ibid.*, pp. 42, 47–49.
20. *Ibid.*, This is a subject throughout most of the book, but pp. 21–36 offer a leading example.
21. *Ibid.*, p. 2.
22. For the result of such programs in other countries and tendencies here see Helmut Schoeck, ed., *Financing Medical Care: An Appraisal of Foreign Programs* (Caldwell, Idaho: Caxton Printers, 1962), and Marvin H. Edwards, *Hazardous to Your Health: A New Look at the "Health Care Crisis" in America* (New Rochelle, New York: Arlington House, 1972), especially pp. 266–75 on the "right" to health care.
23. "If You Are Arrested," card available from the ACLU, 633 South Shatto Place, Los Angeles, CA 90005.
24. Sanford Jay Rosen, William Birtles, and David Fine, *Your Rights Before the Grand Jury* (New York: ACLU, February, 1972) and addenda supplement (June, 1972).
25. Coleman A. Blease and Harriet Katz Berman, *Should the Courts Run on Time?*, four–page undated leaflet available from the Los Angeles, San Francisco, and Sacramento offices of the ACLU. There is no pagination; all quotations come from the fourth, or final, page. This article was

reprinted from *Open Forum*, June, 1973, p. 3, the publication of the ACLU's Southern California affiliate in Los Angeles.

26. On the practical record of private arbitration and police protection see William C. Wooldridge, *Uncle Sam, The Monopoly Man* (New Rochelle, New York: Arlington House, 1970), pp. 94–127.

27. Oliver Rosengart with Gail Weinheimer, *The Rights of Suspects* (New York: Avon Books, 1974).

28. "Scandal—Ridden 'Mobilization for Youth,' " *Human Events*, January 2, 1965, pp. 8–9; Alan Stang, *It's Very Simple: The True Story of Civil Rights* (Boston: Western Islands, 1965), pp. 172–93; Shirley Scheibla, *Poverty Is Where The Money Is* (New Rochelle, New York: Arlington House, 1968).

29. U.S. Congress, House, Special Committee on Un–American Activities, *House Report 1311 on the C.I.O. Political Action Committee*, March 29, 1944, p. 149; U.S. Congress, House, Committee on Un–American Activities, *House Report 3123 on the National Lawyers Guild*, September 21, 1950, originally related September 17, 1950 (this contains the quote cited). Also see U.S. Congress, Senate, Senate Judiciary Committee, Internal Security Subcommittee, *Handbook for Americans*, Senate Document 117, April 23, 1956, p. 91.

30. Rosengart, *Rights of Suspects*, p. 17.

31. *Ibid.*, p. 21.

32. *Ibid.*, pp. 40–41. On pp. 34–38 Rosengart discusses the status of "no–knock" search warrants, which rather clearly are subject to objections on Fourth Amendment constitutional grounds.

33. *Ibid.*, pp. 54–59.

34. Those who are inclined to mathematical empiricism might recognize the inequity of *Miranda* if translated as follows: $X=$Miranda's criminal debt to his victim. $X-Y$, such that X is greater than $Y=$the government's "debt" to Miranda for not informing him of all his "rights," that violation being less serious than kidnapping and rape. $O=$the debt that Miranda paid for the harm to his victim. Thus, $X-(X-Y)=O$. For review of the exclusionary rulings and their effects on similar state court rulings as well as the unfortunate details concerning the victims see G. Edward Griffin, *The Great Prison Break: The Supreme Court Leads The Way* (Boston: Western Islands, 1968), pp. 1–77.

35. Rosengart, *Rights of Suspects*, p. 51.

36. The critique being attacked is Fred E. Inbau and John E. Reid, *Criminal Interrogation and Confessions* (Baltimore: Williams and Wilkins Company, 1967). The critical quotation is from an ACLU–distributed reprint of Ed Cray, "Criminal Interrogations and Confessions: The Ethical Imperative," *Wisconsin Law Review*, vol. 1968, no. 1, p. 179.

37. Greene, " 'We Don't Enter Popularity Contests.' "

38. Rosengart, *Rights of Suspects*, pp. 115–16. It is interesting that, with the exception of his comments on searches at airports, Rosengart sees the need for control of local police abuses, but is otherwise oblivious to the danger and threat to *local* control posed by the system of federal controls that is being built around local police forces by the Law Enforcement Assistance Administration in Washington. (See Alan Stang, "Policrats: Plans For A National Police Force," *American Opinion*, February, 1974, pp. 1–16.) Indeed, Rosengart's attack seems to be almost exclusively on our locally controlled police, who are fast losing their locally controlled status. It just so happens that they are also the target of Communist attack. (See W. Cleon Skousen, *The Communist Attack on U.S. Police* [Salt Lake City: Ensign Publishing, 1966].) It is important to note here that the national ACLU strongly supported the legislation that established the LEAA as an incipient national police force. (See "A.C.L.U. Backs Bill to Help Police," *Civil Liberties*, October, 1967, p. 8.)

39. Rosengart, *Rights of Suspects*, p. 42. Such a conversation between a boy and an adult, either another citizen or a police officer, could no more be construed as a violation of rights or deprivation of values than could it be reasonably said that the confessions given in the landmark exclusionary cases were not strictly voluntary.

40. "Prison: Where Is the Law?," New York ACLU, no date.

41. David Rudovsky, *The Rights of Prisoners: The Basic ACLU Guide To A Prisoner's Rights* (New York: Avon Books, 1973).

42. U.S. Congress, House, Committee on Un–American Activities, *Annual Report for 1958, House Report 187*, March 9, 1959, pp. 34–35. Also see Senate Judiciary Committee, *Handbook for Americans*.

43. Rudovsky, *Rights of Prisoners*, pp. 11–12. A recent study contradicts the view that punishment does not deter crime: James Q. Wilson, *Thinking About Crime* (New York: Basic Books, 1975).
44. Rudovsky, *Rights of Prisoners*, p. 16.
45. *Ibid.*
46. *Ibid.*, pp. 19–28. In his plea (p. 25) that prison officials should be ordered to write conduct policies that will prevent arbitrary punishments of prisoners, he fails to explain how we will order those wo do the ordering, to do so nonarbitrarily.
47. *Ibid.*, p. 38. We should note that, by accepting as a standard for "cruel and unusual punishment" a determination of "whether the punishment shocks the general conscience of civilized society" (p. 30), Rudovsky assumes the responsibility of locating the world's first "general conscience" and detailing how one might go about such a survey, and at whose expense.
48. *Ibid.*, pp. 41–55, (p. 47 for quote). On the ludicrous consequences and personal tragedies that have resulted from the very prison "reforms" ACLU spokesman Rudovsky is recommending, see Alan Stang, "Behind Bars: More Revolution in the Prisons," *American Opinion*, May, 1973, pp. 17–32. Rudovsky's lack of worry (expressed on p. 47) is evidence that he is unaware of the facts in this article, the widespread distribution of which in 1973 greatly shocked the "general conscience" of Massachusetts, helping to secure dismissal of John Boone, the Massachusetts corrections administrator, whose policies brought mayhem to the state's prisons.
49. Rudovsky, *Rights of Prisoners*, pp. 52–54, 61–68. A prisoner's religious "rights" also expand to include the free provision of special food or other things that free men outside prisons must provide for themselves. It is odd that Rudovsky does not recognize in such special provisions any unconstitutional government establishment of a particular religion, when identical subsidies from taxpayers' wallets would clearly be viewed as such if exercised outside prisons. But taxpayers must apparently be *forced* to provide for prisoners what other men are free to provide for themselves.
50. *Ibid.*, pp. 55–60, 85–91 (p. 90 for quote). A prisoner's legal "rights" are not limited by Rudovsky to correspondence with his attorney, but also include his "right" to take up the practice of amateur law in prison. Other ACLU publications urge that prisoners have a "right" to high–quality legal assistance, as is the issue in *Wallace* v. *Kern*. On this, see "Jailhouse Lawyers Gains," *On The Line*, Summer, 1974, published by the ACLU of Southern California and the Greater Watts Justice Center.

Chapter 6: ACLU Positions on "Victimless Crimes"

1. Annas, *Rights of Hospital Patients* pp.79–91. The ACLU's position on the right to commit suicide, is, at best, confusing and inconsistent. Adopted by the ACLU National Board at its December 6–7, 1975, meeting, it holds suicide to be a victimless crime, not a criminal act. This means that someone who unsuccessfully attempts suicide should not be prosecuted unless some-one else was harmed. However, the same statement recognized the "right" of society to intervene in an act of suicide to make sure that the person attempting it has been shown other rational alternatives prior to completing this irreversible act. By "society" the Union meant, as always, individuals in and out of government, which means the Union upholds government exertion of force to prevent the commission of what they recognize as a victimless crime. Applied to the victimless crime of pornography, this position would uphold the "right" of those in and out of government to force people to listen to moral lectures before permitting them to enter pornographic movie houses. The Union's resolution closed with a separate proposition that implicitly confirms its sanction of another antilibertarian practice. They held that an abortive suicide attempt should not be the *sole* basis for involuntary commitment.
2. *Ibid.*, p. 79. The distinction I make between "active" and "passive" euthanasia, referring to whether or not the victim has initiated the decision rather than to whether the death is accomplished by harmful actions or withholding further treatment, is also called by some the difference between involuntary and voluntary euthanasia. The use of these terms and problems involved in claiming

that a victim really did give consent for his execution are to be found in Charles E. Rice, *The Vanishing Right To Live: An Appeal for a Renewed Reverence for Life* (Garden City, New York: Doubleday, 1969), pp. 51–72. I should state here that I am in firm disagreement with most of Rice's positions. He argues for the illegality of many immoral human actions, not on the basis of anyone's rights being violated by them, but because of a desire to force others to follow what is part of his religious convictions or what he believes is, although undefined, for the "common good of society."

3. *Ibid.*, Annas, *Rights of Hospital Patients*, p. 83.
4. Rice, *Vanishing Right to Live*, pp. 55–57 in particular.
5. Annas, *Rights of Hospital Patients*, p. 84.
6. *Ibid.*, p. 85.
7. *Ibid.*
8. For a complimentary look at "medical services" in the Third Reich see Lothrop Stoddard, *Into the Darkness* (New York: Duell, Sloan and Pearce, 1940).
9. Among other places, the Union's position on the death penalty is presented in "The Death Penalty & Civil Liberties," a one–sheet flyer, New York ACLU, dated July, 1965; Washington Research Project, *The Case Against Capital Punishment (Washington, D.C.: Washington Research Project, 1971), distributed by the ACLU; Hugo A. Bedau, The Case Against the Death Penalty,* pamphlet, New York ACLU, dated January, 1973; and Philip A. Hart, "Why Kill Capital Punishment? Sen. Hart Explains in Introducing the Federal Abolition Bill," *Civil Liberties,* October, 1967, p. 3.
10. ACLU, "The Death Penalty & Civil Liberties"; Bedau, *Case Against the Death Penalty,* p. 1.
11. "ACLU Backs Right to Abortion: Plenary Board Session Adopts New Policies on Four Issues," *Civil Liberties*, January, 1968, pp. 3–4. This is detailed more recently in Susan Deller Ross, *The Rights of Women: The Basic ACLU Guide to a Woman's Rights* (New York: Avon Books, 1973), pp. 192–207.
12. Thomas W. Hilgers and Robert P.N. Shearin, *Induced Abortion: A Documented Report, Written for Presentation to the Minnesota State Legislature* (privately published by the authors, 1971).
13. Ruth Jane Zuckerman, *Abortion and the Constitutional Rights of Minors*, ACLU Reports, Juvenile Rights Project (New York, 1973).
14. The best assembly of medical evidence on the humanity of the unborn child is to be found in one of the friend–of–the–court briefs submitted to the U.S. Supreme Court prior to the decision in *Roe* v. *Wade* and *Doe* v. *Bolton*; apparently it was totally ignored: Dennis J. Horan *et al.*, "Motion and Brief Amicus Curiae of Certain Physicians, Professors and Fellows of the American College of Obstetrics and Gynecology in support of Appellees," in the Supreme Court of the United States, October Term, 1971, *Roe* v. *Wade; Doe* v. *Bolton*.
15. Ayn Rand, "Of Living Death," *The Objectivist*, October, 1968, pp. 1–6. For evidence that the unborn child's unconscious mind is functioning, within the limits of its development and environment, significantly before the arbitrary and fictitiously static point of "viability," see Horan *et al.*, "Motion and Brief," pp.15–28.
16. Ross, *Rights of Women*, pp. 20–21. For a record of recent ACLU work on behalf of the ERA's ratification, see *A.C.L.U. Annual Report* (New York: ACLU) 7/70–7/71, p. 12; 7/71–6/72, p. 9; 1972–1973, p. 31.
17. *Marijuana,* (New York: ACLU 1971, revised 1973). The Union's omissions on the subject of marijuana are glaring. While not claiming that the drug is without potential harm for its users, the Union fails to caution against the practice in spite of the overwhelming proof of its serious dangers, as shown in U.S. Congress, Senate, Committee on the Judiciary, Internal Security Subcommittee, *Marijuana–Hashish Epidemic and Its Impact on United States Security*, 93rd Congress, 2nd session, 1974. Although the subcommittee's recommendation is for outlawing the drug, this study is one of the most complete ever prepared concerning what has been learned in recent years on the harmful effects of marijuana. Also see Jane E. Brody, "Male Sex Debility Traced to Marijuana," *New York Times,* September 16, 1975. A relationship, though not strictly deterministic, between use of marijuana and the commission of crimes is indicated in James C. Munch, "Marijuana and Crime," *Bulletin on Narcotics,* April–June, 1966, pp. 15–22. The proven record of the utility of such drugs in Communist revolutionary activities is given in A. H. Stanton Candlin, *Psycho-Chemical Warfare: The Chinese Communist Drug Offensive Against the West* (New Rochelle, New York: Arlington House, 1973), pp. 45–52.
18. ACLU, *Marijuana.* According to Linda Hunt, public relations director of the Southern California

ACLU affiliate in Los Angeles, this policy was reaffirmed by the National Board in September, 1975.

19. Michael L. Culbert, *Vitamin B–17: Forbidden Weapon Against Cancer* (New Rochelle, New York: Arlington House, 1974). For far more comprehensive coverage of the political issues and motivations involved, see G. Edward Griffin, *World Without Cancer: The Story of Vitamin B 17*, 2 vol. (Thousand Oaks, Calif.: American Media, 1974). A review of some legal issues in the laetrile cases in also available: Martin J. Cooper, "The Cancer Drug Controversy—U.S. v. Laetrile," *University of San Fernando Valley Law Review*, vol. 3, no. 2 (1974), pp. 51–63.

20. The only indication of ACLU involvement in the battle for freedom of choice in cancer therapy is the fact that some Union members in San Diego have decided *locally* to oppose California laetrile regulations. Letter, George W. Kell, attorney for laetrile users, to Carolyn Anagnos, Los Angeles office, ACLU of Southern California, May 5, 1975.

21. "City Councilman Joins ACLU in Fluoride Fight," *Open Forum*, December, 1973, p. 4; "Fluoridation Victory," *Open Forum*, October, 1974, p. 6. Fortunately, thanks to the voters of Los Angeles, the ACLU is still awaiting its "victory."

22. The most damning indictment of misinformation still used to promote fluoridation as beneficial in preventing tooth decay is P.R.N. Sutton, *Fluoridation, Errors and Omissions in Experimental Trials* (Melbourne, Australia: Melbourne University Press, 1960).

23. John Lear, "New Facts on Fluoridation," *Saturday Review*, March 1, 1969, pp. 51–56.

24. G.L. Waldbott, *A Struggle With Titans: Forces Behind Fluoridation* (New York: Carlton Press, 1965).

25. The works of Thomas S. Szasz are recommended on this subject, including the following, which discuss the inconsistent policy of the ACLU: *Law, Liberty, and Psychiatry: An Inquiry into the Social Uses of Mental Health Practices* (New York: Macmillan, 1963), pp. 64–65; *Psychiatric Justice* (New York: Collier Books, 1965), pp. 64, 183, 232, 237; and *The Manufacture of Madness: A Comparative Study of the Inquisition and the Mental Health Movement* (New York: Harper & Row, 1970), pp. 65–66, 141n. A rational definition of "mental health" and "mental illness" is given by another libertarian specialist in psychology: Nathaniel Branden, *The Psychology of Self-Esteem* (Los Angeles: Nash, 1969), pp. 89–101.

26. Bruce Ennis and Loren Siegel, *The Rights of Mental Patients: The Basic ACLU Guide to a Mental Patient's Rights* (New York: Avon Books, 1973), p. 13.

27. The Union's failure to be consistent on this issue was indicated in an exchange between Szasz and ACLU Executive Director Neier. Thomas S. Szasz, "The A.C.L.U.'s 'Mental Illness' Cop–Out," *Reason*, January, 1974, pp. 4–9; Aryeh Neier and Thomas S. Szasz, "The A.C.L.U. & Involuntary Commitment: Response and Reply," *Reason*, April, 1974, pp. 28–30.

28. Ennis and Siegel, *Rights of Mental Patients*, pp. 40–43, 49–50, 82–83.

29. Robert J. Kukla, *Gun Control* (Harrisburg, Pa.: Stackpole, 1973), pp. 352, 407–9, 434. This book provides many competent answers to the excuses usually put forth for gun control. During the San Francisco police strike of August, 1975, CBS Radio network reporter Charles Osgood, on his morning "Newsbreak" on KNX radio in Los Angeles (August 20, 1975), reported that David Fishlow, executive director of the Northern California ACLU, was advocating that the police be disarmed while on strike in order to avoid the violence that he feels results from the ownership of guns by persons not actively under government command.

30. The Bill of Rights was modeled after the Virginia Declaration of Rights. The author of the Declaration, George Mason of Virginia, conceived of the militia, referred to in the Second Amendment, as consisting of "the whole people except a few public officials." This was the concept generally held at the time. In Noah Webster, *An American Dictionary of the English Language*, 2 vol. (New York: S. Converse, 1828; reprinted 1967, Anaheim, California: Foundation for American Christian Education) we find under *Militia:* "The body of soldiers in a state enrolled for discipline, but not engaged in actual service except in emergencies; as distinguished from regular troops, whose sole occupation is war or military service. The militia of a country are the able bodied men organized into companies, regiments, and brigades, with officers of all grades, and required by law to attend military exercises on certain days only, but at other times to pursue their usual occupations." In other words, the people were the militia, not the enlisted soldiers of a regular branch of the armed services attached to a state or the nation. Even if such were not historically true, the constitutional protection of one's right to keep and bear arms is guaranteed in the Ninth Amendment. From the positivist statutory standpoint we must note that the National Guard was not established until the twentieth century. It could therefore not be equated with the

militia mentioned in this amendment, which is defined as follows: "The militia of the United States consists of all able-bodied males at least 17 years of age and . . . under 45 years of age who are or who have a declaration of intent to become citizens of the United States." (U.S. Code, Chapter 13, Article 311. See cross references in this chapter of the code for other material on the militia.) This definition clearly distinguishes the National Guard, or so-called organized militia, from the "unorganized militia," which is the people themselves. The Second Amendment is, of course, all inclusive. However, the Supreme Court has ruled in *Presser* v. *State of Illinois* (6 S.C. 580; 116 U.S.C. 252; 29 L.E. 615) that a state may pass laws prohibiting private or unorganized militia activities, including the keeping and bearing of arms by such groups, unless such legislation is forbidden by a state constitution. This decision and others have abridged Second Amendment rights in numerous states. This situation could be reversed if every state added an amendment to its constitution or if the Supreme Court chose to assert the predominance of the federal Constitution and laws over those of the states in this area, as has been done in matters of racial discrimination.

31. "Union Says Guns Kill Free Speech, Calls for Stiffest Possible Controls," *Civil Liberties*, July, 1968, p. 8.
32. *Ibid.*
33. Franklyn S. Haiman, *The First Freedoms: Speech, Press, Assembly* (New York: ACLU, 1971, with updated corrections, September, 1974); *How Americans Protest: A Statement on the Civil Rights Demonstrations* (New York: ACLU, August, 1963); Dissent in Crisis: The Anti–Riot Act (New York: ACLU, 1969).
34. J. Edward Bond, *Whose Rights?* (Menlo Park, Calif.: Institute for Humane Studies, 1967).
35. Haiman, *First Freedoms*, pp. 20–22; Fred Powledge, *An ACLU Guide to Cable Television* (New York: ACLU, 1972), pp. 31–36.
36. Rand *et al.*, *Capitalism*, pp. 117–24.
37. Kenneth P. Norwick, *Lobbying for Freedom: Censorship* (Chicago: Playboy Foundation, 1974), an excerpt from the book by the same name published in February, 1975, by St. Martin's Press. Pages numbers used here are those of the pamphlet excerpt, which is made available by the ACLU.
38. This position is called "The Freedom to Read," a joint statement of the American Library Association and the Association of American Publishers; on this, see Norwick, *Lobbying for Freedom*, p. 45.
39. *Ibid.*, p. 43. Apparently some do, including the members of the ACLU in San Diego, who chose to show *Deep Throat* and *Behind the Green Door* at a special fund raising party. See Ruth Abraham, "Deep Throat Attracts San Diego ACLUers," *Open Forum*, May, 1974, p. 7. A similar attitude is expressed in "In the Eyes of the Beholder," *Civil Liberties*, September, 1974, p. 8.
40. Norwick, *Lobbying for Freedom*, pp. 36, 46.
41. *Ibid.*, pp. 36–37, 46–49.
42. Ayn Rand, "Censorship: Local and Express," *Ayn Rand Letter*, August 13 and 27 and September 10 and 24, 1973; "Thought Control," *Ayn Rand Letter*, October 8 and 22, 1973.
43. Some of their views on this are expressed in U.S. Congress, Senate, Committee on the Judiciary, Subcommittee on Administrative Practice and Procedure, *Invasions of Privacy (Government Agencies)*, 89th Congress, 1st session, 1965, pp. 300–306, testimony of the ACLU. Frank Donner, "The Theory and Practice of American Political Intelligence," reprinted by the ACLU in 1971 from *The New York Review of Books*; John Shattuck, Patricia Brown, and Stephen Carlson, *The Lie Detector As A Surveillance Device*, ACLU Reports (New York, 1973); and Frank Donner, "Rx for Surveillance," *The Civil Liberties Review*, Summer, 1974, pp. 8–78. (The authors of articles in this issue, including conservative Rep. Barry Goldwater, Jr. (who does point to big government as a danger to privacy), all look to more government controls as the solution. None seem to recognize that it is because such media of communication as the postal system and the telephone companies are effectively under government monopoly controls that it is so easy for snooping bureaucrats to get access to personal data. None seem to recognize that the only solution lies in removing these vital institutions from government affiliation and control. An IRS agent may be able to pressure a local government postmaster into letting him read somebody's mail, but would find it far more difficult to get the same letter from a private business.) "Surveillance: Is This the Law?," ACLU flyer, no date, summarizes the manner in which the Union believes the collection of data on observable events effects "civil liberties": "By the very act of snooping,

these agencies caution the people. They warn they may sometime employ their force against individuals who lawfully use their freedom of speech, conscience, press and assembly. The threat creates fear. Fear chills political dissent. And the chilling of dissent cracks the foundation of a democratic society, expanding the power of government beyond its lawful bounds to control its master, the people. The American Civil Liberties Union is dedicated to preserving the foundations of democracy. The ACLU is determined that the people shall think, speak and live freely and fearlessly.'' A masterpiece of figurative language argumentation, this statement fails to explain just how the collection of data on the actions of others is in any way an *initiation of force* to deprive those others of their rights. Such is obviously not the case. But, by the logic of the Union's advocacy of outlawing surveillance because its existence will make timid someone afraid of the possible uses of that data, we might argue that all persons with a criminal record in New York should be locked up so that we law-abiding folks will not have chilled our rightful desire to stroll ungarded in Central Park at midnight. The difference in this analogy is that what muggers do violates human rights, whereas the mere *collection* of data made possible by actions of others does not. In essence, the Supreme Court agreed. In *Laird* v. *Tatum* (408 U.S. 1 [1972]) the high court failed to recognize, or outlaw, any "chilling effect" of intelligence–gathering activities. For further views of ACLU representatives, see U.S. Congress, House, Committee on Government Operations, *The Computer and Invasion of Privacy*, 89th Congress, 2nd session, 1966, pp. 158–59, 182–84. A recent hearing disclosed the ACLU's role in the left-wing attack on all law enforcement intelligence operations, as well as making reference to the fact that Frank Donner, the Union's political surveillance project research director, was identified three times in sworn testimony as a Communist Party member: U.S. Congress, Senate, Committee on the Judiciary, Internal Security Subcommittee, *The Nationwide Drive Against Law Enforcement Intelligence Operations, Hearings*, 94th Congress, 1st session, 1975, pp. 1, 35–37.

44. Aryeh Neier, *Dossier: The Secret Files They Keep On You* (New York: Stein and Day, 1975), p. 192.
45. *Ibid.*, p. 193.
46. *Ibid.*, p. 198.
47. *Ibid.*, p. 11.
48. Joel M. Gora, *The Rights of Reporters: The Basic ACLU Guide to a Reporter's Rights* (New York: Avon Books, 1974). Also see Ron Ridenour, ed., *The Press—Freedom's Test: 50th Anniversary ACLU 1973 Bill of Rights Journal* (Los Angeles: ACLU of Southern California, 1973).
49. Gora, *Rights of Reporters*. pp. 71–104, 117–23.
50. *Ibid.*, pp. 25–70.
51. David Rubin, *The Rights of Teachers: The Basic ACLU Guide to a Teacher's Constitutional Rights* (New York: Avon Books, 1968); Alan Levine, Eve Cary, and Diane Divoky, *The Rights of Students: The Basic ACLU Guide to a Student's Rights* (New York: Avon Books, 1973); *Academic Freedom in the Secondary Schools* (New York: ACLU, 1971); *Academic Freedom and Civil Liberties of Students in Colleges and Universities* (New York: ACLU, 1974). The consequences of the full application of the Union's positions on "students' rights" are indicated in the personal testimony of a victim, a public high school principal who dared challenge the dictates of the New York affiliate: Howard L. Hurwitz, "Student Rights: ACLU Formula for School Disruption," *Human Events*, September 13, 1975.
52. Levine, Cary, and Divoky, *Rights of Students*, pp. 15–20. On so–called public education, see Zach. Montgomery, *The School Question* (New York: Arno Press and the *New York Times*, 1972 reprint of 1889 edition); Murray N. Rothbard, *Education, Free and Compulsory: The Individual's Education* (Wichita, Kansas: Center for Independent Education, no date).
53. Joseph B. Robison, *The Case Against Parochiaid* (New York: ACLU, 1972), expecially pp. 11–13; George R. LaNoue, *Public Funds for Parochial Schools?: A Resource Document* (New York: National Council of Churches, 1963), pp. 1–2, 33–36. The LaNoue monograph is made available by the ACLU. It is remarkable that the Union recognizes the validity of appealing to what the Founding Fathers said and wrote (as is done on pp. 5–14 of LaNoue's work) in the context of this issue, but not on gun control.
54. LaNoue, *Public Funds for Parochial Schools?*, pp. 1–2.
55. Rubin, *Rights of Teachers*, passim; Levine, Cary, and Divoky, *Rights of Students*, pp. 21–138;

Alan Reitman, Judith Follman, Edward T. Ladd, *Corporal Punishment in the Public Schools: The Use of Force in Controlling Student Behavior*, ACLU Reports (New York, 1972).

56. ACLU, "Academic Freedom and Civil Liberties of Students in Colleges and Universities," pp. 37–39; Edward O. Miller, *No Constitutional Amendment to Allow Prayers in Public Schools* (New York: ACLU, 1965).

57. *Southern Manifesto . . . Massive Resistance . . . Freedom of Choice Pupil Placement . . . Interposition Busing* (New York: ACLU, no date).

58. Robert S. Rivkin, *The Rights of Servicemen: The Basic ACLU Guide to Servicemen's Rights* (New York: Avon Books, 1972).

59. Position papers on these issues include: *Why End the Draft: Questions and Answers* (New York: ACLU, no date); Randolph N. Jonakait, *The Abuses of the Military Chaplaincy*, ACLU Reports (New York, 1973). The ACLU's sanction of conscription laws became a controversial crisis within the organization during the late 1960s: "A 'Liberal' Group Speaks Out Against Draft Violation, Rioting," *U.S. News & World Report*, February 12, 1968, pp. 68–69.

60. Rivkin, *Rights of Servicemen*, pp. 15–16.

61. Henry Schwarzschild, *Amnesty: Questions & Answers* (New York: ACLU, no date); Edwin J. Oppenheimer, compilor, *The Clemency Program: A Manual of Materials on Procedures and Defenses*, ACLU Reports (New York, 1974); Arlie Schardt, "Amnesty for All," reprinted from the *Los Angeles Times* by the ACLU of Southern California, no date.

62. *The War Against the Law* (New York: ACLU, 1971). The unconstitutionality of any form of conscription is demonstrated in Henry Mark Holzer and Phyllis Holzer, "The Constitution and the Draft," *The Objectivist*, October and November, 1967.

63. Ross, *Rights of Women*. Also see *Sexual Equality: This is the Law* (New York: ACLU, no date); Trudy Hayden, *Punishing Pregnancy: Discrimination in Education, Employment, and Credit*, ACLU Reports, Women's Rights Project (New York, 1973); Kathleen Peratis, *Employment Discrimination*, ACLU Reports, Women's Right Project (New York, 1974).

64. E. Carrington Boggan *et al.*, *The Rights of Gay People: The Basic ACLU Guide to a Gay Person's Rights* (New York: Avon Books, 1975). Also see Jay Murley, "Gay Rights Pressed," *Open Forum*, July, 1974, reprinted for distribution as an ACLU recruitment pamphlet. As of this writing, the Union and its allies are approaching success in overcoming the "problem" of police oppression of "gays" in Los Angeles by forcing the Los Angeles Police Department to hire admitted homosexuals in spite of the department's opposition on personnel and security grounds. The Union's interest in "gay rights" as another excuse for forcing individuals to do things with their property against their will is made clear in a statement that also implies the need for "public education" to correct "widespread ignorance of homosexual motivations and activities": undated form letter to ACLU members from Marilyn G. Haft, director, Sexual Privacy Project, ACLU, New York.

65. Ross, *Rights of Women*, pp. 31–38; Boggan *et al.*, *Rights of Gay People*, pp. 263–68 and passim.

66. Ross, *Rights of Women*, primarily pp. 31–147; Boggan *et al.*, *Rights of Gay People*, pp. 21–32, 85–102.

67. Sylvia Law and Burt Neuborne, *The Rights of the Poor* (New York: Avon Books, 1974). Law was an employee of Mobilization for Youth and other OEO programs and recommends that her readers consult the National Welfare Rights Organization. Also see Trudy Hayden, *The Immigration and Naturalization Service and Civil Liberties: A Report on the Abuse of Discretion*, ACLU Reports (New York, 1974).

68. Law and Neuborne, *Rights of the Poor*, pp. 12–13.

69. *Ibid.*, pp. 11–12.

70. Examples of economic–rights issues of a valid nature that the Union has overlooked or avoided include those discussed in Monroe H. Freedman, "A Civil Libertarian Looks at the S.E.C.," *Reason*, February, 1975, pp. 22–27; and Dan Smoot, *The Business End of Government* (Boston: Western Islands, 1973), passim. A rare case in which the Union said something about the threat to property rights posed by the regulatory agencies of the federal executive branch concerned the administrative abuses of the Federal Trade Commission. See *Congressional Record–Appendix*, August 8, 1962, pp. A6059–A6061, quoting from the *St. Louis Globe–Democrat*, June 2–3,

1962. The force of this position is considerably undercut by the admission by then ACLU Executive Director Pemberton of "the need for Government involvement in the lives of citizens . . . , the growth . . . of Government agencies required to deal with the complexity of today's economic and social problems. . . ."

71. The Union's inactivity in the field of protecting private property rights against government has, no doubt, helped to maintain tax exemption for the American Civil Liberties Union Foundation, the foundation affiliate that provides support for the Union's work. The ACLU does awaken to the issue when the IRS starts knocking on its doors: "IRS Seeks to Audit ACLU Books," *ACLU Newsletter* (Portland, Oregon), Fall, 1975, p. 1.

72. See my tentatively titled *No Civil War at All: Eighty Years of Conspiracy to Destroy the United States* (Boston: Western Islands, forthcoming).

Chapter 7: Some Considerations Prior to a Verdict

1. Joseph W. Bishop, Jr., "Should the ACLU Be So Political?," *Human Events*, January 22, 1972, pp. 8–9. This article originally appeared in the December, 1971, issue of *Commentary*.
2. *Ibid.*, p. 8.
3. Seymour Martin Lipset and Earl Raab, "Watergate: The Vacillation of the President," *Psychology Today,* November, 1973, pp. 77–84. Another interesting article in this connection is Mark Harris, "Conspiracy to the Left of Us! Paranoia to the Right of Us!," *New York Times Magazine,* August 24, 1975, as discussed in Medford Evans, "Conspiracy Revealed in *New York Times,*" *Review of the News,* September 17, 1975, pp. 31–38.
4. See my forthcoming *No Civil War at All.*
5. The record of the Union's work is available in many libraries in the collection of *A.C.L.U. Annual Reports, 1920*–1969, reprinted recently by Arno Press and the *New York Times.*
6. I shall not attempt to list an exhaustive bibliography concerning the spread of world communism, which should be obvious to the reader. Other issues of controversy, such as the question of any fundamental changes in the methods, goals, or authoritarian structure of the conspiracy, are not vital for our purposes here. However, the reader can gauge the extent to which communism has been dependent upon those in the West for its success by consulting, among others, Antony C. Sutton, *National Suicide: Military Aid to the Soviet Union* (New Rochelle, New York: Arlington House, 1973), which well summarizes Sutton's extensive work. Also see Antony C. Sutton, *Wall Street and the Bolshevik Revolution* (New Rochelle, New York: Arlington House, 1974), the conclusions in which are unfortunately limited by the range of the factual material discussed in the book.
7. Among the many sources of evidence from personal testimony and investigation concerning the nature of the Communist Party in America, its relationship to the world Communist movement, and the nature of its fronts are: U.S. Congress, Senate, Committee on the Judiciary, Internal Security Subcommittee, *The Communist Party of the United States of America, What It Is, How It Works, A Handbook for Americans*, 84th Congress, 2nd session, 1956; U.S. Congress, House, Committee on Un-American Activities, *Manipulation of Public Opinion by Organizations Under Concealed Control of the Communist Party (National Assembly for Democratic Rights and Citizens Committee for Constitutional Liberties),* 87th Congress, 1st session, 1961; U.S. Congress, Senate, Committee on the Judiciary, Internal Security Subcommittee, *Communist Party, U.S.A.—Soviet Pawn*, 90th Congress, 1st session, 1967; J. Edgar Hoover, *Masters of Deceit: The Story of Communism in America and How to Fight It* (New York: Holt, Rinehart and Winston, 1958); Louis F. Budenz, *Men Without Faces: The Communist Conspiracy in the U.S.A.* (New York: Harper & Brothers, 1950); Bella V. Dodd, *School of Darkness* (New York: Devin–Adair, 1963); Benjamin Gitlow, *The Whole of Their Lives* (New York: Charles Scribner's Sons, 1948); Whittaker Chambers, *Witness* (New York: Random House, 1952); Julia Brown, *I Testify: My Years as an Undercover Agent for the F.B.I.* (Boston: Western Islands, 1966); Maurice L. Malkin, *Return to My Father's House* (New Rochelle, New York: Arlington House, 1972).

Chapter 8: 1920-1929: Origins of the ACLU and Struggle Between Warring Collectivists

1. *The Fight for Free Speech: A brief statement of present conditions in the United States, and of the work of the AMERICAN CIVIL LIBERTIES UNION against the forces of suppression* (New York: ACLU, 1921), pp. 4–5, as reprinted in *American Civil Liberties Union, Annual Reports, Volume 1, January 1920–May 1930* (New York: Arno Press & the *New York Times,* 1970).
2. My major source of information on Baldwin and the early years is Bean's *Pressure For Freedom.* The early years are covered quite well on pp. 1–42, and a good biographical sketch of Baldwin's background and early views is given on pp. 47–56, including the influence of Goldman (p. 54), see also footnote 27, p. 54. Two government investigative reports also detailed this early period (these have been reproduced, in part, in the Appendix to this volume): U.S. Congress, Senate, Subcommittee on the Judiciary, *Brewing and Liquor Interests and German and Bolshevik Propaganda, Report and Hearings,* 3 vol., 66th Congress, 1st session, 1919, vol. 2, pp. 2254–2256, 2707–2717, 2729–2735, 2782–2785. As the subcommittee was headed by Senator Lee Overman, this report will be referred to as the *Overman Report. Revolutionary Radicalism, Its History, Purpose and Tactics, with An Exposition and Discussion of the Steps Being Taken and Required to Curb It, Being the Report of The Joint Legislative Committee Investigating Seditious Activities, Filed April 24, 1920, In the Senate of the State of New York, Part I, Revolutionary and Subversive Movements Abroad and at Home,* 4 vol. (Albany, N.Y.: J.B. Lyon Company, 1920), vol. I, pp. 1051–1104. This report is known as the *Lusk Committee Report* after its head, State Senator Clayton R. Lusk. Volume II contains transcripts of two early ACLU documents, one of which (reproduced in the Appendix) reflects Marxist rhetoric similar to that in the 1921 *Annual Report* (see pp. 1979–1989 of the *Lusk Committee Report*). It should be stated that this report was the most influential investigation of subversion on the basis of the information available prior to 1922. Although often criticized for its conclusions and some inconsistent assumptions on the part of its authors, who were caught up in the wartime propaganda campaign, the factual content is massive and extensively documented. For the relationship of Emma Goldman to Bolshevism see vol. I, pp. 844–60, and vol. II, pp. 1295–1966. Another source is Nesta H. Webster, *The Socialist Network* (London: Boswell, 1926), pp. 54, 58, 70, the last page referring to an anti–Semitic Soviet attack on Goldman after she found Communist Russia unappealing.
3. The best source on Wall Street interest in the war's profitability is Charles Callan Tansill, *America Goes to War* (Gloucester, Mass.: Peter Smith, 1963, reprint of 1938 edition), pp. 67–134. Along with British historians like Francis Neilson, other Americans exposed the myth of the German "war–guilt" thesis quite effectively after the war. Professor Sidney B. Fay did so with his *The Origins of the World War,* published in 1929. Others, such as Charles A. Beard and Harry Elmer Barnes, carried the "revisionist" school of diplomatic history up through and after the Second World War. Both Beard and Barnes were left–wing "liberals" active in the ACLU during its earlier decades.
4. Bean, *Pressure for Freedom,* pp. 1–10; *Lusk Committee Report,* vol. I, pp. 1051–1076, on People's Council of America. Also see *Overman Report,* pp. 2254–2256, 2705–2785. Excerpts are included in the Appendix. Derived from these investigations were many secondary studies with biographical information on most of the people involved. One of the most reliable recent compilations is Francis X. Gannon, *Biographical Dictionary of the Left,* 4 vol. (Boston: Western Islands, 1969–1973). On Max Eastman, also see Max Eastman, *Reflections on the Failure of Socialism* (New York: Devin–Adair, 1962), pp. 7–20. One of Eugene Debs' professions of Bolshevism was published in an issue of Eastman's *Liberator,* May, 1919, p. 3.
5. Bean, *Pressure for Freedom,* p. 11. See also information on a number of these persons in: Gannon, *Biographical Dictionary of the Left.*
6. Bean, *Pressure for Freedom,* p. 21.
7. The major source of evidence on German propaganda, espionage, and sabotage in the U.S. during the war is the *Overman Report.* Much of this is summarized in a recently reprinted work that both covers this subject and illustrates the kind of vigilance that can easily result in the loss of civil liberties if not thoughtfully conducted: Emerson Hough, *The Web: The Authorized History of The*

American Protective League (New York: Arno Press & the *New York Times,* 1969 reprint of 1919 edition), pp. 62–140. It is important to keep in mind that this book was published before Wall Street's role in promoting the war was generally known. Another source on the early years of radical subversion in this century is William J. Burns, *The Masked War* (New York: Arno Press & the *New York Times,* 1969 reprint of 1913 edition). Although this account of cases investigated by Burns' National Detective Agency is obiously written to be self–serving, it provides a valuable balance to other accounts that suggest there was no justification for a "Red Scare" during these years. Burns later became the Justice Department's director of the Bureau of Investigation and led the 1922 raid at Bridgman, Michigan, which exposed widespread Communist activities and gained him the hatred of the ACLU and its dubious allies. (See pp. 320–24 of *The Masked War* for an interesting ethical sidelight on later ACLU attorney Clarence Darrow.) A major connection between the German General Staff and the Bolshevik movement was made public as the war ended. The "Sisson Papers," which were supposed to be communications between the Germans and Lenin's entourage in Petrograd, indicated that the coup had been under German control. These papers were later published in Edgar Sisson, *One Hundred Red Days: A Personal Chronicle of the Bolshevik Revolution* (New Haven, Conn.: Yale University Press, 1931), appendix. Although the authenticity of these documents has been fairly questioned since that time (on the basis of internal flaws), other evidence corroborates the conclusion that if the copies Sisson received were not the originals, they were carelessly prepared from some that were real, or otherwise reflected what was substantially the truth. The problem is that they helped obscure the fact that it was not only prominent Germans who helped ensure the revolt's success.

 8. *A.C.L.U. Anual Reports,* vol. I, p. vii.
 9. Rose L. Martin, *Fabian Freeway: High Road to Socialism in the U.S.A., 1884*–1966 (Boston: Western Islands, 1966), pp. 145–54. This study is probably the best documented survey of the growth and influence of the Fabian socialist movement and the hundreds of prominent persons who have been affiliated with it in many organizations. It is a helpful source on many persons active in the ACLU. It is a revision of the earlier work by Mary Margaret Patricia McCarren, *Fabianism in the Political Life of Britian, 1919*–1931 (Chicage: Heritage Foundation, 1954).
10. Bean, *Pressure for Freedom,* pp. 1–11. Compare early leaders with persons in Gannon, *Biographical Dictionary of the Left;* and Martin, *Fabian Freeway,* pp. 176—94.
11. Martin, *Fabian Freeway,* pp. 155–75; Jennings C. Wise, *Woodrow Wilson: Disciple of Revolution* (New York: Paisley Press, 1938), pp. 77–553; George Sylvester Viereck, *The Strangest Friendship in History: Woodrow Wilson and Colonel House* (London: Duckworth, 1933), passim. If these fascinating and detailed studies are found too polemical by the reader, or their authors unreliable, the same influence is clearly indicated throughout the official work of Charles Seymour, *The Intimate Papers of Colonel House*, 4 vol. (Boston: Houghton Mifflin Company, 1926–1928). As Seymour was an associate of House's Inquiry group, he was not a critical compilor.
12. Seymour, *Intimate Papers,* vol. III, pp. 170–73.
13. Anonymous (Edward Mandell House), *Philip Dru: Administrator, A Story of Tomorrow, 1920–1935* (New York: B.W. Huebsch, 1912), p. 45, as an example of the Marxist overtones. This incredible book, published by socialist Huebsch, who was active in the ACLU from its earliest days, is an eerie picture of much of what was in store for the future. For a discussion of the extent to which the story of Philip Dru was played out by the Wilson Administration, see Seymour, *Intimate Papers,* vol. I, pp. 152–59.
14. Martin, *Fabian Freeway,* pp. 157–60. Also see Edward Mandell House, "Does America Need a Dictator?—A Warning to Selfish Wealth and Narrow—Minded Politicians to Uplift Our Capitalistic Civilization," *Liberty*, January 7, 1933, pp. 4–6, in which House smiles upon the economic fascism of Italy that FDR was beginning to install here. In spite of the fact that plans in *Philip Dru* resemble the New Deal almost as much as they do the New Freedom, another study has shown a similar Wall Street plan to have been the basis for Roosevelt's takeover of the economy: Antony C. Sutton, *Wall Street and FDR* (New Rochelle, New York: Arlington House, 1975). House's support for the success of the Bolshevik revolution was affirmed several times, including his official telegram from Paris to the President and the secretary of state (dated November 28, 1917), which read: "There has been cabled over and published here statements made by American papers to the effect that Russia should be treated as an enemy. It is exceedingly important that such

criticisms should be suppressed. It will throw Russia into the lap of Germany if the Allies and ourselves express such views at this time." See United States State Department Decimal Files, National Archive Microfilm File 316, roll 10. That House supported the establishment of Bolshevism in Russia apart from any concern about wartime strategy is made clear by the fact that he strongly opposed any Allied military intervention in Russia after November, 1917, and continued to oppose offers of anti–Bolshevist interventions by Japan after the Germans were defeated. This is reflected in numerous pieces of correspondence. He insisted that Russia should not be freed from the Bolsheviks because their fighting spirit "was burnt out" and the Reds were in control "because they satisfied the only real demand of the Russian peasants." See Seymour, *Intimate Papers,* vol. 3, pp. 386–422; Sutton, *Wall Street and the Bolshevik Revolution.*

15. *Lusk Committee Report*, vol. I, pp. 988–92.
16. *Overman Report*, vol. II, p. 2717. For mention of Crystal Eastman's work as director of New York City branch of the Women's Peace Party, see Bean, *Pressure for Freedom,* p. 10. Louis Fraina was a U.S. Communist delegate at the founding of the Third Communist International in 1919 (Webster, *Socialist Network,* p. 44).
17. Sutton, *Wall Street and the Bolshevik Revolution,* passim.
18. The plans and work of Rhodes and Milner have been revealed in Carroll Quigley, *Tragedy and Hope: A History of the World in Our Time* (New York: Macmillan, 1966), pp. 130–37 and passim. Also see Walter Nimocks, *Milner's Young Men: The "Kingergarten" in Edwardian Imperial Affairs* (Durham: Duke University Press, 1968). The fact that the Round Table, whose leaders were instrumental in encouraging the war in 1914, controlled such papers as the *London Times,* made it possible to exaggerate the role of Germany in the war and the Bolshevik revolution, while concealing that of the Round Table groups. One series which promoted this partial confusion is Adolphe Smith, "The Pan–German Internationale," *London Times,* July 29–31, 1919. The connection between the Round Table groups (particularly such members as William T. Stead), the British Fabian Society, and the Wall Street crowd including House and Marburg is presented in Wise, *Woodrow Wilson,* pp. 32–39.
19. Sutton, *Wall Street and the Bolshevik Revolution*, pp. 174–75.
20. *Ibid.*, pp. 172—74. Sutton's conclusion is reasonable, based on the limited range of evidence and subject matter covered in his book. However, it becomes inadequate when considered with much other evidence concerning the domestic movements and collectivist programs that were also promoted in the U.S. by these same Wall Street interests. Such promotion of domestic statism, like the establishment of a worldwide revolutionary movement, was *not* in the long–range economic interest of the Wall Street crowd, and thus suggests that some of them had a political objective similar to that of Rhodes and Milner.
21. Andrew Carnegie clearly expressed a political vision indistinguishable from the Round Table goals. This he did in his book *Triumphant Democracy* and in a most unusual article: "Drifting Together—Will the United States and Canada Unite?," *London Express*, October 14, 1904, reprinted in "Steps Toward British Union, a World State, and International Strife—Part I," remarks of Rep. J. Thorkelson of Montana, *Congressional Record,* House of Representatives, 76th Congress, 3rd session, August 19, 1940. The reader is cautioned against Thorkelson's unfortunate interpretations in this and later speeches.
22. Wise, *Woodrow Wilson,* p. 64. On other activities of Baruch, Warburg, and Kahn, see Sutton, *Wall Street and the Bolshevik Revolution*, passim. Butler became head of the Carnegie Endowment for International Peace, founded in 1910 to promote, among other things, "the international mind" (*1920 Yearbook* [New York: Carnegie Endowment for International Peace, 1920], p. 62). More information on the international coordination of the forces at work for world government at this time is found in Nesta H. Webster, *The Surrender of an Empire* (London: Boswell, 1931), pp. 35, 52–65. This is a very detailed and important, if not unique, study of anticolonialism in the British Empire, in spite of the fact that the author was at the time only beginning to sense the influence of the Round Table groups (see pp. 153, 329–30, 374).
23. Wise, *Woodrow Wilson,* p. 64.
24. *Ibid.*, p. 70–71.
25. Marburg's associate, Rabbi Stephen S. Wise, had been in on the earliest AUAM activities, but

later left the group during the war. Bean, *Pressure for Freedom,* pp. 3–4. Of assistance to the AUAM after Baldwin began work in New York in 1917, was Assistant Secretary of War Frederick P. Keppel, former secretary of Marburg's American Association for International Conciliation and later important in the Rockefeller Foundation. (Bean, pp. 23, 68.) Carnegie's Church Peace Union was used to gather information for Baldwin's National Civil Liberties Bureau of the AUAM, although it apparently wished to avoid public connections with the revolutionaries at the Bureau. On this, see the *Overman Report*, vol. II, p. 2711; *Lusk Committee Report*, vol. I, p. 1082; letter, Frederick Lynch to Louis Lochner, May 10, 1917, declining to have his name used for Lochner's First American Conference for Democracy and Terms of Peace, *Lusk Committee Report,* pp. 992–93. Pages 967–1104 of the *Lusk Committee Report* contain one of the most detailed examinations anywhere of the interlocking directorates of the various organizations in the "peace" movement, including the AUAM–ACLU. This fact was early recognized by Baldwin as a potential liability. He was elected a member of the executive committee of Lochner's Communist People's Council, but requested that it not be advertised publicly, saying, "I think we all work more effectively in separate groups without giving our critics a chance to claim that the same little bunch is running all these organizations." (Bean, p. 83, footnote.) Within three years, the Lusk Committee would prove just that. (See p. 32 of the committee report re their shared offices.) One piece of evidence that indicated the collaboration of such distant personalities as Baldwin, John D. Rockefeller, Jr., and Military Intelligence Chief Heber Blankenhorn was the report issued by the Interchurch World Movement on the 1919 steel strike, an outstanding example of deceptive left–wing propaganda on labor: Marshall Olds, *Analysis of the Interchurch World Movement Report on the Steel Strike* (New York: Arno Press and the *New York Times*, 1972 reprint of 1922 edition), pp. 425–55 and passim.

26. Bean, *Pressure for Freedom,* p. 40. Support for this group from the foundations continued after it became the FPA. See U.S. Congress, House, Special Committee to Investigate Tax–Exempt Foundations and Comparable Organizations, *Tax–Exempt Foundations, Report,* 83rd Congress, 2nd session, 1954, pp. 168–81. The report includes material on the CFR.

27. Quigley, *Tragedy and Hope.* There have developed popular conceptions of the CFR as an organization in which many of the world's real rulers meet and plan their strategies. This is expressed in Gary Allen, *None Dare Call It Conspiracy* (Seal Beach, Calif.: Concord Press, 1972), passim, and the forthcoming *Rockefeller File,* by the same author. Such a view is not confined to journalists with a conservative or libertarian perspective, as is indicated by the comments on CFR in Ferdinand Lundberg, *The Rockefeller Syndrome* (New York: Lyle Stuart, 1975). The internationalism of the CFR is reflected well in its journal *Foreign Affairs,* not necessarily by any corporate view held by *all* of its resident and nonresident members (letter, Carroll Quigley to William Lander, October 31, 1972). Nonmembers have no other source but the Council's publications for judging its general positions, since meetings are conducted in secret and members are forbidden to reveal what is said. See *Annual Report, Council on Foreign Relations* (New York: CFR, 1969), p. 91, article two of the by–laws.

28. Sutton, *Wall Street and the Bolshevik Revolution,* passim.

29. Tansill, *America Goes to War,* passim; Viereck, *Strangest Friendship,* pp. 106–193. A recent bestseller proves this claim even more firmly with the latest evidence: Colin Simpson, *The Lusitania* (Boston: Little, Brown and Company, 1972).

30. Tansill, *America Goes to War,* p. 651. The Carnegies and the Morgans felt some effects from the revolutionaries they were financing. In 1915 both families were subject to attacks that were apparently assassination attempts. On this, see John Dos Passos, *Mr. Wilson's War* (Garden City, New York: Doubleday, 1962), pp. 147–48. Dos Passos, who was active in the ACLU, k describes the early pre–ACLU "peace" movements on pp. 161–63.

31. John Foster Dulles, *U.S. News and World Report,* September 7, 1956, p. 110. The idea that representatives of the Establishment would finance radical "antiwar" agitation to make their own policies look more respectable—both factions moving to the left—was even more obvious in the "peace" movements organized on college campuses during the 1960s to protest the Vietnam War. See James Kunen, *The Strawberry Statement: Notes of a College Revolutionary* (New York: Random House, 1968), p. 130:

241

In the evening I went to the U. to check out a strategy meeting. A kid was giving a report on the SDS convention. He said that . . . at the convention men from Business International Round Tables, the meeting sponsored by Business International for their client groups and heads of government, tried to buy up a few radicals.

These men are the world's leading industrialists and they convene to decide how our lives are going to go. These are the guys who wrote the Alliance for Progress. They are the left wing of the ruling class.

They offered to finance our demonstration in Chicago. We were also offered ESSO (Rockefeller) money. They want us to make a lot of radical commotion so they can look more in the center as they move to the left.

32. Bean, *Pressure for Freedom*, p. 29, italics in the original letter.
33. *Ibid.*, p. 31.
34. *Ibid.*, p. 32.
35. See Chapter 8, footnote 25, above.
36. *Ibid.*, pp. 56–57. The reader can review the political careers of many of these people and others to be mentioned later in Gannon, *Biographical Dictionary of the Left*. I feel that a detailed listing of their Communist affiliations either before or after this time is a far better commentary on themselves than it is on the ACLU, particularly when it is obvious that, at least for its first thirty years, if the Union's work reflected the thinking or purposes of any one man, that man was Baldwin, who, we should remember, was never necessarily representing any member of the organization.
37. Stokes was a member of a wealthy family of outstanding revolutionaries during this period. On her Fabian connections in America, see the *Lusk Committee Report*, vol. II, p. 1247.
38. On Baldwin's spirit as the moving force behind the group, see Bean, *Pressure for Freedom*, p. 47.
39. *Lusk Committee Report*, vol. I, p. 1088. The full text of the communication is quoted, without any typographical errors, on pp. 1057.
40. *Ibid.*, p. 1058.
41. For Baldwin's correspondence concerning the IWW see the *Lusk Committee Report*, vol. I, pp. 1089–1095. There is no more complete source of evidence on the IWW than this report. Some of this material was republished evidence from the *Overman Report*. This indicated the relationship between those in the IWW and the NCLB. Another published expose is Webster, *The Socialist Network*, pp. 72–76. The affiliations of the IWW with Bolshevik activities in Great Britian were obvious even before Webster's book was published in 1926. See "The I.W.W. and Ireland. Imported Agitators," the *London Times*, June 30, 1922, and R.M. Whitney, *Reds in America* (Boston: Western Islands, 1970 reprint of 1924 edition). The recent reprint of this work makes easily available a well-documented survey of the evidence on such groups as the IWW and the ACLU that was available at the time, a fact which earned for its author the ire of the Union. See *1923 A.C.L.U. Annual Report* (New York: ACLU, 1924), p. 4, reprinted in *A.C.L.U. Annual Reports*, vol. I. Also see Joseph J. Mereto, *The Red Conspiracy* (New York: National Historical Society, 1920), pp. 105–137, 247–48. Baldwin's interest in the IWW was increased by his tour of America during the ACLU's first decade, which allowed him to meet with representatives of the "Wobblies" and other labor groups. See Bean, *Pressure for Freedom*, pp. 175–76 on his statement "The cause we now serve is labor" and p. 28 on his former IWW membership.
42. *Lusk Committee Report*, vol. I, pp. 1088–1089, and the ACLU pamphlet "The Challenge." Both are reproduced in the Appendix.
43. See Chapter 8, footnote 24, above.
44. Bean, *Pressure for Freedom*, p. 77, footnote 91. Bean points out that NCLB files were seized by investigators on August 31, 1918, and were the source of the Lusk Committee's evidence. Apparently the files were mixed up during the confiscation, and Baldwin was nice enough to help by being brought handcuffed to the files for a number of days to get them back in order. In recounting this, Bean takes the opportunity to attack Archibald Stevenson, the federal investigator who testified before the Overman Senate Committee (see Appendix) and who was involved in the NCLB raid. This Bean does by referring the reader to an anti–anti–Communist polemic published in 1927 by a socialist publishing company. Bean loses all objectivity here by assuming that unfavorable description of Stevenson's methods somehow eradicates the evidence he possessed.

Being in jail was not sufficient to quiet the energetic Baldwin. Two of his poems were published in Max Eastman's Leninist journal, accompanying articles in the same issues by Lenin and others. A personal portrait of Eugene Debs as a man was given by Harry M. Daugherty and Thomas Dixon, *The Inside Story of the Harding Tragedy* (Boston: Western Islands, 1975 reprint of 1932 edition), pp. 108–113.

45. *Lusk Committee Report*, vol I, p. 844. Palmer discussed the legal issues in his raids and deportations in A. Mitchell Palmer, "The Case Against The 'Reds,' " *The Forum*, February, 1920, pp. 173–85.

46. There is reason to think that the Ku Klux Klan, although after 1915 a major portion of what historians have called the "nativist" movement, was unrelated in its purposes to other groups. See my forthcoming *No Civil War At All*.

47. Daugherty and Dixon, *Inside Story*. Certainly it might be suggested that this work by Daugherty is a self–serving whitewash written to remove the scandal that fell on its author and the whole Harding Administration. That might be maintained were its arguments not independently corroborated by this well–documented study: Blair Coan, *The Red Web* (Boston: Western Islands, 1969 reprint of 1925 edition).

48. Gannon, *Biographical Dictionary of the Left*, for background of individuals Harry Ward being an important example. Some of these early leaders later wrote accounts that, however personally colored, discussed this period. They include: Arthur Garfield Hays, *Let Freedom Ring* (New York: Liveright, 1937); Lucille Milner, *Education of an American Liberal* (New York: Horizon Press, 1954); Louis F. Budenz, *This Is My Story* (New York: McGraw–Hill, 1947). Budenz was later a top American Communist. He left the party to become an outspoken anti–Communist author and government witness. These persons comprised the National Committee. For a complete listing of its members, 1920–1951, see Bean, *Pressure for Freedom*, pp. 398–401.

49. Bean, *Pressure for Freedom*, pp. 395–97 for complete list, 1917–1951.

50. Whitney, *Reds in America*, pp. 15–36, passim; Daugherty and Dixon, *Inside Story*, pp. 95–132. Daugherty's conclusions on the strikes of 1922 are confirmed in Coan, *Red Web*, pp. 58–76.

51. Whitney, *Reds in America*, pp. 19–30.

52. *Ibid.*, pp. 29–30.

53. *Civil Liberties*, January, 1960, p. 2.

54. Whitney, *Reds in America*, pp. 127–28; Benjamin Gitlow, *The Whole of Their Lives* (Boston: Western Islands, 1965 reprint of 1948 edition), pp. 16, 20 on Paterson silk weavers strike and pp. 130–34 on Passaic textile workers strike. These two cases were important because they involved participation by, respectively, Baldwin and Thomas, both of whom were arrested. *Ibid.*, p. 1.

55. The early history in Los Angeles was favorably told in Edsel Newton, "Report on Civil Liberties: An Historical Sketch of the American Civil Liberties Union in Southern California," *Los Angeles Daily Journal*, July 7–10, 13–17, 1959, reprinted for distribution by the Southern California ACLU affiliate. On Sinclair see Whitney, *Reds in America*, pp. 63–64, 84, 155, 158; Coan, *Red Web*, pp. 64, 67; *Lusk Committee Report*, vol. I, p. 1115, vol. II, p. 1384.

56. *A.C.L.U. Annual Report*, 1922 and 1923, introductory sections.

57. *1923 A.C.L.U. Annual Report*, pp. 4–5, 8–9.

58. The entire incredible story of the smear and frame–up of Harding and Daugherty has remained, in spite of overwhelming evidence, virtually unknown to the public and contemporary historians. It was a combined assault of the Establishment and its radical pawns that recalls similar events of recent years. See Daugherty and Dixon, *Inside Story*, passim; Coan, *Red Web*, passim. The skeptical reader is urged to study these books.

59. See these examples of the ACLU promotion of the myth: *1924 A.C.L.U. Annual Report*, p. 38; *Civil Liberties*, January, 1960, p. 2.

60. The whole case has been very judiciously reviewed by a veteran attorney: Robert H. Montgomery, *Sacco–Vanzetti: The Murder and The Myth* (Boston: Western Islands, 1965 reprint of 1960 edition).

61. *Ibid.*, pp. 58–59.

62. *Ibid.*, p. 59.

63. *Ibid.*, passim; Bean, *Pressure for Freedom*, p. 399. Frankfurter's Fabian association with Baldwin and others is revealed in Paul W. Shafer and John Howland Snow, *The Turning of The Tides* (New Canaan, Connecticut: The Long House, 1962), pp. 160–61.

64. Maurice L. Malkin, *Return To My Father's House: A Charter Member of the American Communist Party Tells Why He Joined—And Why He Later Left to Fight Communism* (New Rochelle, New York: Arlington House, 1972), pp. 127, 136–37, 172 on ACLU Communists Bailey and Robert W. Dunn.
65. Montgomery, *Sacco–Vanzetti*, p. 65. The Union had IWW Defense and Publicity funds in 1922. See *1922 A.C.L.U. Annual Report*, p. 55. On Garland funds see *1923 A.C.L.U. Annual Report*, pp. 20–21, and *1928 A.C.L.U. Annual Report*, pp. 44–45. The latter shows that during 1928 the Union received slightly more from the Garland Fund than was made available to the ILD. The *1929 A.C.L.U. Annual Report* (pp. 49–53) illustrates the trend of cases financed at this time with Garland money including the Mooney–Billings, Schwimmer, and Gastonia, North Carolina, labor–riot murders. The report contains rather lengthy statements on several of these cases, which were then current, as well as a list of court decisions and laws in opposition to civil liberties by the Union's standards. It also contains statements on the work which lay ahead (pp. 32–39), which illustrate a significantly better understanding of the inherent issues than is found in the Union's positions of recent years, as discussed in the first part of this book.
66. Gitlow, *The Whole Of Their Lives*, pp. 130–131.
67. See Chapter 8, footnote 7, above.
68. *Civil Liberties*, January, 1960, p. 1; Bean, *Pressure for Freedom*, pp. 102, 262–63.
69. The inevitable injustice today is a monopolized teaching in government schools of a *belief* in Darwinism, under the pretense of separation of church and state.
70. Bean, *Pressure for Freedom*, p. 96. On Untermyer's role in the attack on Daugherty see Coan, *Red Web*, pp. 75, 92, 104.
71. Bean, *Pressure for Freedom*, p. 96.
72. Michel Sturdza, *The Suicide of Europe* (Boston: Western Islands, 1968), p. 23.
73. C.A. Phillips, T.F. McManus, and R.W. Nelson, *Banking and the Business Cycle: A Study of the Great Depression in the United States* (New York: Arno Press and the *New York Times*, 1972 reprint of 1937 edition).

Chapter 9: 1930-1939:
Depression Years and the United Front

1. *American Civil Liberties Union Annual Reports*, vol. I, p. xxix.
2. "Guilt By Collaboration," *News and Views*, September, 1957, p. 1. The Union never seemed to find any essential violation of rights in antitrust prosecutions, which they regarded as an "economic issue" outside their concern—in spite of the problems of fixing blame on businessmen for conspiring in the course of associated marketing activities that are essential for successful business operation. On this see A.D. Neale, *The Antitrust Laws of the United States of America: A Study of Competition Enforced by Law* (Cambridge, England: Cambridge University Press, 1970), pp. 79–91. Also see D.T. Armentano, *The Myths of Antitrust: Economic Theory and Legal Cases* (New Rochelle, New York: Arlington House, 1972); Ambrose Paré Winston, *Judicial Economics (New York: Arno Press and the New York Times*, 1972). From the Union's point of view, people often conspire for economic values, but rarely, if ever, for political values. At least only the latter seem exclusively worthy of constitutional protection.
3. The structure and functioning of the ACLU is reviewed in Bean, *Pressure for Freedom*, pp. 122–57, 246–73. Also see *American Civil Liberties Union Annual Reports*, vol. I, p. xvi.
4. In addition to sources mentioned in this chapter, see Gannon, *Biographical Dictionary of the Left*, particularly the discussion of the ACLU and the composition of its leadership, vol. l, pp. 1–17.
5. Bean, *Pressure for Freedom*, pp. 153, 185. See also pp. 85, 131.
6. *Ibid.*, p. 6.
7. *Ibid.*, p. 277. The excerpt is quoted by Bean from Harold Lord Varney, "The Civil Liberties Union—Liberalism á la Moscow," *American Mercury*, December, 1936, p. 395. On the suit that the Union threatened as a result of this article and the resulting commentary, see Bean, p. 158, footnote 2. Apparently Varney managed that rare accomplishment, for the Union, of going beyond

free speech to libel. For more of Baldwin's reflections on his observations in Russia, see Roger N. Baldwin, *Liberty Under the Soviets* (New York: Vanguard Press, 1928), pp. 24–32, 105–134.

8. Bean, *Pressure for Freedom*, p. 277, footnote 8, for the appraisal of the article published in vol. 3, no. 7 (September, 1934).

9. *Ibid.*, p. 177. Baldwin's thoughts were strangely echoed by Colonel House: See Chapter 8, footnote 14, above.

10. Martin, *Fabian Freeway*, pp. 306–322.

11. J.B. Matthews, *Odyssey of a Fellow Traveler* (New York: published by the author, 1938, reprinted by American Opinion in 1961), p. 121 of reprint edition. As chairman of the American League Against War and Fascism, one of the most important Communist fronts, Matthews was quite qualified to write this portrait of the United Front during the 1930s. The reader should note that it was published over a decade before Matthews became subject to criticism for his work for Sen. Joseph R. McCarthy. This book is a major primary source document for the period. Also see all of Baldwin's contributions in this elite leftist anthology: Harry W. Laidler and Norman Thomas, ed., *The Socialism of Our Times, A Symposium* (New York: Vanguard Press–League for Industrial Democracy, 1929), pp. 76–82, 144–67. This collection contains representative writings by a number of persons influential in the Union.

12. Bean, *Pressure for Freedom*, pp. 287–88. ACLU contributions to the ILD are listed in *A.C.L.U. Annual Report, 1929*–1930, pp. 48–53. One major joint project at this time was the criminal–case defense of Tom Mooney and Warren K. Billings. On the ILD and its work in this case see U.S. Congress, House, Special Committee on Un-American Activities, *Investigation of Un-American Propaganda Activities in the United States, Appendix—Part IX Communist Front Organizations with Special Reference to The National Citizens Political Action Committee*, 78th Congress, 2nd session, 3 vol., 1944, vol. 1, pp. 814–46, 842–46. This report will be referred to henceforth as the *Dies Committee Report*, after Congressman Martin Dies, the committee chairman. This special committee later became the House Committee on Un-American Activities and has always been a prime target for extinction by the Communists and the ACLU. The ACLU's work on the Mooney–Billings case was well indicated in its contributions to *The Mooney–Billings Report—Suppressed by the Wickersham Commission* (New York: Gotham House, 1932), congratulatory letters from prominent ACLU personalities on the first few unnumbered pages.

13. U.S. Congress, House, Special Committee to Investigate Communist Activities in the United States, *Investigation of Communist Propaganda, Report,* 71st Congress, 3rd session, 1931, pp. 56–57. This is the *Fish Committee Report* (reproduced in the Appendix). The Union's response was illustrative of the same anti–anti–Communist line it had published during the earlier years, but this time aimed at the hearings conducted by Congressman Hamilton Fish, Jr.'s committee: *A.C.L.U. Annual Reports*, vol. II, pp. 3–4. The Fish Committee findings and other material on the ACLU were included in a book, which also provoked the Union's displeasure: Edwin Marshall Hadley, *T.N.T.* (Chicago: The Tower Press, 1932), pp. 20–40 in particular.

14. See Appendix.

15. "Unmasked," *New York American*, October 17, 1935, corrected according to Bean, *Pressure for Freedom*, p. 277, footnote 7, omitting only Baldwin's statement that he had been active in the fight for conservation of birds, animals, and forests, which could just as easily have stemmed from his hobby of birdwatching as from a desire to expand government controls over private property.

16. He would still hold this perspective in 1970. See *American Civil Liberties Union Annual Reports,* pp. xii, xxi, xxv, which include the incredible statement that "experience shows that the further government is removed from direct local pressures, the more favorable it is to civil rights." By this standard, the Soviet Union should be overflowing with civil rights! The welfare state policies of Nazi Germany were touted in *Facts in Review* (New York: German Library of Information), representative issues, 1939–1941. One of the leading New Deal economic "brain trusters" who would remain close to the ACLU and other leftist organizations was Rexford Guy Tugwell. According to the testimony of Dr. William Wirt, later factually confirmed in large part, Tugwell and his boss, Secretary of Agriculture Henry Wallace, later vice–president, were looked to by the Communists in Washington to assist in the Red takeover of the New Deal. The strategy was to cover up the facts concerning the nation's remarkable degree of economic recovery in 1932–33 so as to justify more controls over the economy, which would keep the U.S. in depression and provide excuses for still further controls. Although Wirt was to die in a mental institution shortly thereafter,

he was able to reveal the truth about the conspiracy as it was admitted to him at a dinner party in Washington on September 1, 1933. Representatives of a number of federal agencies were present at the gathering, including a former ACLU official, Laurence Todd, who was Washington representative of the Soviet News Agency, TASS. The Department of Agriculture employee who, according to Wirt, did most of the talking about the Communist plans to take over the New Deal was Hildegarde Kneeland, a member of the ACLU. See U.S. Congress, House, Select Committee, *Hearings to Investigate Certain Statements of Dr. William Wirt*, 73rd Congress, 2nd session, 1934, passim. Those in attendance admitted that the party was held, but denied the conversation Wirt reported. Adolph A. Berle, Jr., another New Deal official who would later do work for the ACLU, admitted that the conversation had occurred, but that the guests were just pulling Wirt's leg. The joke ended in 1953, with the disclosure of the Silvermaster and Ware Communist cells in the Agriculture Department during the New Deal and the evidence that Alice P. Barrows had been a Communist agent since her original government employment in the U.S. Office of Education in 1919. It was in Barrows' home that the 1933 dinner party was held. The best survey of the period is James Burnham, *The Web of Subversion: Underground Networks In The U.S. Government*, (Boston: Western Islands, 1965 reprint of 1954 edition), pp. 80–91. On Barrows see U.S. Congress, Senate, Committee on the Judiciary, Internal Security Subcommittee, *Interlocking Subversion in Government Departments, Hearings—Part 12*, 83rd Congress, 1st session, pp. 823–40, passim. This reference to Barrows later was obscured by being listed incorrectly as "Alice P. Borrows" in U.S. Congress, Senate, Committee on Government Operations, *Congressional Investigations of Communism and Subversive Activities, Summary--Index, 1918–1956*, 84th Congress, 2nd session, 1956, pp. 43, 160, 343, 345.

17. *Dies Committee Report*. This is the most comprehensive source of all, but much of the intricate details are told in Eugene Lyons, *The Red Decade* (New Rochelle, New York: Arlington House, 1970 reprint of 1941 edition), pp. 148, 367 on Baldwin. Matthews, *Odyssey*, passim. An excellent summary of the interlocking structures of the United Front, under the leadership of Matthews' American League Against War and Fascism is contained in Gannon, *Biographical Dictionary of the Left*, vol. 4, pp. 30–62 for the coordination of Communist efforts in the fields labor, education, racial agitation, and support of foreign Communist movements. A similar United Front had come to power in Spain by 1936, but was defeated in the Spanish Civil War by Franco's forces, a Communist defeat that became the cause celebre of anti–Fascism in America even after 1939 and the Stalin-Hitler Pact, well illustrating the international level of Communist coordination. On this United Front in Spain and the fact that Franco's falangist movement was by no means essentially Fascist see Conzalo Rodriguez Castillo, *Notes for Posterity—Communist World Offensive Against Spain (A Report on the "Spanish Case" in the United Nations Organization), January–April, 1946* (Madrid, Spain: Deplomatic Information Office, 1949), passim; *The General Cause—The Red Domination in Spain, Preliminary Information Drawn Up By The Ministry of Justice*, (Madrid, 1946); Richard A.H. Robinson, *The Origins of Franco's Spain: The Right, the Republic and Revolution, 1931–1936* (Devon, England: David & Charles, 1970). In spite of the fact that its leaders, particularly Baldwin and Ward, were active in pro-Communist movements regarding Spain, the ACLU was not brought into them as an organization.

18. Gannon, *Biographical Dictionary of the Left*, vol. 4, pp. 630–36 on Ward's record, including chairmanship of the American League Against War Fascism by 1936 and his early work as a founder of the Communist–front Methodist Federation for Social Service. On this, see Rembert Gilman Smith, *Moscow Over Methodism* (published by the author, 1936) as well as other secondary sources already listed relating to the information published in the *Dies Committee Report*. The dishonesty of Ward's position as chairman of the ACLU was illustrated in his attack, using the abusive *ad hominem* method so denounced when employed by anti–Communists, on Harold Lord Varney after the publication of Varney's article referred to in Chapter 9, footnote 7, above. Ward accused Varney of being a Fascist in " 'American Mercury' Goes Berserk," *A.C.L.U.—News*, January, 1937, p. 3. Perhaps Ward's anger resulted from the fact that Varney had defected from the extreme left, having been a writer for Max Eastman's *Liberator* years earlier. Varney's interest in fascism was illustrated in a subsequent article in which he showed how similar the New Deal was to Mussolini's policies and how useful one IWW leader had been to Mussolini: Harold Lord Varney, "The Truth About American Fascism," *American Mercury*, August, 1937, pp. 385–98. On the Communist front Ward founded, see U.S. Congress, House,

Committee on Un–American Activities, *Review of The Methodist Federation for Social Action, Formerly The Methodist Federation For Social Service*, 82nd Congress, 2nd session, 1952.

19. Gannon, *Biographical Dictionary of the Left*, vol. 4, pp. 415–18. Also see *Dies Committee Report*, index references. A number of Holmes' later affiliations were listed with sources given in Myers G. Lowman, compilor, *A Compilation of Public Records: 42% of the Unitarian Clergymen and 450 Rabbis* (Cincinnati: Circuit Riders, Inc., 1961), pp. 65–68.

20. Baldwin's affiliations are listed in Gannon, *Biographical Dictionary of the Left*, vol. 1, pp. 220–22, including those which continued after 1939 and cast unfavorably upon Baldwin's claim that such associations were long since "abandoned." The extent to which he and others abandoned these movements is the extent to which they were no longer used as the primary tools for accomplishing Communist purposes, or got their work done and went out of business. The Union's officers and National Board members are listed on its letterhead of the period as well as in Bean, *Pressure for Freedom*, pp. 395–401. Also see Bean, pp. 278–86 on Baldwin and Ward and their work with Communists. The Union had published Leon Whipple, *The Story of Civil Liberty in the United States* (New York: Vanguard Press–ACLU, 1927), but it sold poorly. On this and other publications of the period, see Bean, pp. 318–48. Later accounts by ACLU leaders attracted more attention, and they provide portraits of the different views present in the organization during the 1930s. These include Arthur Garfield Hays, *Let Freedom Ring* (New York: Liveright, 1937), a panoramic first-hand review of many leading cases, and Osmond K. Fraenkel, *Our Civil Liberties* (New York: Viking Press, 1944), which, in spite of its blindness to the Communist conspiracy, contains much sensible libertarian thought, particularly in reviewing the Jehovah's Witnesses cases, pp. 51–63. Fraenkel's devotion to "economic democracy," or socialism, is indicated on pp. 257–59.

21. *Dies Committee Report*, vol. 1, p. 961, vol. 2, pp. 1141, 1148, 1372.

22. *Ibid.*, volume 1, pp. 384–85, 764.

23. *Ibid.*, pp. 310–11.

24. *Ibid.*, pp. 380–81. Lamont's identity as a Communist derives directly from his unswerving support of Communist causes rather from any evidence that he ever joined the Communist Party, something he always denied. See Gannon, *Biographical Dictionary of the Left*, vol. 1, pp. 409–10.

25. *Dies Committee Report*, vol. 1, pp. 390–91, 404–5, 416–17, 423–28, p. 423 including a joint ALAWF–ACLU meeting p. 409, and vol. 2, p. 1300 on the National Peoples Committee Against Hearst of the ALAWF, pp. 1090–1095, on activities concerning partisan support for the war in China.

26. *Ibid.*, vol. 1, p. 472.

27. *Ibid.*, pp. 518–22, and vol. 2, pp. 1312–1313 on the virtual group, the National Student League.

28. *Ibid.*, vol. 1, pp. 534–37.

29. *Ibid.*, pp. 588–89.

30. *Ibid.*, pp. 618–19. This involved the view that would prevail in all later Smith Act cases. The Union advanced Baldwin's position that, regardless of any evidence that the Communist Party is a disciplined cadre or conspiracy, no verbal utterances may be legally proscribed, only violent actions. See Fraenkel, *Our Civil Liberties*, pp. 64–108 for an airing of these views. See Baldwin's testimony before the Fish Committee in 1931 (Appendix). With such a view, we might wonder why the Union ever tried to sue anyone for libel.

31. *Dies Committee Report*, vol. 1, pp. 658–59. See also index references to Consumers Union in vol. 3.

32. *Ibid.*, vol. 1, pp. 758–59.

33. *Ibid.*, p. 949.

34. *Ibid.*, p. 1037.

35. *Ibid.*, pp. 772–73.

36. *Ibid.*, vol. 2, pp. 1162–1164. Anna Rochester was the author of one Book Union selection from the Communist press, *Rulers of America: A Study of Finance Capital* (New York: International Publishers, 1936), which resembled Gustavus Myer's classic *History of the Great American Fortunes* and contained much detail on the Wall Street crowd that had actually financed so many of the revolutionary activities in which Rochester would take part.

37. *Dies Committee Report*, vol. 2, p. 1171.

38. *Ibid.*, pp. 1186–1191.
38. *Ibid.*, p. 1367. For more on the Communist campaign for Social Insurance see Marjorie Shearon, *Wilbur J. Cohen: The Pursuit of Power, A Bureaucratic Biography* (Chevy Chase, Maryland: Shearon Legislative Service, 1967), pp. 1–33.
40. *Dies Committee Report*, Vol. 2, pp. 1471–1472, p. 1471 providing an example of what could quite reasonably appear to be a hasty evaluation by the committee of a group merely on the basis of its having certain persons as members. This report, as with all others, must be read critically, with attention to the logical strength of its conclusions, and also in the context of subsequently corroborating evidence in other books.
41. *Ibid.*, vol. 3, p. 1774. My mother knew and worked with Rose Schneiderman in the Labor Department in Washington during the mid–1930s when it was practically a recruiting ground for the Communist Party. She remembers Rose as a very kind woman.
42. The best book reviewing the case with an interest in showing the manner in which the ILD and ACLU made the case into a legendary crusade similar to that of Sacco–Vanzetti is Files Crenshaw, Jr., and Kenneth A. Miller, *Scottsboro: The Firebrand of Communism* (Montgomery, Alabama: Brown Printing Company, 1936). On the front here mentioned, see the *Dies Committee Report*, vol. 2, p. 1309. On the Fellowship of Reconciliation, in addition to Matthews' own *Odyssey of a Fellow Traveler*, see Gannon, *Biographical Dictionary of the Left*, vol. 1, pp. 74–85, showing its resemblance to the Carnegie–financed Foreign Policy Association. The Fellowship's link to the Communist American Student Union is shown in California State Legislature, Senate, Investigating Committee on Education, *Fourteenth Report—Patriotism or Pacifism, Which?* (Sacramento: State of California, 1956), p. 67, passim. The numerous reports of this body of the California State Senate, the Nelson Dilworth Committee, republished much material on the ACLU and other groups over the years. I have not made much use of them because much of the same material on the ACLU was published in the reports of the California Fact–Finding Committee on Un–American Activities, the Tenney–Burns Committee, and often presented better in those. One Communist protest related to the Scottsboro case agitation was the New York Harlem riots of March 19, 1935. See Varney, "The Civil Liberties Union," pp. 390–92. Negro former Communist Leonard Patterson admitted the role he played in these disturbances on party orders during his speaking tours on behalf of the John Birch Society's Truth About Civil Turmoil Committees during the mid–1960s. One of his speeches is reprinted in Leonard Patterson *et al.*, *A Conservative Civil Rights Seminar* (Belmont, Mass.: American Opinion Speakers Bureau, no date).
43. On the Communist-controlled Bonus March riot, see Gitlow, *The Whole Of Their Lives*, pp. 229–34; Douglas MacArthur, *Reminiscences* (New York: McGraw–Hill, 1964), pp. 92–97; Frazier Hunt, *The Untold Story of Douglas MacArthur* (Old Greenwich, Conn.: Devin-Adair, 1973 rev. ed.), pp. 136, 141–47.
44. The best quick source for these case activities during the 1930s is the sections on "gains," "setbacks," and "work ahead" listed in the ACLU annual reports for those years. The decision in the *Ulysses* case is reprinted in James Joyce, *Ulysses* (New York: Modern Library, 1961), pp. v–xv. More of Morris Ernst's influential thoughts are contained in Morris L. Ernst, *The First Freedom* (New York: Macmillan, 1946).
45. See Appendix. The ACLU was quick to make use of Dies' conclusion, although ridiculing most of his other conclusions: *Civil Liberties*, January, 1960, p. 2. This impression that the ACLU spread of Dies giving the Union a clean bill of health was a bit dishonest, since he had "strongly recommended" that it be "thoroughly investigated," something it managed to avoid. On this, and the work of the Dies Committee see Martin Dies, *Martin Dies' Story* (New York: Bookmailer, 1963), p. 182, passim. Also see the earlier Martin Dies, *The Trojan Horse in America* (New York: Dodd, Mead & Company, 1940), passim.
46. In addition to his many other revealing revisionist studies on the causes of both world wars, Barnes' hardest-hitting material were his essays and monographs on the latest studies concerning World War II and the official "blackout" on their findings in the academic world and other establishment centers of national life. See Harry Elmer Barnes, *Selected Revisionist Pamphlets* and *Pearl Harbor After A Quarter Of A Century* (both New York: Arno Press and the *New York Times*, 1972 reprint editions). These are highly recommended to the student of contemporary diplomatic history.

Chapter 10: 1940-1959: The Stalin-Hitler Pact and the ACLU's Temporary "Anticommunism"

1. The story of this crisis, as derived from ACLU files now located at Princeton University, is told in Bean, *Pressure for Freedom*, pp. 294–316.
2. The resolution barred from ACLU governing bodies and staff any person "who is a member of any political organization which supports totalitatian dictatorship in any country (including the American Communist Party, the German–American Bund and native organizations with obvious anti–democratic objectives or practices), or who by his public declarations indicates his support of such a principle." A similarly worded resolution was adopted on January 17, 1949, against all police states and all movements supporting them. See ACLU letter for submission to corporation members, "Statement No. 1 on: Nature of Communist Party, Defense of Civil Liberties Regardless of Associations, Allowable Consideration of Associations (In General)," May 8, 1953, the first of three 1953 Resolutions (as hereafter cited), copies of which are in the archives of the ACLU's New York headquarters. In December, 1974, I was able to copy these with the assistance of Richard Gibboney, ACLU archivist. Norman Thomas' curious socialist anticommunism was clearly defined. See Norman Thomas, *The Test of Freedom* (New York: W.W. Norton, 1954), pp. 86–90, on his reasons for not outlawing the Communist Party, but for thinking that Communists do not have the right to teach in public schools or hold other "sensitive" positions. Reading this book, which contains views on the larger events of the ACLU's history, as well as the predictable attack on "McCarthyism," I could only conclude that, if sincere, Thomas' major error was in not recognizing that his "democratic" socialist goals would, in practice, lead inevitably to the same police state advocated by the rival collectivists he opposed. On this point, see Friedrich A. Hayek, *The Road to Serfdom* (Chicago: University of Chicago Press, 1944); James Burnham, *Suicide of the West: An Essay on the Meaning and Destiny of Liberalsim* (New York: John Day Company, 1964), pp. 164–71.
3. Flynn herself carried the torch, as can be seen in one of many articles: "Life of the Party," *Daily Worker*, April 27, 1949, p. 10. A very left–wing staff secretary of the Union from its earliest days to 1945 wrote of the "trial" in Lucille Milner, *Education of An American Liberal* (New York: Horizon Press, 1954), pp. 261–94. An indication of the tone of this book might be gauged by its warm review in the publication of the Communist Emergency Civil Liberties Committee: Corliss Lamont, "ACLU Founder Writes Own Story," *Rights*, June, 1954, p. 14. Lamont would later take up this cause and others in Corliss Lamont, *Freedom Is As Freedom Does* (New York: Horizon Press, 1956), pp. 273–77, and publish the "trial" transcript in Corliss Lamont, ed., *The Trial of Elizabeth Gurley Flynn by the American Civil Liberties Union* (New York: Horizon Press, 1968), which was dedicated to Dr. Harry F. Ward.
4. Forster was ACLU staff counsel from 1941 to 1950 and its special counsel from 1950 to 1954, when he resigned from the Union. Herbert Levy became staff counsel in 1950. My information about Clifford Forster comes from an interview he was kind enough to grant in his New York apartment on December 21, 1974. With his permission, the interview was recorded and I prepared an abridged transcript of it—condensing primarily my own questions rather than his answers—as well as my interview that same day with C. Dickerman Williams. The single-spaced transcript runs twenty–seven pages, and it will be referred to henceforth as the Forster–Williams Transcript. Both Forster and Williams provided me with documentary material concerning their work in connection with the ACLU. Clifford Forster made his views known through his numerous articles and letters to newspapers and magazines during his tenure with the Union and after. Some of his expressed views provide a basis for understanding why he broke with the ACLU. Had he not publicized his opinions, his views might not have been reflected regardless of what course was taken by the Union, since he, as staff counsel, like Baldwin and his successor as director, sat in on Board meetings, but did not debate or vote on policies. Forster was not deceived by the tide of Communist propaganda during the Spanish Civil War. And he insisted on pointing our hypocrisies in propaganda put forth in opposition to Franco's anti–Communist cause: form letter to the editor,

written by Forster on stationery of his "The Open Mind," December 20, 1938. He opposed all efforts to outlaw anti–Semitic speech and writings, although upholding the validity of laws requiring authorship disclosure on material representing foreign interests, a position also taken by such Union Leaders as Morris Ernst: Clifford Forster, "Should Anti–Semitism Be Outlawed?," *New Europe*, December, 1944, p. 31. (Also see, Forster–Williams Transcript, p. 4.) He was very much aware of Communist inroads in Mexico and Western Europe and of the serious need for an effective U.S. anti–Communist educational strategy to be waged against the problem in these areas: Clifford Forster, "We Still Need a Good Neighbor Policy: Anti–Americanism in Mexico," *The New Leader*, December 27, 1947, p. 5; Clifford Forster, "The Dirty Little Street–Corner Battle," *The New Leader*, June 4, 1951, p. 11. Consequently, he looked with dismay on the efforts of those Americans who were assisting in the Communist drives to undermine the position of our allies, in particular the campaign against French Algeria: Clifford Forster, "Our Relations With France: United States Activities in Morocco and Algeria Queried," *New York Times*, December 1, 1956. He was objective enough to see through the emotionalism that surrounded the injustice of the Nuremberg trials: Clifford Forster, "Holds Arab Criticism of France Is a Case of Pot and Kettle," *The New Leader*, November 17, 1952, p. 26. He also knew the hypocrisy of many Rosenberg trial crusaders: Clifford Forster, "Reactions to Crime," *New York Herald Tribune*, November 30, 1953. And he saw that it was a matter of "equal protection under the laws" rather than political persecution when the offices and assets of the Communist *Daily Worker* were seized: Clifford Forster, "Seizing The Daily Worker: Issue Seen as Refusal of Party to Comply with Tax Statutes," *New York Times*, March 31, 1956. He viewed the Truman Loyalty Review Board as a politically ill–inspired maneuver plagued by many unclear details but posing no threat to civil liberties. He viewed any government job as potentially useful for Communist espionage purposes, but regretted the FBI's policy of withholding the identity of accusers in such cases. He pointed out that, because prosecutions would not be forthcoming without such disclosures in court, civil liberties were still not in danger. See Clifford Forster, "Is Loyalty Program Hurting Civil Liberties?," *The Liberal*, January, 1948, p. 8. He firmly believed the Communists posed a serious espionage threat to the United States—an activity not protected by the Bill of Rights—although he knew the party could never take power in America as was done in Russia: Clifford Forster, "Is There a Danger of Communism in America?," *Paris Continental Daily Mail*, July 30, 1950, under "The Experts Answer." From his dissatisfactions with the Smith Act, he derived an argument by which he felt the Communist Party might be outlawed without violating the civil liberties of innocent dupes: Clifford Forster, "To Outlaw Communists: Statute Advocated Declaring Party a Criminal Conspiracy," *New York Times*, April 15, 1954. (This appeared about the time of his resignation from the ACLU.) He, like Harry Elmer Barnes, was among those who were recognizing that the American "liberal" establishment was being quite effective in censoring anti–Communist books from public attention, but was ever eager to protest attempts to encourage a departure from such censorship: E.F. Tompkins, "Hiding The Truth: Left–Wing Censorship," *New York Journal–American*, March 26, 1953; Clifford Forster, "Defends Threatened Boycott Over James Burnham Book," *The New Leader*, May 11, 1953, p. 27. Forster was instrumental in helping one former Soviet sympathizer get his story published: Isaac Don Levine, *The Mind Of An Assassin* (New York: Farrar, Straus and Cudahy, 1959), p. vi. Another humanitarian effort he undertook voluntarily was the defense of the family of an unintended victim of the Social Security program's loyalty restrictions: Frederick Woltman, "U.S. Praised Ex-Red—His Orphans Pay," *New York World Telegram*, May 3, 1956, pp. 1–2; Peter Kihss, "Ex–Red's Family Loses U.S. Benefit: Checks for Children Halted Despite Father's Service as Government Witness," *New York Times*, May 4, 1956. Forster's principled position gained him the warm regard and respect of his fellow ACLU staff members by the time he became special counsel, even from those significantly less anti–Communist than he: letter, Patrick Murphy Malin, George E. Rundquist, Herbert M. Levy, Alan Reitman, Jeffrey Fuller to Clifford Forster, on ACLU stationery, March 3, 1950. There are very few issues that Forster today believes to be proper functions of government, particularly in the field of victimless crimes. He does think government has a role to play in restricting the availability of obscene materials to children. He also acknowledges having run into the problem discussed in the first part of this book, the absence of admissibility of constitutional issue pleading in the courts, when he tried to raise a constitutional argument in a magistrate court. He is more optimistic on the chances in higher federal courts. (See Forster–Williams Transcript, pp. 6–7.)

5. My source for information on Williams is the Forster–Williams Transcript. C. Dickerman Williams, a member of the New York bar, was employed in the U.S. Attorney's office, 1925–1927. Like the young Roger Baldwin, he was interested in municipal reform and civil liberties. He joined the ACLU in 1927 as a result of his sympathetic interest in the Gastonia case. (He took depositions for the defendants in New York.) In 1944 he was invited to take a position on the ACLU Board, which he did, although he was unable to serve actively for several months. (Ironically that same year the Consumer–Farmer Milk Cooperative, Inc., which earlier had used his name among many others as a sponsor, was identified as a Communist front. See *Dies Committee Report*, vol. 3, pp. 1771–1777.) In 1951 he left the Board to go to Washington and serve af general counsel at the Department of Commerce, having resigned from the Board because he was unable to attend meetings. He returned to New York and the ACLU Board in 1954, right at the time the controversy that would soon result in the resignations of himself, Forster, and several others was brewing. Because Williams was on the Board he was far less in touch with the Union's daily adminsitrative work than Forster. He commented that Baldwin would rarely state his own views on resolutions at Board meetings, but Williams was close enough to sense that, as I implied earlier, "It was sometimes suspected that if Roger Baldwin didn't like a particular resolution, it would just lie dormant." (Forster–Williams Transcript, p. 20.)

6. Forster–Williams Transcript, p. 26. Williams believes that Lamont was never taken very seriously by many of his fellow Board members. An interesting and revealing anecdote on Lamont, who taught for years at Columbia University, concerns Hede Massing, former wife of Soviet agent Gerhardt Eisler. Hede told Lamont at a dinner in Moscow of the purge trials and her fear for her own life. She reported later he "was completely unprepared to be told" the truth "by someone he knew to be a 'party functionary' … he looked aghast, as though I had really lost my mind." She asked him to tell Baldwin on his return to notify the State Department if she should "disappear," and later learned that Baldwin had received the message as follows: "You know, Roger, I had dinner with Hede. *My! She has gone sour!*" See E. Merrill Root, *Collectivism on the Campus* (New York: Devin–Adair, 1961), pp. 153–54.

7. On these people and others, see, among other sources, Gannon, *Biographical Dictionary of the Left*. The later pro–Communist work of Aubrey Williams, another New Deal bureaucrat, was covered in Joint Legislative Committee on Un–American Activities, *Activities of the Southern Conference Educational Fund, Inc., in Louisiana* (Baton Rouge, La.: State of Louisiana, 1963–1965), Reports 4, 5, 6.

8. The story of those intellectuals who *kept* trying to keep us out of war is in Wayne S. Cole, *Charles A. Lindbergh and the Battle Against American Intervention in World War II* (New York: Harcourt Brace Jovanovich, 1974). The best source on the American left's role in promoting the war against Germany, after it would help Stalin, is unquestionably James J. Martin, *American Liberalism and World Politics, 1931–1941, Liberalism's Press and Spokesmen on the Road Back to War Between Mukden and Pearl Harbor*, 2 vol. (New York: Devin– Adair, 1964). This important study contains much detail on the influence of many ACLU leaders, including Baldwin and Lamont. Angell succeeded Holmes as chairman of the Board in 1950. The ACLU annual reports of the war years review his work on cases of conscientious objectors.

9. *The Right to Advocate Violence* (New York: ACLU, 1931); *Fish Committee Report* (see Appendix).

10. The Union published a review of the subject a decade later: *The Smith Act and the Supreme Court, An American Civil Liberties Union Analysis, Opinion and Statement of Policy* (New York: ACLU, 1952). This summarized the objections that had been made to the act's outlawing of utterances and the ambiguous standards of valid enforcement listed by the Supreme Court, which had been argued in various ACLU annual reports since 1940.

11. Forster–Williams Transcript, pp. 4, 19. Forster and Baldwin did offer the Union's assistance to anti–Semite Gerald L.K. Smith and the German–American Bund in cases of government harrassment against them during the war. At the outset of the war, Arthur Garfield Hays successfully challenged a New Jersey statute that prohibited the Bund's anti–Semitic propaganda activities. Letter, Clifford Forster to William H. McIlhany, November 4, 1975.

12. Forster–Williams Transcript, p. 20. Williams recalls Arthur Garfield Hays getting assurances of better behavior in the future from Dies (Transcript, p. 5); Forster recalls no Board discussions of Stalinist terror.

13. Forster–Williams Transcript, pp. 3, 17–19. Both gentlemen agree about the fact that the Union dodged this case when it should not have.

14. The two major sources on this trial are certainly partisan: Maximilian St. George and Lawrence Dennis, *A Trial on Trial: The Great Sedition Trial of 1944* (National Civil Rights Committee, 1946); Anonymous, *The Sedition Case* (Lowell, Arizona: Lutheran Research Society, 1953), recently reprinted by the anti–Semitic "Sons of Liberty" in Los Angeles. A number of the defendants had written books, which we shall not take space here to catalog. The best–known was Elizabeth Dilling of Chicago, who would later become the female Gerald L.K. Smith. She exposed the ACLU and its Red connections in two books she wrote and published in 1936, *The Red Network* and *The Roosevelt Red Record,* which are largely free of the anti–Semitism contained in her other works. A case that involved the British opponents of war who lost their civil liberties under the heel of Churchill between 1939 and 1946, included an American acting in a manner that the Union would later respect in those who surfaced to expose the Watergate cover–up, but the case was too hot for the ACLU to touch: John Howland Snow, *The Case of Tyler Kent* (New Canaan, Conn.: The Long House, 1962). The Union's Board may have been influenced at the time by the very libelous "John Roy Carlson," *Undercover* (Cleveland and New York: World, 1943).

15. *A.C.L.U. Annual Reports,* vol. 1, p. xiii: "It was a gesture of appeasement to some of our worried friends, but, practically, it meant little."

16. St. George and Dennis, *A Trial on Trial,* pp. 90–91. A similar, but lesser known, government policy was that of using the pretense of Axis collaboration as an excuse for further police–state measures. During the war, government agents arrested hundreds of persons of German descent in Central and South American countries, who were secretly brought to the United States for internment. Clifford Forster became convinced that they were persecuted, not for aiding Nazi war efforts, but because they were resented by local business competitors in their new Spanish–speaking homelands. After the war, they were prepared for deportation to Germany, many to Communist East Germany. Forster learned of this from a letter written by a German who had acquired Guatamalan citizenship after marrying a citizen of that country. Forster immediately pressed for an arrangement by the Department of Justice, by which several hundred Germans were permitted to return to their adopted Latin American nations. In doing so, Forster probably spared them execution or imprisonment in concentration camps, and he was formally honored by the German community of Guatamala for having done so. Letter, Clifford Forster to William H. McIlhany, November 4, 1975.

17. The standard study on this tragedy is Allan R. Bosworth, *America's Concentration Camps* (New York: Norton, 1967). See also *ACLU Annual Reports,* vol 1, Baldwin, p. xiii. Perhaps the reason the ACLU "could do little" about this was related to the fact that the governor of California who was administering it was the late Earl Warren, who, in 1945, foreshadowing his views as Supreme Court chief justice the following decade, bowed to the Union's request and vetoed a bill requiring state employees to state their views on war. This reasonable measure for *government* employment during wartime was viewed by the Union in California as an attack on resisters, and Warren said it encouraged "witch–hunting," which indicated that he had already picked up the left's smear word for investigation of subversive activities.

18. Sutton, *Wall Street and F.D.R..*

19. John W. Scoville, *Labor Monopolies—OR Freedom* (New York: Arno Press and the *New York Times,* 1972 reprint of 1946 edition), pp. 113–117, quoted from the 1943 ACLU pamphlet *Democracy in Trade Unions.*

20. Forster–Williams Transcript, pp. 15–16, 20–22. Arthur Garfield Hays and Whitney North Seymour saw the danger. Hays was also opposed to the Securities Act, which established the SEC, because he recognized, as the Union today does not, that a person has a *right* to make stupid and poor investments with a stock broker, just as he does to do the same in Las Vegas or at a race track.

21. The 1944 Texas White Primary Case and the 1948 effort to secure the right to vote for Indians in Arizona and New Mexico were among the leading cases featured in the Union's annual reports. A convenient list of Supreme Court cases on these and other issues was prepared, with those decisions favored by the Union marked. One "landmark" was *Shelly* v. *Kraemer* (1948), which the ACLU hailed, and which I reviewed in Chapter Four, well indicating the approaches taken by the Union for "civil rights": Osmond K. Fraenkel, *The Supreme Court and Civil Liberties: How*

Far Has The Court Protected The Bill of Rights? (New York: ACLU 1955, revised edition), pp. 91–106.

22. A report that covers most of these issues representatively is "Our Uncertain Liberties," *Annual Report, 1947–1948* (New York: ACLU, 1948), pp. 3–19. The report (p. 18) cites the UN Genocide Treaty as desirable. This treaty would outlaw prosecution of utterances in favor of racial hatred, discrimination, and violence, the same sort of abuse that the report complains about in reference to the Smith Act. Page 87 of the report lists Laurence Duggan and A.A. Berle, Jr., as being in charge of the Union's Committee on Civil Rights in American Colonies. In spite of the strong anti–Communists also present, the Union had been infiltrated by an agent of the Soviet espionage apparatus within the Communist Party, U.S.A. He was not destined to live long: "Hull's Ex–Aid Dies in Plunge; Tied to Spies," *New York Daily News,* December 21, 1948. Also see Chambers, *Witness*, pp. 30, 334, 339, 341, 381–82, 467, 469; Burnham, *Web of Subversion*, pp. 65, 123, 136.

23. The best recent survey of this material is G. Edward Griffin, *The Fearful Master: A Second Look at The United Nations* (Boston: Western Islands, 1964), pp. 67–122.

24. For an interesting look at the Allied occupation of Germany see Guenther Reinhardt, *Crime Without Punishment: The Secret Soviet Terror Against America* (New York: Hermitage House, 1952), pp. 221–39. See p. 255 on the ACLU. Arthur Garfield Hays also tried to bring justice to the case of Chetnik leader Drazha Mihailovich prior to his betrayal by the U.S. and execution by Tito. The story is told by a disheartened socialist: David Martin, *Ally Betrayed: The Uncensored Story of Tito and Mihailovich* (New York: Prentice–Hall, 1946), p. 345.

25. Charles A. Willoughby and John Chamberlain, *MacArthur, 1941–1951* (New York: McGraw-Hill, 1954), p. 330. Baldwin's presence was also used as a means of defending MacArthur from recent criticisms.

26. The best judicial review of the great injustices is in F.J.P. Veale, *Advance to Barbarism: The Development of Total Warfare From Sarajevo to Hiroshima* (New York: Devin–Adair, 1968), which also discusses a few of the Allied war crimes. The worst Soviet atrocity of conquest, committed at the end of the war with American assistance, was Operation Keelhaul. See Julius Epstein, *Operation Keelhaul: The Story of Forced Repatriation from 1944 to the Present* (Old Greenwich, Conn.: Devin-Adair, 1973). Although there were innumerable other incidents the Union could have condemned, this one remained so secret throughout the 1950s that it was brought to public attention by only one other author, Robert Welch (*The Politician* [Belmont, Mass.: Belmont, 1964, revised from pre–1958 private letter], chapter four). But the Union could have spotlighted many others. In his ACLU capcity, at the end of the war Clifford Forster got his first awareness of the U.S. policy of forcible repatriation of anti–Communist Europeans in the case of three Russian stowaway deserters who were about to be handed over to the Communist partisan forces in "liberated" France. Forster prevented their deportation "by procurement of a letter from the French Vice–Consul (Mr. Ramin) who was a representative of the Deuxieme Bureau, advising the Immigration and Naturalization Service that the French government would not accept the return of the three stowaways." Letter, Clifford Forster to William H. McIlhany, November 4, 1975.

27. Forster–Williams Transcript, pp. 9, 10, on the affiliates, particularly the Union's action to separate itself from the Communist Chicago Civil Liberties Committee, and p. 24 on the fact that the California affiliates were always consistently more left–wing than the national office. This resulted in the investigation by the State of California's Senate Fact–Finding Subcommittee on Un–American Activities. The Burns Subcommittee's 1961 report (excerpted in the Appendix), surveys the committee's changing evaluations from 1943 to 1961, which reflect the National ACLU's policy of "anti–Communism" far better than the records of the Northern and Southern California affiliates. I have omitted any detailed review of the activities of any affiliate, since such would not necessarily represent the policies and views of the national office, and an organization should be evaluated more on the basis of its national influence and work rather than by examples of affiliations and actions by local members. After 1955, the national ACLU became increasingly more willing to assume the coloration of its most activist affiliates, which we must discuss together in reference to the 1960s and early 1970s as a result of the particular issues that were so influential on both levels. By 1961, the Burns Committee, though still critical of the Union, took a position

reversing its 1943 determination that the group was a Communist front: "Civil Liberties Union Cleared of Red Control—Group Has Been Attacked by Communists, State Senate Subcommittee Report Shows," *Los Angeles Times*, June 13, 1961. An interesting national connection between the Union and the nucleus of the 1930s United Front was the fact that Carey MacWilliams remained a member of the National Committee between 1945 and 1948, although he, like his colleague Francis J. McConnell of the old Interchurch World Committee, had been a major subject of the *Dies Committee Report*.

28. *Civil Liberties*, January, 1960, p. 4.

29. Forster–Williams Transcript, p. 4, on Baldwin's accumulation of knowledge about constitutional law. Advancing age has apparently effected his store of knowledge rather severely, because about five years ago he could not even identify the Second Amendment of the Constitution when a question was raised about it following a speech he made, but during which he finally admitted the "militia" was the "people": Susan L.M. Huck, "The Day Mr. Baldwin Flipped His Wig," *Review of the News*, March 3, 1971, p. 35–40.

30. A sketch of Malin is given in Booton Herndon, "Patrick Murphy Malin: The Lawyer You Didn't Know You Had," *True*, April, 1961, pp. 18–20, 22, 24, 26, 28, 98. Baldwin felt him qualified to take over the leadership because "we don't fight the same way today. Then you could get your hands on the bastards. Today it's all remote—you file briefs. Pat Malin fits into a time like this. He's got courage, fidelity, and a lot more tact than I ever had." (Herndon, p. 24). A recruitment pamphlet published as Malin resumed control at the outset of his second decade of leadership was most revealing, especially regarding the elite support the Union had collected from key Establishment figures. See *What Is The American Civil Liberties Union? An Idea, Beliefs, Action, Organization, People* (New York: ACLU, 1960), p. 4: "It is a pleasure to send my cordial greetings to all present at the dinner celebrating the 40th Anniversary of the American Civil Liberties Union. This is an occasion that well merits public observance. It is of the utmost importance that our civil liberties be preserved intact and untarnished. This we need not only for individual self–realization but, also, as an example to the rest of the world."—Nelson A. Rockfeller.

31. An interesting research challenge is to find out very much about the International League for the Rights of Man, to the leadership of which Baldwin was retired in 1950. The story of its roots is too lengthy to review here, but should the reader compare the information contained in the following authoritative source with the material cited in Chapter 8, footnote 21, above, he may get the impression that this change of pace for Baldwin constituted not a satisfying hobby for retirement years but, rather, a graduation of sorts. The reader can compare Mildred J. Headings, *French Freemasonry Under The Third Republic* (Baltimore: Johns Hopkins University Press, 1949), pp. 237–72, published in vol. LXVI of The Johns Hopkins University Studies in Historical and Political Science, no. 1; McIlhany, *No Civil War At All*. Baldwin's work with the group included in the 1950s not only steady promotion of the image and strength of the UN but a major role in the propaganda campaign against anti–Communist Gen. Rafael Trujillo of the Dominican Republic. See Harold Lord Varney, "What is Behind the Galindez Case?," extension of remarks of Rep. B. Carroll Reece, June 26, 1957, *Congressional Record—Appendix*, House of Representatives, pp. A5141–A5143. On this case, see Arturo R. Espaillat, *Trujillo: The Last Caesar* (Chicago: Henry Regnery, 1963), pp. 77, 126, 163–76. Possibly the only case of interference with Communist objectives by the International League and Roger Baldwin was another outrage that motivated Clifford Forster to action. It was the case of Povl Bang–Jensen, a Danish deputy secretary of the UN Special Committee on Hungary. He was assigned the task of interviewing eyewitnesses of the Soviet suppression of the 1956 Budapest revolt. They had given him information on the condition that their names be withheld from Communists at the UN because many of them had relatives still living in Communist Hungary. On December 6, 1957, the UN Special Committee suspended Bang–Jensen from his duties without pay because he refused their demand to deliver the names. He was unwilling for them to fall into the hands of Khrushchev's agents in the UN Secretariat. Bang–Jensen later "committed suicide" in New York after making clear that he would never do so. Forster was able to get Baldwin and others at the International League to recognize the injustice in the UN's suspension of Bang–Jensen and prepared for the League a strong statement of protest. Forster had also been Bang–Jensen's attorney in an unsuccessful attempt to resist the U.N. firing.

Letter, Clifford Forster to William H. McIlhany, November 4, 1975; Brutus Coste, Clifford Forster, Benjamin Gim, "Memorandum of the International League for the Rights of Man," March, 1958. The story of Bang–Jensen is told in Julius Epstein, "The Bang–Jensen Tragedy: A Review Based on the Official Records," *American Opinion,* May, 1960; DeWitt Copp and Marshall Peck, *Betrayal At the UN: The Story of Paul Bang–Jensen* (New York: Devin–Adair, 1963), pp. 6–11, 20, 229, and 274 on Clifford Forster's work for Bang–Jensen.

32. Dan Smoot, *The Invisible Government* (Boston: Western Islands, 1965 reprint of the 1962 edition), p. 105, quoted from CFR *Annual Report*.

33. Communist strategy since about 1945. U.S. Congress, House, Committee on Un–American Activities, *The New Role of National Legislative Bodies in the Communist Conspiracy, Reprint of "How Parliament Can Play A Revolutionary Part in the Transition to Socialism" and "The Role of the Popular Masses" by Jan Kozak, Historian of the Communist Party of Czechoslovakia,* 87th Congress, 1st session, 1962; reprinted as Jan Kozak, *And Not a Shot is Fired* (New Canaan, Conn.: The Long House, 1972).

34. Smoot, *Invisible Government*, p. 105. On Thomas Lamont, see Sutton, *Wall Street and the Bolshevik Revolution*.

35. William F. Buckley, Jr., and L. Brent Bozell, *McCarthy and His Enemies: The Record and Its Meaning* (New Rochelle, New York: Arlington House, 1970 reprint of 1954 edition), pp. 295–97, 306, 333, on James Wechsler and pp. 343–46 on Judge Dorothy Kenyon. This evidence did not seem to mean much to the ACLU in 1950. See *Civil Liberties*, January, 1960, p. 4. Clifford Forster took an interest in discussing the matter of Wechsler with McCarthy (Forster–Williams Transcript, p. 11). J. Robert Oppenheimer, a most distinguished member of the ACLU National Committee, would later be accused of substantial Communist ties. See *St. Louis Globe–Democrat*, July 4, 1963; Personnel Security Board, United States Atomic Energy Commission, *In the Matter of J. Robert Oppenheimer, Texts of Principal Documents and Letters*, (Washington D.C.: G.P.O., 1954).

36. These are discussed in detail in the early 1950s annual reports, as far back as the *1947–1948 Annual Report* (pp. 23–26), and in Henry Steele Commager, "The Real Danger—Fear of Ideas," *New York Times Magazine*, June 26, 1949. The Union leadership confined most of its interest to cases involving statements and organizational affiliations rather than offering any opposition to such espionage cases as that of the Rosenbergs (Forster–Williams Transcript, p. 13). In fact, the Rosenbergs may have been scapegoats for others in more influential positions, including Oppenheimer. See Medford Evans, *The Secret War for the A–Bomb* (Chicago: Henry Regnery, 1953).

37. The object of the Union's attack in 1952 was the highly influential and very factual *Red Channels: The Report of Communist Influence in Radio and Television* (New York: American Business Consultants, 1950). The Union's critique, Merle Miller's *The Judges and the Judged,* had to be revised to remove a number of "unintentional errors." See Ernest Angell and H. William Fitelson, "ACLU Officials Deny Communist Infiltration," *The New Leader,* November 17, 1952, p. 27. A few Union members of note, like Carey McWilliams, had even taken part in such Communist–front attacks as Hollywood Arts, Sciences & Professions Council, P.C.A., *Conference on Thought Control in the U.S.A.*, 6 vol. (Los Angeles: Progressive Citizens of America, Southern California Chapter, 1947). Many Union leaders could not recognize in this issue the essential matter of an employer's right to hire or fire anyone for any reason, especially when the public climate would make it wise for him to do so. One gets the impression that some believed that jobs should be guaranteed in the relevant industries. Forster, Pitzele, Williams, and a few others disagreed. In fact, Pitzele charged that Merle Miller's book contained "half-truths, distortions, and lies."

38. Roy Cohn, *McCarthy* (New York: New American Library, 1968).

39. Forster–Williams Transcript, p. 8, on debates between Miller and Pitzele over the issue of "blacklisting" as anyone's *right*. In a report to the Board, Forster supported the reasoning that such was an employer's right. He found out how much of a minority view this was, as the report was never published. The best review of the evidence McCarthy had is Buckley and Bozell, *McCarthy and His Enemies*. Also see Joseph R. McCarthy, *The Fight for America* (Hamilton, Montana: Poor Richard's Book Shop, reprint of 1952 edition). The evidence from other sources is

255

found in Robert E. Stripling and Bob Considine, *The Red Plot Against America* (Drexel Hill, Pa.: Bell, 1949), which covers the findings of the HCUA; Jack B. Tenney, compilor, *Red Fascism* (Los Angeles: Federal Printing, 1947), which is based on the earlier work of Tenney's California Senate Fact–Finding Subcommittee.

40. On this academic censorship of World War II revisionism, see Barnes, "The Struggle Against the Historical Blackout," *Selected Revisionist Pamphlets*, pp. 8–9. Here Barnes refers to the Rockefeller Foundation *Annual Report, 1946,* from which Charles Austin Beard drew the conclusion I stated in the text. The all–out effort to "get" McCarthy is covered in Buckley and Bozell, *McCarthy and His Enemies,* and expanded upon in a more recent work, which discusses the theory that McCarthy was murdered: Medford Evans, *The Assassination of Joe McCarthy* (Boston: Western Islands, 1970).

41. *Civil Liberties*, January, 1960, p. 4.

42. The best source of information on the foundations at this time is U.S. Congress, House, Special Committee to Investigate Tax-Exempt Foundations and Comparable Organizations, *Tax–Exempt Foundations, Report,* 83rd Congress, 2nd session, 1954, the "infamous" Dodd Report of the Reece Committee. The committee's general counsel later published a summary: Rene A. Wormser, *Foundations: Their Power and Influence* (New York: Devin-Adair, 1958). After reviewing these publications, the reader should note the number of representatives of such foundations who were ACLU leaders at the time. They included: Twentieth–Century Fund Vice-Chairman–President August Hecksher; Fund for the Republic consultant Walter Millis; Fund for the Republic President Robert M. Hutchins; Fund for the Republic Chairman Elmo Roper; John Finerty of the Robert Marshall Civil Liberties Trust; United World Federalists Vice–President Grenville Clark; former CFR President Walter T. Fisher; Institute for Pacific Relations Trustee Benjamin H. Kizer; and Agnes Brown Leach of the Foreign Policy Association Board. See "What is The American Civil Liberties Union?," pp. 16–19. The influence of such persons was felt at the ACLU although it was not obvious that they were directing the Union's policies and work for their ends (Forster–Williams Transcript, pp. 6, 24, 26).

43. C. Dickerman Williams, "Problems of the Fifth Amendment," *Fordham Law Review*, Summer, 1955, pp. 19–52. In this article, Williams advanced a number of excellent arguments, including the simple fact that the wording of the Fifth Amendment protects one's right to be free from self–incrimination in *criminal cases* on trial, not in the case of a legislative investigation. Whittaker Chambers refuted the claim that such investigations were repressive to American freedoms in his "Is Academic Freedom in Danger?," *Life,* June 22, 1953, pp. 91–104. The Union's general view was expressed rather well in Zechariah Chafee, Jr., "Freedom and Fear," *Bulletin of American Association of University Professors,* Autumn, 1949, which was distributed by the ACLU in reprint. On the Fund for the Republic's unequal debate, see Wormser, *Foundations,* pp. 274–75. Also see Clifford Forster, "Fifth Amendment," *The New Leader*, March 14, 1955, in which Forster noted Griswold's main objection to possibly mistaken inferences that could be made from one's exercise of Fifth Amendment protections. The missing book was Sidney Hook, *Common Sense and the Fifth Amendment* (Chicago: Henry Regnery, 1963 reprint of 1957 edition). However, a copy of the ACLU *1955–1956 Annual Report* I have seen, had an attached card from the Fund for the Republic, which distributed 10,000 copies, "Additional copies are available on request." Furthermore, a book praising the ACLU and its record of case interests (Robert E. Cushman, *Civil Liberties in the United States: A Guide to Current Problems and Experience* [Ithaca, N.Y.: Cornell University Press, 1956], p. v) was inspired and subsidized by the Fund for the Republic. The whole interrelationship between the Fund and the ACLU on this front is well summarized in Harold Lord Varney, "Where is the 'Liberty' in Civil Liberties?," *American Mercury*, January, 1956, pp. 17–27. The Fund's major effort on the "blacklisting" problem was John Cogley, *Report on Blacklisting, I Movies, II Radio-Television,* 2 vol. (Santa Barbara, Calif.: Fund for the Republic, 1956). This work is quite laudatory of the ACLU.

44. Letter, Norman Dodd to Dr. Howard E. Kershner, December 29, 1962, copy in "Foundations" file, Research Department, John Birch Society, San Marino, California.

45. ACLU staffer Irving Ferman, another member of the anti–Communist minority there, was seen to be unfit by the Union's leaders by virtue of his support of Brent Bozell's political campaign in

Maryland, a classic commentary on the Union's lords of "academic freedom": "Who Promoted Ferman?," *National Review*, July 5, 1958. In 1950, Ernest Angell replaced Holmes as chairman of the Board. Angell, despite his association with the American Legion, held rather consistently to policies of the Establishment crowd mentioned above. On Ferman's criticism of Bertrand Russell's procommunism, see Fulton Lewis, Jr., "Liberals Take Russell to Task," *Los Angeles Herald–Examiner,* April 12, 1956.

46. Forster–Williams Transcript, pp. 9–10, 22–25; 1953 Resolutions, ACLU letters to corporation members, May 8, June 3, 1953. Resolution 2 was titled, "Allowable Consideration of Associations (In Educational and United Nations Employment)," and 3, "Propriety of Questions and Competency of Authority Refusals to Answer Questions About Associations, Allowable Considerations of Such Refusals (In Government, United Nations and Educational Employment)." The minutes of special and regular Board meetings, March 17, April 15, and May 4, 1953, which I copied at ACLU headquarters, chronicle the debates over revisions of the resolutions and their adoption. This was summarized in *A.C.L.U. Annual Report, 1953–1954,* pp. 25–29.

47. See Chapter 8, footnotes 49, 50, Chapter 7, footnote 6, above.

48. Griffin, *Fearful Master.* See also U.S. Congress, Senate, Committee on the Judiciary, Internal Security Subcommittee, *Activities of United States Citizens Employed by the United Nations, Two Reports*, 82nd Congress, 2nd session, 1953–1954, which show extensive employment of Communists among U.S. personnel at the UN. Another report appropriate to these resolutions is Hamilton A. Long, *Permit Communist–Conspirators to Be Teachers?*, U.S. Congress, House, House Document 213, 1953.

49. Chapter 5, footnote 42, above. The Union staff during this period regarded the ECLC generally as what it was and stayed clear of association with other similar–sounding Communist fronts, such as the Hawaii Civil Liberties Committee. (See U.S. Congress, House, Committee on Un–American Activities, *Report on Hawaii Civil Liberties Committee, A Communist Front,* 81st Congress, 2nd session, 1950, p. 23.) After the resolutions were adopted, the Union supported the Hawaii statehood movement, in spite of the pervasive Communist political influence there, which the ACLU glossed over. See *A.C.L.U. Annual Report, 1954–1955,* pp. 98–99; *"Communism in Hawaii" A Summary of the 1955 Report of the Territorial Commission on Subversive Activities*, published by IMUA, the Hawaii Resident's Association, Inc., which opposed statehood to the end.

50. *A.C.L.U. Annual Report, 1953–1954,* p. 120. Others who were disappointed by the resolutions and did not stay with the Union were Whitney North Seymour, Varian Fry, and H. William Fitelson. Fitelson had initiated the three proposals originally, but from a far stronger anti–Communist position. He was bitterly disappointed when they were watered down and amounted to reversals of his position. Letter, Clifford Forster to William H. McIlhany, November 4, 1975.

51. The record of pro–Communist positions on foreign and domestic issues which followed after 1954 is so lengthy that a scrapbook of examples was compiled by merely quoting from A.C.L.U. reports and other publications: Charles C. Polenick, *Does the American Civil Liberties Union Serve the Communist Cause? What Do You Think?* (Phoenix, Arizona: FACT—A Committee For All Comprehensive Truth, 1962). This compilation makes clear the answer, although some of the policies quoted express positions that are philosophically valid in spite of their promoting general Communist objectives. Many are clearly not of this mixed nature. A typical example of this orientation was an incident of ACLU collaboration with perjurer Harvey Matusow, whose recanting was part of a major Communist propaganda campaign. See Finis Farr, "To the Aid of the Party," *National Review*, May 31, 1958, pp. 517–19. The Union attacked deportations of some phoney Hungarian Freedom Fighters in 1956, the first 6200 of whom, according to Congressman Francis E. Walter, were Communist agents given immigration numbers of other people so they could settle here. See *Manchester Union Leader* (New Hampshire), February 11, 1957. The Union's protest against subsequent deportations is discussed in "ACLU Hits U.S. Treatment of Hungary Exiles," *The Worker*, October 6, 1957. If Walter was correct, the Communist paper would naturally be interested. After 1954, the Union became more tolerant of pro–Communist activities by leading members of its local affiliates. A major example was its sanction of the

conduct of the Southern California affiliate's "Roger Baldwin," A.L. Wirin, a worker for some time in the New York national office, who would become active in both the Communist National Lawyers Guild and the Fair Play for Cuba Committee. On Wirin's record, in addition to the Tenney–Burns Committee reports, summaries of which are excerpted in the Appendix, see "Union Asks CIO Council to Dismiss Its Attorney," *Los Angeles Times,* November 7, 1951. In 1957 Wirin took the case of John and Sylvia Powell, journalists for the Red *China Monthly Review* who were being prosecuted under laws concerning foreign Communist agents. Not only did Wirin make use of taxpayers' money for a trip to Communist China to gather evidence for his defendants, but he also made speeches on his return about how wonderful was the People's Republic, providing pure Communist propaganda on China that was picked up and used in the Communist press: "Attorney Wirin Sues for Right to Visit China," *Los Angeles Times,* January 3, 1957; "Judge OK's Wirin's Trip to Red China," *Los Angeles Times,* January 5, 1957; "Wirin Issued Passport for Red China Trip," *Los Angeles Times,* November 21, 1957. On the use of taxpayers' money see *U.S.A.* v. *Powell, Powell, Schuman,* U.S. District Court, Northern District, California, Southern Division, Criminal No. 35065, Order, December 5, 1957, by U.S. District Judge Louis E. Goodman, ordering that the U.S. pay Wirin's traveling expenses. On the propaganda, see "Red China Nice Place, as Mr. Wirin Tells It," *Los Angeles Times,* April 21, 1958; "Three Mothers Report Reception 'Wonderful' on Arrival in China," *Daily Worker,* January 7, 1958; "U.S. Captives' Mothers Cross Into Red China," *Los Angeles Times,* January 6, 1958; Sidney Shapiro, "Letter From China: The Powell 'Sedition' Case–A View from Peking," *People's World,* April 5, 1958; Philip M. Connelly, "Back from China, Wirin Tells of Germ War Data," *People's World,* March 8, 1958; "Atty. A.L. Wirin Talks on China Before ACLU," *Los Angeles Times,* April 14, 1958; Philip M. Connelly, "An American Lawyer Looks at China," *People's World,* March 22, 1958; "Ex–Chiang Aides Willing to Testify for Powells," *People's World,* March 29, 1958; and "Jewish Center's Use for Wirin Talk Hit," *Los Angeles Times,* April 11, 1958.
52. Greene, " 'We Don't Enter Popularity Contests.' "
53. "Red-Baiting Held Losing Support," *People's World,* May 8, 1950; "Gains in Struggle for Human Freedoms Told," *Los Angeles Times,* October 25, 1956.
54. *ACLU Annual Reports,* pp. xxx, p. xi, the latter for Baldwin's view that anti–Communist fears have never been really well-founded in the facts, one of which he says, incredibly, was that no Communist was ever convicted of anything worse than exercise of free speech and association rights!

Chapter 11: 1960-1975: "Civil Liberties" Become Leftist Activism

1. The executive order was very effective in discouraging further government investigations by McCarthy and others. See Evans, *Assassination of Joe McCarthy*; Buckley and Bozell, *McCarthy and His Enemies.*
2. On this controversy, see U.S. Congress, House, Committee on Un–American Activities, *Issues Presented By Air Reserve Center Training Manual, Hearings,* 86th Congress, 2nd session, 1960.
3. On the Committee and the United Front against it, see U.S. Congress, House, Committee on Un-American Activities, *The House Committee on Un-American Activities, What It Is—What it Does*, 86th Congress, 1st session, 1958; U.S. Congress, House, Committee on Un–American Activities, *The Communist Party's Cold War Against Congressional Investigation of Subversion, Report and Testimony of Robert Carrillo Ronstadt,* 87th Congress, 2nd session, 1962. An excellent general defense of the Committee's work, including articles by former ACLU officials, C. Dickerman Williams and Irving Ferman, is William F. Buckley, Jr., ed., *The Committee and Its Critics: A Calm Review of The House Committee on Un-American Activities* (Chicago: Henry Regnery, 1962).
4. In addition to the Union's annual reports after 1961, we find Roger Baldwin as recently as 1970 saying, "Of all the volunteer saviors opposed by the ACLU, the anti–Communists are the most

numerous and the most influential because they play upon fears of revolution. Ever since the Russian Revolution, wave after wave of witch–hunting has marked the country, stimulated by a host of private patriots, often in rival competing agencies, some outright racketeers living off the money of scared property–owners. Others, such as veterans organizations, feel it their patriotic duty to fight against Communism. Extremists like the John Birch Society fight all advocates of change identifying Communism with socialism, socialism with liberalism and liberalism with the centralized powers of the welfare state.''

5. On the riots and "Operation Abolition," see U.S. Congress, House, Committee on Un–American Activities, *The Communist*–Led Riots Against The House Committee on Un–American Activities in San Francisco, Calif., May 12–14, 1960, Report, 86th Congress, 2nd session, Washington: G.P.O., 1960; U.S. Congress, House, Committee on Un–American Activities, "Operation Abolition", The Campaign Against The House Committee on Un–American Activities, The Federal Bureau of Investigation, The Government Security Program, By The Emergency Civil Liberties Committee And Its Affiliates, 85th Congress, 1st session, 1957; U.S. Congress, House, Committee on Un–American Activities, *The Truth About The Film "Operation Abolition"*, Report, Part 1, 87th Congress, 1st Session, 1961.

6. This would be freely and proudly admitted by the Union and its affiliates. A National Board policy on HCUA is expressed in "Board Statement on Wilkinson and Braden Cases, and on HUAC," *Civil Liberties*, April, 1961, p. 3. The extent of the Union's participation in this drive is clear to anyone who examines the Union's annual reports, 1959–1973, or George Robnett, *The Crusade Against Government Investigating Agencies* (Pasadena, Calif.: Institute for Special Research, no date). News items on the ACLU and this activity are numerous. Much of the work was spearheaded in California years before against the State Senate Delworth Committee. See "Spurns Flag When School Board Hears Protests on Red Quiz," *Los Angeles Herald*–Examiner, December 15, 1953; John Stone, "1,000 Meet to Take a Whack at HUAC," *People's World*, March 18, 1961; ACLU news release, "HUAC," New York, December 8, 1962. The A.C.L.U.'s bluff was called on the issue of whose rights had been violated by any misrepresentation of the Committee. See Edward J. Mowery, "The Facts About HUAC: ACLU Ignores Political Evaluation of Witnesses," *Torrance Daily Breeze* (California), November 15, 1961. Mowery wrote Alan Reitman, the Union's associate director, asking to be informed about who had been falsely charged in or harmed by the Committee's statements. Mowery's analysis of the summary of cases furnished by Reitman yielded no cases in which false accusations were made. The only basis for the listings in the ACLU's response was that these people had been hurt. But with a notion of misplaced agency similar to their stand on gun control, the Union was blaming the committee for actions taken by others in response to the listed persons' testimonies, usually discharges from government or private employment positions. Reitman has edited two collections of essays that reflect, but do not necessarily represent, recent ACLU policies: Alan Reitman, *The Price of Liberty* (New York: W.W. Norton, 1968); *The Pulse of Freedom, American Liberties: 1920–1970s* (New York: W.W. Norton, 1975).

7. An adequate, though popular, discussion of most of these cases is Rosalie M. Gordon, *Nine Men Against America: The Supreme Court and Its Attack On American Liberties* (Boston: Western Islands, 1965 reprint of 1958 edition).

8. See a portion of this report excerpted in the Appendix. Many of the yearly California reports of the Tenney–Burns Committee contained material on the Union in California. I have not concentrated on that because it primarily concerned local affiliates that were long more pro–Communist than the national ACLU. The reader can check most of these citations in the cumulative *Index to the California State Senate Committee Reports, 1943–1963*.

9. "Civil Liberties Union Cleared of Red Control." The Union even protested a considered JBS investigation by the HCUA, which never occured, and did this "holding our noses": financial appeal form letter to members from Patrick Murphy Malin, no date, but obviously 1961.

10. Elliot Carlson, "Civil Liberties Guard: ACLU Goes Increasingly to Aid of Right-Wing Groups," *Wall Street Journal*, March 29, 1965. One such case involved the involuntary commitment of Major General Edwin A. Walker after he was arrested by the Justice Department in Oxford, Mississippi, in 1962 during the crisis of federal intervention on behalf of James Meridith. The story is told in Earl Lively, Jr., *The Invasion of Mississippi* (Belmont, Mass.: American Opinion,

1963). Although the Union did not oppose the "invasion," they agreed with the John Birch Society that Walker had been deprived of his constitutional protections. They got some publicity for saying so: "Civil Liberties Head Hails Walker's Release," *Los Angeles Times*, October 9, 1962, in which Director Pemberton took the opportunity to link the Birch Society with Nazis and Communists. General Walker quipped, "They have showed up vaguely in a minor release and of course followed by editorials as having in some way defended my constitutional rights. It is the usual double twist of a front organization." *Timber*, September, 1967, p. 35. (*Timber* is a private anti–Communist newsletter published in Seattle, Washington, by ACLU–watcher Lawrence Timber).

11. Alan Stang, *It's Very Simple: The True Story of Civil Rights* (Boston: Western Islands, 1965), pp. 210–22, well documented; Carlson, "Civil Liberties Guard." Only on this issue do the ACLU and the Anti–Defamation League of B'nai B'rith differ. Both view, otherwise, anti–anticommunism and collectivist propaganda as somehow related to their professed goals. On this similar pattern in the ADL, see Nathaniel Weyl, *The Jew in American Politics* (New Rochelle, New York: Arlington House, 1968), pp. 85–87, 142.

12. Sam H. Bowers, Jr., Imperial Wizard of the White Knights of the Ku Klux Klan of Mississippi, admitted to his top–level assistants that he was working to promote racial hatred and violence in Mississippi to help justify the imposition of federal control and martial law over that state. He also admitted that he was a member of the Communist Party. See my *Klandestine: The Untold Story of Delmar Dennis and His Role in the F.B.I.'s War Against the Ku Klux Klan* (New Rochelle, New York: Arlington House, 1975).

13. *A.C.L.U. Annual Report, 1961*–1962, pp. 35–37, which also includes a statement on protecting the rights of Birchers, but at the same time implying JBS responsibility in a bombing case, something called prejudgment, or almost. The "muzzling" was thoroughly investigated. See U.S. Congress, Senate, Armed Services Committee, Special Preparedness Subcommittee, *Military Cold War Education and Speech Review Policies, Hearings*, 6 vol., 87th Congress, 2nd session, 1962. Also see "ACLU Raps Navy Story on Socialism," *Pasadena Star-News* (California), November 23, 1961.

14. Recruitment form letter from ACLU Executive Director Aryeh Neier, no date, but obviously 1975.

15. U.S. Congress, Senate, Committee on the Judiciary, Internal Security Subcommittee, *The New Drive Against The Anti–Communist Program, Hearings*, 87th Congress, 1st session, 1961. These hearings made clear that the Birch Society was bearing the brunt of a smear campaign in accord with recent Kremlin orders.

16. Both of these affiliations were given in the *Warren Commission Report*, though casual readers missed Oswald's ACLU membership because for some reason the ACLU was not listed in the index.

17. *A.C.L.U. News* (Seattle, Washington), October 22, 1965; "Liberties Union Urged to Right an Old Wrong," *Daily World*, February 29, 1969.

18. "Liberties Union Urged to Right an Old Wrong"; Sam Kushner, "An Appeal to Right an Old Wrong," *Daily World*, February 1, 1969.

19. *A.C.L.U. Annual Report, 1958–1959*, pp. 18–19.

20. At least two local affiliates in Illinois and California prepared "guidelines" for instructing local school superintendents on what they must do. One of these was a letter from ACLU of Southern California Executive Director Eason Monroe to Superintendent Fullmar of the Huntington Beach Union High School District, (November 16, 1971). One guideline advised that "Jingle Bells" should be sung in place of "Hark the Herald Angels," which expert Monroe noted was "entirely religious." Not only does this reflect utter ignorance of the non–Christian religious roots of much of secular Christmas celebrations, but it is also a pathetically absurd piece of intimidation, well worthy of a police–state bureaucrat. This "guideline" was answered and largely debunked in letters by State Senator James E. Whetmore; George Murphy, California Legislative Counsel; and the California Justice Foundation. The rebuttals demonstrated that Monroe's guidelines were more wishful thinking than constitutional law.

21. The best survey of the leadership of the "civil rights" alliance in which so many ACLU people worked, is Stang, *It's Very Simple*.

260

22. In addition to these issues as discussed in Chapter 6, above, see Van Alstyne Brown, "Opposition to Law and Order," *American Mercury*, September, 1961, pp. 19–24; Homer Bigart, "Liberties Union Asks Friends and 'Responsible' Foes of Review Board to Ombudsman Talks," *The New York Times*, November 15, 1966; "ACLU Urges Police Gun Curbs," *San Francisco Examiner*, July 17, 1968; William Schulz, "Cop–Killer Slain: ACLU Official Protests," *Human Events*, November 2, 1963, p. 8; Eve Cary, "Cops & Rebels: Provoking Crime," *Civil Liberties*, July, 1972, pp. 1, 5; "House acts on Civil Rights: Predict Attempt to Weaken Measure," and A.L. Wirin, "Realty Boards and Racial Bias," both in *Open Forum*, February, 1964. On the issue of "open housing" see George Slaff, "Prop. 14 and the Sacred Rights of Private Property," *Open Forum*, August, 1964, p. 3. Slaff, Communist Flynn's fan and vice–president of the Southern California ACLU Board of Directors, let it all out with the claim that a person has "absolutely no right to do anything with his property which society deems socially undesirable."

23. *A.C.L.U. Annual Report, 1958–1959*, pp. 9, 26; *ACLU Annual Report, 1959–1960*, p. 2, 20. Note that Union favors all views being expressed over the "public utility" of the airwaves, but protested the posting of a morally critical appraisal of the ACLU–defended novel, *Lady Chatterly's Lover*, in a "public" post office building.

24. On many of these people, see Gannon, *Biographical Dictionary of the Left*; Martin, *Fabian Freeway*. This by no means exhausts the overlap between the ACLU, the CFR and recent federal administrations. See Dan Smoot, "The American Civil Liberties Union," *The Dan Smoot Report*, July 27, 1964, p. 238. This weekly *Dan Smoot Report*, well documented in spite of the attacks it receives, provides occasional commentary on the ACLU's activities from 1955 to the present. The National Lawyers Guild, which has recently been plagued by internal power struggles between Moscow and Peking sympathizers, operates something called the Peoples College of Law at 2228 West Seventh Street, Los Angeles. It really looks the part, and I found out about it from its literature which was kept in Ron Ridenhour's former Public Relations office at the ACLU's Los Angeles headquarters.

25. Patrick Murphy Malin first proposed this departure from the Union's limited concerns into a broad range of issues for leftist activism. Pemberton and Neier have followed suit, trying to keep pace with some of their more "progressive" local affiliates, bringing criticism from friends of the Union. These departures have involved taking positions on the Vietnam War, on economic issues from a statist standpoint, on environmental controls and "consumer protection" legislation, as well as on the impeachment of Richard Nixon, all somehow justified as "civil liberties" concerns. See Morrie Ryskind, "The ACLU Syndrome," *Los Angeles Herald–Examiner*, June 4, 1972; Nick Thimmesch, "The ACLU Veers to the Left, and Loses Some Credibility," *Los Angeles Times*, January 28, 1972; Lawrence Feinberg, "ACLU a Stormy Center of Rights—and Politics: Critics Say 'Nonpartisan' Group Is More Eager to Fight for Liberal Cause," *Los Angeles Times*, August 20, 1972; David Shaw, "New Direction for ACLU: How Far Will It Go?: Vulnerability to Criticism Increases as Scope of Concerns Grows Steadily," *Los Angeles Times*, October 25, 1972; U.S. Study Team on Religious and Political Freedom in Vietnam, "Findings on Trip to Vietnam, May 25–June 10, 1969," *Congressional Record*, Senate, July 2, 1969, pp. S7493, footnote. Participating in the Study Team, which generally reported a Communist line against South Vietnam on its return, were former ACLU Executive Director John Pemberton and ACLU official Robert F. Drinan. See also Joseph W. Bishop, Jr., "Should the ACLU Be So Political?," *Commentary*, December, 1971 (reprinted in *Human Events*, January 22, 1972), highly recommended; Shirley Scheibla, "Pros and Cons: The Curious Story of the American Civil Liberties Union," "Liberty or License?—The ACLU Sometimes Has Trouble Telling Them Apart," "Defense to Offense: The ACLU is Rapidly Expanding Its Sphere of Influence," *Barron's*, August 26, September 9, September 30, 1968. This series is possibly the best coverage of the Union's contemporary leftist activism in print. Malin announced the goal of the new departure, in the field of Southern agitation, in the *ACLU Annual Report, 1955–1956*.

26. *ACLU Annual Reports*, pp. xxvi–xxxiii. Clifford Forster related to me that one of the things that caused him to lose interest in Baldwin's International League for the Rights of Man was the fact that Baldwin was all for anticolonialist movements that were pro–Communist, but condemned the 1961–1962 independence struggle of the State of Katanga against the Congo central government

261

and UN troops as the "Balkanizing" of states, which, apparently, were not supposed to be independent if under an anti–Communist pro–American leader. On the UN's war against Katanga see Griffin, *The Fearful Master,* pp. 3–66.

27. *ACLU Annual Reports,* pp. xxvi– xxxiii. Also see his statement that there "isn't even an international communism movement left" in Flora Lewis, "Looking Ahead at 87," *Los Angeles Times,* September 10, 1971. Baldwin viewed the invasion of Czechoslovakia in 1968 as proof the Communist sattelite empire was collapsing. The Czechs saw it differently. The theme of our "interdependence" in "a new world order" is now echoed by ACLU historian Commager. See *Review of the News,* October 22, 1975, p. 60.

28. *ACLU Annual Reports,* pp. xxxii– xxxiii.

29. V.I. Lenin, "Left–Wing Communism, an Infantile Disorder" (1920), *Selected Works* (New York: International Publishers, 1943), vol. X, pp. 94, 138, on zigzags and sacrifices, or two steps forward, one step backward.

30. Convicted "Watergator," Jeb Stuart Magruder, *Los Angeles Times,* October 23, 1975.

Index

265

Fund for the Republic, 149-50
Furuseth, Andrew, 141

Gaither, Rowan, 149
Gale, Zona, 115, 120
Garland Fund, 127, 135
Gastonia, N.C., 127
German General Staff, 120
Germany, Nazi, 49, 86-7, 115-7, 119,
135, 141, 145-6
Gibbons, Cardinal, 118
Ginn, Edward, 118
Goldman, Emma, 114-5, 123
Gore, Albert, 159
Greater New York Emergency Conference
on Inalienable Rights, 137
Greene, Nathan, 140
Griswold, Erwin, 149

Hague, Mayor ("I Am the Law"), 138
Hague, The 117-9
Hallinan, Charles T., 115-6
Hamilton, Alexander, 32, 35
Hammer, Fannie Lou, 159
Hapgood, Norman, 124
Harding, Warren G., 124-6
Harris poll, 84
Harvard, 114, 127
Harvard Class Book, 134
Hart, Philip, 159
Hays, Arthur Garfield, 124, 136, 140
143, 146
Hepburn, A. Barton, 118
Henry, Aaron, 159
Henry, Patrick, 32
Hillman, Sidney, 135
Hillquit, Morris, 115, 117, 120, 124
Hirschkop, Philip, 159

Hitler, Adolf, 58, 139, 140-1, 143,
145
Hobbes, Thomas, 21-3, 25-6
Holmes, John Haynes, 121, 135-6, 140-4
Holmes, Sherlock, 56
Hook, Sidney, 149
Hooker, Richard, 30
Hoover, Herbert, 138
House Committee on Un-American Activi-
ties, 144, 146, 151, 156
House, Edward Mandell, 116-9
Hoyt, Palmer, Jr., 148
Huebsch, B.W., 124, 136, 143
Hutchins, Robert M., 143

Inbau, Fred E., 74
Industrial Workers of the World, 122-4
126-7
Institutes, 30
Intercollegiate Socialist Society, 116-7
Internal Revenue Service, 162
International Labor Defense, 127, 133-5
International League for the Rights
of Man, 148
International School of Peace, 118
Isserman, Abraham, 140-1
Italy, 135

Jackson, Robert H., 130
James I, King, 30
Japan, 147
Japanese, repression of in California,
146
Jefferson, Thomas, 32, 34
Jehovah's Witnesses, 116, 125, 138, 146
John Birch Society, 155-7
Johnson administration, Lyndon, 159
Johnson, James Weldon, 124

Joint Committee for the Defense of the
Brazilian People, 137
Jordan, David Starr, 115, 136
Joyce, James, 138
Jungle, The, 126
Justice Department, 123-6

Kahn, Otto, 118, 128
Kant, Immanuel, 25, 35, 54
Keller, Helen, 124
Kellogg, Paul, 115-6, 120
Kennedy administration, John F., 157,
159
Kenyon, Dorothy, 142
Knox, 118
Korea, 147
Ku Klux Klan, 123, 141, 156
Kunstler, William, 159

"Labor Defender," 133
Labor Defense Council, 135
Lamont, Corliss, 136-7, 140, 143, 148,
150, 152, 157
Lamont, Mrs. Thomas W., 152
Lamont, Thomas, 148
Lancaster, Burt, 159
Laski, Harold, 132-3
Law, Sylvia, 102-3
Leach, Agnes Brown, 121
League of Nations, 119
League of Young Southerners, 137
Lenin, V.I., 116, 161
Lerner, Max, 143, 159
Lewisohn, 120
Liberator, 115
Liberty Under the Soviets, 132
Lindbergh, Charles, 145
Linville, Henry P., 124

Lippman, Walter, 117
Llewellyn, Karl, 127
Lochner, Louis P., 115, 117, 122-3, 125
Locke, John, 20-6, 31-2, 35
Lovejoy, Owen, 115
Lovett, Robert Morss, 124, 136-7, 143
Lusk Committee, 123
Lynch, Frederick, 115

MacArthur, Douglas, 138, 147
McCarthy, Joseph, 147-50, 154
McConnell, Francis J., 143
McDonald, Duncan, 124
McGhee v. *Sipes,* 59
MacKay, Clarence, 118
MacLeish, Archibald, 136, 143
McWilliams, Carey, 159
Madison, James, 32
Magna Carta, 32, 34, 57
Magnes, Judah Leon, 121
Malin, Patrick Murphy, 147-8, 150 159
Mallory v. *U.S.,* 72
Manson, Charles, 79
Marburg Theodore, 118-9
Marchetti, Vincent, 156 .
Maritain, Jacques, 55, 57
Marshall, Louis, 128
Marx, Karl, 76
Maryland Peace Society, 118
Mason, George, 32
Massachusetts Circular Letter of
1768, 33
Masses, 115
Mass Sedition Trial, 144, 147
Matthews, J.B., 136-7
Maurer, James H., 115
Medicaid, 66
Medicare, 66
Middle Ages, 29

Milner Lord Alfred, 117
Milner, Lucille B., 124
Mink, Patsy, 159
Minneapolis, 121-2
Miranda v. *Arizona,* 72-4
Mobilization for Youth, 71
Mooney-Billings case, 135
Morgan, J.P. 114-5, 119-20, 126
Moscow, 162
Mother Bloor Celebration Committee, 137
Municipal Court, Los Angeles, 70
Mussey, Henry S., 115, 120
Muste, A.J., 124, 143

Napoleon, 58
National Advisory Council (ACLU), 159
National Civil Liberties Bureau, 121, 123-4
National Civil Rights Committee, 145
National Committee Against Censorship of the Theater Arts, 137
National Committee to Abolish HUAC, 155
National Congress for Unemployment and Social Insurance, 137
National Emergency Civil Liberties Committee, 77
National Labor Relations Board, 138
National Lawyers Guild, 71, 76, 159
National Observer, 63
Nearing, Scott, 115, 121, 127, 136-7
Neier, Aryeh, 64, 99, 100, 159
Nelles, Walter, 121, 124
New Deal, 134-5, 138, 144, 146
New York Economic Club, 118
New York Life Insurance Company, 117
New York Professional Workers Conference on Social Insurance, 137

New York Times, 132-3
Ninth Amendment, 95
Nixon administration, Richard, 108, 159
Non-Partisan League, 123
Number One, 125, 127, 151
Number Two, 125-6, 151
Nuremberg War Crimes Trials, 147

Odets, Clifford, 137
Office of Economic Opportunity, 71
Office of Strategic Services, 149
Open Mind discussion group, 142
Operation Abolition, 155
Oppenheimer, J. Robert, 143, 148
Oswald, Lee Harvey, 157
Otis, James, 32-3
Overman Committee, 123
Oxnam, G. Bromley, 143

Palace Guard, 108
Palmer, A. Mitchell, 123-4
Panthers, Black, 64
Paris, 118
Parliament, 30, 33, 57
Patterson, William, 32
Patton, James G., 159
Peace Mission, 117
Peace Movement Practical, 118
Pearl Harbor, 145
Peking, 162
Pelley, William Dudley, 145
Pemberton, John de J., Jr., 159
People's Council of America, 115, 121-2, 125
Permanent Court of Arbitration, 118
Philip Dru: Administrator, 117
Pickens, William H., 124